FEB 1 0 2009

746.434 EPS
Epstein, Nicky.
Crocheting on the edge : ribs & bobbles, ruffles, flora, fringes, points & scallops...

PALM BEACH COUNTY
LIBRARY SYSTEM
3650 Summit Boulevard
West Palm Beach, FL 33406-4198

crocheting on the edge

ribs & bobbles • ruffles • flora • fringes • points & scallops

crocheting on the edge

ribs & bobbles • ruffles • flora • fringes • points & scallops

the essential collection of more than 200 decorative borders

nicky epstein

author of *Knitting On the Edge, Knitting Over the Edge* and *Knitting Beyond the Edge*

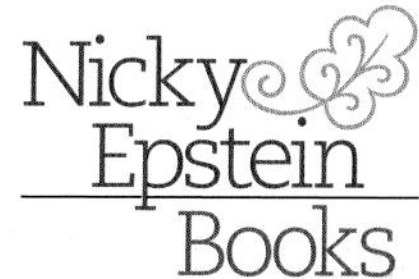

To my seven DeFazio Uncles—Frank, Marty, Joe, Syl, Gus, Anthony, and Johnny—all of whom teased me as a child, and still tease me…but with love!

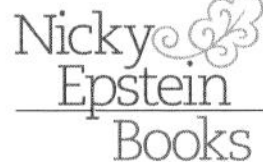

Editorial Director
ELAINE SILVERSTEIN

Book Division Manager
ERICA SMITH

Senior Editor
MICHELLE BREDESON

Art Director
DIANE LAMPHRON

Associate Art Director
SHEENA T. PAUL

Graphic Designer
MICHAEL YONG

Yarn Editor
TANIS GRAY

Instructions Editor
EVE NG

Technical Illustrations
KAREN MANTHEY

Instructions Checker
JEANNIE CHIN

Proofreaders
JO BRANDON
NANCY HENDERSON

Copy Editor
KRISTINA SIGLER

Bookings Manager
RACHAEL STEIN

Photography
JACK DEUTSCH STUDIO

Fashion Stylist
LAURA MAFFEO
JULIE HINES

Vice President, Publisher
TRISHA MALCOLM

Creative Director
JOE VIOR

Production Manager
DAVID JOINNIDES

President
ART JOINNIDES

Copyright © 2008 by Nicky Epstein
All rights reserved. No part of this publication may be reproduced or used in any form or by any means—graphic, electronic, or mechanical, including photocopying, recording, or information storage-and-retrieval systems—without written permission of the publisher.

The written instructions, photographs, designs, projects and patterns are intended for the personal, noncommercial use of retail purchaser and are under federal copyright laws; they are not to be reproduced in any form for commercial use. Permission is granted to photocopy patterns for the personal use of the retail purchaser.

Library of Congress Control Number: 2007937748

ISBN 1-933027-35-5

ISBN-13: 978-1-933027-35-7

Manufactured in China

3 5 7 9 1 0 8 6 4 2

First Edition

contents

introduction

When I wrote *Knitting On the Edge*, the first book in what would become a trilogy of books on knitted edgings, I had no idea what a wild success it would become. Knitters of all skill levels have made all three books in the series perennial bestsellers, and the books have been translated into many languages. The kind messages that I have received from knitters around the world have validated all the hard work put into those books.

Shortly after the first book was released I began hearing from my crochet friends: "Hey, where's our edging book?" Well, it took three years to get there, but here it is.

I've been inspired by the patterns in the knit book and have given them a new twist (pun intended) to translate them beautifully into the art of crocheting. You'll find ribs, bobbles, ruffles, classic vintage, fringes, flora and lots more, along with original design pieces that I've created just for this book. I've covered traditional techniques and come up with some of my own, and have given you easy-to-follow instructions for each and every edging.

I have always been a fan of all kinds of edgings, and I believe that they can take handcrafted pieces from ordinary to extraordinary, or from special to sublime. I think with a little effort and a little imagination, you'll soon be enhancing your pieces as never before. Most of all, I hope this book inspires you to try your own variations and innovations. I know you'll find it fascinating and fun.

Happy crocheting,

textures

The following edgings illustrate the difference yarn texture and weight can make in how an edging looks. I used a variety of yarns of different weights and textures along with corresponding needle sizes for each yarn. The swatches are made using the original instructions (see page 140).

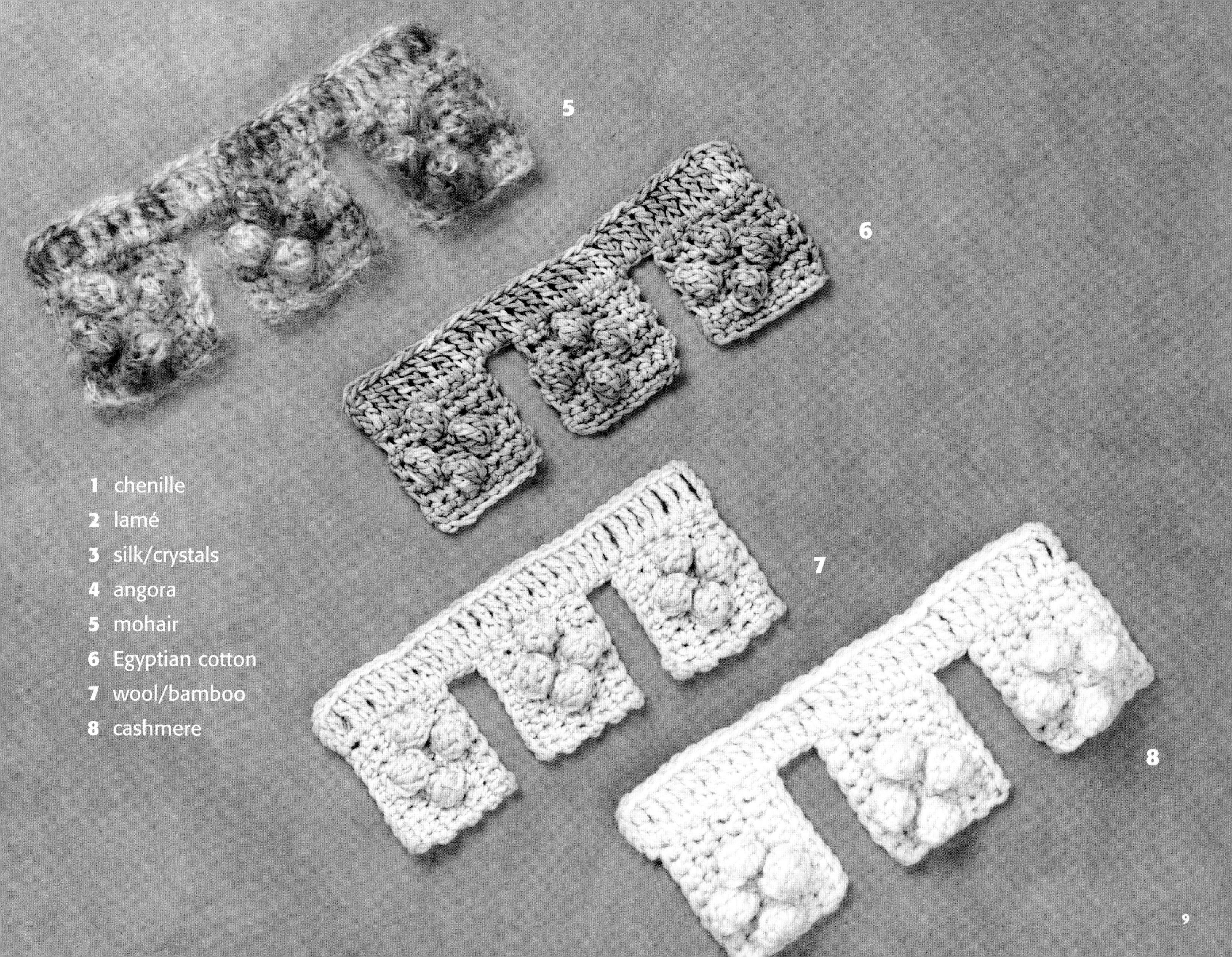
5
6
7
8
1 chenille
2 lamé
3 silk/crystals
4 angora
5 mohair
6 Egyptian cotton
7 wool/bamboo
8 cashmere

s i z e

9 wool (bulky weight)
10 cotton/rayon
11 cotton DMC

notes on using this book

Directional Symbols

In the instructions, we have used the symbols shown below to indicate the direction in which the edging was worked. The direction is based on having the project at the top and the edging at the bottom. In many cases, the edgings in this book are reversible.

- ▲ Work from bottom up: Foundation row is the lower edge.
- ▼ Work from the top down: Fastened-off edge is the lower edge.
- ▶ Work from left to right.
- **E** Embellishment: Work separately and sew onto piece.

Standard Yarn Weights

In the Patterns chapter, next to the suggested yarn in the Materials section, we have used the Standard Yarn Weight System for ease in substitution. If you plan to substitute a yarn, be sure to crochet a gauge swatch and check that it matches the original gauge in the pattern and has a similar appearance to the original yarn used in the pattern. These standard yarn weights can be used for any pattern.

Working Directly onto a Project

If an edging requires a specific number of repeat stitches, the multiple will be noted in parentheses just under the edging name. The accompanying heading (if used instead) is written to accommodate that multiple.

For abbreviations used in this book, see page 12.

Placement of Charts

All swatches are photographed with the heading on top for consistency. However, many charts show the heading on the bottom. This is to facilitate working the swatch from the heading outward.

Explanation of Charts

Basic stitch patterns have been added to most of the edgings. The stitch patterns are indicated in the lightened portion of each chart. You can work them with the finished edging, if desired, or you can continue in the pattern of your choice.

Standard Yarn Weight System

Categories of yarn, gauge ranges, and recommended needle and hook sizes

Yarn Weight Symbol & Category Names	0 Lace	1 Super Fine	2 Fine	3 Light	4 Medium	5 Bulky	6 Super Bulky
Type of Yarns in Category	Fingering 10 count crochet thread	Sock, Fingering, Baby	Sport, Baby	DK, Light Worsted	Worsted, Afghan, Aran	Chunky, Craft, Rug	Bulky, Roving
Knit Gauge Range* in Stockinette Stitch to 4 inches	33 –40** sts	27–32 sts	23–26 sts	21–24 sts	16–20 sts	12–15 sts	6–11 sts
Recommended Needle in Metric Size Range	1.5–2.25 mm	2.25–3.25 mm	3.25–3.75 mm	3.75–4.5 mm	4.5–5.5 mm	5.5–8 mm	8 mm and larger
Recommended Needle U.S. Size Range	000 to 1	1 to 3	3 to 5	5 to 7	7 to 9	9 to 11	11 and larger
Crochet Gauge* Ranges in Single Crochet to 4 inch	32-42 double crochets**	21–32 sts	16–20 sts	12–17 sts	11–14 sts	8–11 sts	5–9 sts
Recommended Hook in Metric Size Range	Steel*** 1.6–1.4mm Regular hook 2.25 mm	2.25–3.5 mm	3.5–4.5 mm	4.5–5.5 mm	5.5–6.5 mm	6.5–9 mm	9 mm and larger
Recommended Hook U.S. Size Range	Steel*** 6, 7, 8 Regular hook B–1	B–1 to E–4	E–4 to 7	7 to I–9	I–9 to K–10½	K–10½ to M–13	M–13 and larger

* Guidelines only: The above reflect the most commonly used gauges and needle or hook sizes for specific yarn categories.

** Lace weight yarns are usually knitted or crocheted on larger needles and hooks to create lacy, openwork patterns. Accordingly, a gauge range is difficult to determine. Always follow the gauge stated in your pattern.

*** Steel crochet hooks are sized differently from regular hooks--the higher the number, the smaller the hook, which is the reverse of regular hook sizing.

This Standards & Guidelines booklet and downloadable symbol artwork are available at: **YarnStandards.com**

stitch key

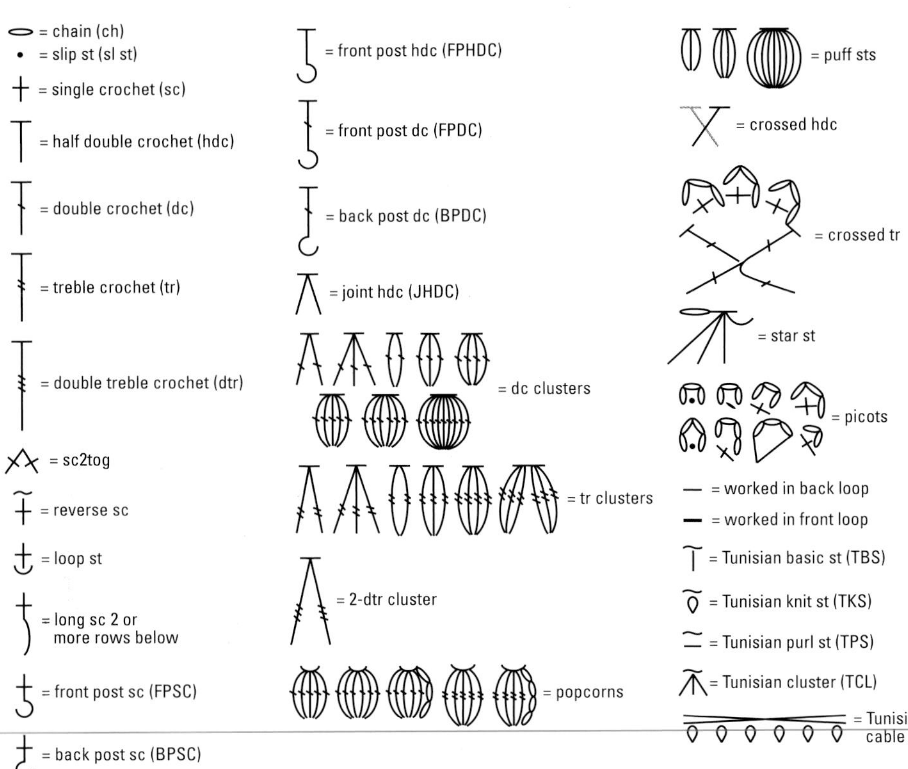

abbreviations

Beg	begin(ning)
Ch(s)	chain(s)
Cont	continue
Dc	double crochet
Dtr	double treble (or triple) crochet
Hdc	half double crochet
Lp(s)	loop(s)
Patt	pattern
Rem	remain
Rep	repeat
Reverse sc	reverse single crochet
Rnd(s)	round(s)
RS	right side
Sc	single crochet
Sl st	slip stitch
Sl	slip
Sp(s)	space(s)
St(s)	stitch(es)
Tr	treble (or triple) crochet
WS	wrong side
Yo	yarn over

conversion chart

U.S. Term	U.K./AUS Term
sl st slip stitch	**sc** single crochet
sc single crochet	**dc** double crochet
hdc half double crochet	**htr** half treble crochet
dc double crochet	**tr** treble crochet
tr treble crochet	**dtr** double treble crochet
dtr double treble crochet	**trip** tr or trtr triple treble crochet
trtr triple treble crochet	**qtr** qaudruple treble crochet
rev sc reverse single crochet	**rev dc** reverse double crochet
yo yarn over	**yoh** yarn over hook

The following crocheted edges are on knitted pieces. The edgings are a lovely, quick way to finish a knitted edge or a crocheted edge. The beauty of crocheting these small edgings is that they can be used in any number of layering combinations to enhance your projects.

cluster

▼ (multiple of 2 sts + 1 for patt row)

Row 1 (RS) Ch 1, sc evenly across, working 3 sc in corner. Turn.

Row 2 Ch 1, 1 sc in each sc across, working 3 sc in corner. Turn.

Row 3 (patt) Ch 2, *1 hdc in next sc, [yo, insert hook around stem of hdc just made, yo and draw up a lp] 3 times, yo and draw through all 7 lps on hook, ch 1, skip next sc; rep from *, end 1 hdc in last 2 sc. Fasten off.

cluster

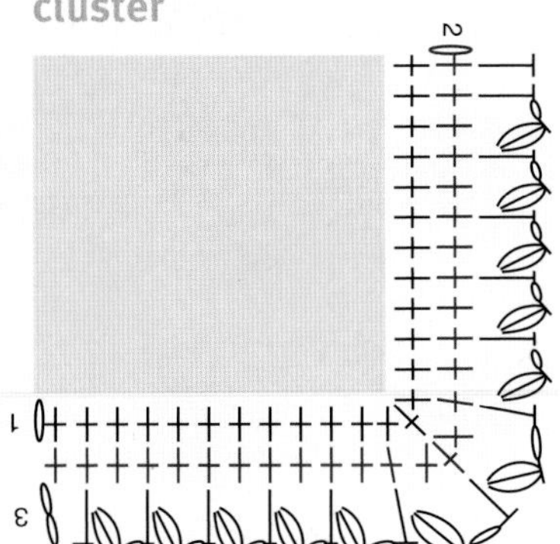

popcorn cluster

▼ (multiple of 2 sts + 1 for patt row)

Row 1 (WS) Ch 1, sc evenly across, working 3 sc in corner. Turn.

Row 2 (patt) Ch 1, 1 sc in first sc, *[yo, insert hook and draw up a lp, yo and draw through 2 lps on hook] 4 times in next sc, yo and draw through all 5 lps on hook, 1 sc in next st; rep from *

popcorn cluster

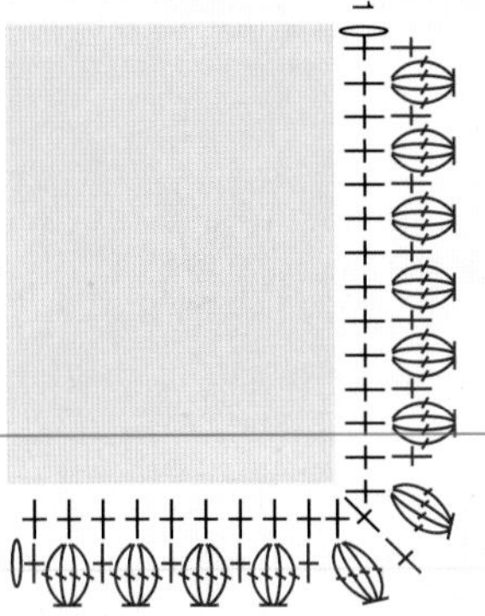

picot arch

▼ (multiple of 3 sts + 1 for patt row)

Row 1 (RS) Ch 1, sc evenly across, working 3 sc in corner. Turn.

Row 2 Ch 1, 1 sc in each sc across, working 3 sc in corner. Turn.

Row 3 Ch 3 (counts as 1 dc), 1 dc in each sc across, working 3 dc in corner. Turn.

Row 4 (patt) Ch 6 (counts as 1 dc, ch 3), skip next 2 dc, 1 dc in next dc, *ch 3, skip next 2 dc, 1 dc in next dc; rep from * to end. Turn.

Row 5 Ch 1, sl st in first ch-3 lp, *ch 6, sl st in 4th ch from hook, ch 2, 1 sc in next ch-3 lp; rep from * to end. Fasten off.

picot arch

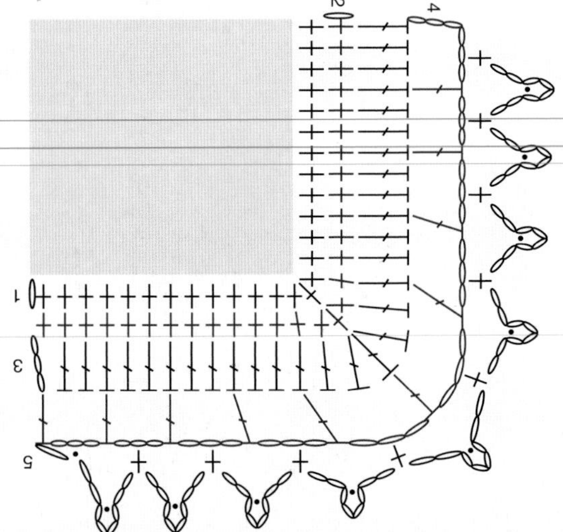

classic picot

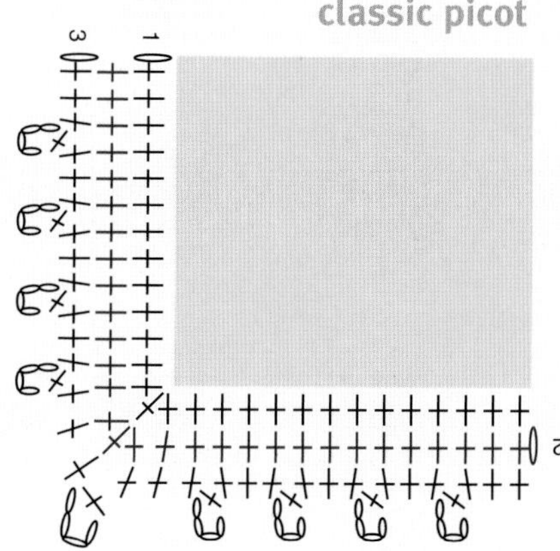

arch

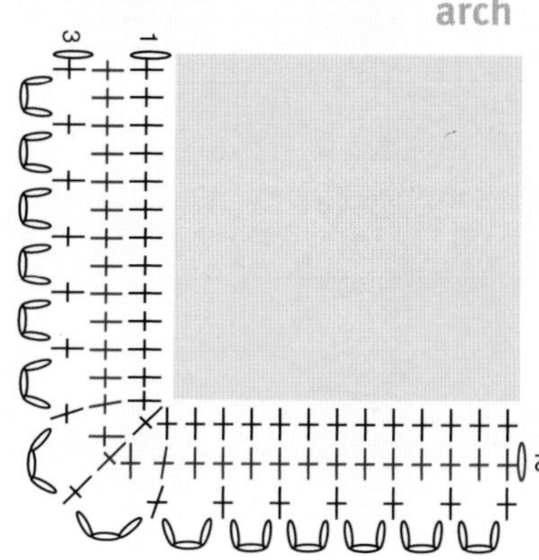

dot picot

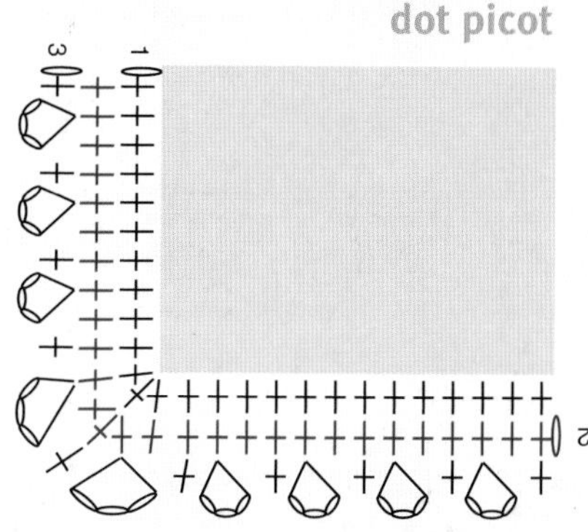

classic picot

▼ (multiple of 3 sts for patt row)

Row 1 (RS) Ch 1, sc evenly across, working 3 sc in corner. Turn.

Row 2 Ch 1, 1 sc in each sc across, working 3 sc in corner. Turn.

Row 3 (patt) Ch 1, 1 sc in first 3 sc, *ch 4, sl st in sc just made, 1 sc in next 3 sc; rep from * to end. Fasten off.

arch

▼ (multiple of 2 sts + 1 for patt row)

Row 1 (RS) Ch 1, sc evenly across, working 3 sc in corner. Turn.

Row 2 Ch 1, 1 sc in each sc across, working 3 sc in corner. Turn.

Row 3 (patt) Ch 1, 1 sc in first sc, *ch 3, skip 1 sc, 1 sc in next sc; rep from * to end. Fasten off.

dot picot

▼ (multiple of 3 sts + 1 for patt row)

Row 1 (RS) Ch 1, sc evenly across, working 3 sc in corner. Turn.

Row 2 Ch 1, 1 sc in each sc across, working 3 sc in corner. Turn.

Row 3 (patt) Ch 1, 1 sc in first sc, *skip next sc, insert hook into next sc and draw up a lp, ch 3 in lp just made, yo and draw through both lps on hook, 1 sc in next sc; rep from * to end. Fasten off.

striped edge

▼ **Colors** A and B

(Any number of sts)

Row 1 (RS) With A, ch 1, sc evenly across, working 3 sc in corner. Turn.

Row 2 Ch 1, 1 sc in each sc across, working 3 sc in corner. Turn.

Fasten off A and attach B.

Row 3 With B, ch 1, sl st in each sc across.

Fasten off.

reverse single crochet

▼ **Colors** A and B

(Over any number of sts)

Row 1 (WS) With A, ch 1, sc evenly across, working 3 sc in corner. Turn.

Row 2 (RS) Ch 1, 1 sc in each sc across, working 3 sc in corner. Turn.

Fasten off A and attach B.

Row 3 (RS) With B, ch 1, working from left to right, 1 reverse sc in each sc across.

Fasten off.

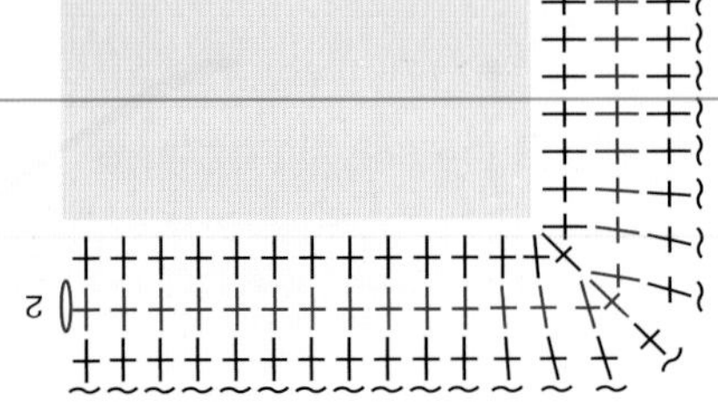

2-color loop

▼ **Colors** A and B

(Multiple of 4 sts + 1 for patt row)

Row 1 (WS) With A, ch 1, sc evenly across, working 3 sc in corner. Turn.

Fasten off A and attach B.

Row 2 With B, ch 1, 1 sc in each st across, working 3 sc in corner. Turn.

Fasten off B and attach A.

Row 3 (patt) With A, ch 1, 1 sc in first sc, *ch 6, skip next 3 sc, 1 sc in next sc; rep from * until 2 sts before corner; [ch 6, skip next sc, 1 sc in next sc] twice; rep from * to end. Turn.

Fasten off A and attach B.

Row 4 With B, ch 1, 1 sc in first sc, *sl st in back lp of next 6 ch, 1 sc in next sc; rep from * to end.

Fasten off.

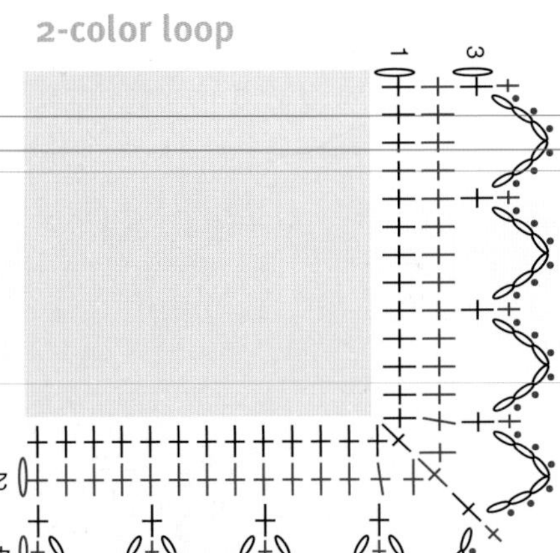

scallop

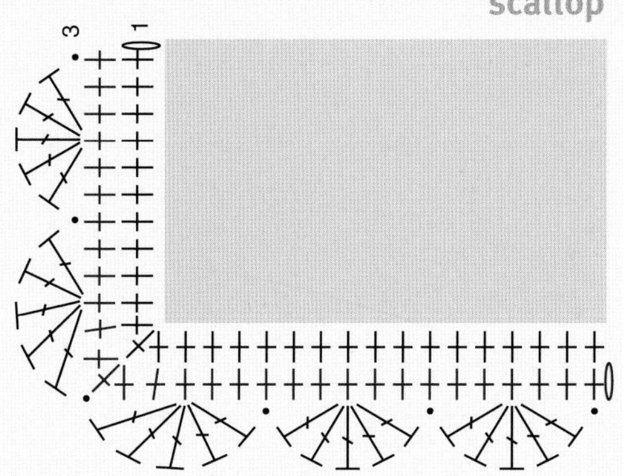

scallop

▼ (multiple of 6 sts + 1 for patt row)

Row 1 (RS) Ch 1, sc evenly across, working 3 sc in corner. Turn.

Row 2 Ch 1, 1 sc in each sc across, working 3 sc in corner. Turn.

Row 3 (patt) Sl st in first sc, *skip next 2 sc, 5 dc in next sc, skip next 2 sc, sl st in next sc; rep from * to end.

Fasten off.

sassy shells

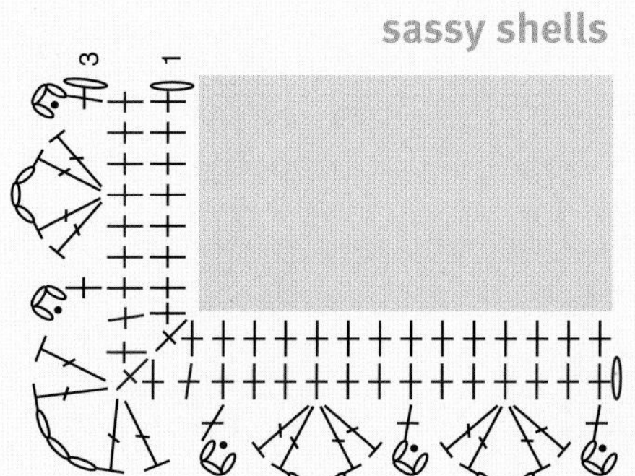

sassy shells

▼ (multiple of 6 sts + 1 for patt row)

Row 1 (RS) Ch 1, sc evenly across, working 3 sc in corner. Turn.

Row 2 Ch 1, 1 sc in each sc across, working 3 sc in corner. Turn.

Row 3 (patt) Ch 1, 1 sc in first sc, ch 3, sl st in sc just made, *skip next 2 sc, [2 dc, ch 3, 2 dc] in next sc, skip next 2 sc, 1 sc in next sc, ch 3, sl st in sc just made; rep from * to end.

Fasten off.

triangle

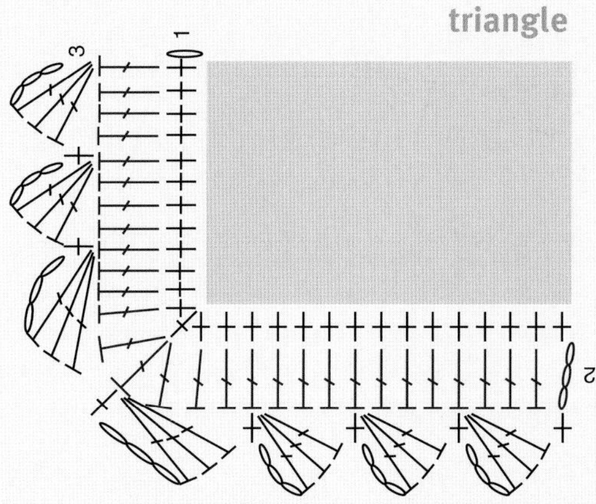

triangle

▼ (multiple of 4 sts + 1 for patt row)

Row 1 (RS) Ch 1, sc evenly across, working 3 sc in corner. Turn.

Row 2 Ch 3, 1 dc in each sc across, working 3 dc in corner. Turn.

Row 3 (patt) Ch 3, 3 dc in same st, *skip next 3 dc, 1 sc in next dc, ch 3, 3 dc in same dc; rep from *, end 1 sc in top of beg ch-3.

Fasten off.

ribs &

bobbles

post rib

▲ (multiple of 2 sts)

FPSC (Front post sc) Insert hook from front to back to front around post of designated st and draw up a lp, yo and draw through both lps on hook.

BPSC (Back post sc) Insert hook from back to front to back around post of designated st and draw up a lp, yo and draw through both lps on hook.

Edging

Make a ch to desired depth in a multiple of 2 sts + 1.

Row 1 1 sc in 2nd ch from hook and in each ch to end. Turn.

Row 2 Ch 1, 1 sc in first sc, *FPSC around next sc, BPSC around next sc; rep from *, end 1 sc in last sc. Turn.

Rep row 2 six times more or to desired depth.

Fasten off, continue with the heading on chart, or continue as desired.

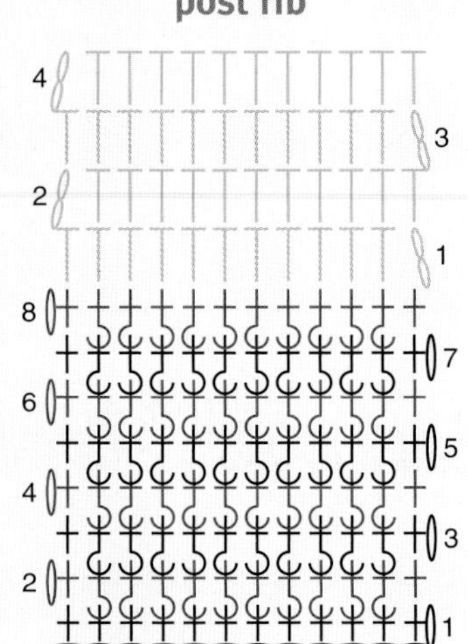

ridge rib

▶ **Edging**

Make a ch to desired depth.

Row 1 1 sc in 2nd ch from hook and in back 1 lp of each ch to end. Turn.

Row 2 Ch 1, 1 sc in back lp of first sc and in each sc to end. Turn.

Rep row 2 to desired width.

Fasten off, continue with the heading on chart, or continue as desired.

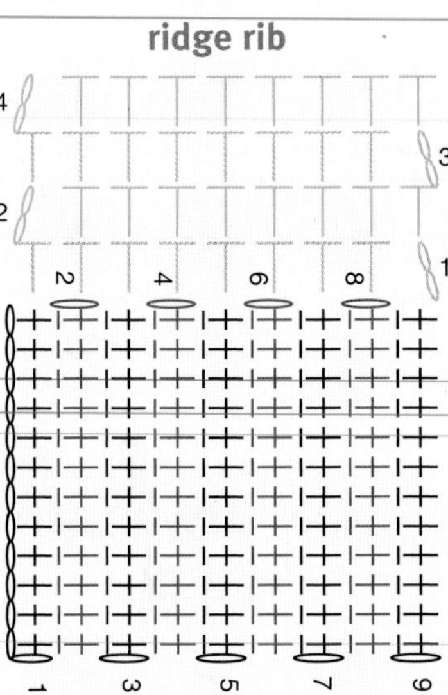

tunisian mock rib

▲ (multiple of 2 sts)

Tunisian Basic St (TBS) On first half rows, insert hook under front vertical bar from right to left, yo and draw up lp.

Edging

Make a ch to desired length in a multiple of 2 sts

Row 1 (first half) Insert hook under top lp only of 2nd ch from hook, forming a lp on hook, keeping all lps on hook, draw up a lp under top strand of each ch to end. There will be the same number of lps on hook as number of chs. *Do not turn.*

Row 1 (second half) Yo, draw through first lp, *yo, draw through 2 lps; rep from * until 1 lp rems. This lp is the first st on next row. *Do not turn.*

Row 2 (first half) Yo, draw through first lp, TBS in next st and each st to end. *Do not turn.*

Row 2 (second half) Rep second half of row 1.

Rep first and 2nd halves of row 2 nine times more or to desired depth.

Fasten off, continue with the heading on chart, or continue as desired.

tunisian mock rib

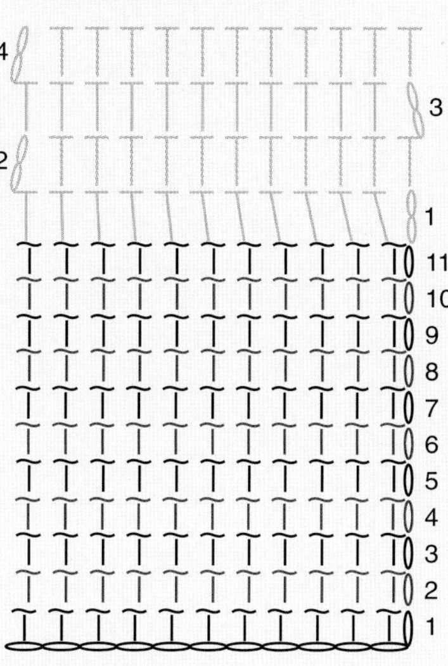

5-stitch loop rib

▲ (Over any number of sts)

JHDC (Joint hdc) Yo, insert hook into same st and draw up a lp, yo, insert hook into next st and draw up a lp, yo and draw through all 5 lps on hook.

Edging

Make a ch to desired length.

Row 1 1 sc in 2nd ch from hook and in each ch to end. Turn.

Row 2 Ch 3 (counts as 1 hdc, ch 1), JHDC in first 2 sts, *ch 1, JHDC over last st worked and next st; rep from *, end ch 1, 1 hdc in last st. Turn.

Row 3 Ch 1, *1 sc in next ch-1 sp; rep from * to end. Turn.

Rep rows 2 and 3 twice more or to desired depth.

Fasten off, continue with the heading on chart, or continue as desired.

5-stitch loop rib

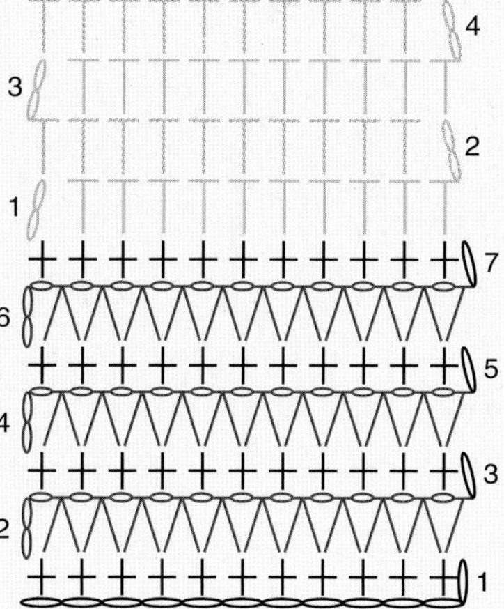

bump rib

▲ (multiple of 2 sts + 1)

FPDC (Front post dc) Yo, insert hook from front to back to front around post of designated st and draw up a lp, [yo and draw through 2 lps] twice.

Edging

Make a ch to desired length in a multiple of 2 sts.

Row 1 (WS) 1 sc in 2nd ch from hook and in each ch to end. Turn.

Row 2 Ch 1, 1 sc in first sc, *FPDC around next sc, 1 sc in next sc; rep from * to end. Turn.

Row 3 Ch 1, 1 sc in first st and in each st to end. Turn.

Row 4 Ch 1, 1 sc in first sc, *FPDC around next st 2 rows below, 1 sc in next sc; rep from * to end. Turn.

Rep rows 3 and 4 three times more or to desired depth. Fasten off, continue with the heading on chart, or continue as desired.

bump rib

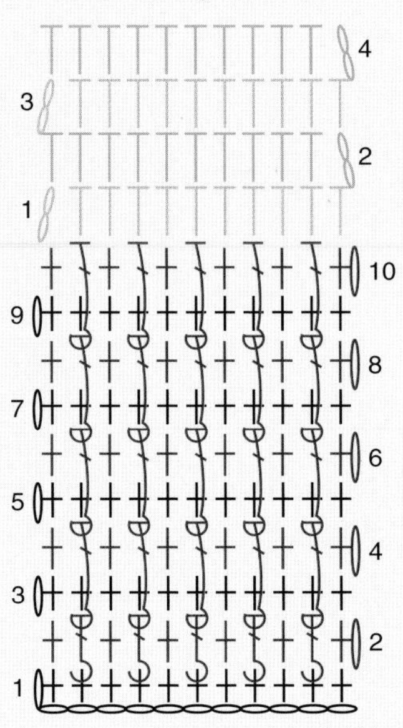

relief rib

▲ (multiple of 2 sts + 1)

FPDC (Front post dc) Yo, insert hook from front to back to front around post of designated st and draw up a lp, [yo and draw through 2 lps] twice.

Edging

Make a ch to desired length in a multiple of 2 sts.

Row 1 (RS) 1 tr in 5th ch from hook and in each ch to end. Turn.

Row 2 Ch 1, 1 sc in first tr and in each tr to end. Turn.

Row 3 Ch 1, Sc in first st, *FPDC around next st 2 rows below, 1 sc in next st; rep from * to end. Turn.

Row 4 Ch 1, 1 sc in first st and in each st to end. Turn.

Rep rows 3 and 4 twice more or to desired depth. Fasten off, continue with the heading on chart, or continue as desired.

relief rib

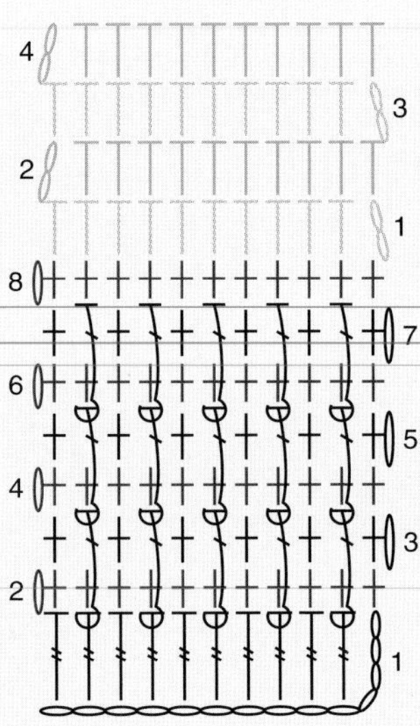

horizontal rib

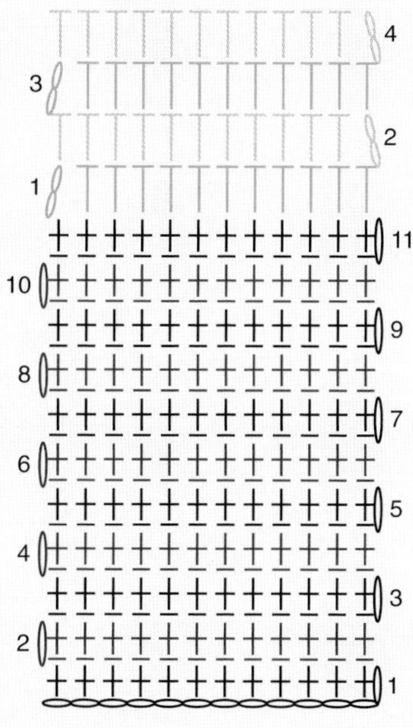

horizontal rib

▲ (over any number of sts)

Edging

Make a ch to desired length.

Row 1 1 sc in 2nd ch from hook and in each ch to end. Turn.

Row 2 Ch 1, 1 sc in back lp of first sc and in back lp of each sc to end. Turn.

Rep row 2 nine times more or to desired depth.

Fasten off, continue with the heading on chart, or continue as desired.

double ridge rib

▲ (over any number of sts)

Edging

Make a ch to desired length.

Row 1 1 dc in 4th ch from hook and in each ch to end. Turn.

Row 2 Ch 3 (counts as 1 dc), 1 dc in back lp of next dc and in each dc to end. Turn.

Rep row 2 four times more or to desired depth.

Fasten off, continue with the heading on chart, or continue as desired.

double ridge rib

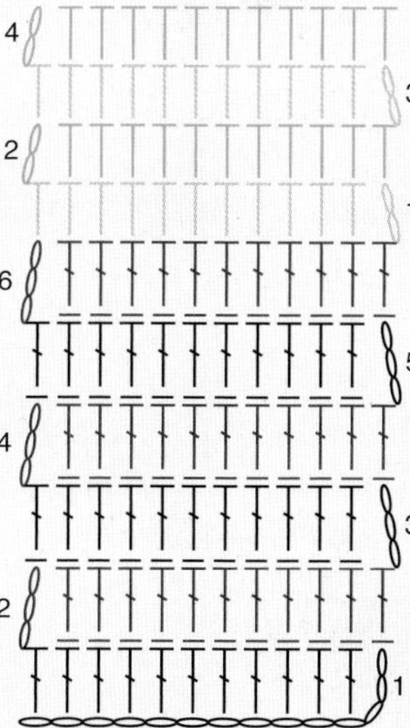

basket stitch rib

▲ (multiple of 4 sts + 3)

Edging

Make a ch to desired length in a multiple of 4 sts.

Row 1 (RS) 1 sc in 2nd ch from hook and in each ch to end. Turn.

Row 2 Ch 1, 1 sc in back lp of first sc and in each sc to end. Turn.

Row 3 Ch 1, 1 sc in back lp of first 3 sc, *1 sc in next sc of row below, 1 sc in back lp of next 3 sc; rep from * to end. Turn.

Row 4 Rep row 2.

Row 5 Ch 1, 1 sc in back lp of first sc, *1 sc in next sc of row below, 1 sc in back lp of next 3 sc; rep from *, end last rep with 1 sc in back lp of last sc. Turn.

Row 6 Rep row 2.

Rep rows 3–6 once more or to desired depth.

Fasten off, continue with the heading on chart, or continue as desired.

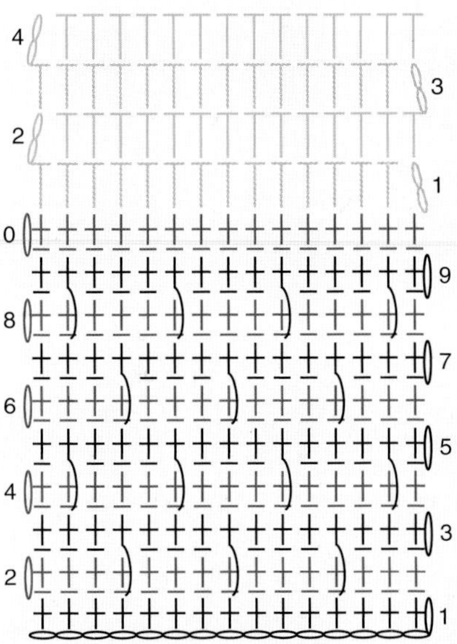

crab stitch rib

▶ (over any number of sts)

Edging

Make a ch to desired length.

Row 1 (WS) 1 sc in 2nd ch from hook and in each ch to end. *Do not turn.*

Row 2 Ch 1, working from left to right, 1 sc in front lp of first sc and in front lp of each sc to end. *Do not turn.*

Row 3 Ch 1, 1 sc in each unworked back lp of row 1. Turn.

Row 4 Ch 1, 1 sc in first sc and in each sc to end. Turn.

Row 5 Ch 1, 1 sc in first sc and in each sc to end. *Do not turn.*

Rep rows 2–5 twice more or to desired depth, then rep rows 2 and 3 once.

Fasten off, continue with the heading on chart, or continue as desired.

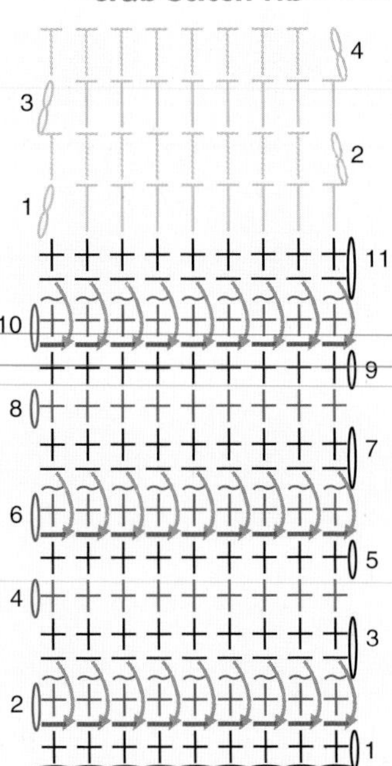

tunisian ladder rib

▲ (multiple of 6 sts + 4)

Tunisian Basic Stitch (TBS) On first half rows, insert hook under front vertical bar, yo and draw up a lp.

Tunisian Purl Stitch (TPS) On first half rows, insert the hook through the back loop of vertical bar from behind work, yo and draw up a lp.

Edging

Make a ch to desired length in a multiple of 6 sts + 4.

Row 1 (first half) Insert hook under top lp only of 2nd ch from hook, forming a lp on hook, keeping all lps on hook, draw up a lp under top strand of each ch to end. There will be the same number of lps on hook as number of chs. *Do not turn.*

Row 1 (second half) Yo, draw through first lp, *yo, draw through 2 lps; rep from * until 1 lp rems. This lp is the first st on next row. *Do not turn.*

Row 2 (first half) Yo, draw through first lp, *TBS in next 3 sts, TPS in next 3 sts; rep from *, end TBS in last 3 sts. *Do not turn.*

Row 2 (second half) Rep second half of row 1.

Rep first and 2nd halves of row 2 six times more or to desired depth. *Do not turn.*

Fasten off, continue with the heading on chart, or continue as desired.

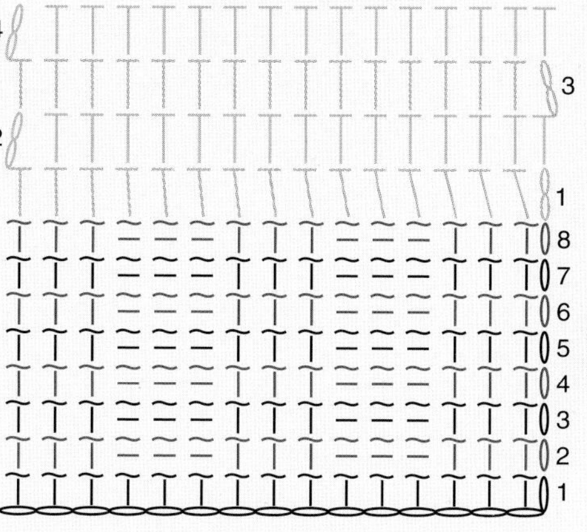

vertical rib

▶ (Over any number of sts)

Edging

Make a ch to desired depth.

Row 1 (WS) 1 sc in 2nd ch from hook and in each ch to end. Turn.

Row 2 Ch 1, 1 sc in front lp of first sc and in front lp of each sc to end. Turn.

Row 3 Ch 1, 1 sc in unworked back lp of first sc of row 1, 1 sc in each unworked back lp of row 1. Turn.

Rows 4 and 5 Ch 1, 1 sc in first sc and in each sc to end. Turn.

Rep rows 2–5 to desired width.

Fasten off, continue with the heading on chart, or continue as desired.

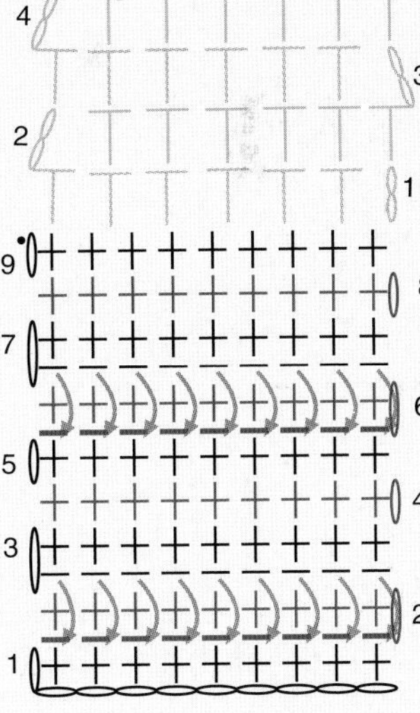

horizontal raised rib

▲ (Over any number of sts)

Edging

Make a ch to desired length.

Row 1 (WS) 1 sc in 2nd ch from hook and in each ch to end. Turn.

Row 2 Ch 1, 1 sc in front lp of first sc and in front lp of each sc to end. Turn.

Row 3 Ch 1, 1 sc in unworked back lp of first sc of row 1, 1 sc in each unworked back lp of row 1. Turn.

Rows 4 and 5 Ch 1, 1 sc in first sc and in each sc to end. Turn.

Rep rows 2–5 twice more or to desired depth. Fasten off, continue with the heading on chart, or continue as desired.

horizontal raised rib

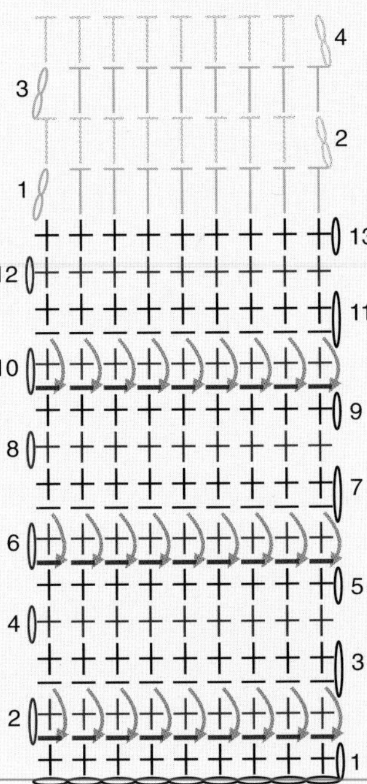

tunisian vertical clock rib

▲ (multiple of 4 sts)

Tunisian Basic Stitch (TBS) On first half rows, insert hook under front vertical bars, yo and draw up a lp.

Tunisian Cluster (TCL) On first half rows, insert hook in sp before next st, yo and draw up lp, TBS in nest st (cluster), insert hook in sp after next st (cluster), yo and draw up lp.

Edging

Make a ch to desired length in a multiple of 4 sts + 3.

Row 1 (first half) Insert hook under top lp only of 2nd ch from hook, forming a lp on hook, keeping all lps on hook, draw up a lp under top strand of each ch to end. There will be the same number of lps on hook as number of chs. *Do not turn.*

Row 1 (second half) Yo, draw through first lp, *yo, draw through 2 lps; rep from * until 1 lp rems. This lp is the first st on next row. *Do not turn.*

Row 2 (first half) Yo, draw through first lp, *TCL, TBS in next st; rep from * to end. *Do not turn.*

Row 2 (second half) Yo, draw through first lp, *yo and draw through 4 lps, (TCL made), yo and draw through 2 lps; rep from * to end. *Do not turn.*

Row 3 (first half) Yo, draw through first lp, *TCL, TBS in next st; rep from * to end. *Do not turn.*

Row 3 (second half) Rep second half of row 2.

Rep both halves of row 3 six times more or to desired depth. Fasten off, continue with the heading on chart, or continue as desired.

vertical clock rib

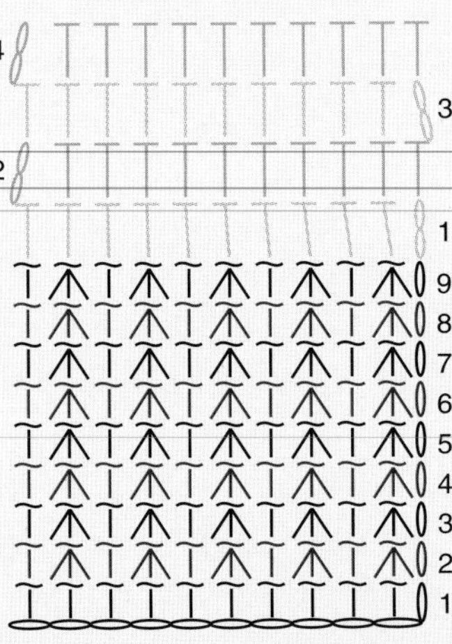

horizontal rib eyelet

▲ (multiple of 2 sts)

Edging

Make a ch to desired length in a multiple of 2 sts + 1.

Row 1 1 sc in 2nd ch from hook and in each ch to end. Turn.

Row 2 Ch 2 (counts as 1 hdc), *skip next sc, 1 hdc in next sc, 1 hdc in skipped sc *(crossed hdc made)*; rep from *, end 1 hdc in last sc. Turn.

Row 3 Ch 1, 1 sc in front lp of first hdc and in front lp of each hdc to end. Turn.

Rep rows 2 and 3 twice more or to desired depth. Fasten off, continue with the heading on chart, or continue as desired.

horizontal rib eyelet

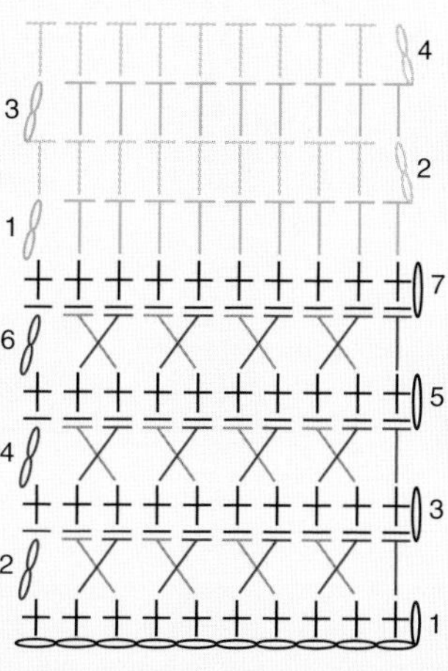

wave rib

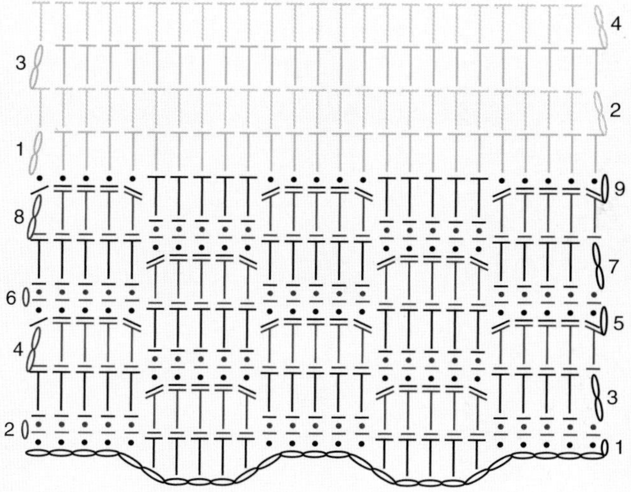

wave rib

▲ (multiple of 10 sts + 5)

Edging

Make a ch to desired length in a multiple of 10 sts + 6.

Row 1 Sl st in 2nd ch from hook and in next 4 ch, *1 hdc in next 5 ch, sl st in next 5 ch; rep from * to end. Turn.

Row 2 Ch 1, sl st in back lp of next 5 sl sts, *1 hdc in back lp of next 5 hdc, sl st in back lp of next 5 sl st; rep from * to end. Turn.

Row 3 Ch 2, 1 hdc in back lp of next 4 sl sts, *sl st in back lp of next 5 hdc, 1 hdc in back lp of next 5 sl st; rep from * to end. Turn.

Row 4 Ch 2, 1 hdc in back lp of next 4 sl sts, *sl st in back lp of next 5 hdc, 1 hdc in back lp of next 5 sl sts; rep from * to end. Turn.

Row 5 Ch 1, sl st in back lp of next 5 hdc, *1 hdc in back lp of next 5 sl sts, sl st in back lp of next 5 hdc; rep from * to end. Turn.

Row 6 Rep row 2.

Rows 7, 8 and 9 Rep rows 3, 4 and 5.

Fasten off, continue with the heading on chart, or continue as desired.

blind rib

▲ (multiple of 2 sts + 1)

FPHDC (Front post hdc) Yo, insert hook from front to back to front around post of designated st and draw up a lp, yo and draw through all 3 lps on hook.

Edging

Make a ch to desired length in a multiple of 2 sts + 1.

Row 1 (RS) 1 dc in 4th ch from hook and in each ch to end. Turn.

Row 2 Ch 1, 1 sc in first dc and in each dc to end. Turn.

Row 3 Ch 3, FPHDC around next st 2 rows below, 1 dc in next st; rep from * to end. Turn.

Row 4 Ch 1, 1 sc in first dc, *1 sc in FPHDC, 1 sc in sp before next dc; rep from *, end 1 sc in top of beg ch-3. Turn.

Row 5 Ch 3, FPHDC around next st 2 rows below, 1 dc in next st; rep from * to end. Turn.

Rep rows 4 and 5 once more or to desired depth. Fasten off, continue with the heading on chart, or continue as desired.

blind rib

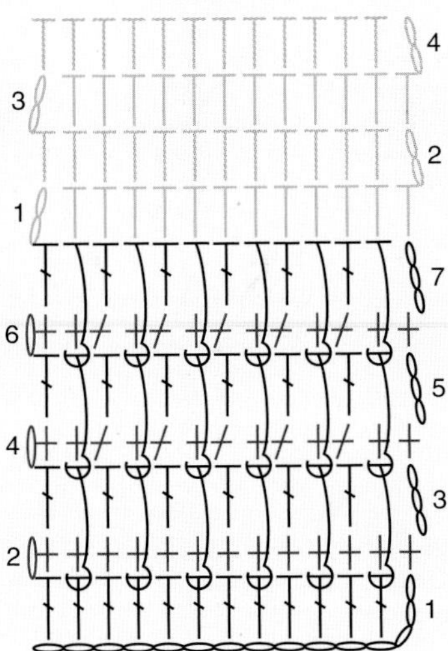

eiffel tower

▲ (multiple of 4 sts + 1)

LS (Long sc) Insert hook in next sc 4 rows below, draw up a lp to top of work, yo and draw through both lps on hook.

Edging

Make a ch to desired length in a multiple of 4 sts + 2.

Row 1 1 sc in 2nd ch from hook and in each ch to end. Turn.

Rows 2, 3, 4 and 5 Ch 1, 1 sc in first sc and in each sc to end. Turn.

Row 6 Ch 1, 1 sc in first 2 sc, *LS in next sc 4 rows below, 1 sc in next 3 sc; rep from *, end last rep with 1 sc in last 2 sc. Turn.

Rows 7, 8, 9 and 10 Ch 1, 1 sc in first sc and in each sc to end. Turn.

Row 11 Ch 1, 1 sc in first 4 sc, *LS in next sc 4 rows below, 1 sc in next 3 sc; rep from *, end 1 sc in last sc. Turn.

Rep rows 2–11 to desired depth.

Fasten off, continue with the heading on chart, or continue as desired.

eiffel tower

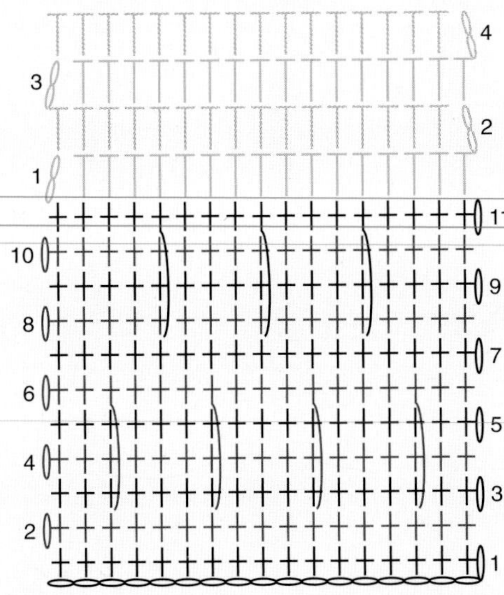

step rib

▲ (multiple of 8 sts + 2)

FPDC (Front post dc) Yo, insert hook from front to back to front around post of designated st and draw up a lp, [yo and draw through 2 lps] twice.

BPDC (Back post dc) Yo, insert hook from back to front to back around post of designated st and draw up a lp, [yo and draw through 2 lps] twice.

Edging

Make a ch to desired length in a multiple of 8 sts + 4.

Row 1 (WS) 1 dc in 4th ch from hook and in each ch to end. Turn.

Rows 2 and 3 Ch 3, *FPDC around next 4 sts, BPDC around next 4 sts; rep from *, end 1 dc in top of beg ch-3. Turn.

Row 4 Ch 3, FPDC around next 3 sts, BPDC around next 4 sts, *FPDC around next 4 sts, BPDC around next 4 sts; rep from *, end FPDC in next st, 1 dc in top of beg ch-3. Turn.

Row 5 Ch 3, BPDC around next st, FPDC around next 4 sts, *BPDC around next 4 sts, FPDC around next 4 sts; rep from *, end BPDC around next 3 sts, 1 dc in top of beg ch-3. Turn.

Row 6 Ch 3, FPDC around next 2 sts, BPDC around next 4 sts, *FPDC around next 4 sts, BPDC around next 4 sts; rep from *, end FPDC around next 2 sts, 1 dc in top of beg ch-3. Turn.

Row 7 Ch 3, BPDC around next 2 sts, FPDC around next 4 sts, BPDC around next 4 sts, FPDC around next 4 sts; rep from *, end BPDC around next 2 sts, 1 dc in top of beg ch-3. Fasten off, continue with the heading on chart, or continue as desired.

Note For a deeper edging, rep row 6 working 1 less FPDC at beg and 1 more at end of row and row 7 working 1 more BPDC at beg and 1 less at end of row.

step rib

basket rib

▲ (multiple of 6 sts + 5)

FPDC (Front post dc) Yo, insert hook from front to back to front around post of designated st and draw up a lp, [yo and draw through 2 lps] twice.

BPDC (Back post dc) Yo, insert hook from back to front to back around post of designated st and draw up a lp, [yo and draw through 2 lps] twice.

Edging

Make a ch to desired length in a multiple of 6 sts + 1.

Row 1 (RS) 1 dc in 4th ch from hook and in each ch to end. Turn.

Rows 2 and 3 Ch 3, *FPDC around next 3 sts, BPDC around next 3 sts; rep from *, end FPDC around next 3 sts, 1 dc in top of beg ch-3. Turn.

Rows 4 and 5 Ch 3, *BPDC around next 3 sts, FPDC around next 3 sts; rep from *, end BPDC around next 3 sts, 1 dc in top of beg ch-3. Turn.

Rep rows 2–5 to desired depth.

Fasten off, continue with the heading on chart, or continue as desired.

basket rib

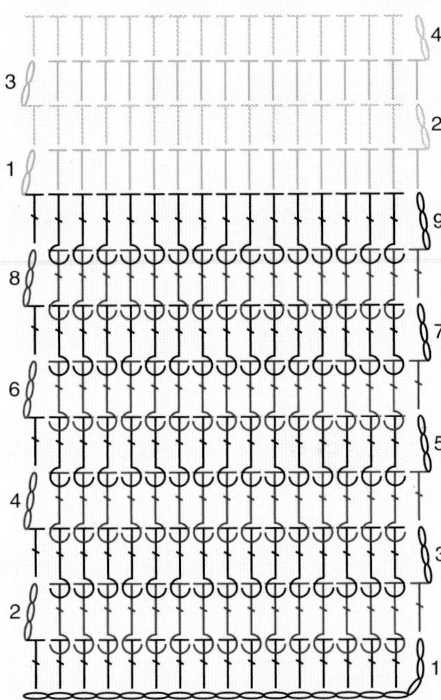

herringbone rib

▲ (multiple of 12 sts + 3)

Edging

Make a ch to desired length in a multiple of 12 sts + 4.

Row 1 (RS) 1 sc in 2nd ch from hook, *ch 1, skip next ch, 1 sc in next ch; rep from * to end. Turn.

Row 2 Ch 1, 1 sc in first sc, *ch 1, 1 sc in next sc; rep from * to end. Turn.

Row 3 Ch 1, 1 sc in first sc, *ch 1, 1 sc in next sc, ch 6, skip next 2 ch-1 sp, sl st in next ch-1 sp 2 rows below, ch 6, skip next 2 ch-1 sp, 1 sc in next sc; rep from *, end ch 1, 1 sc in last sc. Turn.

Row 4 Ch 1, 1 sc in first sc, *ch 1, 1 sc in next sc, [ch 1, 1 dc in next sc of row 2] 4 times, ch 1, 1 sc in next sc; rep from *, end ch 1, 1 sc in last sc. Turn.

Rep rows 3 and 4 three times more or to desired depth.

Fasten off, continue with the heading on chart, or continue as desired.

herringbone rib

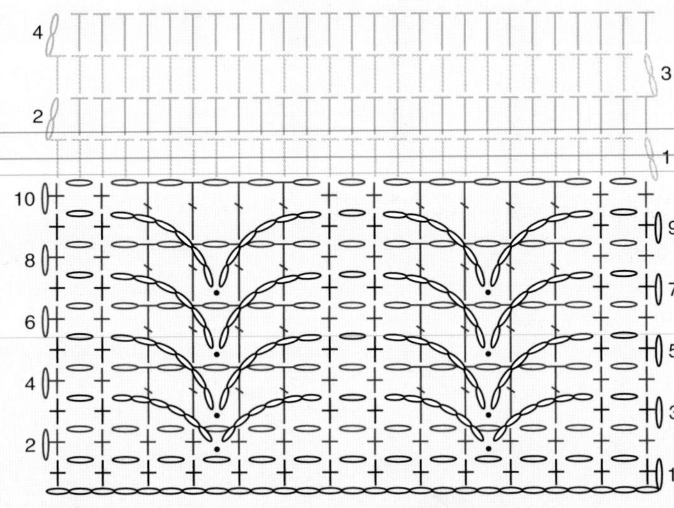

mock rib cable

▲ (multiple of 6 sts + 1)

FPDC (Front post dc) Yo, insert hook from front to back to front around post of designated st and draw up a lp, [yo and draw through 2 lps] twice.

MC (Mock cable) Skip next 2 sc, FPDC around next sc, 1 sc in 2nd skipped sc, FPDC around first skipped sc.

Edging

Make a ch to desired length in a multiple of 6 sts + 2.

Row 1 (WS) 1 sc in 2nd ch from hook and in each ch to end. Turn.

Row 2 Ch 1, 1 sc in first 2 sc, *MC, skip next sc, 1 sc in next 3 sc; rep from *, end 1 sc in last 2 sc. Turn.

Row 3 Ch 1, 1 sc in first sc and in each st to end. Turn.

Row 4 Ch 1, 1 sc in first 2 sc, *FPDC around 2nd post of cable below, skip next sc, 1 sc in next sc, FPDC around first post of cable below, skip next sc, 1 sc in next 3 sc; rep from *, end 1 sc in last 2 sc. Turn.

Rep rows 3 and 4 three times more or to desired depth.

Fasten off, continue with the heading on chart, or continue as desired.

mock rib cable

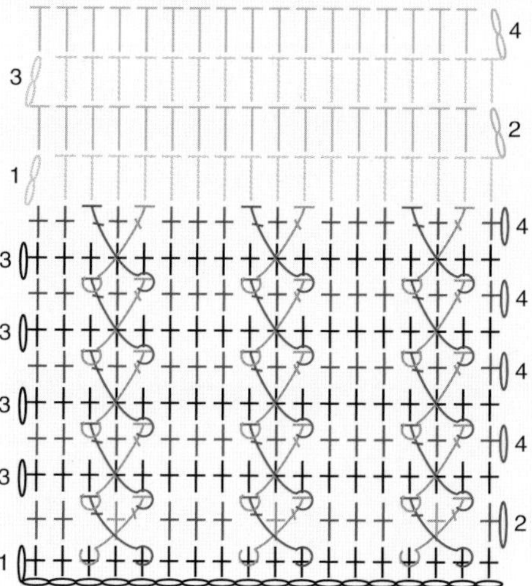

hopscotch band

▲ **Colors** A and B

(multiple of 10 sts + 5)

FPSC (Front post sc) Insert hook from front to back to front around post of designated st and draw up a lp, yo and draw through both lps on hook.

Edging

With A, make a ch to desired length in a multiple of 10 sts + 7.

Row 1 1 dc in 4th ch from hook and in each ch to end. Turn.

Fasten off A and attach B.

Row 2 With B, ch 1, 1 FPSC around first 5 dc, *[1 dc in next dc, 1 sc in next dc] twice, 1 dc in next dc, 1 FPSC around next 5 dc; rep from * to end. Turn.

Fasten off B and attach A.

Row 3 With A, Ch 3, 1 dc in next st and in each st to end. Turn.

Fasten off A and attach B.

Row 4 Ch 3, [1 sc in next dc, 1 dc in next dc] twice, *FPSC around next 5 dc, [1 dc in next dc, 1 sc in next dc] twice, 1 dc in next dc; rep from * to end. Turn.

Fasten off B and attach A.

Row 5 With A, rep row 3.

Rep rows 2–5 to desired depth.

Fasten off, continue with the heading on chart, or continue as desired.

hopscotch band

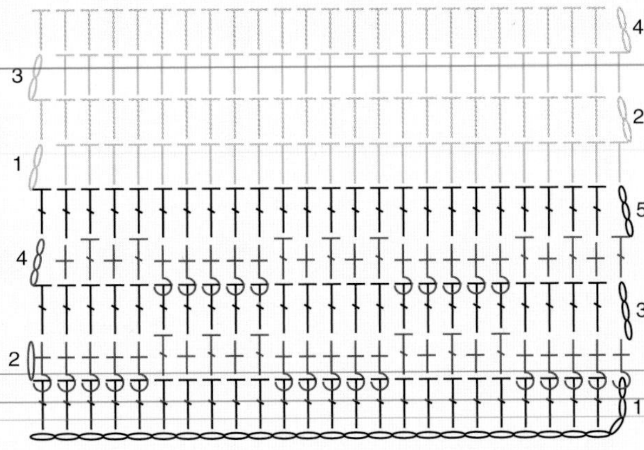

oyster rib

▼ (multiple of 4 sts + 2)

Edging

Make a ch to desired length in a multiple of 4 sts + 3.

Row 1 1 sc in 2nd ch from hook, 1 sc in next ch, ch 2, 2 dc in sc just made, *skip 2 ch, 1 sc in next 2 ch, ch 2, 2 dc in sc just made; rep from *, end last rep with skip 2 ch, 1 sc in last 2 ch. Turn.

Row 2 Ch 1, 1 sc in first 2 sc, *ch 2, 2 dc in sc just made, 1 sc in next 2 sc; rep from * to end. Turn.

Rep row 2 once more or to desired depth.

Fasten off.

Heading

Working along foundation ch, attach yarn to right-hand edge.

oyster rib

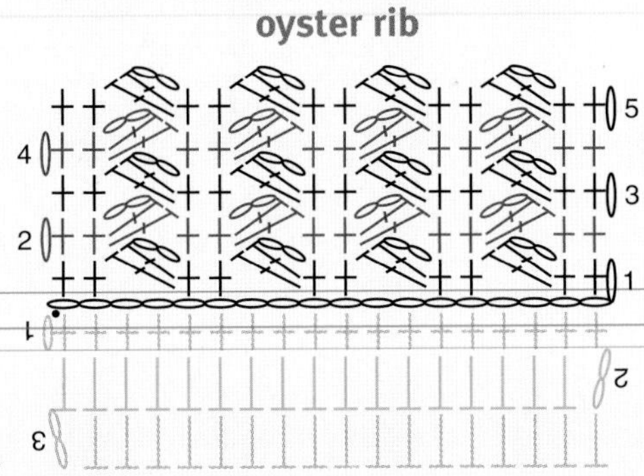

Row 1 Ch 1, 1 sc in first ch and in each ch to end. Turn.

Row 2 Ch 2 (counts as 1 hdc), 1 hdc in next sc and in each sc to end. Turn.

Row 3 Ch 2, 1 hdc in next hdc and in each hdc to end.

Fasten off or continue as desired.

slanty rib

▲ (multiple of 4 sts + 3)

FPDC (Front post dc) Yo, insert hook from front to back to front around post of designated st and draw up a lp, [yo and draw through 2 lps] twice.

Edging

Make a ch to desired length in a multiple of 4 sts.

Row 1 (RS) 1 sc in 2nd ch from hook and in each ch to end. Turn.

Row 2 Ch 1, 1 sc in first sc and in each sc to end. Turn.

Row 3 Ch 1, 1 sc in first 3 sc, *FPDC around next sc, 1 sc in next 3 sc; rep from * to end. Turn.

Rows 4, 6 and 8 Ch 1, 1 sc in first st and in each st to end. Turn.

Row 5 Ch 1, 1 sc in first 4 sc, FPDC around first FPDC 2 rows below, skip sc behind FPDC just made, *1 sc in next 3 sc, FPDC around next FPDC 2 rows below, skip sc behind FPDC just made; rep from *, end 1 sc in last 2 sc. Turn.

Row 7 Ch 1, 1 sc in first sc, FPDC around next sc, skip sc behind FPDC just made, *1 sc in next 3 sc, FPDC around next FPDC 2 rows below, skip sc behind FPDC just made; rep from *, end 1 sc in last sc. Turn.

Row 9 Ch 1, 1 sc in first 2 sc, FPDC around first FPDC 2 rows below, *skip sc behind FPDC just made, 1 sc in next 3 sc, FPDC around next FPDC 2 rows below; rep from *, end 1 sc in last 4 sc. Turn.

Rep rows 2–9 to desired depth.

Fasten off, continue with the heading on chart, or continue as desired.

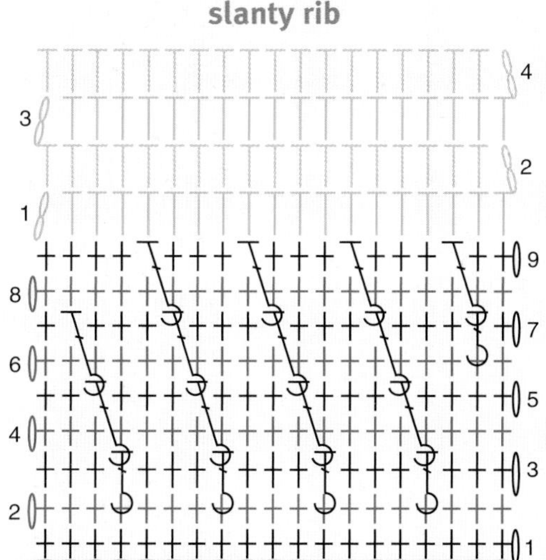

worm rib

▶ **Edging**

Ch 9 or to desired depth.

Row 1 (WS) 1 sc in 2nd ch from hook and in each ch to end. Turn.

Row 2 Ch 1, 1 sc in first sc and in each sc to end. Turn.

Row 3 Ch 4, 1 tr in back lp of next sc and in back lp of each sc to end. Turn.

Row 4 Ch 1, *1 sc in back lps of next tr *and* sc of row below; rep from * to end. Turn.

Row 5 Ch 1, 1 sc in first sc and in each sc to end. Turn.

Rep rows 2–5 to desired length.

Fasten off, continue with the heading on chart, or continue as desired.

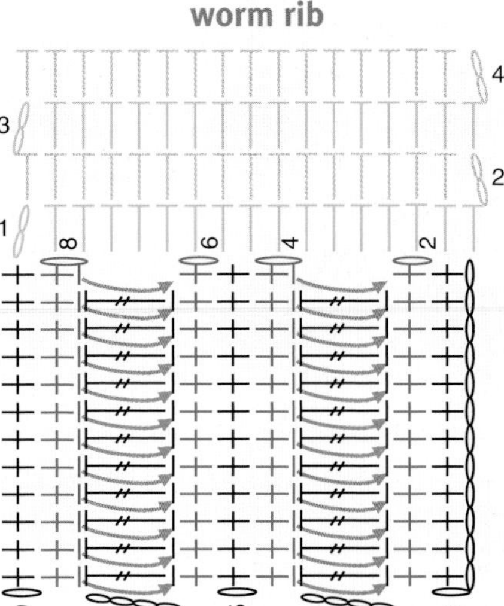

cable rib

▲ (multiple of 4 sts + 2)

Edging

Make a ch to desired length in a multiple of 4 sts + 3.

Row 1 (WS) 1 sc in 2nd ch from hook and in each ch to end. Turn.

Row 2 Ch 3, *skip next sc, 1 dc in next 3 sc, 1 dc in skipped sc; rep from *, end 1 dc in last sc. Turn.

Row 3 Ch 1, 1 sc in first st and in each st to end. Turn.

Rep rows 2 and 3 twice more or to desired depth.

Fasten off, continue with the heading on chart, or continue as desired.

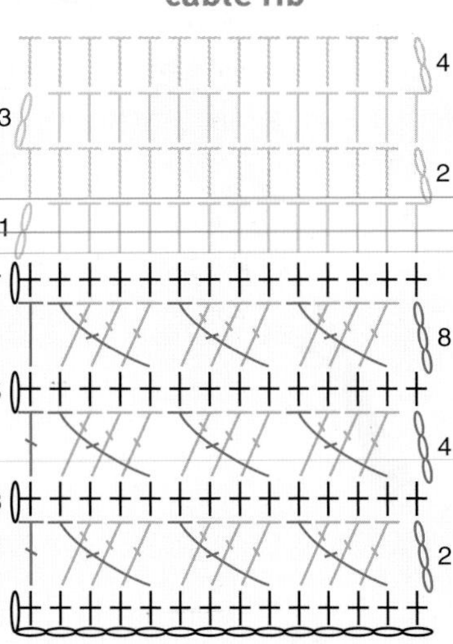

tunisian chain cable rib

▲ (multiple of 10 sts + 4)

Tunisian Knit Stitch (TKS) On first half rows, insert hook from front to back through center of vertical bars (the hook should pass under the chain formed by the second half of the previous row, yo and draw up a lp.

Tunisian Purl Stitch (TPS) On first half rows, insert the hook through the back loop of vertical bar from behind work, yo and draw up a lp.

Edging

Make a ch to desired length in a multiple of 10 sts + 4.

Row 1 (first half) Insert hook under top lp only of 2nd ch from hook, forming a lp on hook, keeping all lps on hook, draw up a lp under top strand of each ch to end. There will be the same number of lps on hook as number of chs.

Do not turn.

Row 1 (second half) Yo, draw through first lp, *yo, draw through 2 lps; rep from * until 1 lp rems. This lp is the first st on next row. *Do not turn.*

Row 2 (first half) Yo, draw through first lp, TPS in next 3 sts, TKS in next 6 sts, * TPS in next 4 sts; rep from *, end last rep with TPS in last 3 sts, draw up a lp in last bar.

Do not turn.

Row 2 (second half) Rep second half of row 1.

Rows 3 and 4 Rep both halves of row 2.

Row 5 (first half) Rep first half of row 2.

Row 5 (second half) Yo, draw through first lp, [yo, draw through 2 lps] 3 times, *drop first lp from hook, then drop next 6 TKS lps, with hook in *front* of work, make right twist by inserting hook through 3 knit sts at left, then 3 knit sts at right, pick up first dropped lp, [yo, draw through 2 lps] 10 times; rep from * to end. *Do not turn.*

Rows 6, 7 and 8 Rep both halves of rows 2, 3 and 4.

Rep both halves of rows 5–8 to depth desired.

Fasten off, continue with the heading on chart, or continue as desired.

tunisian chain cable rib

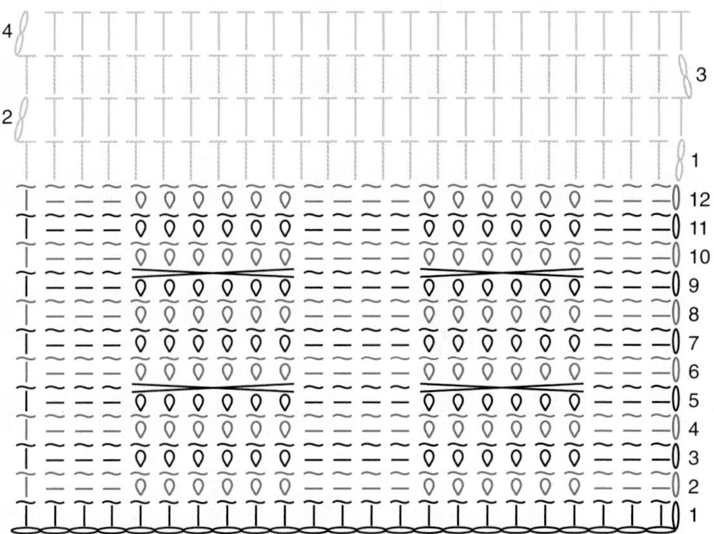

twisted loop rib

▲ (multiple of 3 sts + 2)

Edging

Make a ch to desired length in a multiple of 3 sts.

Row 1 (RS) 1 sc in 2nd ch from hook and in each ch to end. Turn.

Row 2 Ch 1, 1 sc in first sc and in each sc to end. Turn.

Row 3 Ch 1, 1 sc in first sc, *ch 3, skip next 2 sc, 1 sc in next sc, ch 1, TURN, 1 sc in next 3 ch, ch 1, TURN, 1 sc in 2 skipped sc; rep from *, end ch 1, 1 sc in last sc. Turn.

Row 4 Ch 1, 1 sc in first sc, *2 sc in next sc behind lp, 1 sc in next sc behind lp; rep from *, end 1 sc in last sc. Turn.

Row 5 Rep row 2.

Rep rows 2–5 once more or to desired depth.

Fasten off, continue with the heading on chart, or continue as desired.

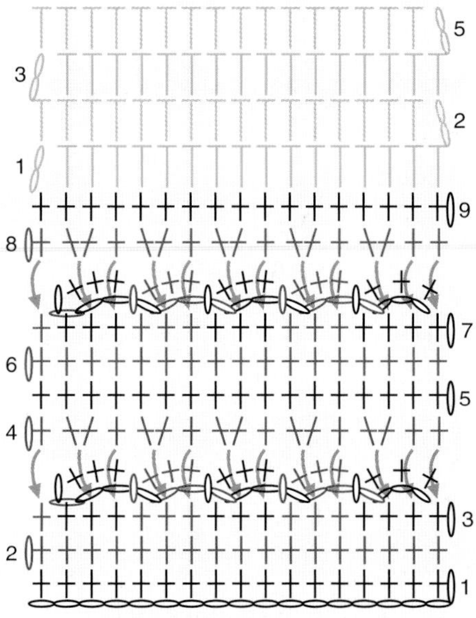

NOTE: REFER TO INSTRUCTION FOR CORRECT STITCH PLACEMENT ON CABLES

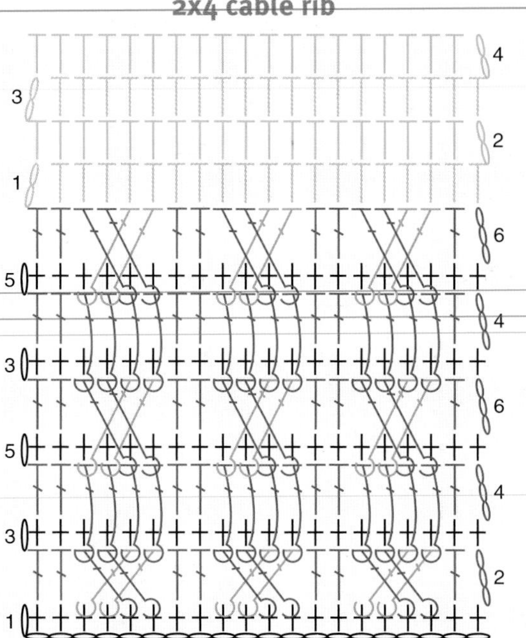

baby cable rib

▲ (multiple of 4 sts + 2)

FPDC (Front post dc) Yo, insert hook from front to back to front around post of designated st and draw up a lp, [yo and draw through 2 lps] twice.

Edging

Make a ch to desired length in a multiple of 4 sts + 3.

Row 1 (WS) 1 sc in 2nd ch from hook and in each ch to end. Turn.

Row 2 Ch 3 (counts as 1 dc), 1 dc in next sc, *skip next sc, FPDC around next sc, FPDC around skipped sc, 1 dc in next 2 sc; rep from * to end. Turn.

Row 3 Ch 1, 1 sc in first dc and in each dc to end. Turn.

Row 4 Ch 3 (counts as 1 dc), 1 dc in next sc, *skip next sc, FPDC around next FPDC in 2d row below, FPDC around FPDC below skipped sc, 1 dc in next 2 sc; rep from * to end.

Rep rows 3 and 4 twice more or to desired depth.

Fasten off, continue with the heading on chart, or continue as desired.

baby cable rib

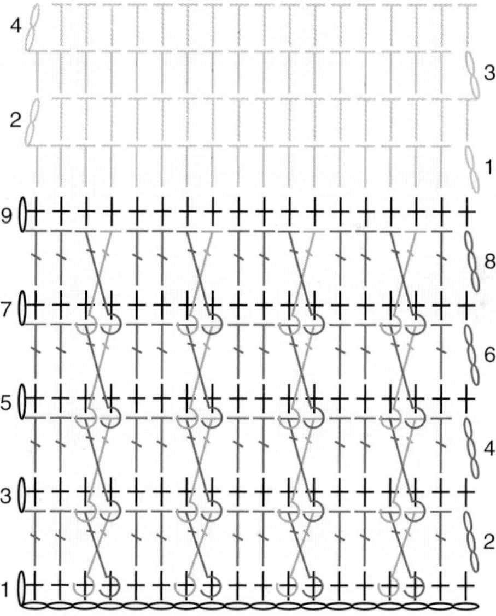

2x4 cable rib

▲ (multiple of 6 sts + 2)

FPDC (Front post dc) Yo, insert hook from front to back to front around post of designated st and draw up a lp, [yo and draw through 2 lps] twice.

Edging

Make a ch to desired length in a multiple of 6 sts + 3.

Row 1 (WS) 1 sc in 2nd ch from hook and in each ch to end. Turn.

Row 2 Ch 3 (counts as 1 dc), 1 dc in next sc, *skip next 2 sc, FPDC around next 2 sc, FPDC around 2 skipped sc, 1 dc in next 2 sc; rep from * to end. Turn.

Row 3 Ch 1, 1 sc in first st and in each st to end. Turn.

Row 4 Ch 3, 1 dc in next sc, *FPDC around next 4 FPDC, 1 dc in next 2 sc; rep from * to end. Turn.

Row 5 Rep row 3.

Row 6 Ch 3, 1 dc in next sc, *skip next 2 sc, FPDC around next 2 FPDC, FPDC around 2 FPDC under 2 skipped sc, 1 dc in next 2 sc; rep from * to end. Turn.

Rep rows 3–6 once more or to desired depth.

Fasten off, continue with the heading on chart, or continue as desired.

chain rib

▲ **Colors** A and B

(multiple of 4 sts)

Edging

With A, make a ch to desired length in a multiple of 4 sts + 1)

Row 1 (RS) 1 sc in 2nd ch from hook, 1 sc in next 3 ch, *ch 12, 1 sc in next 4 ch; rep from * to end. Turn.

Row 2 With ch-lps toward RS, 1 sc in first sc and in each sc across.

Rows 3 and 4 Ch 1, 1 sc in first sc and in each sc to end.

Fasten off A and attach B.

Row 5 1 sc in first sc, 1 sc in next 3 sc, *ch 12, 1 sc in next 4 sc; rep from * to end. Turn.

Rows 6, 7, 8 and 9 Rep rows 2–5.

Fasten off B and attach A.

Rows 10 and 11 Rep rows 2 and 3.

Starting at row 1, chain lps tog by pulling each lp through the one below.

Row 12 Ch 1, 1 sc in first 4 sc, *insert hook in next sc and next ch-lp, yo and draw up a lp, yo and draw through both lps on hook, 1 sc in next 3 sc; rep from * to end.

Fasten off, continue with the heading on chart, or continue as desired.

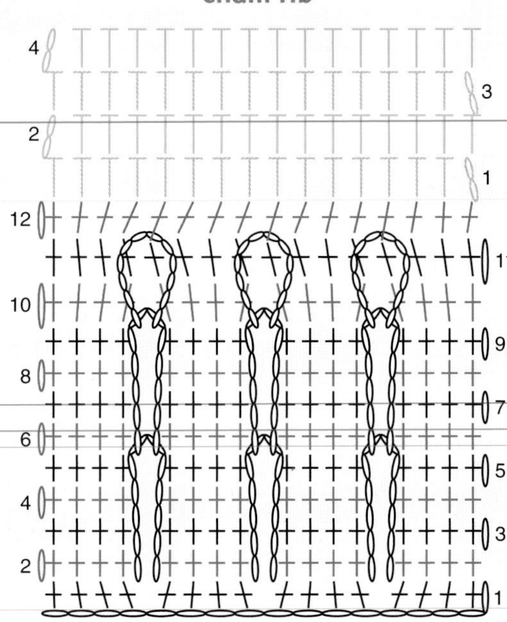

chain loop rib

▲ **Colors** A and B

(multiple of 4 sts)

Edging

With A, make a ch to desired length in a multiple of 16 + 5.

Fasten off A and attach B.

Row 1 (RS) 1 sc in 2nd ch from hook, 1 sc in next 3 ch, *skip next 12 ch, 1 sc in next 4 ch; rep from * to end. Turn.

Row 2 Ch 1, 1 sc in first 4 sc, *ch 12, 1 sc in next 4 sc; rep from * to end. Turn.

Row 3 Ch 1, with ch-lps toward RS, 1 sc in first sc and in each sc to end.

Row 4 Ch 1, 1 sc in first sc and in each sc to end. Fasten off B and attach A.

Row 5 1 sc in first sc, 1 sc in next 3 sc, *ch 12, 1 sc in next 4 sc; rep from * to end. Turn.

Row 6–8 Rep row 3.

Fasten off A and attach B.

Row 9 Rep row 5.

Rows 10 and 11 Rep row 3.

Starting at Row 1, chain lps tog by pulling each lp through the one below.

Row 12 Ch 1, 1 sc in first 4 sc, *insert hook in next sc and next ch-lp, yo and draw up a lp, yo and draw through both lps on hook, 1 sc in next 3 sc; rep from * to end.

Fasten off, continue with the heading on chart, or continue as desired.

chain loop rib

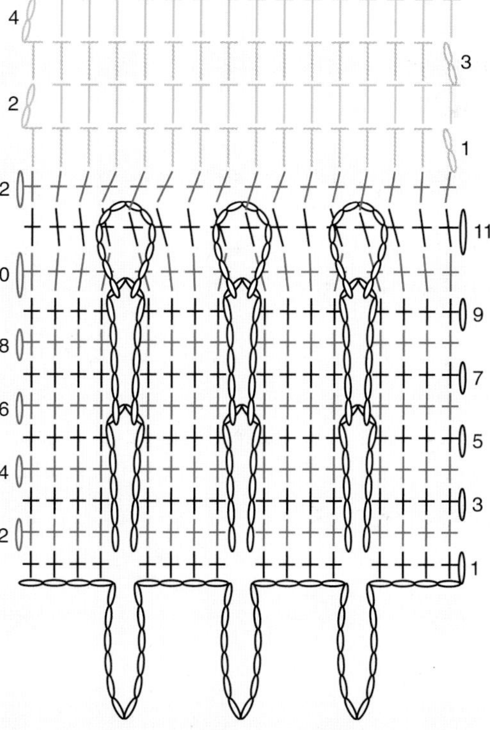

fence rib

▲ (multiple of 5 sts + 3)

FPDC (Front post dc) Yo, insert hook from front to back to front around post of designated st and draw up a lp, [yo and draw through 2 lps] twice.

BPDC (Back post dc) Yo, insert hook from back to front to back around post of designated st and draw up a lp, [yo and draw through 2 lps] twice.

Edging

Make a ch to desired length in a multiple of 5 sts.

Row 1 (WS) 1 dc in 4th ch from hook and in each ch to end. Turn.

Row 2 Ch 3, FPDC around next 2 dc, BPDC around next 2 dc, *FPDC around next 3 dc, BPDC around next 2 dc; rep from *, end FPDC around next 2 dc, 1 dc in top of beg ch-3. Turn.

Row 3 Ch 3, BPDC around next 2 dc, FPDC around next 2 dc, *BPDC around next 3 dc, FPDC around next 2 dc; rep from *, end BPDC around next 2 dc, 1 dc in top of ch-3. Turn.

Rep rows 2 and 3 once more, then row 2 once again; or rep rows 2 and 3 to desired depth.

Fasten off, continue with the heading on chart, or continue as desired.

fence rib

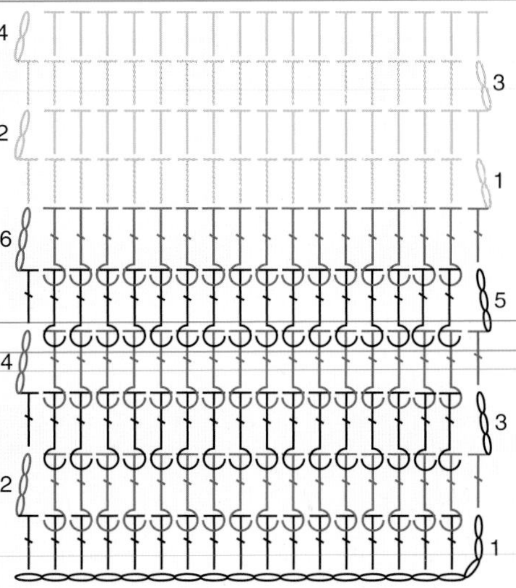

shadow box rib

▲ (multiple of 4 sts + 3)

FPDC (Front post dc) Yo, insert hook from front to back to front around post of designated st and draw up a lp, [yo and draw through 2 lps] twice.

BPDC (Back post dc) Yo, insert hook from back to front to back around post of designated st and draw up a lp, [yo and draw through 2 lps] twice.

Edging

Make a ch to desired length in a multiple of 4 sts + 5.

Row 1 1 dc in 4th ch from hook and in each ch to end. Turn.

Row 2 Ch 3 (counts as 1 dc), FPDC around next 2 dc, * BPDC around next dc, FPDC around next 3 dc; rep from *, end last rep as BPDC around next dc, FPDC around next 2 dc, 1 dc in top of beg ch-3. Turn.

Row 3 Ch 3, 1 dc in next 2 dc, *FPDC around next dc, 1 dc in next 3 dc; rep from * to end. Turn.

Rep rows 2 and 3 once more, then row 2 once again; or rep rows 2 and 3 to desired depth.

Fasten off, continue with the heading on chart, or continue as desired.

shadow box rib

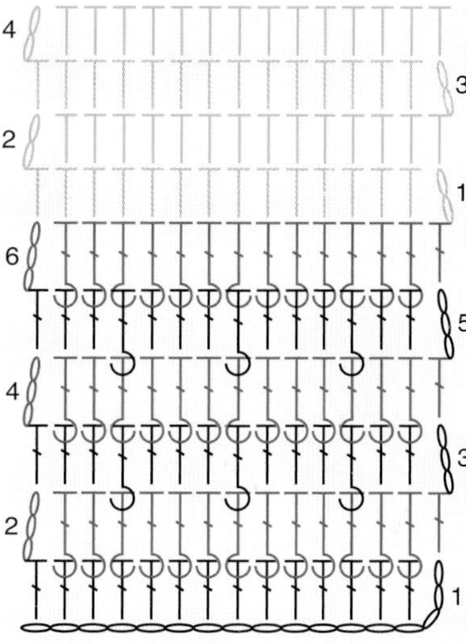

galley rib

▼ (multiple of 8 sts + 5)

Note This edging can be worked directly onto a project or onto the heading as shown and attached.

Heading

Make a ch to desired length in a multiple of 8 + 6.

Row 1 1 hdc in 3rd ch from hook and in each ch to end. Turn.

Row 2 Ch 2 (counts as 1 hdc), 1 hdc in next hdc and in each hdc to end. Turn.

Row 3 Rep row 2.

Fasten off.

Edging

FPDC (Front post dc) Yo, insert hook from front to back to front around post of designated st and draw up a lp, [yo and draw through 2 lps] twice.

With WS facing, attach yarn to right-hand edge of heading or project.

Row 1 (WS) Ch 3, 1 dc in next 4 sts or chs, *skip next st (ch) [2 dc, ch 2, 2 dc] in next st (ch), skip next st, 1 dc in next 5 sts (chs); rep from * to end. Turn.

Row 2 Ch 3, FPDC around next 4 dc, *skip next 2 dc, [2 dc, ch 2, 2 dc] in next ch-2 sp, skip next 2 dc, FPDC around next 5 dc; rep from *, end last rep with FPDC around next 4 dc, 1 dc in top of beg ch3. Turn.

Rep row 2 four times more or to desired depth.

Fasten off or continue as desired.

fence rib

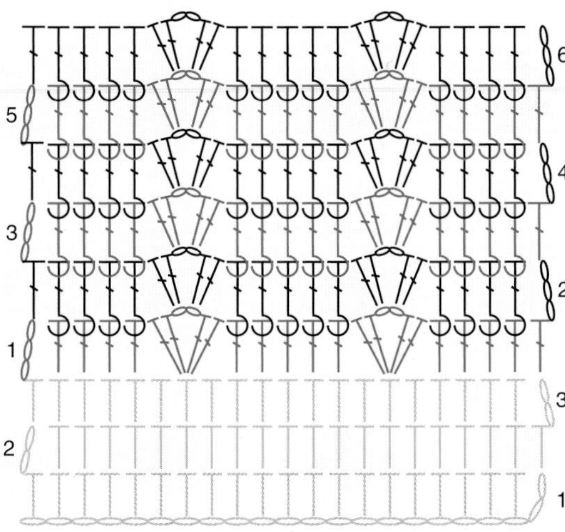

stardust

▲ (multiple of 2 sts + 1)

Tunisian Basic Stitch (TBS) On first half rows, insert hook under front vertical bar, yo and draw up a lp.

Edging

Make a ch to desired length in a multiple of 2 sts + 1.

Row 1 (first half) Insert hook under top lp only of 2nd ch from hook, forming a lp on hook, keeping all lps on hook, draw up a lp under top strand of each ch to end. There will be the same number of lps on hook as number of chs. *Do not turn.*

Row 1 (second half) Yo, draw through first lp, *yo, draw through 2 lps; rep from * until 1 lp rems. This lp is the first st on next row. *Do not turn.*

Row 2 (first half) Yo, draw through first lp, TBS in next st and in each st to end. *Do not turn.*

Row 2 (second half) Rep second half of row 1.

Row 3 Rep both halves of row 2.

Row 4 Ch 2, draw up a lp in 2nd ch from hook and in first 3 bars, yo and draw through all 5 lps, ch 1 for eye (first Star st made), *draw up a lp in center of last eye, draw up a lp in back of last st picked up , draw up a lp in next 2 bars, yo and draw through all 5 lps, ch 1 for eye (Star st made); rep from * to end. Turn.

Row 5 Ch 2, 2 hdc in 3rd ch from hook, *2 hdc in next eye; rep from *, end 1 hdc in top of beg ch-2.

Rows 6, 7 and 8 Rep both halves of row 2.

Fasten off, continue with the heading on chart, or continue as desired.

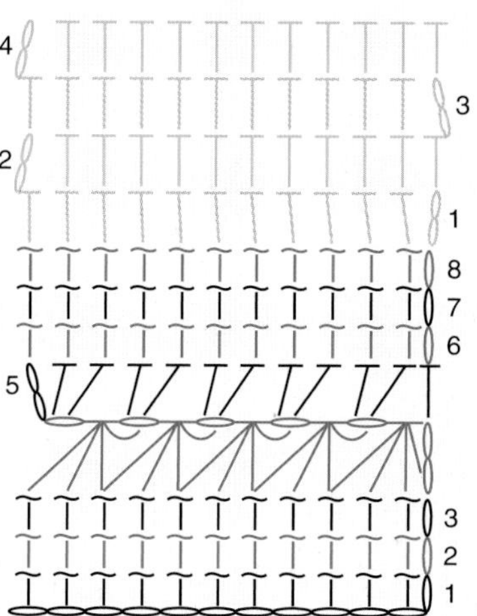

popped border

▲ (multiple of 6 sts + 1)

Popcorn 5 dc in designated st, drop lp from hook, insert hook in first dc of 5-dc group just made and dropped lp, yo and draw through both lps on hook.

Edging

Make a ch to desired length in a multiple of 6 sts + 3.

Row 1 1 dc in 4th ch from hook and in each ch to end. Turn.

Row 2 Ch 1, 1 sc in first dc, *ch 1, skip next dc, 1 sc in next dc; rep from * to end. Turn.

Row 3 Ch 3 (counts as 1 dc), *skip next ch-1 sp, [popcorn, ch 1, 1 dc, ch 1, popcorn] in next ch-1 sp, skip next ch-1 sp, 1 dc in next sc; rep from * to end. Turn.

Row 4 Ch 1, 1 sc in first dc, *1 sc in next popcorn, 1 sc in next ch-1 sp, 1 sc in next dc, 1 sc in next ch-1 sp, 1 sc in next popcorn, 1 sc in next dc; rep from * to end. Turn.

Row 5 Ch 3 (counts as 1 dc), 1 dc in next sc and in each sc to end. Turn.

Fasten off or cont to row 1 of heading.

Heading

Row 1 Ch 2 (counts as 1 hdc), 1 hdc in next dc and in each dc to end. Turn.

Rows 2 and 3 Ch 2 (counts as 1 hdc), 1 hdc in next hdc and in each hdc to end. Turn.

Fasten off or continue as desired.

Optional Sew purchased beaded fringe to WS of edging.

popped border

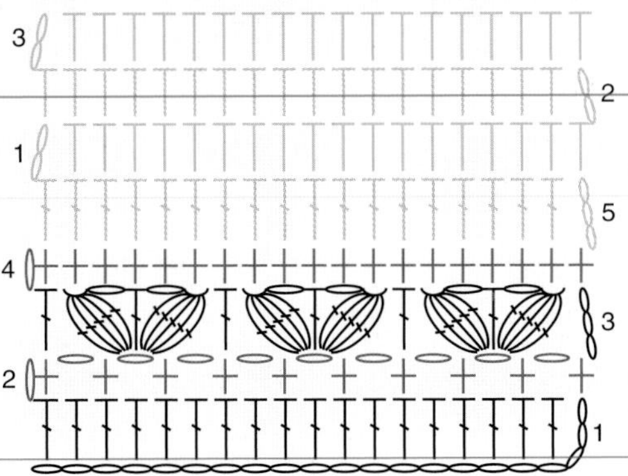

tunisian popcorn with beads

▲ (multiple of 4 sts)

Tunisian Basic Stitch (TBS) On first half rows, insert hook under front vertical bar, yo and draw up a lp.

Edging

Make a ch to desired length in a multiple of 4 sts + 1.

Row 1 (first half) Insert hook under top lp only of 2nd ch from hook, forming a lp on hook, keeping all lps on hook, draw up a lp under top strand of each ch to end. There will be the same number of lps on hook as number of chs. *Do not turn.*

Row 1 (second half) Yo, draw through first lp, *yo, draw through 2 lps; rep from * until 1 lp rem. This lp is the first st on next row. *Do not turn.*

Row 2 (first half) Yo, draw through first lp, TBS in next and each st across to last st, insert hook under 2 (front and back) strands of last st, draw up a lp (this will give a firm edge). *Do not turn.*

Row 2 (second half) Work same as row 1 (second half).

Row 3 (first half) Yo, draw through first lp, TBS in each of next 4 sts, *ch 3, TBS in each of next 4 sts; rep from * to end. *Do not turn.*

Row 3 (second half) Rep row 2 (second half).

Row 4 Rep both halves of row 2.

Row 5 (first half) Yo, draw through first lp, TBS in each of next 2 sts, *ch 3, TBS in each of next 4 sts; rep from *, end last rep with ch3, TBS in each of last 2 sts. *Do not turn.*

Row 5 (second half) Rep row 2 (second half).

Row 6 Rep both halves of row 2.

Row 7 Rep both halves of row 3.

Rows 8 and 9 Rep both halves of row 2.

Cont to row 1 of heading.

Heading

Row 1 Ch 2 (counts as 1 hdc), 1 hdc in vertical bar of next st and in each st to end. Turn.

Rows 2 and 3 Ch 2 (counts as 1 hdc), 1 hdc in next hdc and in each hdc to end. Turn.

Fasten off or continue as desired.

Optional Sew purchased beaded fringe to WS of edging.

tunisian popcorn with beads

buds

▲ (multiple of 6 sts + 5)

Popcorn 6 dc in designated st, drop lp from hook, insert hook in first dc of 6-dc group just made and dropped lp, yo and draw through both lps on hook.

Edging

Make a ch to desired length in a multiple of 6 sts.

Row 1 (WS) 1 sc in 2nd ch from hook and in each ch to end. Turn.

Rows 2 and 3 Ch 1, 1 sc in first sc and in each sc to end. Turn.

Row 4 Ch 1, 1 sc in first 5 sc, *ch 1, popcorn in next sc 2 rows below, 1 sc in next 5 sc; rep from * to end. Turn.

Row 5 Ch 1, 1 sc in first 5 sc, *1 sc in next ch-1 sp, 1 sc in next 5 sc; rep from * to end. Turn.

Rows 6 and 7 Ch 1, 1 sc in first sc and in each sc to end. Turn.

Row 8 Ch 1, 1 sc in first 2 sc, *ch 1, 1 popcorn in next sc 2 rows below, 1 sc in next 5 sc; rep from *, end last rep with ch 1, 1 popcorn in next sc 2 rows below, 1 sc in last 2 sc. Turn.

Row 9 Ch 1, 1 sc in first 2 sc, *1 sc in next ch-1 sp, 1 sc in next 5 sc; rep from *, end last rep with 1 sc in next ch-1 sp, 1 sc in last 2 sc. Turn.

Rows 10 and 11 Rep rows 6 and 7.

Fasten off or cont to row 1 of heading.

Heading

Row 1 Ch 2 (counts as 1 hdc), 1 hdc in next sc and in each sc to end. Turn.

Rows 2 and 3 Ch 2 (counts as 1 hdc), 1 hdc in next hdc and in each hdc to end. Turn.

Fasten off or continue as desired.

buds

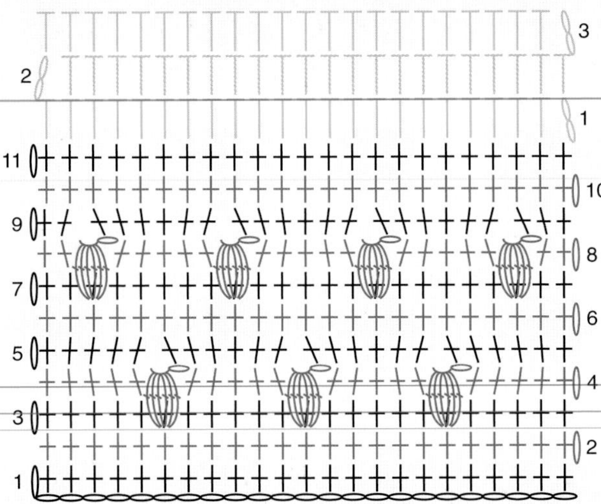

bangles

▲ (multiple of 2 sts)

Puff st [Yo, insert hook in designated st and draw up a lp] 4 times, yo and draw through 8 lps on hook, yo and draw through rem 2 lps on hook.

Edging

Make a ch to desired length in a multiple of 2 sts.

Row 1 1 Puff st in 4th ch from hook, *ch 1, skip next ch, 1 puff st in next ch; rep from * to end. Turn.

Row 2 Ch 3, *1 puff st in next ch-1 sp, ch 1, rep from *, end 1 puff st in turning ch-sp. Turn.

Rows 3 and 4 Rep row 2.

Fasten off or cont to row 1 of heading.

Heading

Row 1 Ch 2 (counts as 1 hdc), 1 hdc in each ch-1 sp and in each puff st to end. Turn.

Rows 2 and 3 Ch 2 (counts as 1 hdc), 1 hdc in next hdc and in each hdc to end. Turn.

Fasten off or continue as desired.

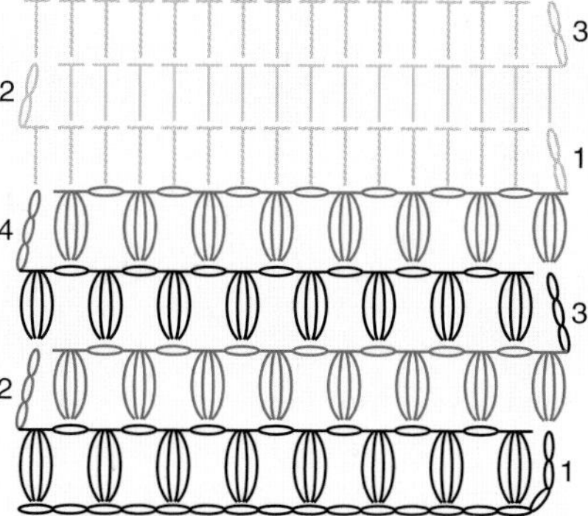

puff stitch

▲ **Colors** A and B

(multiple of 2 sts + 1)

Puff st [Yo, insert hook in designated st and draw up a lp] 4 times, yo and draw through all 9 lps on hook.

Edging

With A, make a ch to desired length in a multiple of 2 sts + 3.

Row 1 1 dc in 4th ch from hook and in each ch to end. Turn.

Fasten off A and attach B.

Row 2 Ch 3 (counts as 1 dc), *puff st in next dc, 1 dc in next dc; rep from * to end. Turn.

Fasten off B and attach A.

Row 3 Ch 3 (counts as 1 dc), *1 dc in next puff st, 1 dc in next dc; rep from * to end. Turn.

Fasten off A and attach B.

Rows 4 and 5 Rep rows 2 and 3.

Fasten off or cont to row 1 of heading.

Heading

Row 1 With A, ch 2 (counts as 1 hdc), 1 hdc in next dc and in each dc to end. Turn.

Rows 2 and 3 Ch 2 (counts as 1 hdc), 1 hdc in next hdc and in each hdc to end. Turn.

Fasten off or continue as desired.

puff stitch

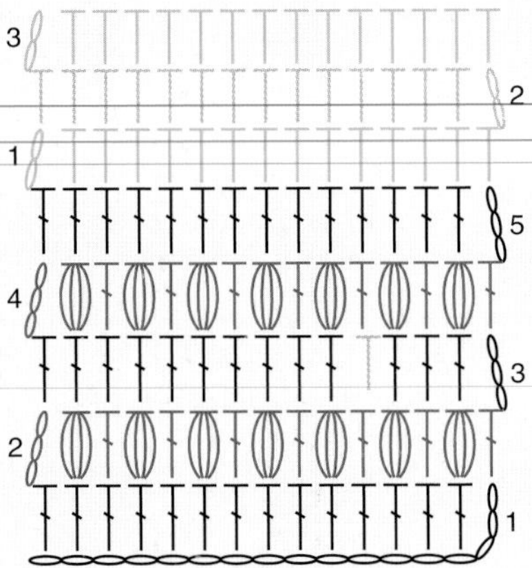

bobbles

bobble slant

▲ (multiple of 4 sts + 3)

Bobble Insert hook into next st and draw up a lp, [yo, insert hook into same st 2 rows below and draw up a lp, yo and draw through 2 lps on hook] 6 times, yo and draw through all 8 lps on hook.

Edging

Make a ch to desired length in a multiple of 4 sts.

Row 1 1 sc in 2nd ch from hook and in each ch to end. Turn.

Rows 2 and 3 Ch 1, 1 sc in first sc and in each sc to end. Turn.

Row 4 Ch 1, 1 sc in first 3 sc, 1 bobble in next sc, 1 sc in next 3 sc; rep from * to end. Turn.

Row 5 Ch 1, 1 sc in first sc and in each sc and bobble to end. Turn.

Rows 6 and 7 Rep rows 2 and 3.

Row 8 Ch 1, 1 sc in first 2 sc, *1 bobble in next st, 1 sc in next 3 sc; rep from *, end 1 bobble in last sc. Turn.

Row 9 Ch 1, 1 sc in first bobble and in each sc and bobble to end. Turn.

Rows 10 and 11 Rep rows 2 and 3.

Row 12 Ch 1, 1 sc in first sc, *1 bobble in next sc, 1 sc in next 3 sc; rep from *, end last rep with 1 bobble in next sc, 1 sc in last sc. Turn.

Row 13 Rep row 5.

Rows 14 and 15 Rep rows 2 and 3.

Row 16 Ch 1, 1 bobble in first sc, *1 sc in next 3 sc, 1 bobble in next sc; rep from *, end 1 sc in last 2 sc. Turn.

Fasten off or cont to row 1 of heading.

Heading

Row 1 Ch 2 (counts as 1 hdc), 1 hdc in next sc and in each sc and bobble to end. Turn.

Rows 2 and 3 Ch 2 (counts as 1 hdc), 1 hdc in next hdc and in each hdc to end. Turn.

Fasten off or continue as desired.

bobble slant

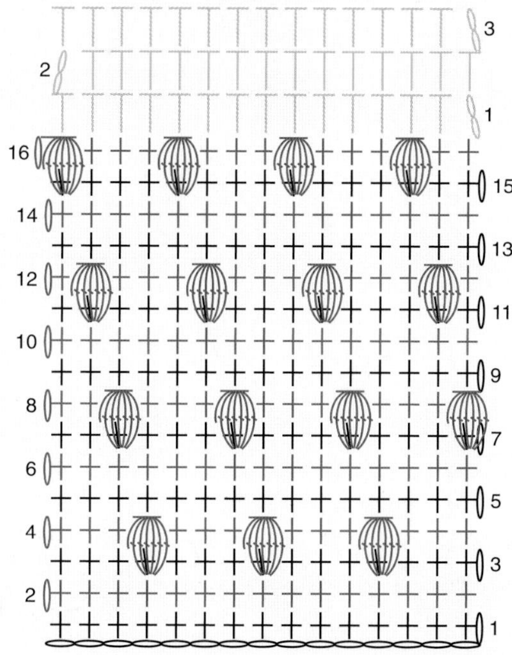

bobble clusters

▲ (multiple of 3 sts)

CL (Cluster) [Yo, insert hook in designated st and draw up a lp, yo and draw through 2 lps on hook] 5 times, yo and draw through all 6 lps on hook.

Edging

Make a ch to desired length in a multiple of 3 sts + 1.

Row 1 1 sc in 2nd ch from hook and in each ch to end. Turn.

Row 2 Ch 1, *CL in next sc, 1 sc in next 2 sc; rep from * to end. Turn.

Row 3 Ch 1, 1 sc in first sc and in each sc and CL to end. Turn.

Row 4 Ch 1, 1 sc in first 2 sc, *CL in next sc, 1 sc in next 2 sc; rep from *, end CL in last sc. Turn.

Row 5 Ch 1, 1 sc in first CL and in each sc and CL to end. Turn.

Rows 6–9 Rep rows 2–5.

Fasten off or cont with row 1 of heading.

Heading

Row 1 Ch 2 (counts as 1 hdc), 1 hdc in next sc and in each sc to end. Turn.

Rows 2 and 3 Ch 2 (counts as 1 hdc), 1 hdc in next hdc and in each hdc to end. Turn.

Fasten off or continue as desired.

bobble clusters

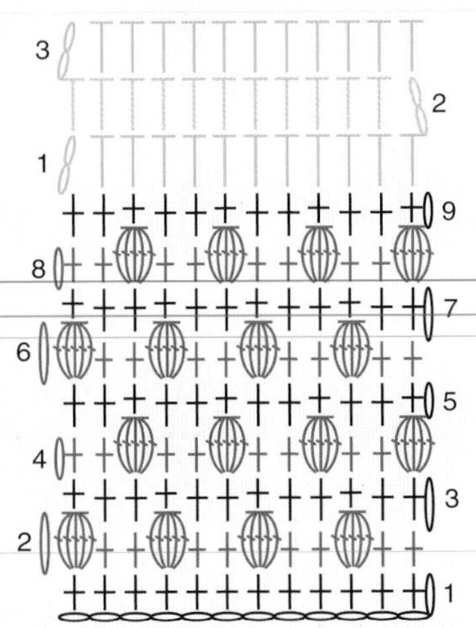

diagonal bobbles/eyelet

▲ (multiple of 3 sts)

Edging

Work same as Bobble Clusters through row 9.

Row 10 Ch 2 (counts as 1 hdc), hdc in next sc and each sc across. Turn.

Row 11 Ch 2 (counts as 1 hdc), hdc in next hdc and in each st across.

Fasten off, continue with the heading on chart, or continue as desired.

Finishing (Optional)

Thread ribbon in and out of sts between row 9 and heading rows 1 and 2.

alternating puffs

▲ (multiple of 4 sts + 3)

Puff st [Yo, insert hook in designated st and draw up a lp] 3 times, yo and draw through all 7 lps on hook.

Edging

Make a ch to desired length in a multiple of 4 sts.

Row 1 (RS) 1 sc in 2nd ch from hook and in each ch to end. Turn.

Row 2 Ch 1, 1 sc in first 3 sc, *1 puff st in next sc, 1 sc in next 3 sc; rep from * to end. Turn.

Row 3 Ch 1, 1 sc in first sc and in each sc and puff st to end. Turn.

Row 4 Ch 1, 1 sc in first sc, *1 puff st in next sc, 1 sc in next 3 sc; rep from *, end last rep with 1 puff st in next sc, 1 sc in last sc. Turn.

Row 5 Ch 1, 1 sc in first sc and in each puff st and sc to end. Turn.

Rows 6–9 Rep rows 2–5.

Fasten off or cont to row 1 of heading.

Optional decorative border

Row 1 Ch 2 (counts as 1 hdc), 1 hdc in next sc and in each sc to end. Turn.

Rows 2 and 3 Ch 2 (counts as 1 hdc), 1 hdc in next hdc and in each hdc to end. Turn.

Fasten off, continue with the heading on chart, or continue as desired.

Optional Sew decorative ribbon to RS of border.

alternating puffs

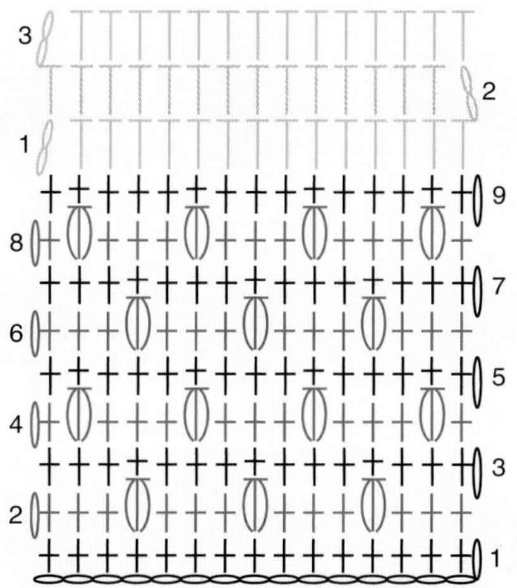

lace puffs

▲ (multiple of 6 sts + 3)

Puff st [Yo, insert hook in designated st and draw up a lp] 4 times, yo and draw through all 9 lps on hook.

Edging

Make a ch to desired length in a multiple of 6 sts + 1.

Row 1 [1 Dc, ch 2, 1 dc] in 5th ch from hook, *skip 2 ch, 1 puff st in next ch, ch 1, skip 2 ch, [1 dc, ch 2, 1 dc] in next ch; rep from *, end skip 1 ch, 1 dc in last ch. Turn.

Row 2 Ch 3, 1 puff st in next ch-2 sp, ch 1, *[1 dc, ch 2, 1 dc] in next puff st, 1 puff st in next ch-2 sp, ch 1; rep from *, 1 dc in top of beg ch-3. Turn.

Row 3 Ch 3, [1 dc, ch 2, 1 dc] in next puff st, *1 puff st in next ch-2 sp, ch 1, [1 dc, ch 2, 1 dc] in next puff st; rep from *, end 1 dc in top of beg ch-3. Turn.

Row 4 Rep row 2.

Fasten off or cont to row 1 of heading.

Heading

Row 1 Ch 2 (counts as 1 hdc), *1 hdc in next ch-1 sp, 1 hdc in next puff st, 1 hdc in next dc, 2 hdc in next ch-2 sp, 1 hdc in next dc; rep from *, end 1 hdc in next ch-1sp, 1 hdc in next puff st, 1 hdc in top of beg ch-3. Turn.

Rows 2 and 3 Ch 2 (counts as 1 hdc), 1 hdc in next hdc and in each hdc to end. Turn.

Fasten off, continue with the heading on chart, or continue as desired.

Optional Sew lace to WS of edging.

lace puffs

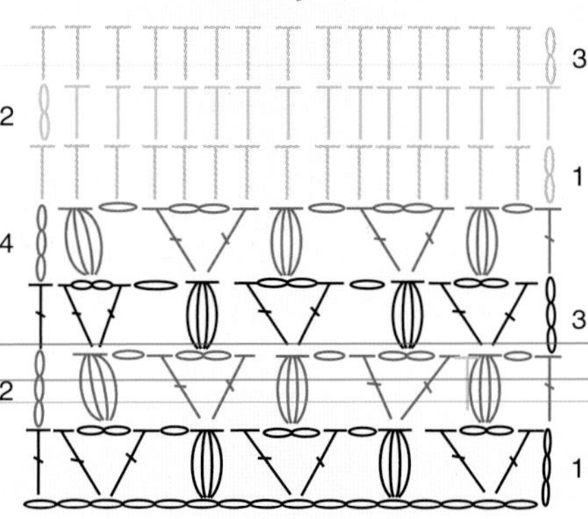

hazelnut point bobbles

▼ Make # required

Popcorn 5 dc in designated st, drop lp from hook, insert in first dc of 5-dc group just made and dropped lp, yo and draw through both lps on hook.

Triangle

Ch 10.

Row 1 1 Popcorn in 4th ch from hook, *ch 2, 1 dc in next ch, 1 popcorn in next ch; rep from * twice more—(*4 popcorns*). Turn.

Row 2 Ch 3, *1 popcorn in next ch-2 sp, ch 2; rep from * twice more, omitting last ch 2—(*3 popcorns*). Turn.

Row 3 Ch 3, 1 popcorn in next ch-2 sp, ch 2, 1 popcorn in next ch-2-sp—(*2 popcorns*). Turn.

Row 4 Ch 3, 1 popcorn in next ch-2 sp.

Fasten off.

Make desired number of triangles.

▲ **Joining**

With RS facing and working across foundation ch, attach yarn to first ch at right-hand edge of any triangle.

Row 1 Ch 2 (counts as 1 hdc), 1 hdc in next 7 ch, *working in next triangle, 1 hdc in next 8 ch; rep from * until all triangles have been joined.

Row 2 Ch 2, 1 hdc in next 6 hdc, *skip next hdc, 1 hdc in next 7 hdc; rep from *, end 1 hdc in top of beg ch-2.

Fasten off, continue with the heading on chart, or continue as desired.

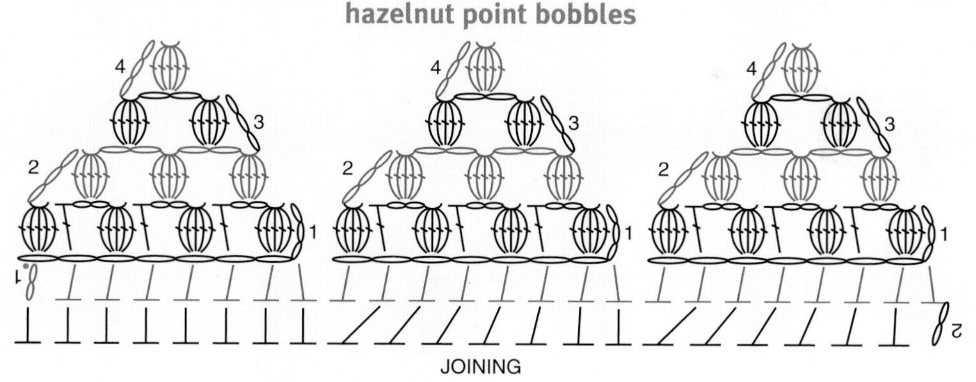

ruffles

petite ruffle

▼ **Colors** A, B and C

(multiple of 2 sts + 1)

Note This edging can be worked directly onto a project or into a chain and attached.

Heading

With A, make a ch to desired length in a multiple of 2 sts.

Row 1 1 hdc in 3rd ch from hook and in each ch to end. Turn.

Rows 2 and 3 Ch 2 (counts as 1 hdc), 1 hdc in next hdc and in each hdc to end. Turn.

Fasten off.

Ruffle

Attach A to right-hand edge of heading project or make a ch to desired length in a multiple of 2 sts.

Row 1 With A, ch 1, 1 sc in each st or ch across. Turn.

Fasten off A. Attach B in same sp.

Row 2 With B, ch 3 (counts as 1 dc), 1 dc in same st, 3 dc in next sc, *2 dc in next sc, 3 dc in next sc; rep from *, end 2 dc in last sc. Turn.

Fasten off B. Attach C in same sp.

Row 3 With C, ch 1, 1 sc in each dc to end.

Fasten off.

petite ruffle

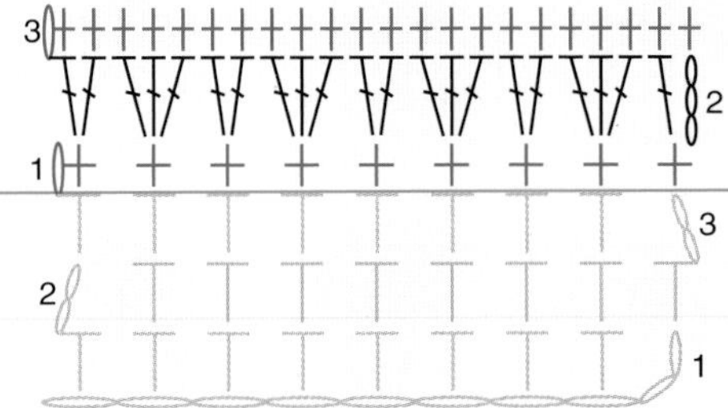

web ruffle

(over any number of sts)

Note This edging can be worked directly onto a project or into a chain and attached.

Heading

Make a ch to desired length.

Row 1 1 hdc in 3rd ch from hook and in each ch to end.

Rows 2 and 3 Ch 2 (counts as 1 hdc), 1 hdc in next hdc and in each hdc to end. Turn.

Fasten off.

Ruffle

Attach yarn to right-hand edge of project or make a chain of desired length.

Row 1 Ch 1, 1 sc in first st or ch and in each st or ch to end. Turn.

Row 2 Ch 1, 1 sc in first sc, *ch 1, 1 sc in next sc; rep from * to end. Turn.

Row 3 Ch 1, 1 sc in first sc, *ch 3, 1 sc in next sc; rep from * to end. Turn.

Row 4 Ch 1, 1 sc in first sc, *ch 5, 1 sc in next sc; rep from * to end. Turn.

Row 5 Ch 1, 1 sc in first sc, *ch 7, 1 sc in next sc; rep from * to end. Turn.

Row 6 Ch 1, 1 sc in first sc, *ch 9, 1 sc in next sc; rep from * to end.

Fasten off.

web ruffle

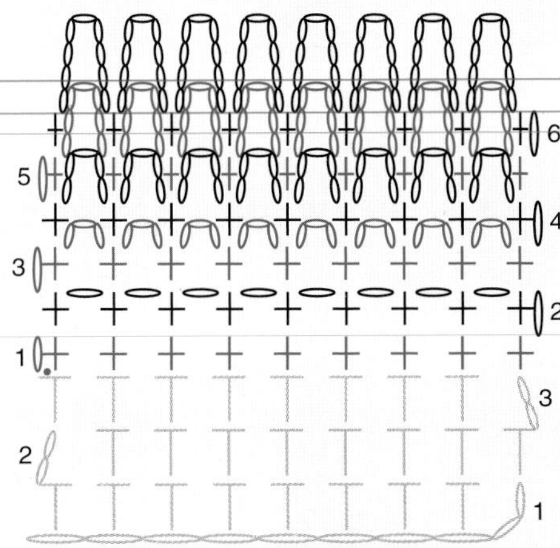

party ruffle

▼ (over an even number of sts)

Note This edging can be worked directly onto a project or into a chain and attached.

Heading

Row 1 1 hdc in 3rd ch from hook and in each ch to end.

Rows 2 and 3 Ch 2 (counts as 1 hdc), 1 hdc in next hdc and in each hdc to end. Turn.

Fasten off.

Ruffle

Attach yarn to right-hand edge of project or make a chain of desired length that is a multiple of 2.

Row 1 Ch 1, 1 sc in each st or ch to end. Turn.

Row 2 Ch 3 (counts as 1 dc), 1 dc in same sc, 2 dc in each sc to end. Turn.

Rows 3 and 4 Ch 3, 1 dc in next dc and in each dc to end. Turn.

Row 5 Ch 5, 1 sc in next dc, *ch 4, skip next dc, 1 sc in next dc; rep from * to end. Turn.

Row 6 Ch 5, 1 sc in first ch-4 lp, *ch 4, 1 sc in next lp; rep from * to end. Turn.

Row 7 Ch 5, 1 sc in first ch-4 lp, *ch 4, 1 sc in next lp; rep from * to end.

Fasten off.

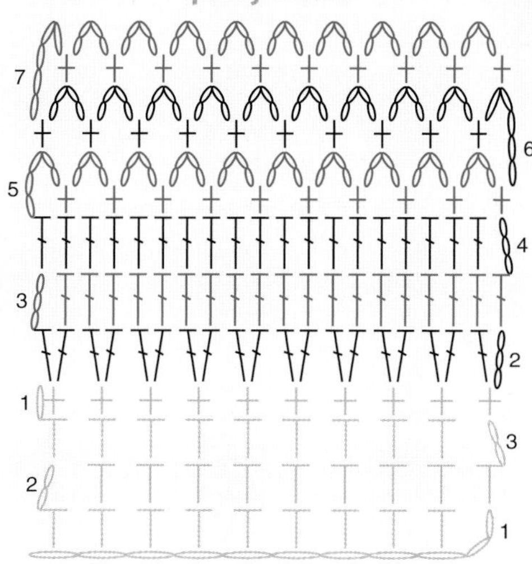

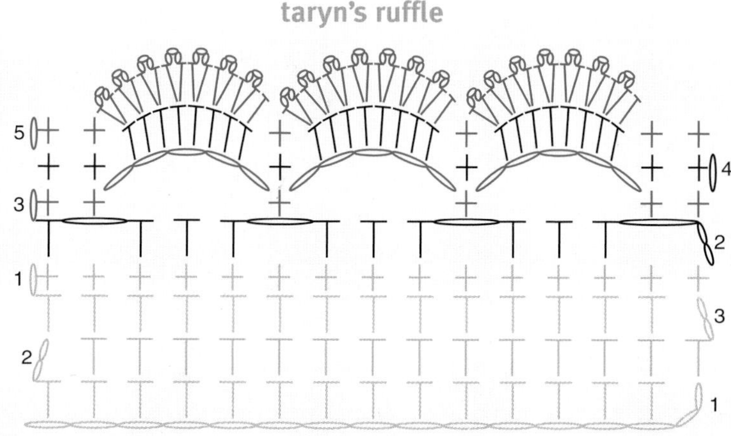

taryn's ruffle

(multiple of 4 sts + 3)

Note This edging can be worked directly onto a project or into a chain and attached.

Heading

Make a ch to desired length in a multiple of 4 sts.

Row 1 (RS) 1 hdc in 3rd ch from hook and in each ch to end.

Rows 2 and 3 Ch 2, 1 hdc in next hdc and in each hdc to end. Turn.

Fasten off.

Ruffle

With WS facing, attach yarn to right-hand edge of project.

Row 1 Ch 1, 1 sc in first st or ch and in each st or ch across. Turn.

Row 2 Ch 3 (counts as 1 hdc, ch 1), skip next sc, *1 hdc in next 3 sc, ch 1, skip next sc; rep from *, end 1 hdc in last sc. Turn.

Row 3 Ch 1, 1 sc in first hdc, 1 sc in ch-1 sp, *ch 5, 1 sc in next ch-1 sp; rep from *, end 1 sc in last hdc. Turn.

Row 4 Ch 1, 1 sc in first 2 sc, *8 hdc in ch-5 sp, 1 sc in next sc; rep from *end 1 sc in last sc. Turn.

Row 5 Ch 1, 1 sc in first 2 sc, *[1 hdc, ch 3, 1 hdc] in next 7 hdc, 1 hdc in next hdc, 1 sc in next sc; rep from *, end 1 sc in last sc.

Fasten off.

samantha's layered ruffle

▼ **Colors** A and B

(multiple of 4 sts + 3)

Note This edging can be worked directly onto a project or into a chain and attached.

Top ruffle

With A, make Taryn's Ruffle (see page 57), working row 2 of ruffle in front lps only.

Bottom ruffle

With ruffle in front of work, attach B to right-hand edge in back lp of first sc in row 1.

Row 1 Ch 5 (counts as 1 tr, ch 1), skip next sc, *1 tr in *back lps* of next 3 sc, ch 1, skip next sc; rep from *, end 1 tr in back lp of last sc. Turn.

Row 2 Ch 1, 1 sc in first tr, 1 sc in ch-1 sp, *ch 5, 1 sc in next ch-1 sp; rep from *, end 1 sc in 4th ch of beg ch-5. Turn.

Row 3 Ch 1, 1 sc in first 2 sc, *8 tr in ch-5 sp, 1 sc in next sc; rep from *, end 1 sc in last sc. Turn.

Row 4 Ch 1, 1 sc in first 2 sc, *[1 tr, ch 3, 1 tr] in next 7 tr, 1 tr in next tr, 1 sc in next sc; rep from *, end 1 sc in last sc.

Fasten off.

samantha's layered ruffle (top)

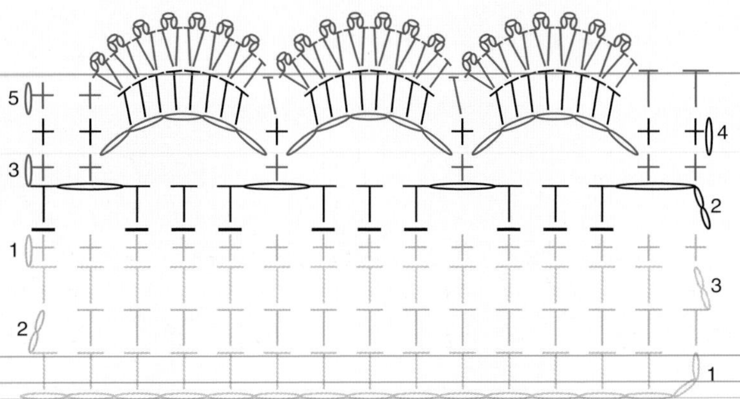

samantha's layered ruffle (bottom)

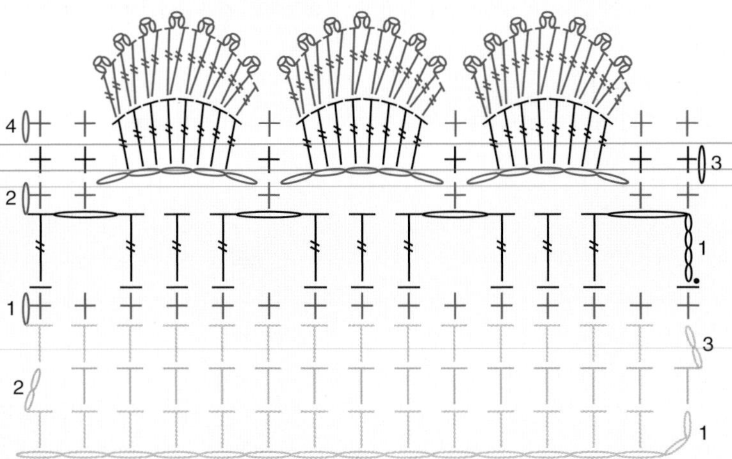

kendall's ruffle

▼ (multiple of 4 sts + 3)

Note This edging can be worked directly onto a project or into a chain and attached.

Heading

Make a ch to desired length in a multiple of 4 sts.

Row 1 1 hdc in 3rd ch from hook and in each ch to end.

Rows 2 and 3 Ch 2 (counts as 1 hdc), 1 hdc in next hdc and in each hdc to end. Turn.

Fasten off.

Ruffle

Attach yarn to right-hand edge of project.

Row 1 Ch 1, 1 sc or ch in first st and in each st or ch across. Turn.

Row 2 Ch 5 (counts as 1 tr, ch 1), skip next sc, *1 tr in next 3 sc, ch 1, skip next sc; rep from *, end 1 tr in last sc. Turn.

Row 3 Ch 1, 1 sc in first tr, 1 sc in ch-1 sp, *ch 5, 1 sc in next ch-1 sp; rep from *, end 1 sc in 4th ch of beg ch-5. Turn.

Row 4 Ch 1, 1 sc in first 2 sc, *8 tr in ch-5 sp, 1 sc in next sc; rep from *, end 1 sc in last sc. Turn.

Row 5 Ch 1, 1 sc in first 2 sc, *[1 tr, ch 3, 1 tr] in next 7 tr, 1 tr in next tr, 1 sc in next sc; rep from *, end 1 sc in last sc.

Fasten off.

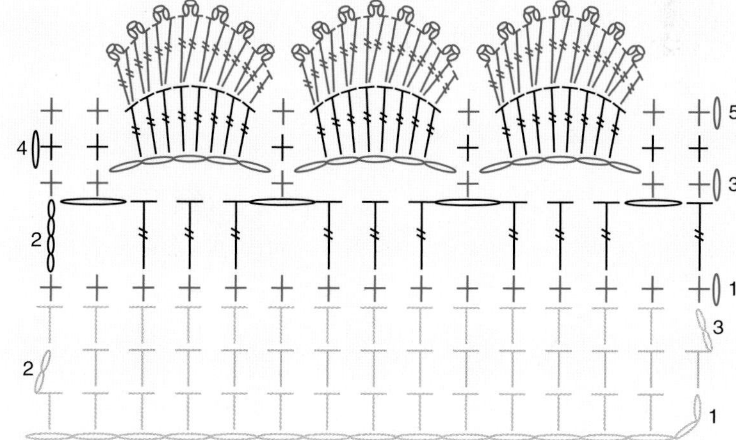

frou frou ruffle (shown 2 ways)

▼ (multiple of 4 sts)

Note This edging can be worked directly onto a project or into a chain and attached.

Heading

Make a ch to desired length in a multiple of 4 sts + 1.

Row 1 1 hdc in 3rd ch from hook and in each ch to end.

Rows 2 and 3 Ch 2 (counts as 1 hdc), 1 hdc in next hdc and in each hdc to end. Turn.

Fasten off.

Ruffle

Dc2tog [Yo, insert hook in designated st(s) and draw up a lp, yo and draw through 2 lps on hook] twice, yo and draw through all 3 lps on hook.

Attach yarn to right-hand edge of project.

Row 1 Ch 4 (counts as 1 dc, ch 1), *dc2tog over next 2 sts or chs, ch 1; rep from *, end 1 dc in last st or ch. Turn.

Row 2 Ch 3 (counts as 1 hdc, ch 1), dc2tog in first ch-1 sp, ch 1, *dc2tog in next dc2tog, ch 1, dc2tog in next ch-1 sp, ch 1, 1 hdc in next dc2tog, ch 1, dc2tog in next ch-1 sp, ch 1; rep from *, dc2tog in next dc2tog, ch 1, dc2tog in last ch-1 sp, ch 1, 1 hdc in 3rd ch of beg ch-4. Turn.

Row 3 Ch 3 (counts as 1 hdc, ch 1), dc2tog in first ch-1 sp, ch 1, *[dc2tog in next dc2tog, ch 1, 1 dc2tog in next ch-1 sp, ch 1] 3 times, 1 hdc in next hdc, ch 1, dc2tog in next ch-1 sp, ch 1; rep from *, end last rep with 1 hdc in 2nd ch of beg ch-3. Turn.

Row 4 Ch 2, dc2tog in first ch-1 sp, ch 1, *[dc2tog in next dc2tog, ch 1, 1 dc2tog in next ch-1 sp, ch 1] 7 times, 1 sc in hdc, ch 1, dc2tog in next ch-1 sp, ch 1; rep from *, end last rep with 1 sc in 2nd ch of beg ch-3. Turn.

Row 5 Ch 1, 1 sc in same st, *[1 dc, ch 3, 1 dc] in next ch-1 sp, *[1 dc, ch 3, 1 dc] in next dc2tog, [1 dc, ch 3, 1 dc] in next ch-1 sp] 15 times, 1 sc in next sc; rep from *, end last rep with 1 sc in first ch of beg ch-2. Fasten off.

frou frou ruffle (rows 1-3)

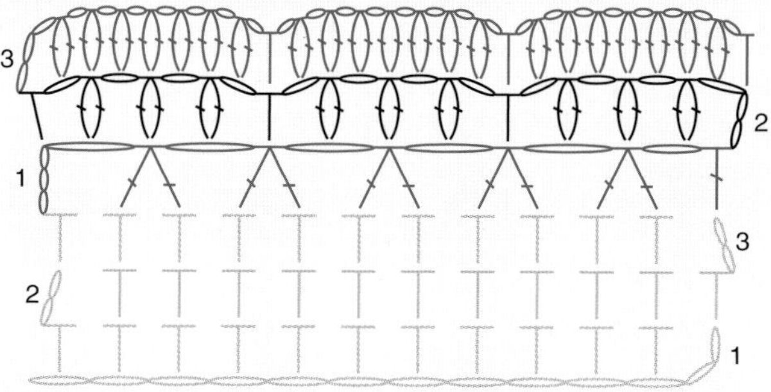

frou frou ruffle (rows 4-5)

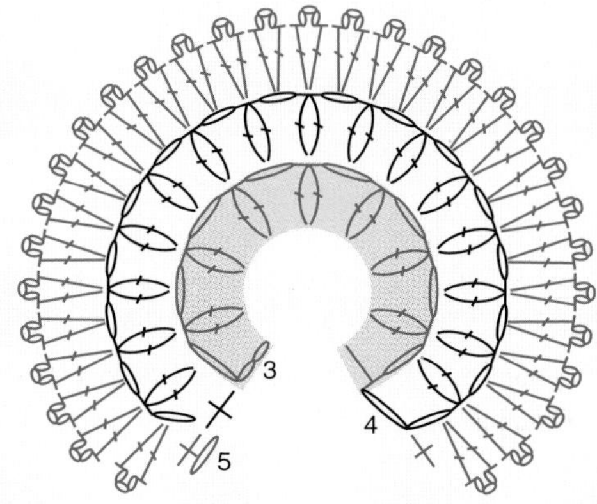

can can ruffle

▼ **Colors** A and B

(over any number of sts)

Note This edging can be worked directly onto a project or into a chain as shown and attached.

Heading

Make a ch to desired length.

Row 1 1 hdc in 3rd ch from hook and in each ch to end.

Rows 2 and 3 Ch 2 (counts as 1 hdc), 1 hdc in next hdc and in each hdc to end. Turn.

Fasten off.

Ruffle

With WS facing, attach yarn to right-hand edge of heading or project.

Row 1 Ch 1, 1 sc in same st and in each st to end. Turn.

Row 2 Ch 1, 2 sc in same sc and in each sc to end. Turn.

Row 3 Ch 1, 1 sc in same sc and in each sc to end. Turn.

Rows 4–8 Rep rows 2 and 3 twice, then rep row 2. Turn.

Fasten off A and attach B.

Row 9 Rep row 3.

Row 10 Ch 1, 1 sc in first sc, *ch 3, 1 sc in next sc; rep from * to end.

Fasten off.

can can ruffle

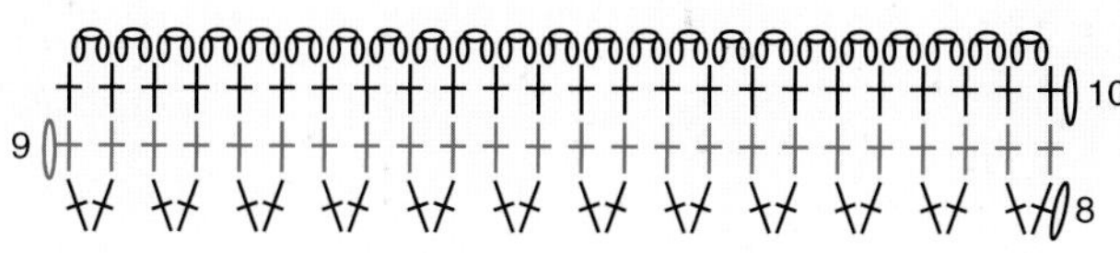

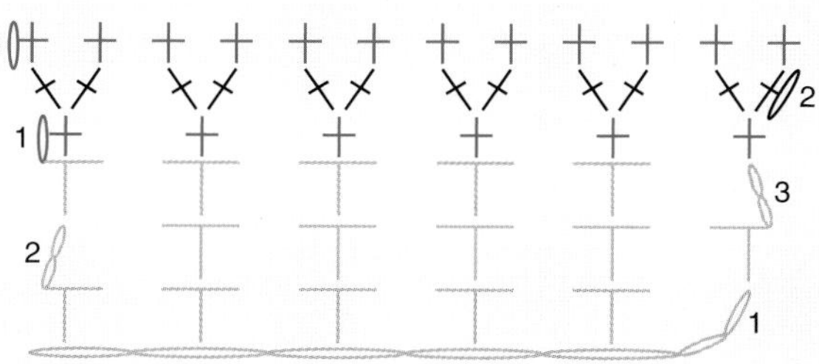

heartbreak ruffle

▼ (multiple of 2 sts + 1)

Note This edging can be worked directly onto a project or into a chain as shown and attached.

Heading

Make a ch to desired length in a multiple of 2 sts.

Row 1 1 hdc in 3rd ch from hook and in each ch to end.

Rows 2 and 3 Ch 2 (counts as 1 hdc), 1 hdc in next hdc and in each hdc to end. Turn.

Fasten off.

Ruffle

Joint dc (JDC) [Yo, insert hook into previous worked st and draw up a lp, yo and draw through 2 lps on hook, yo, insert hook into next st and draw up a lp, yo and draw through 2 lps, yo and draw through all 3 lps on hook.

Row 1 Ch 8, JDC, *ch 5, JDC; rep from *, end ch 5, 1 dc in last st. Turn.

Row 2 Ch 1, 1 sc in first st, *ch 10, 1 sc in next JDC, ch 5, 1 sc in next JDC; rep from *, end ch 10, 1 sc in 3rd ch of beg ch-8. Turn.

Row 3 Ch 8, 1 dc in 6th ch from hook, 1 dc in ch-10 lp, [ch 5, 1 dc in dc just made, 1 dc in same ch-10 lp] 4 times, *1 sc in next ch-5 lp, 1 dc in next ch-10 lp, [ch 5, 1 dc in dc just made, 1 dc in same ch-10 lp] 5 times; rep from * to end.

Fasten off.

heartbreak ruffle

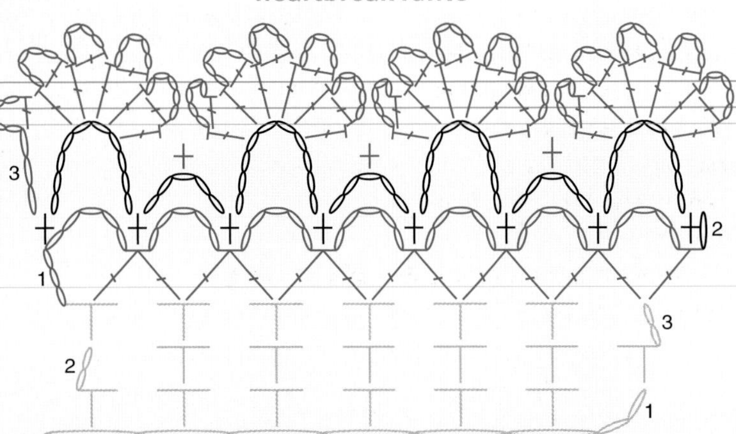

peacock ruffle

▼ (multiple of 8 sts + 1)

Ruffle

Long dc (LDC) Yo, insert hook in next st and draw up lp to ½"/1.25cm, [yo and draw through 2 lps] twice.

Make a ch to desired length in a multiple of 8 sts + 2 or attach to right hand edge of project.

Row 1 1 sc in 2nd ch from hook, *skip 3 ch, 7 LDC in next ch, skip 3 ch, 1 sc in next ch; rep from * to end. Turn.

Row 2 Ch 4 (counts as 1 LDC), 1 LDC in first sc, *ch 2, 1 sc in 4th st of 7-LDC group, ch 2, 2 LDC in next sc; rep from * to end. Turn.

Row 3 Ch 1, *1 sc between 2 LDC, 9 LDC in next sc; rep from *, end 1 sc between last 2 LDC. Turn.

Row 4 Ch 4 (counts as 1 LDC), 1 LDC in first sc, *ch 3, 1 sc in 5th st of 9-LDC group, ch 3, 2 LDC in next sc; rep from * to end. Turn.

Row 5 Ch 1, *1 sc between 2 LDC, 11 LDC in next sc; rep from *, end 1 sc between last 2 LDC. Turn.

Row 6 Ch 4 (counts as 1 LDC), 1 LDC in first sc, *ch 4, 1 sc in 6th st of 11-LDC group, ch 4, 2 LDC in next sc; rep from * to end. Turn.

Row 7 Ch 1, *1 sc between 2 LDC, 13 LDC in next sc; rep from *, end 1 sc between last 2 LDC. Fasten off.

Note For a deeper ruffle, rep row 6 working 1 sc in center st of LDC group and row 7 working 2 more LDC in each LDC group.

Heading

With RS facing and working along opposite side of foundation ch, attach yarn to right-hand edge of ruffle.

Row 1 Ch 2 (counts as 1 hdc), *3 hdc in ch-3 sp, 1 hdc in base of LDC-group, 3 hdc in ch-3 sp, 1 hdc in base of sc; rep from * to end. Turn.

Rows 2 and 3 Ch 2 (counts as 1 hdc), 1 hdc in next hdc and in each hdc to end. Turn.

Fasten off.

Optional Thread ribbon in and out of sts of row 2 of heading.

peacock ruffle

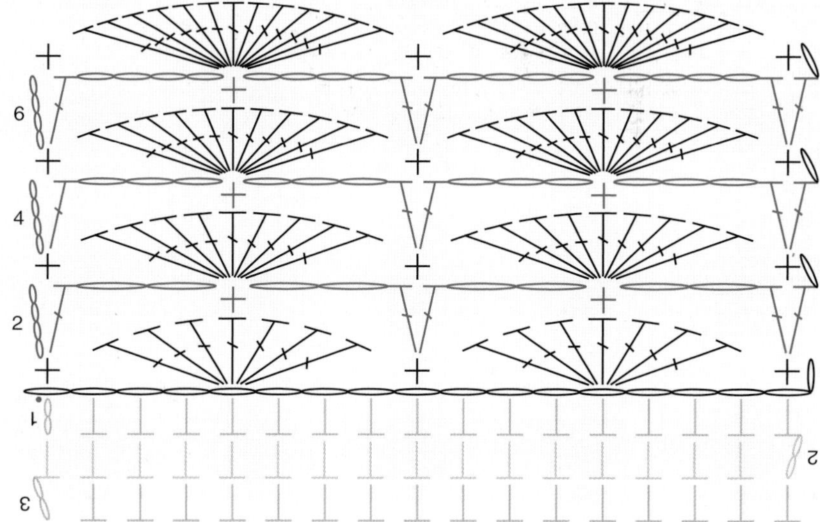

roman ruffle

▼ **Colors** A and B

(multiple of 8 sts)

FPDC (Front post dc) Yo, insert hook from front to back to front around post of designated st and draw up a lp, [yo and draw through 2 lps] twice.

BPDC (Back post dc) Yo, insert hook from back to front to back around post of designated st and draw up a lp, [yo and draw through 2 lps] twice.

Ruffle

With A, make a ch to desired length in a multiple of 8 sts + 2.

Row 1 (WS) 2 dc in 6th ch from hook, *ch 2, 2 dc in next ch, skip 2 ch, 1 dc in next 2 ch, skip 2 ch, 2 dc in next ch; rep from *, end last rep with ch 2, 2 dc in next ch, skip 2 ch, 1 dc in last ch. Turn.

Row 2 Ch 4, *[2 dc, ch 2, 2 dc] in next ch-2 sp, FPDC around next 2 dc; rep from *, end last rep with ch 1, 1 dc in last ch-sp. Turn.

Row 3 Ch 4, *[2 dc, ch 2, 2 dc] in next ch-2 sp, BPDC around next 2 dc; rep from *, end last rep with ch 1, 1 dc in last ch-sp. Turn.

Rep rows 2 and 3 to length desired.

Fasten off.

Top rows

With RS facing and working along foundation ch, attach B to right-hand edge of ruffle.

Row 1 (RS) Ch 2, 1 hdc in next ch and in each ch to end.

Fasten off and re-attach to first st of row 1.

Row 2 Ch 2, 1 hdc in *back lp* of next hdc and each hdc to end.

Fasten off and re-attach to first st of row 2.

Row 3 Ch 2, 1 hdc in next hdc and in each hdc to end.

Fasten off.

roman ruffle

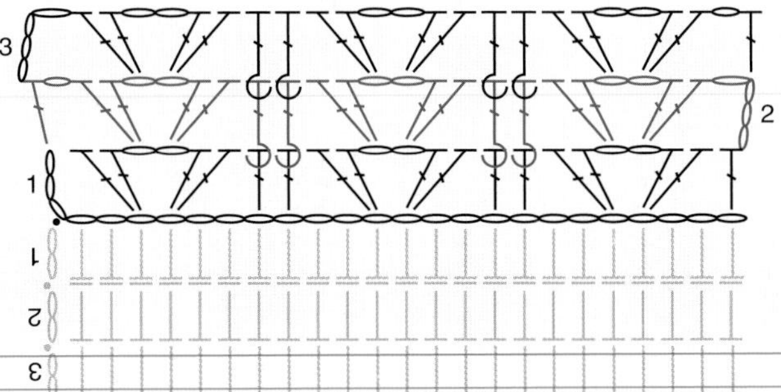

laura's ruffle

▼ (multiple of 4 sts + 3)

Note This edging can be worked directly onto a project or into a chain as shown and attached.

Heading

Make a ch to desired length in a multiple of 4 sts.

Row 1 1 hdc in 3rd ch from hook and in each ch to end.

Rows 2 and 3 Ch 2 (counts as 1 hdc), 1 hdc in next hdc and in each hdc to end. Turn.

Fasten off.

Ruffle

Attach yarn to right-hand edge of project.

Row 1 Ch 1, 1 sc in same st and in each st to end. Turn.

Row 2 Ch 4, skip next sc, *1 dc in next 3 sc, ch 1, skip 1 sc; rep from *, end 1 dc in last sc. Turn.

Row 3 Ch 1, 1 sc in first dc, 1 sc in next ch-1 sp, *ch 5, 1 sc in next ch-1 sp; rep from *, end 1 sc in 3rd ch of beg ch-4. Turn.

Row 4 Ch 1, 1 sc in first 2 sc, *8 dc in ch-5 sp, 1 sc in next sc; rep from *, end 1 sc in last sc. Turn.

Row 5 Ch 1, 1 sc in first 2 sc, *[1 dc, ch 3, 1 dc] in next 7 dc, 1 dc in next dc, 1 sc in next sc; rep from *, end 1 sc in last sc.

Fasten off.

Optional Thread ribbon through spaces of row 2 of ruffle.

laura's ruffle

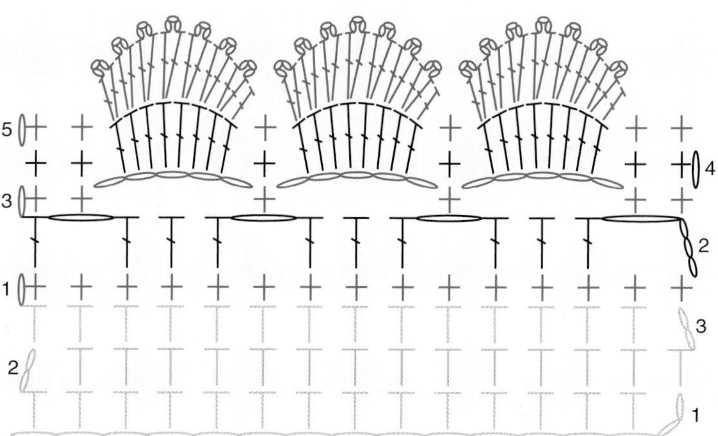

apron lace

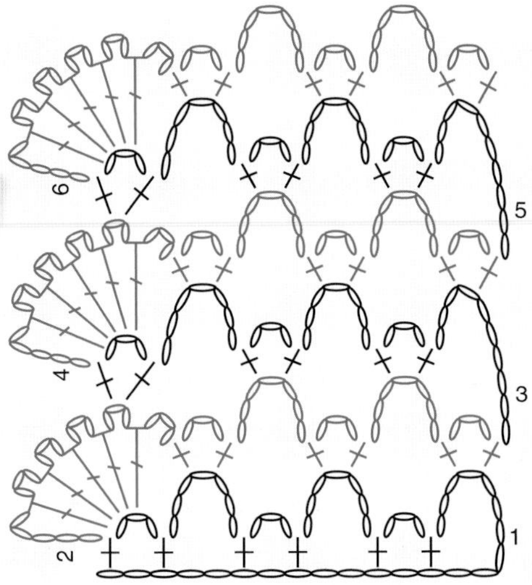

apron lace

Ruffle

Ch 23.

Row 1 1 sc in 11th ch from hook, [ch 3, skip next ch, 1 sc in next ch, ch 7, skip 2 ch, 1 sc in next ch] twice, ch 3, skip next ch, 1 sc in last ch. Turn.

Row 2 Ch 5, [1 dc, ch 3] 5 times in first ch-3 lp, ([1 sc, ch 3, 1 sc, ch 7] in next ch-7 lp) twice, [1 sc, ch 3, 1 sc] in last lp. Turn.

Row 3 Ch 10, ([1 sc, ch 3, 1 sc, ch 7] in next ch-7 lp) twice, skip next ch-3 lp and sp, [1 sc, ch 3, 1 sc] in next sp. Turn.

Rep rows 2 and 3 to desired length, ending with row 2. Fasten off.

Optional Thread ribbon through loops along straight edge of ruffle.

wave ruffle

▼ (multiple of 4 sts + 2)

Note This edging can be worked directly onto a project or onto the heading as shown and attached.

Heading

Make a ch to desired length in a multiple of 4 sts + 3.

Row 1 1 hdc in 3rd ch from hook and in each ch to end.

Rows 2 and 3 Ch 2, 1 hdc in next hdc and in each hdc to end. Turn.

Fasten off.

Ruffle

Dc2tog [Yo, insert hook in designated st(s) and draw up a lp, yo and draw through 2 lps on hook] twice, yo and draw through all 3 lps on hook.

Attach yarn to right-hand edge of heading or project.

Row 1 Ch 4 (counts as 1 dc, ch 1), dc2tog over next 2 sts, ch 1; rep from *, end 1 dc in last st. Turn.

Row 2 *Ch 5, sl st in next dc2tog; rep from *, end last rep with ch 5, sl st in 3rd ch of beg ch-4. Turn.

Row 3 Ch 3 (counts as 1 dc), [2 dc, ch 3, 3 dc] in first ch-5 lp, *ch 2, sl st in next ch-5 lp, ch 2, [3 dc, ch 3, 3 dc] in next ch-5 lp; rep from * to end. Turn.

Row 4 Ch 1, 1 sc in same dc, 1 sc in next 2 dc, *5 sc in ch-3 sp, 1 sc in next 3 dc, 1 sc in next 2 ch, 1 sc in sl st, 1 sc in next 2 ch, 1 sc in next 3 dc; rep from *, end last rep with 5 sc in last ch-3 sp, 1 sc in last 3 dc. Turn.

Row 5 Ch 3, 1 dc in next 3 sc, *2 dc in next 3 sc, 1 dc in next 13 sc; rep from *, end last rep with 2 dc in next 3 sc, 1 dc in last 4 sc.

Fasten off.

Optional String beads and sew to RS at top.

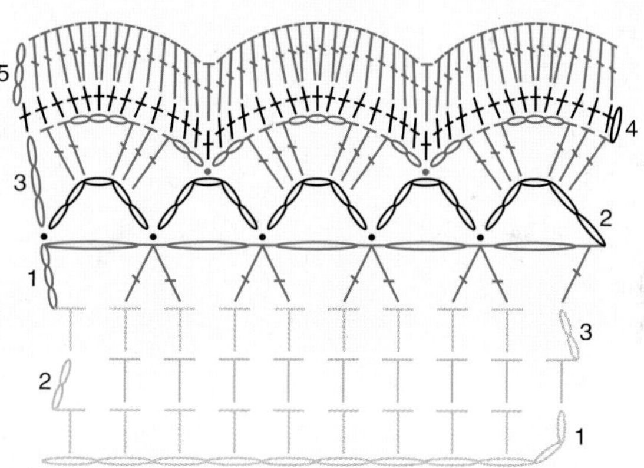

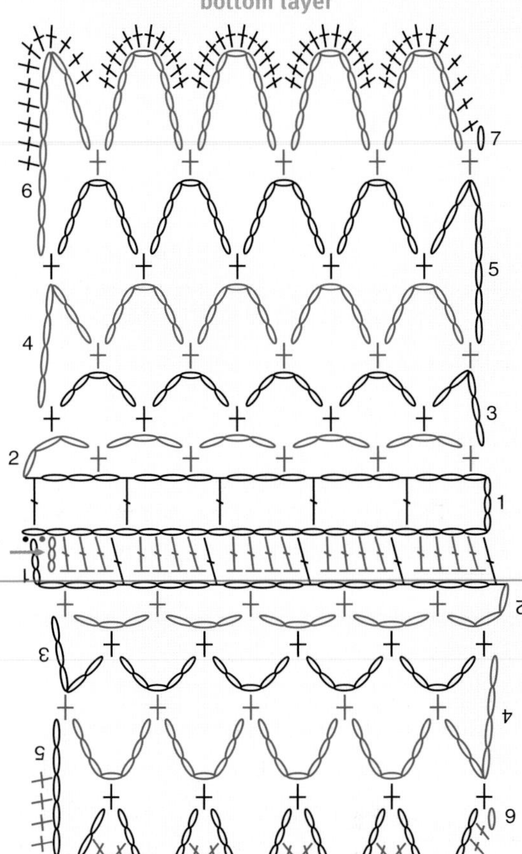

double dutch layered ruffle

▼ **Colors** A and B

(multiple of 4 sts + 1)

Ruffle

Bottom layer

With A, make a ch to desired length in a multiple of 4 sts + 2.

Row 1 *1 dc in 10th ch from hook, *ch 3, skip 3 ch, 1 dc in next ch; rep from * to end. Turn.

Row 2 *Ch 3, 1 sc in next ch-3 sp; rep from * to end. Turn.

Row 3 *Ch 5, 1 sc in next ch-3 sp; rep from * to end. Turn.

Row 4 *Ch 7, 1 sc in next ch-5 sp; rep from * to end. Turn.

Row 5 *Ch 9, 1 sc in next ch-7 sp; rep from * to end. Turn.

Row 6 *Ch 11, 1 sc in next ch-9 sp; rep from * to end. Turn.

Row 7 Ch 1, *12 sc in next ch-11 sp; rep from * to end.

Fasten off.

Top layer

Attach B to end of foundation ch.

Row 1 Ch 6 (counts as 1 dc, ch 3), *1 dc in next ch-sp, ch 3; rep from *, end 1 dc in last ch-sp. Turn.

Rows 2–5 Rep rows 2–5 of bottom layer.

Row 6 Ch 1, *11 sc in next ch-9 sp; rep from * to end.

Fasten off.

Eyelet row

With RS facing, attach B to right-hand edge of foundation chain.

Row 1 Ch 3, 3 dc in first ch-sp, *4 dc in next ch-sp; rep from * to end.

Fasten off.

Optional Weave ribbon through eyelets.

buttoniere ruffle

▼ Colors A, B and C

Purchased bead and button fringe

(over any number of sts)

Note This edging can be worked directly onto a project or into a chain and attached.

Heading

With A, make a ch to desired length.

Row 1 (RS) 1 hdc in 3rd ch from hook and in each ch to end.

Rows 2 and 3 Ch 2, 1 hdc in next hdc and in each hdc to end. Turn. Fasten off.

Ruffle

With RS facing, attach A to right-hand edge of heading or project.

Row 1 Ch 1, 1 sc in same st or ch and in each st or ch to end. Turn. Fasten off A. With RS facing, attach B to right-hand edge.

Row 2 *Ch 5, 1 sc in front lp of next sc; rep from * to end.

Fasten off B. With RS facing, attach C to right-hand edge of row 1.

Row 3 *Ch 7, 1 sc in back lp of next sc of row 1; rep from * to end.

Fasten off C.

Optional Sew bead and button fringe to WS of ruffle.

buttoniere ruffle

ruffle row 3

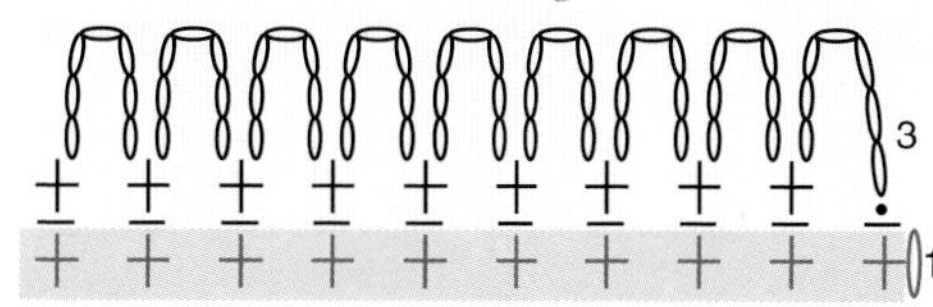

ruffle rows 1-2

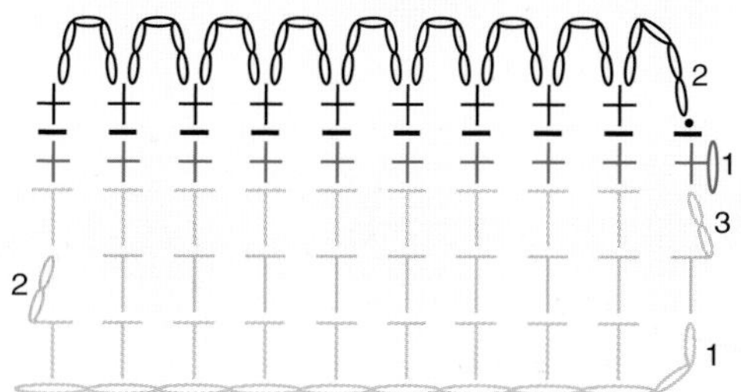

striped ruffle

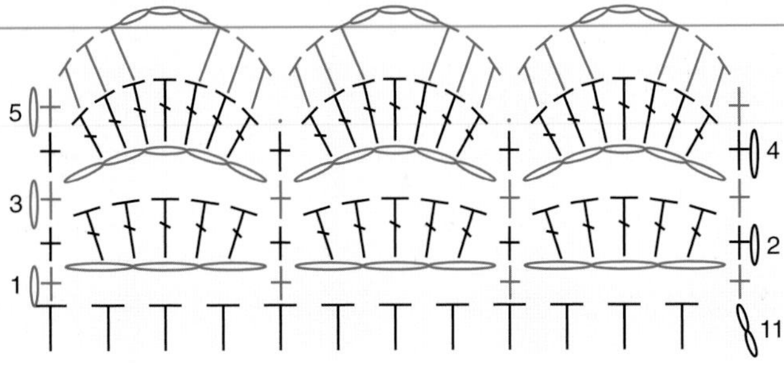

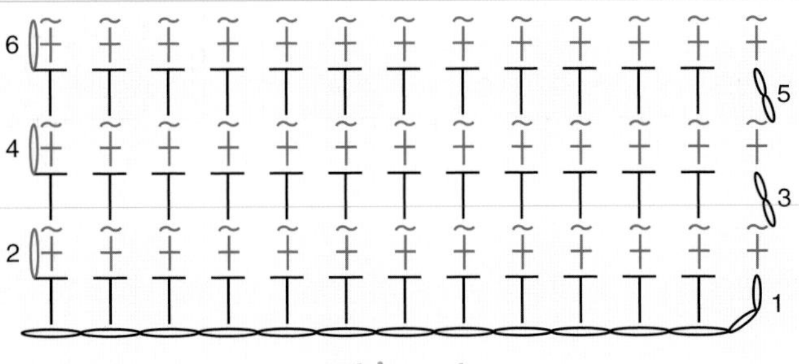

stripe pat

striped ruffle

▼ **Colors** A and B

(multiple of 4 sts + 1)

Stripe pat

With A, make a ch to desired length in a multiple of 4 sts +2.

Row 1 With A, 1 hdc in 3rd ch from hook and in each ch to end. *Do not turn.*

Row 2 With A, ch 1, 1 Reverse sc in next hdc and in each hdc to end, 1 Reverse sc in top of beg ch-2. *Do not turn.*

Row 3 With A, ch 2, 1 hdc in next st and in each st to end. *Do not turn.*

Row 4 With A, ch 1, 1 Reverse sc in next hdc and in each hdc to end. *Do not turn.*

Row 5 With B, ch 2, 1 hdc in next st and in each st to end. *Do not turn.*

Row 6 With B, ch 1, 1 Reverse sc in each hdc to end. *Do not turn.*

Rows 7–10 Rep rows 3–6.

Row 11 Rep row 3.

Fasten off.

Ruffle

With WS facing, attach B to right-hand edge of stripe pat or project.

Row 1 Ch 1, 1 sc in first sc, *ch 3, skip next 3 sts, 1 sc in next st; rep from *, end last rep with 1 sc in top of beg ch-2. Turn.

Row 2 Ch 1, 1 sc in first sc, 5 dc in first ch-3 sp, *1 sc in next sc, 5 dc in next ch-3 sp; rep from *, end 1 sc in last sc. Turn.

Row 3 Ch 1, 1 sc in first sc, *ch 5, skip next 5 dc, 1 sc in next sc; rep from * end last rep with 1 sc in top of beg ch-2. Turn.

Row 4 Ch 1, 1 sc in first sc, *7 dc in next ch-5 sp, 1 sc in next sc; rep from * to end. Turn.

Fasten off B and attach A.

Row 5 With A, ch 1, 1 sc in first sc, *1 hdc in next 3 dc, ch 3, skip next dc, 1 hdc in next 3 hdc, sl st in next sc; rep from *, end last rep with 1 sc in last sc.

Fasten off.

bell ruffle I

▼ **Colors** A and B

(multiple of 6 sts + 4)

FPDC (Front post dc) Yo, insert hook from front to back to front around post of designated st and draw up a lp, [yo and draw through 2 lps] twice.

BPDC (Back post dc) Yo, insert hook from back to front to back around post of designated st and draw up a lp, [yo and draw through 2 lps] twice.

With A, make a ch to desired length in a multiple of 6 sts + 2.

Row 1 (WS) 1 hdc in 3rd ch from hook and in each ch to end. Turn.

Row 2 Ch 2, *BPDC around next st, FPDC around next st; rep from *, end last rep with BPDC around next st, 1 hdc in top of beg ch-2. Turn.

Row 3 Ch 2, *FPDC around next st, BPDC around next st; rep from *, end last rep with FPDC around next st, 1 hdc in top of beg ch-2. Turn.

Note When changing colors in the following rows, keep unworked color on WS of work.

Row 4 Ch 2, [BPDC around next st, FPDC around next st] twice, *drop A and ch 1 with B, skip next st, 3 hdc in next st, drop B and ch 1 with A, skip next st, FPDC around next st, BPDC around next st, FPDC around next st; rep from *, end BPDC around next st, 1 hdc in top of beg ch-2. Turn.

Row 5 Ch 2, *[FPDC around next st, BPDC around next st] twice, *drop A and ch 1 with B, 1 hdc in ch-1 sp, 1 hdc in next 3 hdc, 1 hdc in ch-1 sp, drop B and ch 1 with A, BPDC around next st, FPDC around next st, BPDC around next st; rep from *, end FPDC around next st, 1 hdc in top of beg ch-2. Turn.

Row 6 Ch 2, [BPDC around next st, FPDC around next st] twice, *drop A and ch 1 with B, 1 hdc in next ch-1 sp, 1 hdc in next 5 hdc, 1 hdc in next ch-1 sp, drop B and ch 1 with A, FPDC around next st, BPDC around next st, FPDC around next st; rep from *, end BPDC around next st, 1 hdc in top of beg ch-2. Turn.

Row 7 Ch 2, *[FPDC around next st, BPDC around next st] twice, *drop A and ch 1 with B, 1 hdc in ch-1 sp, 1 hdc in next 7 hdc, 1 hdc in ch-1 sp, drop B and ch 1 with A, BPDC around next st, FPDC around next st, BPDC around next st; rep from *, end FPDC around next st, 1 hdc in top of beg ch-2. Turn.

Row 8 Ch 2, *[BPDC around next st, FPDC around next st] twice, *ch 1, 1 hdc in ch-1 sp, 1 hdc in next 9 hdc, 1 hdc in ch-1 sp, ch 1, FPDC around next st, BPDC around next st, FPDC around next st; rep from *, end with BPDC around next st, 1 hdc in top of beg ch-2. Turn.

Fasten off.

bell ruffle I

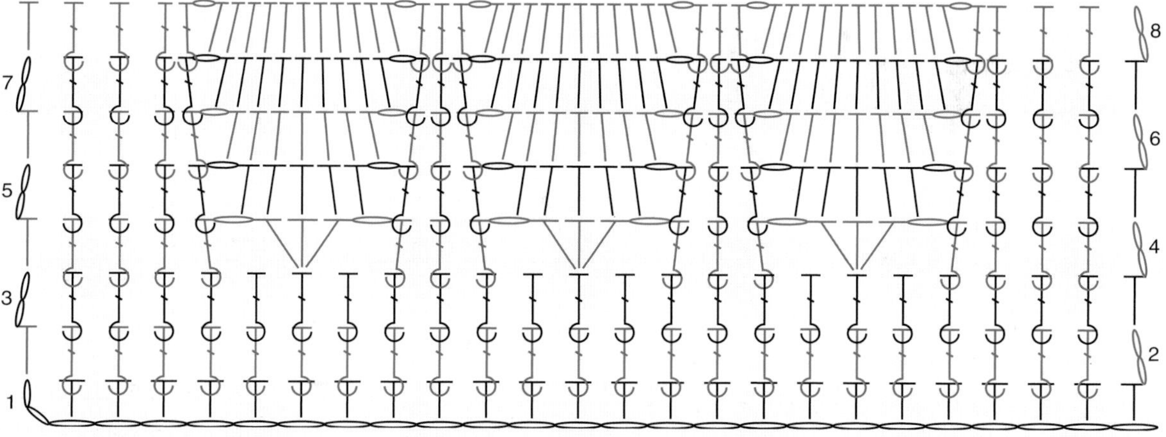

bell ruffle II

▼ (multiple of 6 sts + 2)

FPDC (Front post dc) Yo, insert hook from front to back to front around post of designated st and draw up a lp, [yo and draw through 2 lps] twice.

BPDC (Back post dc) Yo, insert hook from back to front to back around post of designated st and draw up a lp, [yo and draw through 2 lps] twice.

With A, make a ch to desired length in a multiple of 6 sts + 2.

Row 1 (WS) 1 hdc in 3rd ch from hook and in each ch to end. Turn.

Row 2 Ch 2, *FPDC around next st, BPDC around next st; rep from *, end last rep with FPDC around next st, 1 hdc in top of beg ch-2. Turn.

Row 3 Ch 2, *BPDC around next st, FPDC around next st; rep from *, end last rep with BPDC around next st, 1 hdc in top of beg ch-2. Turn.

Row 4 Ch 2, *[FPDC around next st, BPDC around next st] twice, FPDC around next st, ch 1, 3 hdc in next st, ch 1; rep from *, end last rep with [FPDC around next st, BPDC around next st] twice, FPDC around next st, 1 hdc in top of beg ch-2. Turn.

Row 5 Ch 2, *[BPDC around next st, FPDC around next st] twice, BPDC around next st, ch 1, 1 hdc in ch-1 sp, 1 hdc in next 3 hdc, 1 hdc in ch-1 sp, ch 1; rep from *, end last rep with [FPDC around next st, BPDC around next st] twice, FPDC around next st, 1 hdc in top of beg ch-2. Turn.

Row 6 Ch 2, *[FPDC around next st, BPDC around next st] twice, FPDC around next st, * ch 1, 1 hdc in ch-1 sp, 1 hdc in next 5 sts, 1 hdc in ch-1 sp, ch 1; rep from *, end last rep with [FPDC around next st, BPDC around next st] twice, FPDC around next st, 1 hdc in top of beg ch-2. Turn.

Row 7 Ch 2, *[BPDC around next st, FPDC around next st] twice, BPDC around next st, * ch 1, 1 hdc in ch-1 sp, 1 hdc in next 7 hdc, 1 hdc in ch-1 sp, ch 1; rep from *, end last rep with [BPDC around next st, FPDC around next st] twice, BPDC around next st, 1 hdc in top of beg ch-2.

Fasten off.

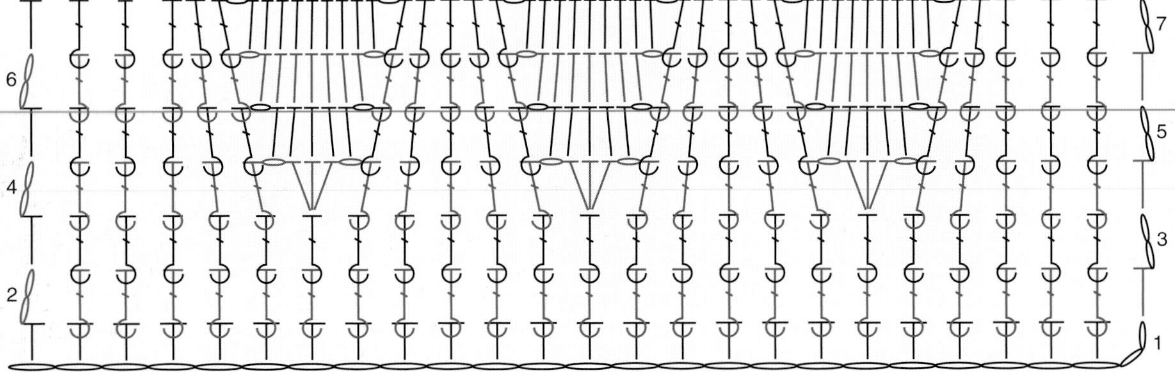

daisy may ruffle

▼ **Colors** A, B and C

Ruffle

With A, make a ch to desired length.

Row 1 1 Hdc in 3rd ch from hook and in each ch to end. Turn.

Rows 2 and 3 Ch 2 (counts as 1 hdc), 1 hdc in next hdc and in each hdc to end. Turn.

Rows 4 and 5 Ch 1, *1 sc in front lp of next st, 1 sc in back lp of same st; rep from * to end. Turn.

Fasten off.

Heading

Working across foundation ch, attach B to right-hand edge.

Row 1 Ch 2, 1 hdc in next ch and in each ch to end. Turn.

Rows 2 and 3 Ch 2, 1 hdc in next hdc and in each hdc to end. Turn.

Fasten off.

Finishing

With C, embroider flowers across heading using daisy chain st. Sew a pearl bead to the center of each flower.

daisy may ruffle

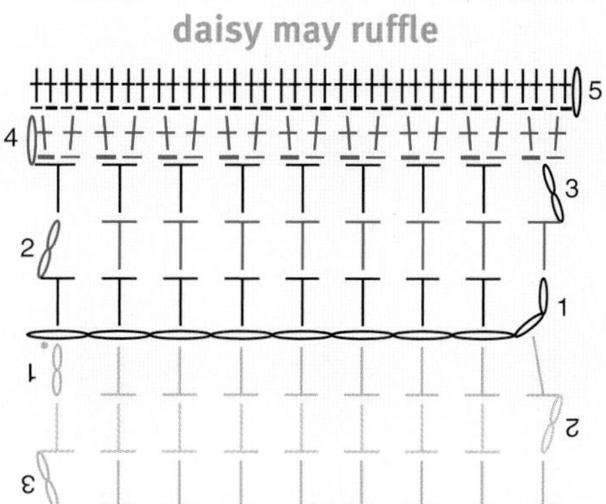

girly ruffle

▼ **Colors** A and B

Ruffle

With A, make a ch to desired length.

Row 1 1 hdc in 5th ch from hook, [ch 3, 1 hdc, ch 3, 1 hdc] in each ch to end. Turn.

Row 2 Ch 1, [1 sc, ch 3, 1 sc] in first ch-3 lp, [ch 3, 1 sc, ch 3, 1 sc] in each ch-3 lp to end.

Fasten off.

Heading

Working across foundation ch, attach B to right-hand edge.

Row 1 Ch 3, 1 dc in next ch and in each ch to end. Turn.

Row 2 Ch 3 (counts as 1 dc), 1 dc in next dc and in each dc to end. Turn.

Fasten off.

girly ruffle

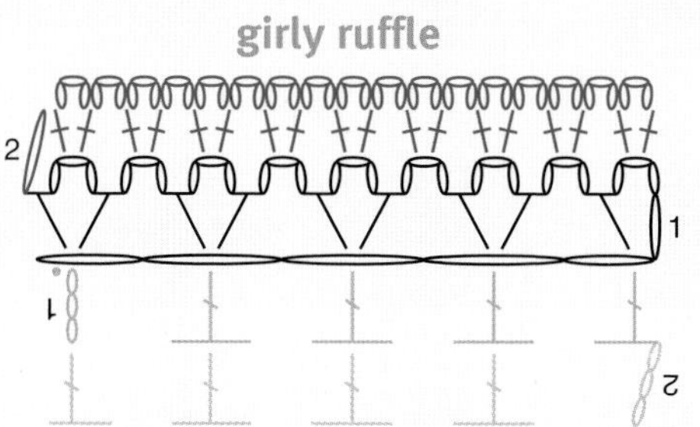

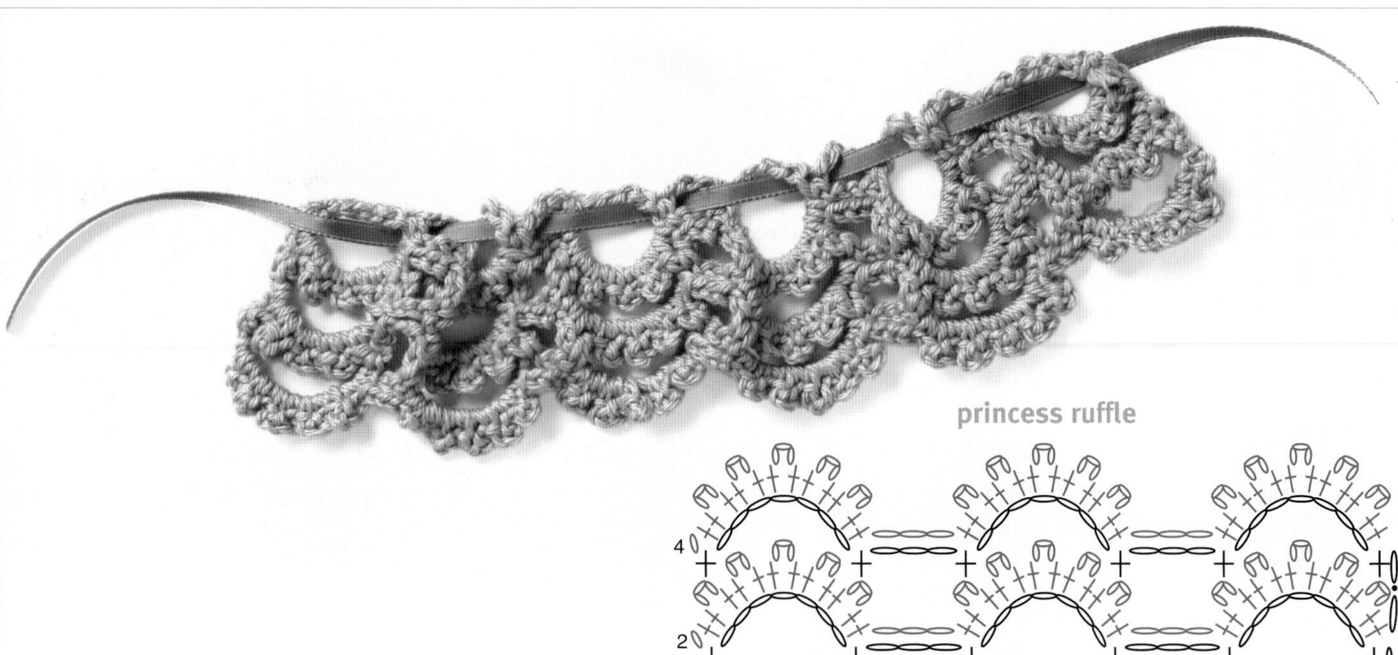

princess ruffle

princess ruffle

▼ (multiple of 9 sts + 6)

Ruffle

Make a ch to desired length in a multiple of 9 sts + 7.

Row 1 1 sc in 2nd ch from hook, *ch 7, skip 4 ch, 1 sc in next ch, ch 3, skip 3 ch, 1 sc in next ch; rep from *, end last rep with ch 7, skip 4 ch, 1 sc in last ch. Turn.

Row 2 Ch 1, *[2 sc, ch 3] 5 times in next ch-7 lp, 2 sc in same lp, ch 3, skip next ch-3 sp; rep from *, end last rep with 2 sc in same lp. Turn.

Row 3 Ch 1, sl st in first ch-3 lp, ch 1, sc in same lp, *ch 7, skip 3 lps, 1 sc in next ch-3 lp, ch 3, skip next ch-3 sp, 1 sc in next ch-3 lp; rep from *, end last rep with 1 sc in last ch-3 lp. Turn.

Rep rows 2 and 3 to desired depth, ending with row 2. Fasten off.

Optional Weave ribbon through loops along straight edge of ruffle.

baby doll ruffle (rows 1-3)

baby doll ruffle (rows 4-7)

baby doll ruffle

▼ **Colors** A and B

With A, make a ch to desired length.

Row 1 1 dc in 4th ch from hook and in each ch to end. Drop A and turn.

Row 2 With B, ch 1, 1 sc in same dc and in each dc to end. Turn.

Row 3 With B, ch 3, 4 dc in first sc, 5 dc in next sc and in each sc to end. Fasten off B and fold ruffle down over previous dc row.

Row 4 Working behind ruffle with A, ch 3, 1 dc in next dc of previous dc row and in each dc to end. Turn.

Row 5 Ch 3, 1 dc in next dc and in each dc to end. Turn.

Row 6 Ch 1, 1 sc in same dc andd in each dc to end. Turn.

Row 7 With A, same as Row 3.

Fasten off.

candy corn

▶ **Colors** A and B

Candy corn

With A, ch 5.

Row 1 1 sc in 2nd ch from hook, 1 hdc in next ch, 1 dc in next ch, 1 tr in last ch.

Fasten off.

Make desired number of candy corn.

With RS facing, attach A in top of tr of first candy corn.

Joining row Ch 1, *5 sc around tr; rep from * until all candy corn are joined.

Fasten off.

Heading

With WS facing, attach yarn to tip of candy corn at right-hand edge.

Row 1 Ch 4 (counts as 1 tr), 1 tr in same sp, *2 tr in tip of next candy corn; rep from * to end. Turn.

Row 2 Ch 1, sc2tog over first 2 sts, *sc2tog over next 2 sts; rep from * to end. Turn.

Row 3 Ch 3 (counts as 1 dc), 1 dc in first st, *2 dc in next st; rep from * to end. Turn.

Row 4 Ch 3, 1 dc in next dc and in each dc to end.

Fasten off.

candy corn

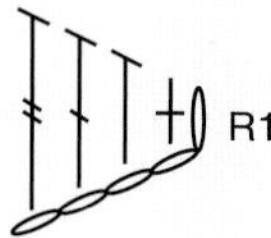

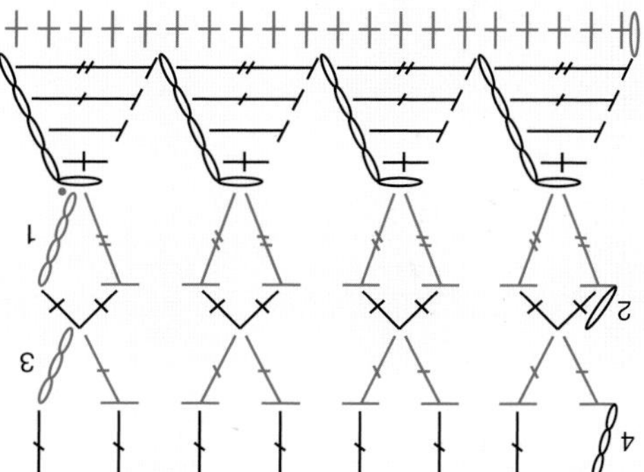

deco ruffle

▼ **Colors** A and B

Ruffle

With A, make a ch to desired length.

Row 1 1 sc in 6th ch from hook, *ch 5, 1 sc in next ch; rep from * to end. Turn.

Row 2 *Ch 6, 1 sc in next ch-5 lp; rep from * to end. Turn.

Fasten off A and attach B.

Row 3 *Ch 7, 1 sc in next ch-6 lp; rep from * to end. Turn.

Row 4 *Ch 8, 1 sc in next ch-7 lp; rep from * to end.

Fasten off.

Heading

Working along foundation ch, attach B to right-hand edge.

Row 1 Ch 2, 1 hdc in next ch and in each ch to end. Turn.

Row 2 Ch 2, 1 hdc in next hdc and in each hdc to end.

Fasten off.

deco ruffle

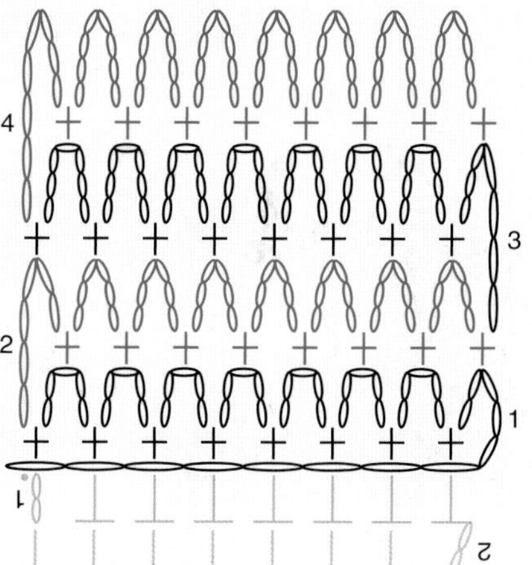

flora

simple bouquet

Note Work chart as for tricolor bouquet, omitting heading.

Edging

Ch 21.

Row 1 (WS) 1 dc in 8th ch from hook, [ch 2 , skip 2 ch, 1 dc in next ch] 3 times, ch 5, skip 3 ch, [1 dc, ch 3] 3 times in last ch, 1 dc in same ch. Turn.

Row 2 Ch 1, ([1 sc, 1 hdc, 1 dc, 1 tr, 1 dc, 1 hdc, 1 sc] in next ch-3 sp) 3 times, ch 5, 1 dc in ch-5 lp, [ch 2, 1 dc in next dc] 4 times, ch 2, skip 2 ch, 1 dc in next ch. Turn.

Row 3 Ch 5, [1 dc in next dc, ch 2] 5 times, 1 dc in ch-5 lp, ch 7, [1 dc, ch 3] 3 times in tr at center of 2nd petal, 1 dc in same tr. Turn.

Row 4 Ch 1, ([1 sc, 1 hdc, 1 dc, 1 tr, 1 dc, 1 hdc, 1 sc] in next ch-3 sp) 3 times, ch 5, 1 dc in ch-7 lp, *ch 2, 1 dc in next dc; rep from *, end 1 dc in 3rd ch of beg ch-5. Turn.

Row 5 Ch 5, [1 dc in next dc, ch 2] 7 times, 1 dc in ch-5 lp, ch 7, [1 dc, ch 3] 3 times in tr at center of 2nd petal, 1 dc in same tr. Turn.

Row 6 Rep row 4.

Row 7 Ch 5, 1 dc in next dc, [ch 2, 1 dc in next dc] 3 times, ch 7, skip next 4 ch-2 sp, [1 dc, ch 3] 3 times in next ch-2 sp, 1 dc in same sp. Turn.

Rep rows 2 to 7 to desired length, ending with row 6.

Fasten off.

Optional Sew a bead to the base of each set of petals.

tricolor bouquet

Colors A, B and C

Edging

With A, work rows 1–6 of simple bouquet (above).

*Fasten off A and attach B. With B, work row 7, then rows 2–6.

Rep from * for each color change to length desired.

Fasten off.

Heading

With RS facing and working along straight length of edging, attach yarn to right-hand edge.

Row 1 Ch 4, *1 tr into side of first dc, 1 tr in next 2 ch of turning ch; rep from * to end.

Fasten off.

tricolor bouquet

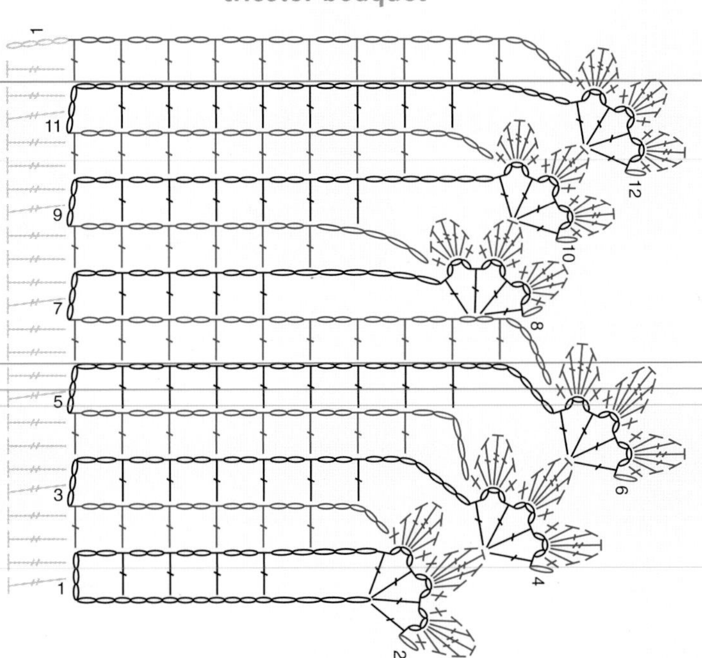

florette on lace

▶ **Florette**

Ch 5. Join with sl st in first ch to form a ring.

Rnd 1 Ch 1, 6 sc in ring. Join with sl st in first sc.

Rnd 2 Ch 4 (counts as 1 sc, ch 3), *1 sc in next sc, ch 3; rep from * around. Join with sl st in 2nd ch of beg ch-4.

Rnd 3 Ch 1, *[1 sc, 1 hdc, 3 dc, 1 hdc, 1 sc] in ch-3 sp; rep from * around. Join with sl st in first sc.

Rnd 4 Ch 1, 1 sc in same sp, *ch 5, 1 sc in back of next sc of rnd 2, ch 5, skip next sc of rnd 2, 1 sc in back of next sc of rnd 2; rep from * once more, end last rep sl st in first sc—4 lps. Join with sl st in first sc.

Rnd 5 Ch 1, *[1 sc, 1 hdc, 1 dc, 4 tr, ch 3, 1 sc in last tr made, 4 tr, 1 dc, 1 hdc, 1 sc] in next ch-5 lp; rep from * around. Join with sl st in first sc.

Rnd 6 Ch 1, 1 sc in same sp, *ch 7, 1 sc in ch-3 lp, ch 7, 1 sc in space between petals; rep from *, end last rep with omit 1 sc in space between petals. Join with sl st in first sc. Fasten off.

Make desired number of flowers.

Heading

Attach yarn in sc at tip of any petal.

Row 1 (join) Ch 1, 1 sc in same sp, *ch 7, 1 dtr in ch-7 lp of next petal, 1 dtr in corresponding ch-7 lp of next flower, ch 7, 1 sc in next sc at tip of next petal; rep from * until all flowers are joined. Turn.

Row 2 Ch 1, 1 sc in first sc and in each ch and st to end. Turn.

Rows 3 and 4 Ch 1, 1 sc in first sc and in each sc to end. Turn.

Fasten off.

Optional Sew beads to center of florettes.

florette on lace

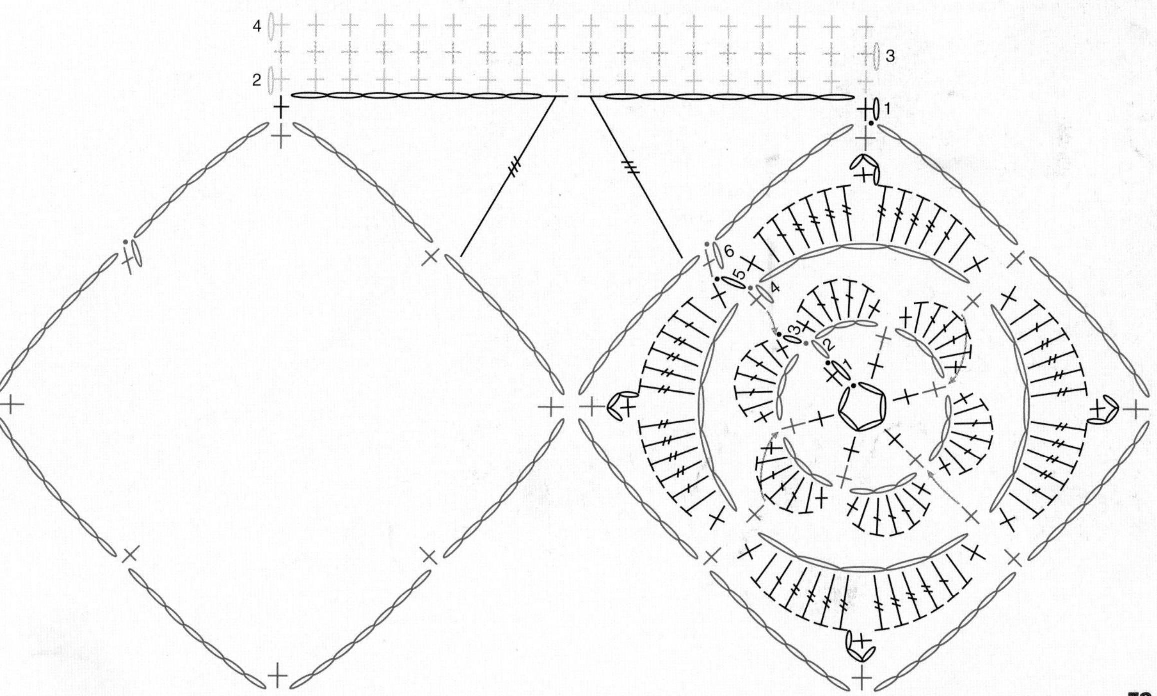

fantasy blossom

Beg TC (Beg Tr Cluster) (Yo twice, insert hook into designated st, yo and draw up a lp, [yo and draw through 2 lps on hook] twice) twice, yo and draw through all 3 lps on hook.

TC (Tr Cluster) (Yo twice, insert hook into designated st, yo and draw up a lp, [yo and draw through 2 lps on hook] twice) 3 times, yo and draw through all 4 lps on hook.

DTC (Dtr Cluster) ([Yo] 3 times, insert hook into designated st, yo and draw up a lp, [yo and draw through 2 lps on hook] 3 times) twice, yo and draw through all 3 lps on hook.

First motif

Ch 10. Join with sl st in first ch to form a ring.

Rnd 1 Ch 1, 20 sc in ring. Join with sl st to first sc.

Rnd 2 Ch 1, 2 sc in each sc around—40 sc. Join with sl st to first sc.

Rnd 3 Ch 1, 1 sc in each sc around. Join with sl st to first sc.

Rnd 4 *Ch 5, skip next sc, 1 sc in next sc; rep from * around. Join with sl st to base of beg ch-5—20 lps.

Rnd 5 Ch 1, sl st in first ch-5 lp, ch 4, beg TC in same lp, *ch 5, TC in next ch-5 lp; rep from * around, ch 5. Join with sl st in top of beg TC.

Fasten off.

Second motif

Work same as First Motif through rnd 4.

Rnd 5 Ch 1, sl st in first ch-5 lp, ch 4, beg TC in same lp, *ch 2, sl st in ch-5 lp of previous motif, ch 2, TC in next lp of current motif; rep from * twice more, complete as for first motif.

Make desired number of motifs following instructions for second motif, leaving 7 lps free at top and bottom of each motif between the 3 joining lps.

Heading

With RS facing, attach yarn in 7th lp to the left of join on first motif.

Joining row Ch 9, 1 tr in next ch-5 lp, *[ch 4, 1 sc in next ch-5 lp] 3 times, ch 4, 1 tr in next ch-5 lp, ch 4, DTC over next ch-5 lp and next ch-5 lp of next motif, ch 4, 1 tr in next ch-5 lp; rep from * across all motifs to last motif, [ch 4, 1 sc in next ch-5 lp] 3 times, ch 4, 1 tr in next ch-5 lp, ch4, 1 dtr in next ch-5 lp. Turn.

Next row Ch 7, *1 dc in next tr, [ch 4, 1 dc in next sc] 3 times, ch 4, 1 dc in next tr, ch 4, 1 dc in DTC, ch 4; rep from *, end last rep with 1 dc in 5th ch of beg ch-9.

Fasten off.

Optional If desired, sew 8 beads evenly around rnd 2 of each motif.

fantasy blossom

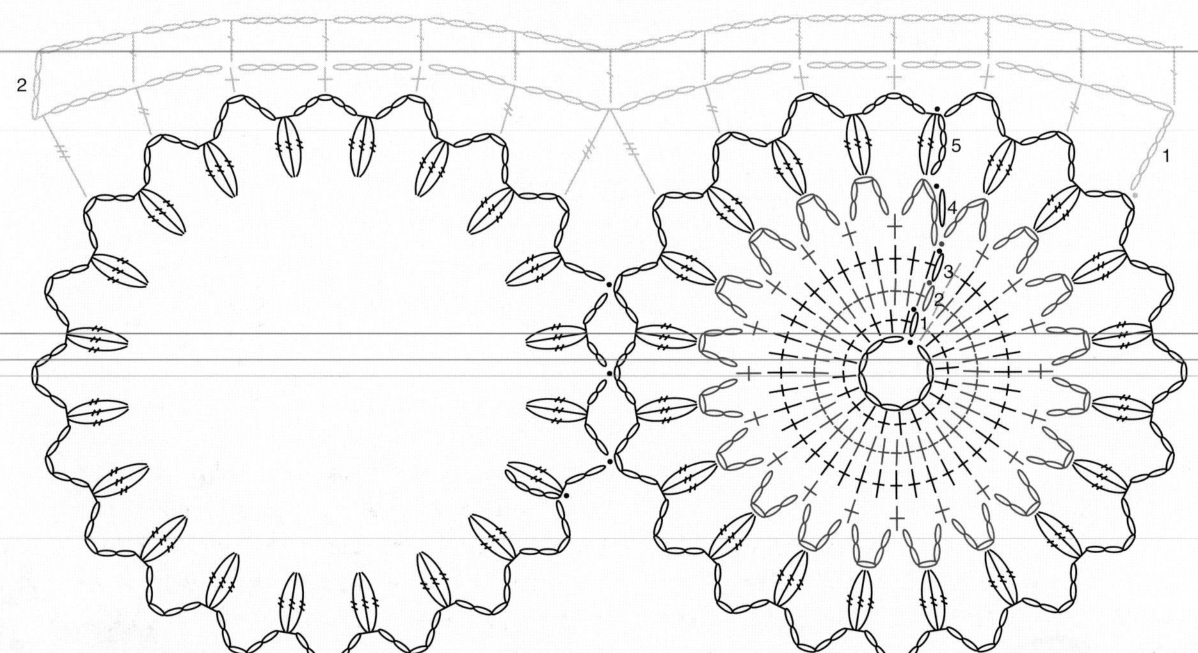

trinidad rose

▶ **Picot** After chaining the specified # of chs, 1 sc in 3rd ch from hook.

Picot Lp Ch 4, picot, ch5, picot, ch 2.

First motif

Ch 8. Join with sl st in first ch to form a ring.

Rnd 1 Ch 1, 12 sc in ring. Join with sl st in first sc.

Rnd 2 Ch 1, 1 sc in same sp, *ch 5, skip next sc, 1 sc in next sc; rep from * 4 times more, ch 5, skip next sc. Join with sl st in first sc.

Rnd 3 Ch 1, *[1 sc, 1 hdc, 5 dc, 1 hdc, 1 sc] in ch-5 lp; rep from * around—*6 petals. Do not join.*

Rnd 4 *Working behind petals of rnd 3,* ch 1, 1 sc in first sc of rnd 2, *picot lp, 1 sc in next sc of rnd 2 between petals; rep from * 4 times more, picot lp. Join with sl st in first sc. Fasten off.

Second motif

Rep rnds 1–4 of first motif. Do not fasten off.

Joining Motifs

Row 1 (RS) In first picot lp of rnd 4, sl st in (sp before 1st picot, 1st picot, after 1st picot), ch 1, 1 sc in same sp, picot lp, 1 sc between picots of next picot lp. Turn.

Row 2 Picot lp, 1 sc between picots of picot lp in row 1, picot lp, 1 sc in first sc of row 1. Turn.

Row 3 In first picot lp, sl st in (sp before 1st picot, 1st picot, after 1st picot), ch 1, 1 sc in same sp, picot lp, 1 sc between picots of next picot lp. Turn.

Row 4 (Joining) Ch 4, picot, ch 1, with RS facing of previous motif, sl st between picots of any picot lp, ch 3, picot, ch 2, 1 sc between picots of picot lp of row 3 of current motif, ch 4, picot, ch 1, sl st between picots of next picot lp of previous motif, ch 3, picot, ch 2,
1 sc in last sc of row 3 of current motif. Fasten off.

Make desired number of motifs following instructions for second motif and joining, keeping one picot lp free on either side of joined picot lps.

Heading

With RS facing, attach yarn between picots of top picot lp at right-hand edge.

Row 1 Ch 8, *1 dc in st between next 2 picot lps, ch 5; rep from * across, end 1 dc in sp between picots of last picot lp of last motif. Fasten off.

Scallop edging

With RS facing and working along bottom edge, attach yarn to sc at base of top picot lp at right-hand edge.

Row 1 Ch 5, picot, ch 3, *[1 tr, ch 3, 1 sc in top of tr just made] 6 times between picots of picot lp, 1 tr in same picot lp, ch 7, skip next picot, 1 sc in next picot, picot lp, 1 sc in next picot, ch 7, skip next picot; rep from *, ending [1 tr, ch 3, 1 sc in top of tr just made] 6 times between picots of picot lp of last motif, 1 tr in same picot lp, ch 5, picot, ch 2, 1 sc in base st of same picot lp. Fasten off.

Optional Sew a bead to the center of each rose.

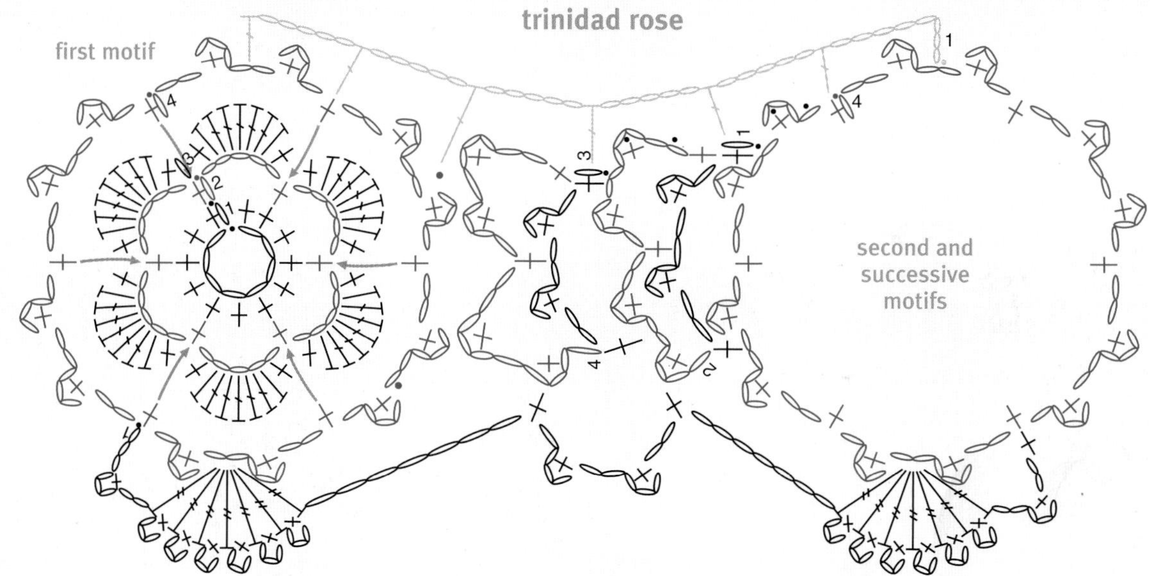

victoria

Note Photo shows only first and last motifs.

First motif

Ch 6. Join with sl st in first ch to form a ring.

Rnd 1 Ch 1, 12 sc in ring. Join with sl st in first sc.

Rnd 2 Ch 1, 1 sc in same st, *ch 5, skip next sc, 1 sc in next sc; rep from * around, ending last rep with ch 5, skip next sc. Join with sl st in first sc.

Rnd 3 Ch 1, [1 sc, 1 hdc, 3 dc, 1 hdc, 1 sc]—(*shell made*), in each ch-5 lp around. Join with sl st in first sc.

Rnd 4 Ch 1, 1 sc in same sp, *ch 5, 1 sc between 2 shells; rep from * around ending last rep with ch 5. Join with sl st in first sc.

Rnd 5 Ch 1, [1 sc, 1 hdc, 5 dc, 1 hdc, 1 sc] in each ch-5 lp around. Join with sl st in first sc.

Rnd 6 Ch 1, 1 sc in same sp, *([ch 5, 1 sc in 3rd ch from hook] twice, ch 2)—(*picot loop*), 1 sc between next 2 shells; rep from *, ending last rep with picot lp. Join with sl st in first sc.

Rnd 7 Ch 1, 1 sc in same sp, make picot lp, 1 sc between picots in next picot lp, make picot lp, 1 sc in sc between picot lps—(*joining picot lps made*), *ch 5, 1 sc between picots in next picot lp, ch 5, 1 sc in next sc; rep from * around, ending last rep with omit 1 sc in next sc. Join with sl st in first sc.

Fasten off.

Second motif

Work same as first motif through rnd 6.

Rnd 7 (Joining) Ch 1, 1 sc in same sp, ch 5, 1 sc in 3rd ch from hook, ch 1, 1 sc between picots on corresponding joining lp of previous motif, ch 4, 1 sc in 3rd ch from hook, ch 2, 1 sc between picots of next picot lp of current motif, ch 5, 1 sc in 3rd ch from hook, ch 1, 1 sc between picots on corresponding joining lp of previous motif, ch 4, 1 sc in 3rd ch from hook, ch 2, [1 sc in sc of current motif, ch 5, 1 sc between picots of next picot lp of current motif, ch 5] twice, 1 sc in sc of current motif, make picot lp, 1 sc between picots in next picot lp, make picot lp, 1 sc in sc between picot lps—(*joining picot lps made*), ch 5, 1 sc between picots in next picot lp, ch 5, 1 sc in next sc, ch 5, 1 sc between picots in next picot lp, ch 5. Join with sl st in first sc.

Fasten off.

Cont to add desired number of motifs following instructions for second motif.

Last motif

Work same as first motif through rnd 6.

Rnd 7 (Joining) Ch 1, 1 sc in same sp, ch 5, 1 sc in 3rd ch from hook, ch 1, 1 sc between picots on corresponding joining lp of previous motif, ch 4, 1 sc in 3rd ch from hook, ch 2, 1 sc between picots of next picot lp of current motif, ch 5, 1 sc in 3rd ch from hook, ch 1, 1 sc between picots on corresponding joining lp of previous motif, ch 4, 1 sc in 3rd ch from hook, ch 2, [1 sc in sc of current motif, ch 5, 1 sc between picots of next picot lp of current motif, ch 5], 5 times. Join with sl st in first sc.

Fasten off.

Top joining

With RS facing, attach yarn to right-hand edge—4 ch-5 lps to right of joining lp.

Row 1 Ch 10, *1 dc in next ch-5 lp, *[ch 3, 1 sc in next ch-5 lp] twice, ch 3, 1 dc in next ch-5 lp, ch 6, dtr in next sc, dtr in sc of current motif, dtr in corresponding sc of next motif, ch 6; rep from *, end last rep with ch 3, 1 dc in next ch-5 lp, ch 10, sl st in next sc. Turn.

Row 2 Ch 5, 1 sc in ch-10 lp, *ch 5, 1 sc in 3rd ch from hook, ch 2, 1 sc in next dc, [ch 5, 1 sc in 3rd ch from hook, ch 2, 1 sc in next sc] twice, ch 5, 1 sc in 3rd ch from hook, ch 2, 1 sc in next dc, [ch 5, 1 sc in 3rd ch from hook, ch 2, 1 sc in next ch-6 lp] twice; rep from *, end last rep with 1 sc in next dc, ch 5, 1 sc in 3rd ch from hook, ch 2, 1 sc in last ch-10 lp, ch 5, sl st in base of ch-10.

Fasten off.

Optional If desired, sew 12 beads evenly around row 1 of each motif.

victoria

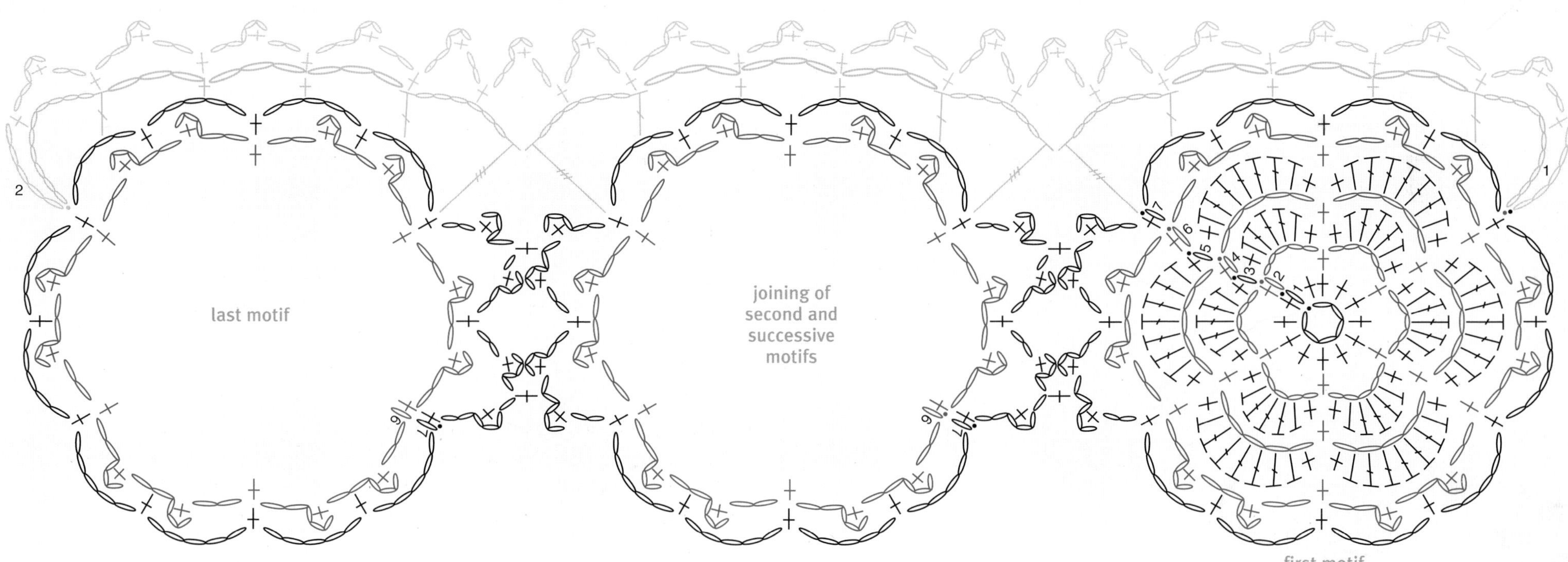

fire flower

fire flower

▶ **DCL (Dc Cluster)** [Yo, insert hook in designated st and draw up a lp, yo and draw through 2 lps on hook] twice, yo and draw through all 3 lps on hook.

TDCL (Tr/Dtr Cluster) [Yo] twice, insert hook in designated st and draw up a lp, [yo and draw through 2 lps on hook] twice, ([yo] 3 times, insert hook in designated st and draw up a lp, [yo and draw through 3 lps on hook] 3 times) twice, [yo] twice, insert hook in designated st and draw up a lp, [yo and draw through 2 lps on hook] twice, yo and draw through all 5 lps on hook.

First flower

Ch 6. Join with sl st in first ch to form 1 ring.

Rnd 1 Ch 1, 12 sc in ring. Join with sl st in first sc.

Rnd 2 Ch 1, 1 sc in same sp, *ch 15, 1 sc in next 2 sc; rep from * around, ending last rep with 1 sc in last sc. Join with sl st in first sc—*6 loops*.

Rnd 3 Ch 1, *[2 sc, ch 3] 9 times in ch-15 lp, 2 sc in same lp, sl st in sp between next 2 sc; rep from * around ending last rep with sl st in first sc.

Fasten off.

Second and successive flowers

Work as for first flower through rnd 2.

Rnd 3 Ch 1, [2 sc, ch 3] 4 times in ch-15 lp, 2 sc in same lp, ch 1, sl st in center ch-3 lp of any petal of previous flower, ch 1, [2 sc, ch 3] 4 times in same ch-15 lp of current flower, 2 sc in same lp, sl st between next 2 sc, *[2 sc, ch 3] 9 times in ch-15 lp, 2 sc in same lp, sl st in sp between next 2 sc; rep from * around ending last rep with sl st in first sc.

Fasten off.

Make desired number of flowers following instructions for second flower, keeping 2 petals between joined petals.

Top joining strip

With RS facing, attach yarn to center ch-3 lp 2 petals to left of joined petal.

Row 1 Ch 1, 1 sc in same sp, *ch 5, skip next ch-3 lp, DCL in next ch-3 lp and in corresponding ch-3 lp of next petal, ch 5, skip next ch-3 lp, 1 sc in next ch-3 lp, ch 7, skip next ch-3 lp, TDCL over next [ch-3 lp, 3rd ch-3 lp of next petal, and corresponding ch-3 lps of 2 petals of next flower], ch 7, skip next ch-3 lp, 1 sc in next ch-3 lp; rep from * until all flowers are joined, ending with DCL, skip next ch-3 lp, 1 sc in next lp. Turn.

Row 2 Ch 6 (counts as 1 dc, ch 3), *1 dc in next ch-sp, ch 3, 1 dc in DCL, ch 3, 1 dc in next ch-sp, ch 3, 1 dc in next sc**, ch 3, 1 dc in next ch-sp, ch 3, 1 dc in TDCL, ch 3, 1 dc in next ch-sp, ch 3, 1 dc in next sc, ch 3; rep from *, ending last rep at **. Turn.

Row 3 Ch 6, *1 dc in next dc, ch 3; rep from *, end skip 3 ch, 1 dc in next ch.

Fasten off.

guinevere

▶ **Colors** A and B

3TCL (3-Tr Cluster) ([Yo] twice, insert hook in designated st and draw up a lp, [yo and draw through 2 lps on hook] twice) 3 times, yo and draw through all 4 lps on hook.

4TCL (4-Tr Cluster) ([Yo] twice, insert hook in designated st and draw up a lp, [yo and draw through 2 lps on hook] twice) 4 times, yo and draw through all 5 lps on hook.

Picot Ch 3, 1 sc in 3rd ch from hook.

Edging

Row 1 With A, *Ch 5, 3TCL in 5th ch from hook; rep from * to desired length with a multiple of 2 clusters.

Rnd 2 *Ch 7, 4TCL between next 2 clusters, ch 7, 1 sc between next 2 clusters; rep from *, end last rep 1 sc in ch at base of last cluster (working around to opposite side of edging), **ch 12, 4TCL between next 2 clusters; rep from **, end ch 12. Join with sl st in base of beg ch-7.

Fasten off A and attach B in same sp.

Rnd 3 With B, ch 1 [4 sc, picot, 4 sc] in each ch-7 lp to end of first side, working around to opposite side, [4 sc, picot, 10 sc] in first ch-12 lp, 12 sc in each ch-12 lp to last lp, end [10 sc, picot, 4 sc] in last ch-12 lp. Join with sl st in first sc.

Fasten off.

Optional If desired, sew 3 beads to center of each flower.

guinevere

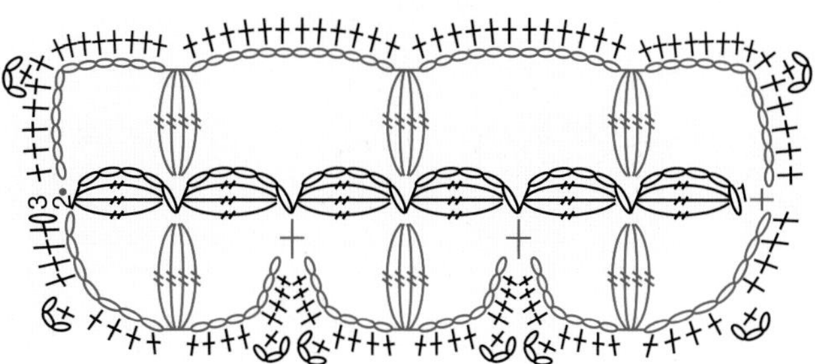

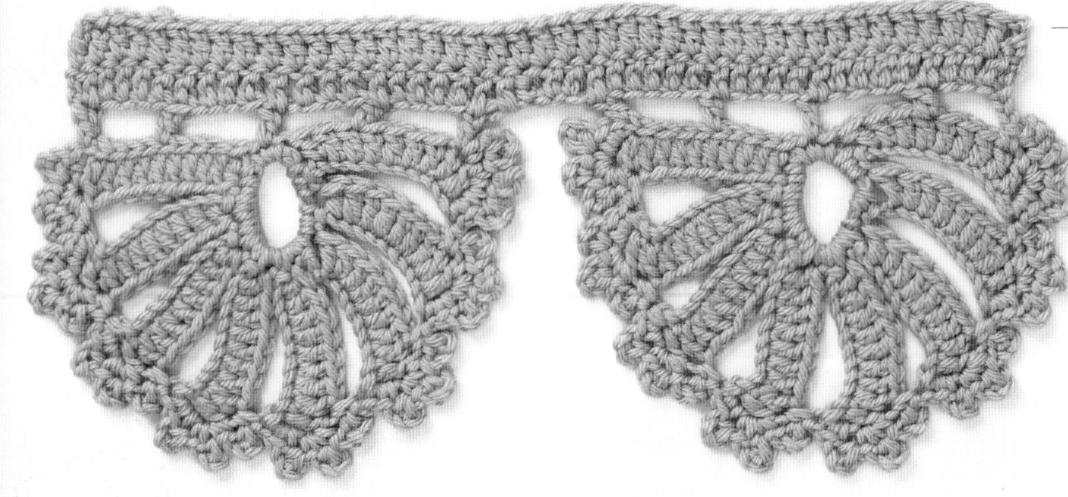

luna flower

Flower

Ch 13. Join with sl st in first ch to form a ring.

Row 1 *Ch 13, 1 dc in 4th ch from hook and in rem 9 ch, 2 sc in ring; rep from * 7 times more—*8 spokes.* Sl st across foundation ch of first spoke.

Row 2 Ch 1, 2 sc in ch-sp at end of spoke, *ch 3, 1 sc in 3rd ch from hook, [1 sc, ch 3, 1 sc in 3rd ch from hook] twice in first dc, 1 sc in next dc, 2 sc in ch-sp at end of next spoke; rep from *, end last rep omit 2 sc in ch-sp at end of next spoke *(3 picots at end of each spoke).*

Fasten off.

Make desired number of flowers. *Do not fasten off after last flower.*

Top joining strip

Row 1 Ch 7 (counts as 1 dc, ch 4), *[skip 4 sts, 1 dc in next st, ch 4] 3 times, 1 dc in next st**, ch 4, 1 dc in last sc of row 2 of next flower, ch 4; rep from * to connect flowers to heading, ending connection of last flower at **.

Rows 2 and 3 Ch 3 (counts as 1 dc), 1 dc in each ch and dc to end. Turn.

Fasten off.

luna flower

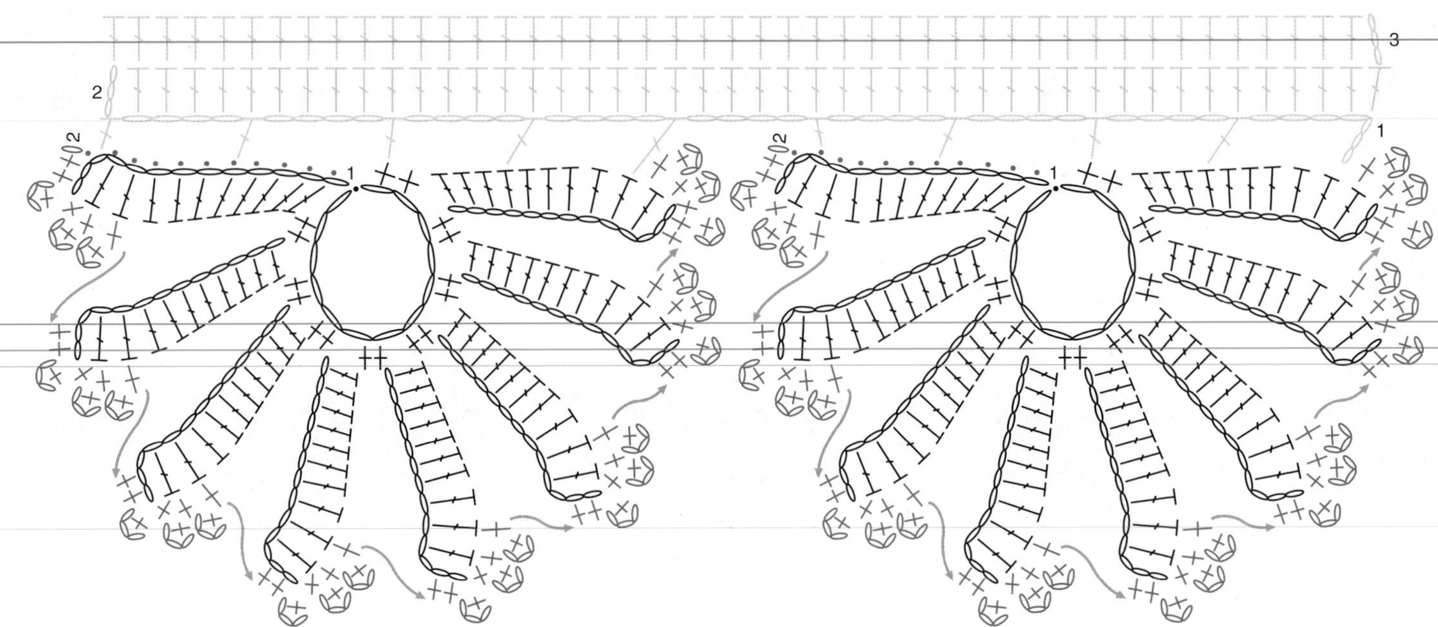

petal edge

▼ **Colors** A and B

(multiple of 18 sts + 7)

4TCL (4-Tr Cluster) ([Yo] twice, insert hook in designated st and draw up a lp, [yo and draw through 2 lps on hook] twice) 4 times, yo and draw through all 5 lps on hook.

3TCL (3-Tr Cluster) ([Yo] twice, insert hook in designated st and draw up a lp, [yo and draw through 2 lps on hook] twice) 3 times, yo and draw through all 4 lps on hook.

With A, make a ch to desired length in a multiple of 18 sts + 1.

Row 1 1 sc in 7th ch from hook, *ch 5, skip 5 ch, 1 sc in next ch; rep from * to last 6 ch, sl st in last ch. Turn.

Row 2 Ch 4, *[4TCL, ch 3] twice in next ch-5 lp, 4TCL in same lp, ch 4, [1 sc in next ch-5 lp, ch 4] twice; rep from *, end last rep [4TCL, ch 3] twice in last ch-5 lp, 4TCL in same lp, ch 4, sl st in last sc.

Fasten off A. With RS facing, attach B in ch-6 lp at right-hand edge of row 1.

Row 3 Ch 4, 3TCL in same lp, *ch 4, 2 sc in next ch-3 sp, ch 6, 2 sc in next ch-3 sp, ch 4, 4TCL in next ch-4 sp; rep from *, end last rep 4TCL in ch-6 lp of Row 1.

Fasten off.

petal edge

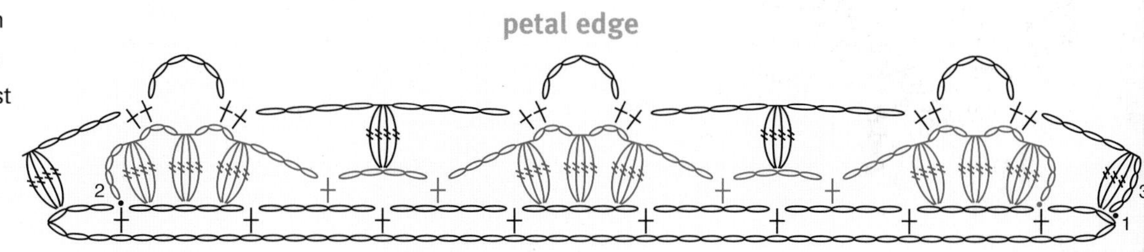

sweet clover

▼ **Colors** A and B

(multiple of 7 sts)

Heading and Clover

With A, make a ch to desired length in a multiple of 7 + 3.

Row 1 (WS) 1 tr in 5th ch from hook and in each ch to end. Turn.

Row 2 Ch 3, 1 dc in next 6 tr, *ch 10, sl st in 7th ch from hook to form a ring, cont around in ring, ch 1, [1 sc, 1 dc, 2 tr, 1 dc] 3 times in ring, 1 sc in same ring, 1 sc in next 3 ch, 1 dc in same tr, 1 dc in next 7 tr; rep from * to end.

Clover Border (optional)

With RS facing, attach B to first sc of clover.

Row 1 *Ch 3, 1 sc in next st; rep from * around. Join with sl st in base of beg ch-3.

Optional Sew bead to center of each clover if desired.

sweet clover

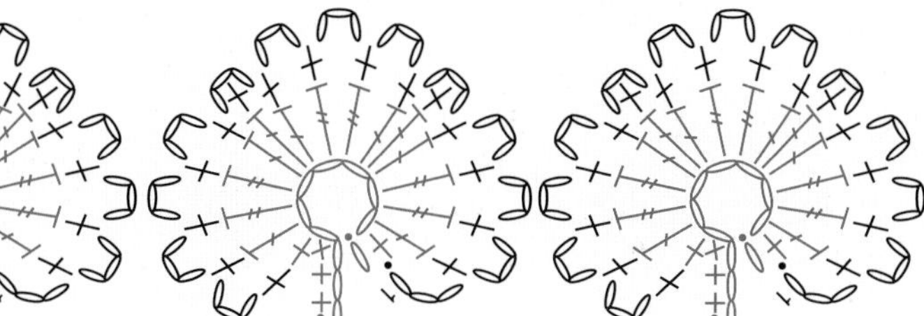

daisy chain

▶ **Colors** A and B

Flowers

Row 1 (RS) With A, *ch 16, 1 sc in 3rd ch from hook, 1 dc in next ch, 1 tr in next 3 ch, 1 dc in next ch, 1 sc in next ch, [ch 9, 1 sc in 3rd ch from hook, 1 dc in next ch, 1 tr in next 3 ch, 1 dc in next ch, 1 sc in next ch]; rep from * to desired length, work between [ ] once more (working around to opposite side), **work between [ ] twice, (1 sc, 1 dc, 3 tr, 1 dc, 1 sc) in next 7 ch; rep from ** to end.

Fasten off.

Top strip

With WS facing, attach B to tip of first upward-pointing petal at right-hand edge.

Row 1 *Ch 7, sl st in tip of next petal, ch 1, sl st in tip of next petal; rep from * ending with ch 7, sl st in tip of last petal. Turn.

Row 2 Ch 5 (counts as 1 dc, ch 2), skip next 2 ch, 1 dc in next ch, *ch 2, skip next 2 ch, 1 dc in next ch, ch 2, skip next ch, 1 dc in next ch, ch 2, skip next 2 ch, 1 dc in next ch; rep from *, end ch 2, skip next 2 ch, 1 dc in last ch.

Fasten off.

daisy chain

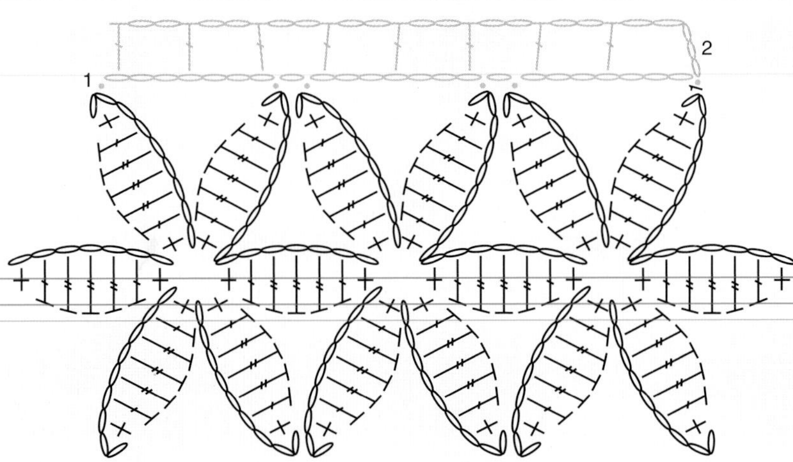

floral flaps

▶ **Colors** A and B

Flower flap

With A, ch 6. Join with sl st in first ch to form a ring.

Rnd 1 Ch 1, [1 sc, ch 1, 1 sc] 8 times in ring. Join with sl st to first sc.

Fasten off A and attach B.

Rnd 2 Draw up lp on hook to ½"/1.25cm, *[yo, insert hook in same lp and draw up a lp to ½"/1.25cm] 3 times in ch-1 sp, yo and draw through all 7 lps on hook—(*bobble made*), ch 4; rep from * around—8 petals. Join with sl st in first bobble.

Fasten off B and attach A in any ch-4 sp.

Rnd 3 Ch 3, 3 dc in same sp, *4 dc in next ch-4 sp; rep from * around. Join with sl st in top of beg ch-3.

Fasten off.

Make desired number of flowers.

Joining strip

With A and RS facing, attach yarn in center of any 4-dc group.

Row 1 Ch 3 (counts as 1 dc), 2 dc in same st, *1 dc in next 8 dc; rep from * for each flower flap until all flaps have been joined, 3 dc in next dc. Turn.

Rows 2 and 3 Ch 3 (counts as 1 dc), 1 dc in next dc and in each dc to end. Turn.

Fasten off.

floral flaps

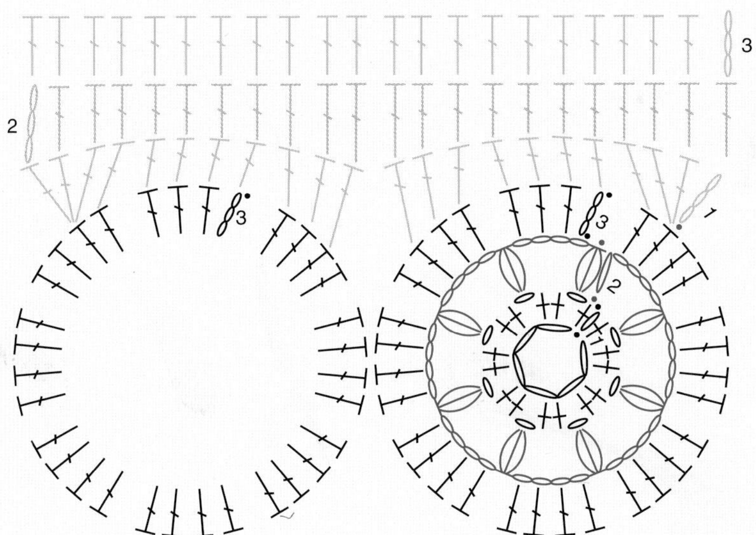

puff flower

▶ **Colors** A and B

Flower

With A, ch 3. Join with sl st in first ch to form a ring.

Rnd 1 [Yo, insert hook in ring and draw up a lp to ½"/1.25cm] 6 times, yo and draw through all 13 lps on hook, ch 4; rep from * 5 times more—6 petals. Join with sl st in top of first petal.

Fasten off A and attach B.

Rnd 2 Ch 1, *[2 sc, ch 1, 3 sc] in next ch-4 sp; rep from * around. Join with sl st in first sc.

Fasten off B and attach A.

Row 3 Ch 3, 1 dc in next sc, *[2 dc, ch 1, 2 dc] in next ch-1 sp, 1 dc in next 5 sc; rep from *, end last rep with 1 dc in last 3 dc. Join with sl st in top of first dc.

Fasten off.

Make desired number of flowers.

Joining tape

Attach B to any ch-1 sp.

Row 1 (join) Ch 3, 2 dc in same sp, *ch 12, 3 dc in ch-1 sp of next flower; rep from * until all fowers have been joined. Turn.

Row 2 Ch 3, 1 dc in next dc and in each dc and ch to end. Turn.

Row 3 Ch 3, 1 dc in next dc and in each dc to end.

Fasten off.

Optional If desired, sew a bead to the center of each flower.

puff flower

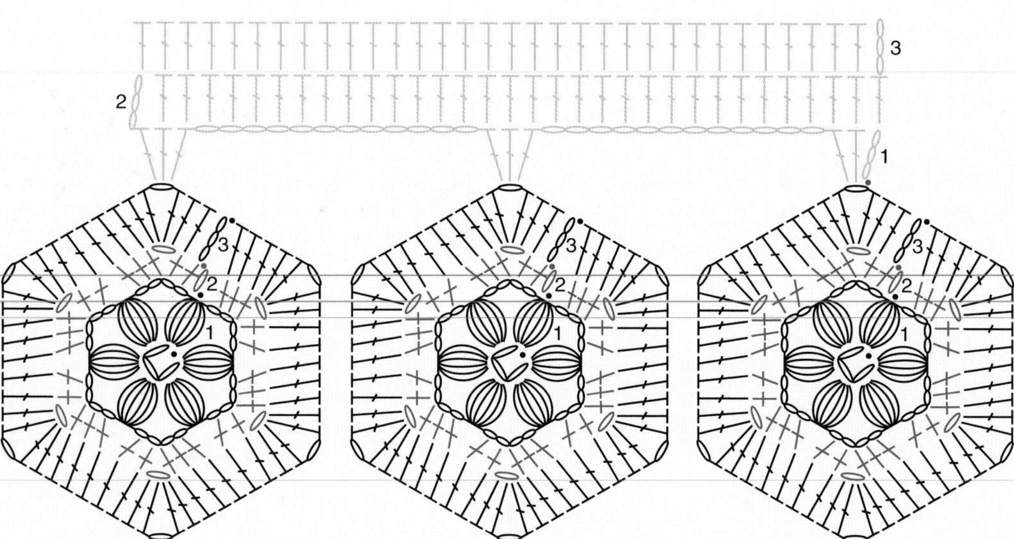

flower wheelies I

▶ **Colors** A and B

First motif

With A, ch 8. Join with sl st in first ch to form a ring.

Rnd 1 Ch 3, *1 dc in ring, ch 3, sl st in top of dc just made—(picot), 1 dc in ring; rep from * 10 times more, 1 dc in ring, ch 3, sl st in top of dc just made. Join with sl st in top of beg ch-3.

Fasten off.

Second motif

With A, ch 8. Join with sl st in first ch to form a ring.

Rnd 1 Ch 3, 1 dc in ring, *ch 2, drop lp from hook, insert hook in any picot of previous motif and dropped lp, drawing lp through, ch 1, sl st in top of dc just made, 2 dc in ring of current motif; rep from * for next picot of previous motif, **ch 3, sl st in top of dc just made, 2 dc in ring; rep from ** 8 times more, ch 3, sl st in top of dc just made. Join with sl st in top of beg ch-3.

Fasten off.

Make desired number of motifs following instructions for second motif, joining first 2 picots to 5th and 6th picots (counting clockwise from last joined picot) of previous motif.

Top joining strip

3TCL (3-Tr Cluster) ([Yo] twice, insert hook in designated st and draw up a lp, [yo and draw through 2 lps on hook] twice) 3 times, yo and draw through all 4 lps on hook.

4TCL (4-Tr Cluster) ([Yo] twice, insert hook in designated st and draw up a lp, [yo and draw through 2 lps on hook] twice) 4 times, yo and draw through all 5 lps on hook.

With RS facing, attach B in 4th picot to right of upper joined picot of motif at right-hand edge.

Row 1 Ch 4, 3TCL over next 3 picots, *ch 8, 4TCL over next 4 picots of next motif; rep from * to end. Turn.

Row 2 Ch 4, *1 tr in TCL, 1 tr in next 8 ch; rep from *, end 1 tr in last TCL, 1 tr in top of beg ch-4.

Row 3 Ch 1, 1 sc in first tr and in each tr to end.

Fasten off.

Optional If desired, sew a bead to the center of each motif.

flower wheelies II

▶ **Colors** A and B

Note When working motifs, alternate colors as you go.

First layer

First motif

Work same as first motif of Flower Wheelies I (see page 91).

Second and subsequent motifs

Work same as second motif of Flower Wheelies I.

Second layer

First motif

Work same as second motif of first layer, EXCEPT joining first 2 picots of motif to 8th and 9th picots (counting clockwise from upper joined picot) of first motif of first layer.

Second and subsequent motifs

With A, ch 8. Join with sl st in first ch to form a ring.

Rnd 1 Ch 3, *1 dc in ring, ch 2, drop lp from hook, insert hook in 8th picot (counting clockwise) of previous motif and dropped lp, drawing lp through, ch 1, sl st in top of dc just made, 1 dc in ring of current motif; rep from * for next picot of previous motif, **1 dc in ring, ch 3, sl st in top of dc just made, 1 dc in ring; rep from ** 6 times more, ***1 dc in ring, ch 2, drop lp from hook, insert hook in corresponding picot of next motif of first layer and dropped lp, drawing lp through, ch 1, sl st in top of dc just made, 1 dc in ring of current motif; rep from * for next picot of corresponding motif, 1 dc in ring, ch 3, sl st in top of dc just made. Join with sl st in top of beg ch-3.

Complete second layer following instructions for second motif, working last motif joining first 2 picots of motif to 5th and 6th picots of last motif and following picots to 3rd and 2nd picots of last motif of first layer.

flower wheelies II

first layer of motifs

second layer of motifs

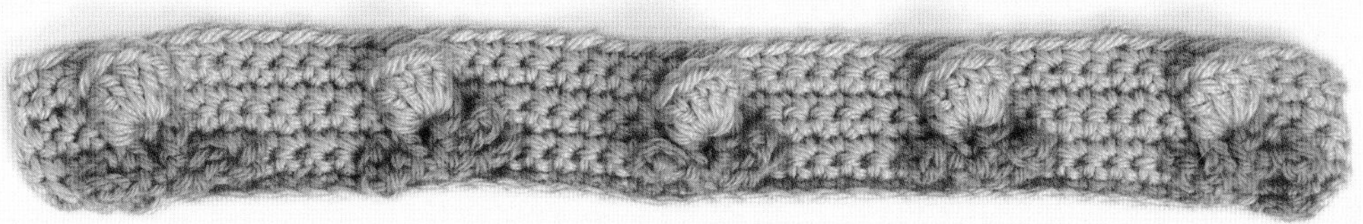

thistle I

▼ Colors A and B

(multiple of 10 sts + 9)

With A, make a ch to desired length in a multiple of 10 sts + 9.

Drop A and attach B.

Row 1 (RS) With B, ch 1, 1 sc in first 4 ch, *[1 sc, ch 8] 3 times in next ch, 1 sc in same ch, 1 sc in next 9 ch; rep from *, end last rep 1 sc in last 4 ch.

Fasten off B.

Row 2 (RS) With A, ch 1, 1 sc in first 4 sc, *ch 1, skip ch lps, skip next sc, 1 sc in next 9 sc; rep from *, end last rep 1 sc in last 4 sc. Turn.

Row 3 Ch 1, 1 sc in first sc, *1 sc through first loop and next sc, 1 sc in next 2 sc, 1 sc in ch-1 sp, 1 sc in next 2 sc, 1 sc through last lp and next sc, 1 sc in next 3 sc; rep from *, end last rep 1 sc in last sc. Turn.

Row 4 Ch 1, 1 sc in first sc and in each sc to end. Turn.

Row 5 Ch 1, 1 sc in first 4 sc, *6 dc through center loop and next sc, 1 sc in next 9 sc,; rep from *, end last rep 1sc in last 4 sc. Turn.

Row 6 Ch 1, 1 sc in first 4 sc, *ch 1, skip 6 dc, 1 sc in next 9 sc; rep from *, end last rep 1 sc in last 4 sc.

Fasten off.

thistle II

▼ Colors A and B

(multiple of 10 sts + 9)

Work same as Thistle I (see left) through row 6.

With RS facing, attach B to right-hand edge.

Row 7 (RS) With B, ch 1, 1 sc in first 9 sts, *[1 sc, ch 8] 3 times in next sc, 1 sc in same sc, 1 sc in next 9 sts; rep from * to end.

Fasten off B. With RS facing, attach A to right-hand edge.

Row 8 (RS) With A, ch 1, 1 sc in first 9 sc, *ch 1, skip ch lps, skip next sc, 1 sc in next 9 sc; rep from * to end. Turn.

Row 9 Ch 1, 1 sc in first 6 sc, *1 sc through first loop and next sc, 1 sc in next 2 sc, 1 sc in ch-sp, 1 sc in next 2 sc, 1 sc through last lp and next sc, 1 sc in next 3 sc; rep from *, end 1 sc in last 3 sc. Turn.

Row 10 Ch 1, 1 sc in first sc and in each sc to end. Turn.

Row 11 Ch 1, 1 sc in first 9 sc, *6 dc through center loop and next sc, 1 sc in next 9 sc; rep from * to end. Turn.

Row 12 Ch 1, 1 sc in first 9 sc, *ch 1, skip 6 dc, 1 sc in next 9 sc; rep from * to end.

Fasten off.

thistle I

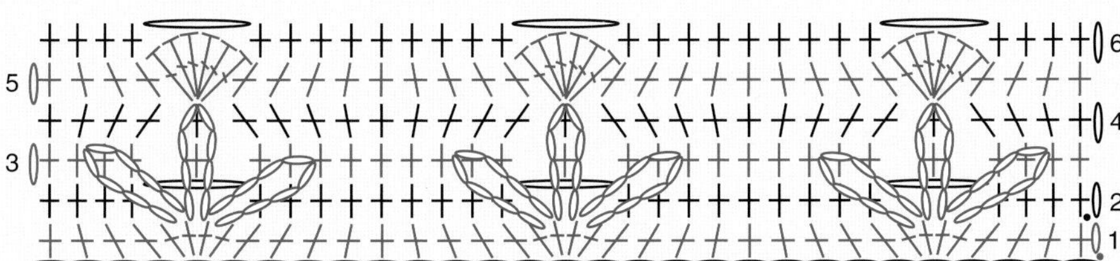

thistle II

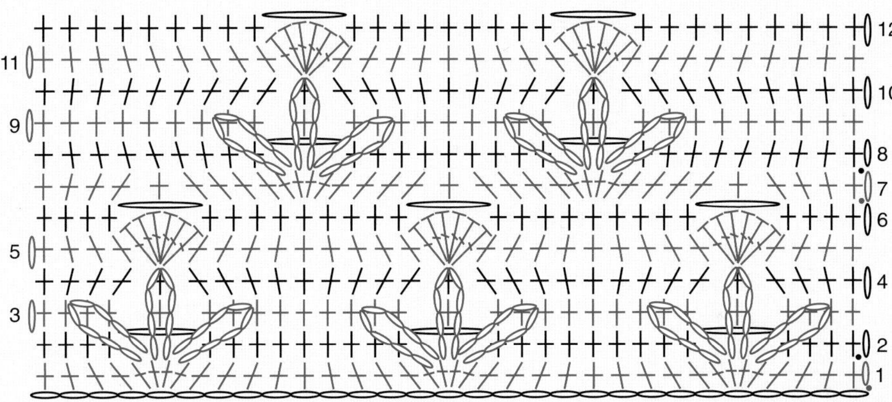

3-d canterbury bell

Colors A and B

(multiple of 8 sts + 1)

Joining strip

With A, make a ch to desired length in a multiple of 8 sts + 7.

Row 1 1 dc in 7th ch from hook (counts as 1 dc, ch 3), *skip 3 ch, [1 dc, ch 3, 1 dc] in next ch; rep from * to end. Turn.

Row 2 Ch 1, [1 sc, 1 hdc, 1 dc, ch 2, 1 dc, 1 hdc, 1 sc] in next ch-3 sp, *[1 sc, ch 5, 1 sc] in next ch 3 sp, [1 sc, 1 hdc, 1 dc, ch 2, 1 dc, 1 hdc, 1 sc] in next ch-3 sp; rep from * to end.

Fasten off.

Bell flower

With RS facing, attach B to in any ch-2 sp of row 2.

Row 1 Ch 3, 5 dc in same sp. Turn.

Row 2 Ch 3 (counts as 1 dc), 1 dc in first dc, 1 dc in next 4 dc, 2 dc in top of beg ch-3—8 dc. Turn.

Row 3 Ch 3 (counts as 1 dc), 1 dc in next dc and in each dc to end. Turn.

Row 4 Ch 3, 1 dc in first dc, 1 dc in next 6 dc, 2 dc in top of beg ch-3—10 dc. Turn.

Row 5 Ch 4 (counts as 1 dc, ch 1), 1 dc in first dc, *ch 1, 1 dc in next dc; rep from *, end ch 1, 1 dc in last dc.

Fasten off.

Work 1 bell flower in each ch-2 sp of row 2.

Edging

Attach A in first ch-1 sp of first flower.

Row 1 Ch 1, 1 sc in same sp, *[ch 4, 1 sc in next ch-1 sp] 10 times, 1 sc in first ch-1 sp of next flower; rep from * until all flowers have been edged.

Fasten off.

Finishing

Using tail ends, sew side seam of each flower.

3-d canterbury bell

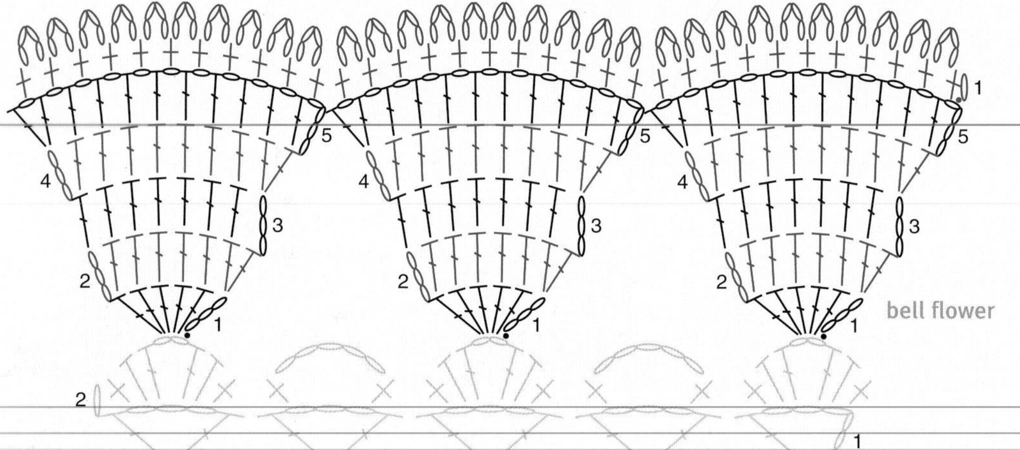

voila

▶ **Colors** A and B

Beg TC (Beg Tr Cluster) (Yo twice, insert hook into designated st, yo and draw up a lp, [yo and draw through 2 lps on hook] twice) twice, yo and draw through all 3 lps on hook.

TC (Tr Cluster) (Yo twice, insert hook into designated st, yo and draw up a lp, [yo and draw through 2 lps on hook] twice) 3 times, yo and draw through all 4 lps on hook.

Motifs

With A, ch 17.

Row 1 1 sc in 17th ch from hook. Turn.

Row 2 Ch 1, 15 sc in lp, 1 sc in 7th ch from joining sc of row 1. Turn.

Row 3 Ch 5, 1 sc in next sc, [ch 5, skip 1 sc, 1 sc in next sc] 7 times—8 lps. Turn.

Row 4 Ch 11, skip 2 lps, 1 sc in next loop. Turn.

Row 5 Ch 1, 16 sc in ch-10 lp, 1 sc in next sc. Turn.

Row 6 Ch 5, 1 sc in next sc, [ch 5, skip 1 sc, 1 sc in next sc] 7 times—8 lps. Turn.

Rep rows 4–6 to desired length, ending with an odd number of motifs.

Fasten off.

Joining tape

With first motif at lower left-hand side and last motif at lower right-hand side, attach B to 2nd free lp on top edge of upper motif at right-hand side.

Row 1 Ch 4, beg TC in same lp, ch 7, skip 2 lps, TC in next lp, *ch 7, skip 1 lp of next motif, TC in next lp, ch 7, skip 2 lps, TC in next lp; rep from * to end. Turn.

Row 2 Ch 4, *[1 dc in next ch, ch 1, skip next ch] 3 times, 1 dc in next ch, ch 1, skip next TC; rep from *, end 1 dc in 4th ch of beg ch-4.

Fasten off.

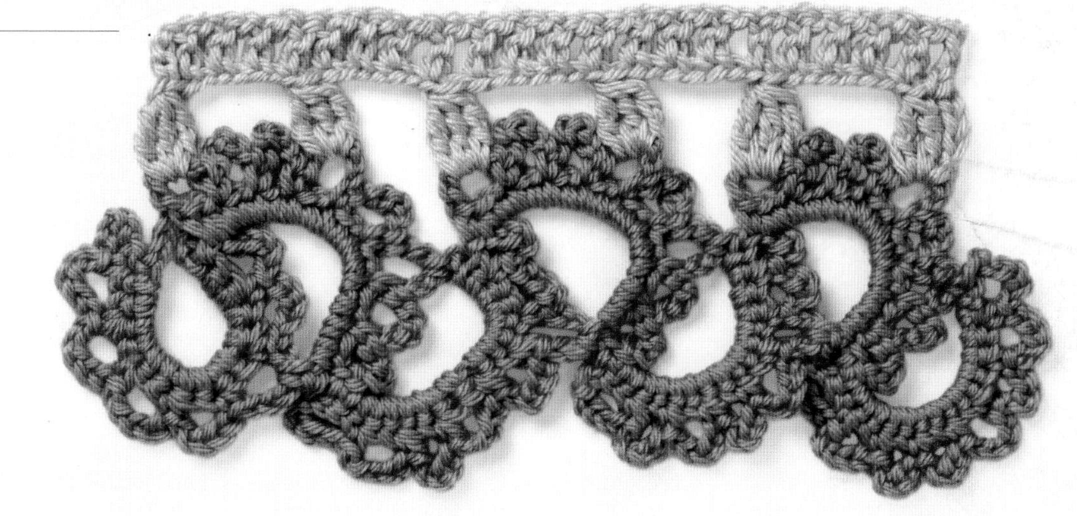

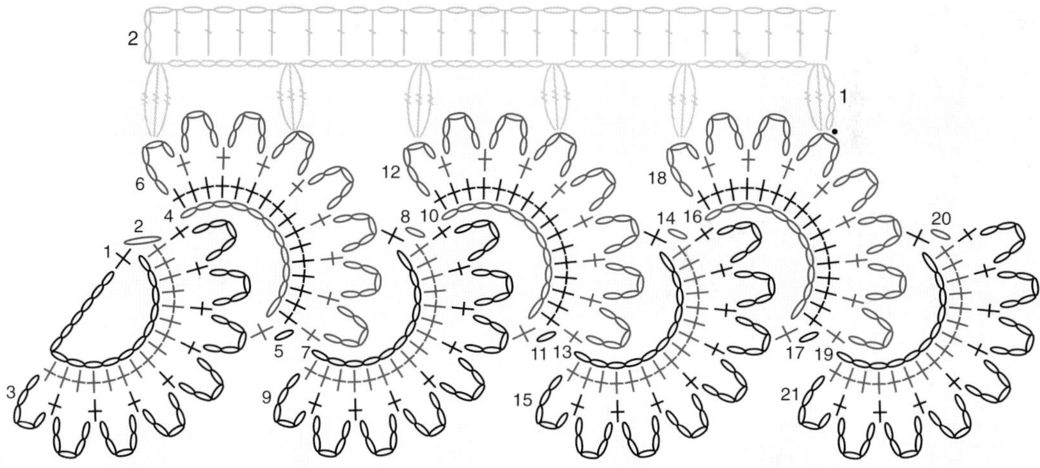

triple chain scallop

▼ **Colors** A and B

(multiple of 4 sts + 1)

Note This edging can be worked directly onto a project or into a chain.

Optional ribbon band

With A, make a ch to desired length in a multiple of 4 sts + 2.

Row 1 (RS) 1 dc in 4th ch from hook and in each ch to end. Turn.

Row 2 Ch 3 (counts as 1 dc), 1 dc in next dc and in each dc to end, 1 dc in top of beg ch-3. Turn.

Fasten off A and attach B.

Row 3 Ch 1, 1 sc in first dc and in each dc to end.

Fasten off.

Scallops

With RS facing, attach A to first st at right-hand edge of ribbon band or project.

Row 1 (RS) Ch 1, 1 sc in first sc, *ch 5, skip 2 sc, 1 sc in next sc; rep from * to end.

Fasten off A. With RS facing, attach B to first sc at right-hand edge.

Row 2 (RS) Ch 1, 1 sc in first sc, *ch 5, drop lp, insert hook into next ch-5 lp from front to back and pick up dropped lp, skip next free sc 2 rows below, 1 sc in next free sc of row 1; rep from *, end ch 5, 1 sc in last sc.

Fasten off B. With RS facing, attach A to first sc at right-hand edge.

Row 3 (RS) Ch 1, 1 sc in first sc, *ch 5, 1 sc in next ch-5 lp of row 2; rep from *, end ch 5, 1 sc in last sc.

Fasten off A. With RS facing, attach B to first sc at right-hand edge.

Row 4 (RS) Ch 1, 1 sc in first sc, *ch 5, drop lp, insert hook into next ch-5 lp 2 rows below from front to back and pick up dropped lp, 1 sc in 4th ch of next ch-5 lp; rep from *, end ch 5, 1 sc in last sc.

Rep rows 3 and 4 to desired length, ending with row 3.

Fasten off.

Optional Sew decorative ribbon to ribbon band.

triple chain scallop

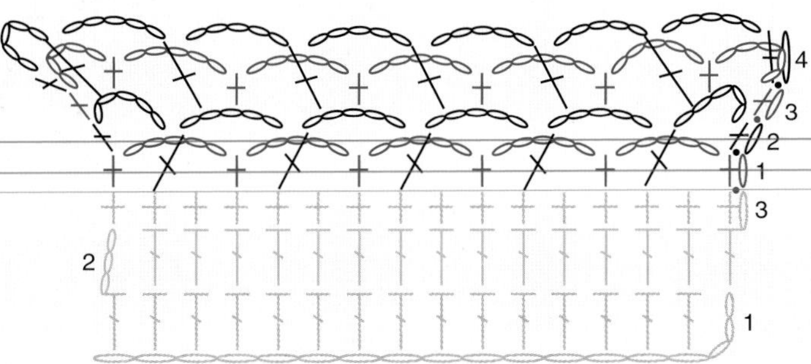

heidi

▶ **Colors** A and B

Flower

With A, ch 2.

Row 1 8 sc in 2nd ch from hook. Join with sl st in first sc.

Fasten off A and attach B in any sc.

Row 2 *Ch 4, 5 tr in same sc, ch 4, sl st in same sc, skip 1 sc, sl st in next sc; rep from * 3 times more.

Fasten off.

Make desired number of flowers.

Top joining rows

With WS facing, attach color A in 5th tr of any petal.

Row 1 *Ch 10, sl st in center tr of next petal, ch 10, sl st in 1st tr of next petal, **ch 3, sl st in 5th tr of any petal of next flower; rep from * until all flowers have been joined, ending last rep at **. Turn.

Row 2 Ch 1, [5 sc, ch 5, 5 sc] in ch-9 lp, *ch 3, [5 sc, ch 5, 5 sc] in next ch-9 lp, 3 sc in next ch-3 lp, 5 sc in next ch-9 lp, ch 2, sl st in last ch-5 lp made, ch 2, 5 sc in same lp; rep from *, end last rep ch 3, [5 sc, ch 5, 5 sc] in last ch-9 lp. Turn.

Row 3 Sl st to center of first picot lp, ch 8, 1 dc in next ch-3 lp, *ch 5, 1 dc in next 2 lps, ch 5, 1 dc in next ch-3 lp; rep from *, end ch 5, 1 dc in last lp.

Row 4 Ch 2, 1 hdc in each ch and dc to end, 1 hdc in 3rd ch of beg ch-8.

Fasten off.

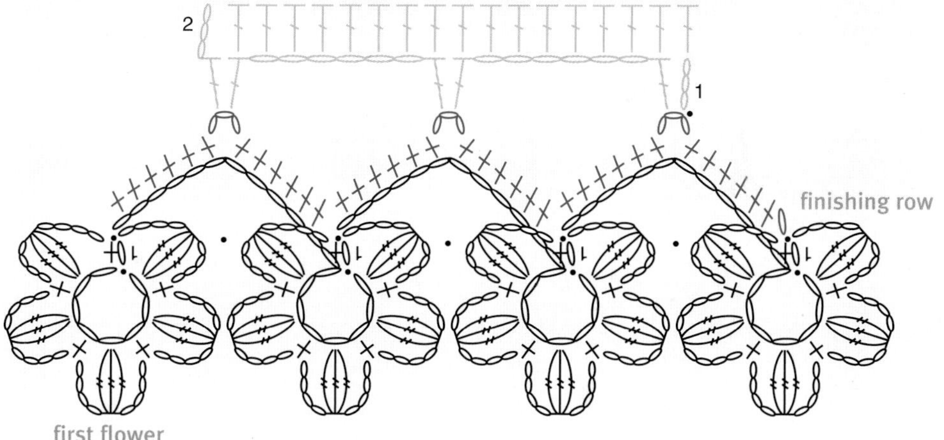

honeysuckle

▶ **Colors** A and B

TC (Tr Cluster) (Yo twice, insert hook into designated st, yo and draw up a lp, [yo and draw through 2 lps on hook] twice) 4 times, yo and draw through all 5 lps on hook.

Picot Ch 5, 1 sc in 3rd ch from hook, ch 2.

Flowers

With A, ch 12.

Row 1 (WS) [1 dc, ch 5, 1 dc] in 12th ch from hook. Turn.

Row 2 Ch 4, *[1 TC, 1 picot] twice in next ch-5 sp, [1 TC, ch 5, 1 TC] in same sp, ch 3, skip next 4 ch, tr in next ch. Turn.

Row 3 Ch 10, [1 dc, ch 5, 1 dc] in ch-5 sp. Turn.

Rep rows 2 and 3 to desired length ending with row 2. *Do not fasten off.*

Finishing row Working along straight length of edging, ch 1, 3 sc in 1st tr, *5 sc in next ch-sp, 3 sc in next tr-sp; rep from *, end 5 sc in last ch-sp. Fasten off.

Heading

With WS facing, attach B to left-hand edge.

Row 1 Ch 2 (counts as 1 hdc), 1 hdc in next sc and in each sc to end. Turn.

Row 2 Ch 2, 1 hdc in next hdc and in each hdc to end. Fasten off

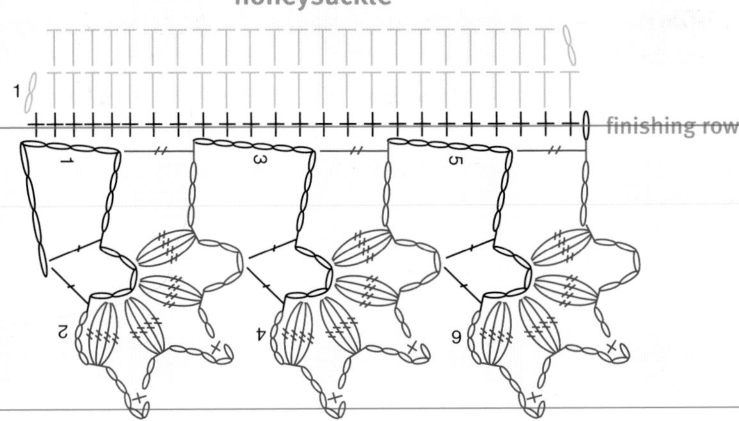

rickrack florette

▶ **2TC (2-Tr Cluster)** (Yo twice, insert hook into designated st, yo and draw up a lp, [yo and draw through 2 lps on hook] twice) twice, yo and draw through all 3 lps on hook.

3TC (3-Tr Cluster) (Yo twice, insert hook into designated st, yo and draw up a lp, [yo and draw through 2 lps on hook] twice) 3 times, yo and draw through all 4 lps on hook.

First flower

Ch 8. Join with sl st in first ch to form a ring.

Rnd 1 Ch 1, *1 sc in ring, ch 4, 3TC in ring, ch 4; rep from * 4 times more—*5 petals*. Join with sl st in first sc. Do not fasten off.

Second and following flowers

Ch 20, sl st in 8th ch from hook to form a ring.

Rnd 1 Ch 1, 1 sc in ring, ch 4, 3TC in ring, sl st in top of corresponding petal of previous flower, ch 4, *1 sc in ring, ch 4, 3TC in ring, ch 4; rep from * 3 times more—*5 petals*. Join with sl st in first sc. Make desired number of flowers following instructions for second flower. *Do not fasten off.* Turn.

Finishing row Ch 1, *[6 sc, ch 3, 6 sc] in next ch-12 lp; rep from * to end. Join with sl st in first sc of first flower.

Fasten off.

Top band

With RS facing, attach B to right-hand edge in first ch-3 lp.

Row 1 Ch 3 (counts as 1 dc), 1 dc in same lp, *ch 6, 2 dc in next lp; rep from * to end. Turn.

Row 2 Ch 3, 1 dc in next dc and in each ch to end. Fasten off.

rickrack florette

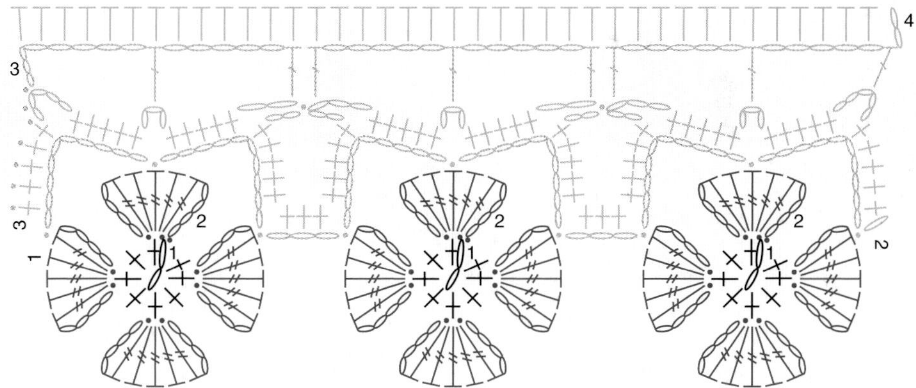

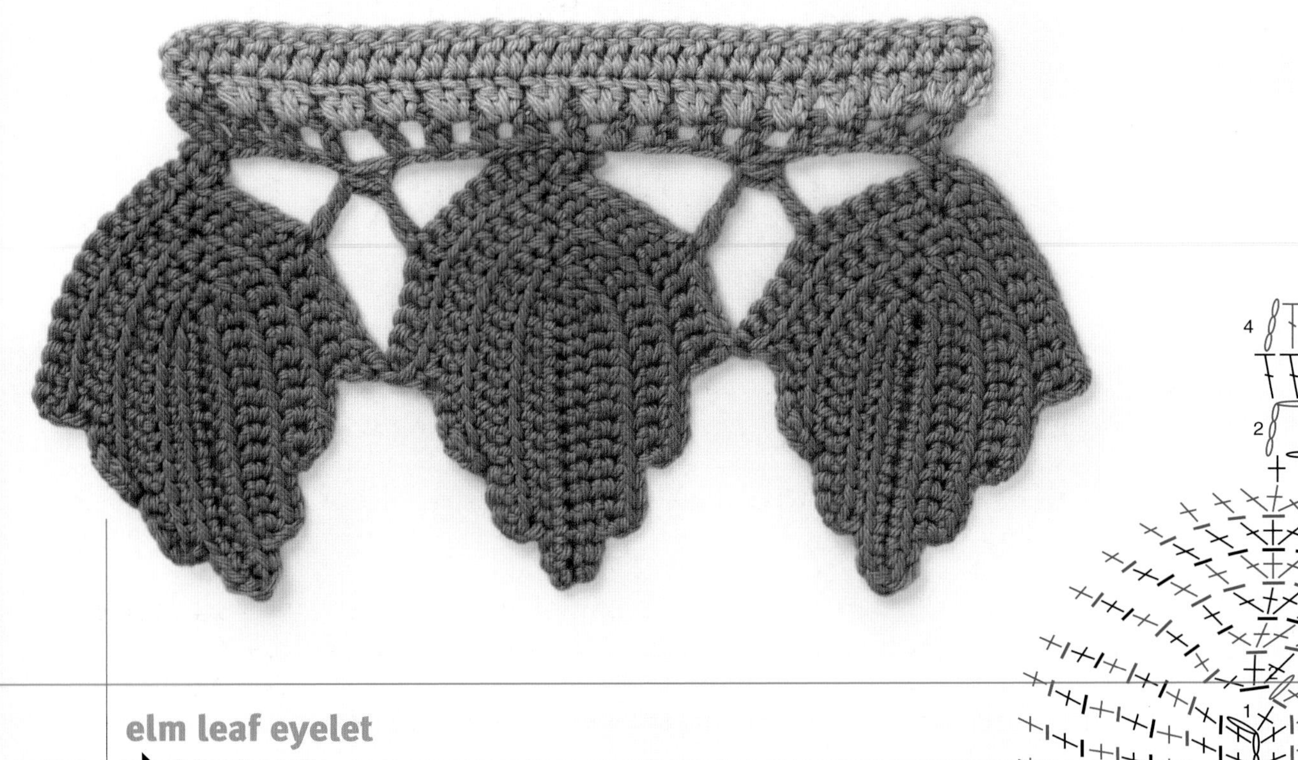

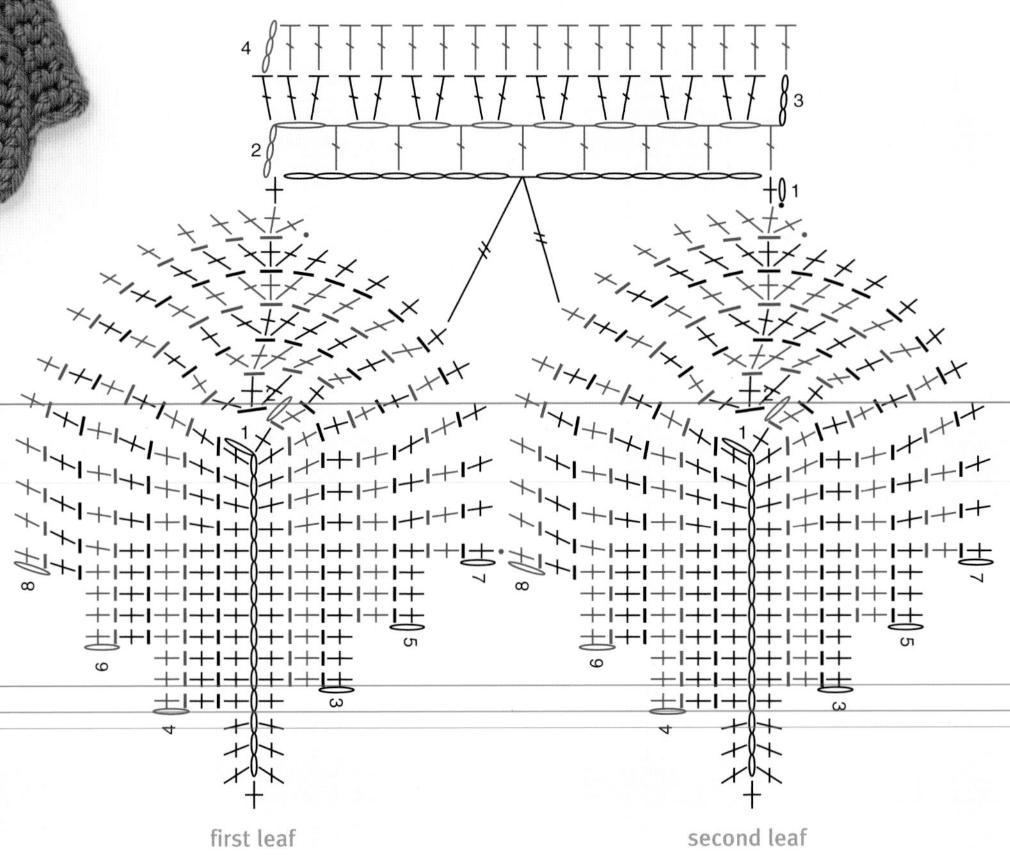

first leaf

second leaf

elm leaf eyelet

▶ **Colors** A and B

2TC (2-Tr Cluster) (Yo twice, insert hook into designated st, yo and draw up a lp, [yo and draw through 2 lps on hook] twice) twice, yo and draw through all 3 lps on hook.

First leaf

With A, ch 16.

Row 1 1 Sc in 2nd ch from hook and in next 13 ch, 3 sc in last ch (working around to other side of foundation ch), 1 sc in next 13 sc, 2 sc in last sc. Turn.

Row 2 Ch 1, 1 sc in front lp of next 12 sc. Turn, leaving rem sc unworked.

Row 3 Ch 1, 1 sc in front lp of next 12 sc, 3 sc in last sc of row 1, 1 sc in front lp of next 12 sc. Turn, leaving rem sc unworked.

Row 4 Ch 1, 1 sc in front lp of next 13 sc, 3 sc in next sc, 1 sc in front lp of next 10 sc. Turn, leaving rem sc unworked.

Row 5 Ch 1, 1 sc in front lp of next 11 sc, 3 sc in next sc, 1 sc in front lp of next 11 sc.

Turn, leaving rem sc unworked.

Row 6 Ch 1, 1 sc in front lp of next 12 sc, 3 sc in next sc, 1 sc in front lp of next 9 sc. Turn, leaving rem sc unworked.

Row 7 Ch 1, 1 sc in front lp of next 10 sc, 3 sc in next sc, 1 sc in front lp of next 10 sc. Turn, leaving rem sc unworked.

Row 8 Ch 1, 1 sc in front lp of next 11 sc, 3 sc in next sc, sl st in next sc.

Fasten off

Second leaf

Work as for first leaf through row 7.

Row 8 Ch 1, sl st in corresponding sc on previous leaf, 1 sc in front lp of next 11 sc of current leaf, 3 sc in next sc, sl st in next sc.

Fasten off.

Make desired number of leaves following instructions for second leaf.

Top joining rows

With RS facing, attach A to center sc of 3-sc group in row 8 of first leaf.

Row 1 Ch 1, 1 sc in same st, *ch 7, skip next 5 sc, 2TC over next sc and corresponding sc of next leaf, ch 7, 1 sc in center sc of 3-sc group in row 8 of next leaf; rep from * until all leaves have been worked, end 1 sc in center sc of 3-sc group in row 8 of last leaf. Turn.

Row 2 Ch 4 (counts as 1 dc, ch 1), *[skip next ch, 1 dc in next ch, ch 1] 3 times, skip next ch, 1 dc in next 2TC, ch 1; rep from * end last rep omit ch 1.

Fasten off A and attach B.

Row 3 Ch 3 (counts as 1 dc), *2 dc in next ch-1 sp; rep from *, end 2 dc in last ch-1 sp, 1 dc in 3rd ch of beg ch-4. Turn.

Row 4 Ch 3, 1 dc in next dc and in each dc to end.

Fasten off.

tooth fairy scallop

Beg TC (Beg Tr Cluster) (Yo twice, insert hook into designated st, yo and draw up a lp, [yo and draw through 2 lps on hook] twice) twice, yo and draw through all 3 lps on hook.

TC (Tr Cluster) (Yo twice, insert hook into designated st, yo and draw up a lp, [yo and draw through 2 lps on hook] twice) 3 times, yo and draw through all 4 lps on hook.

Scallops

Make a ch to desired length in a multiple of 6 sts + 3.

Row 1 (WS) Beg TC over 5th and 6th ch from hook, *ch 5, 1 dc in TC just made, 1 TC over next 3 ch, **ch 3, 1 TC over next 3 ch; rep from *, end last rep at **. Turn.

Row 2 Ch 4, TC in next ch-5 lp, [ch 4, TC] twice in same lp, *1 sc in next ch-3 lp, [1 TC, ch 4] twice in next lp, 1 TC in same lp; rep from * to end.

Fasten off.

Heading

With RS facing and working along foundation ch, attach yarn to right-hand edge.

Row 1 Ch 4, 1 tr in next ch and in each ch to end.

Fasten off.

Optional Sew a bead to the center of each scallop.

tooth fairy scallop

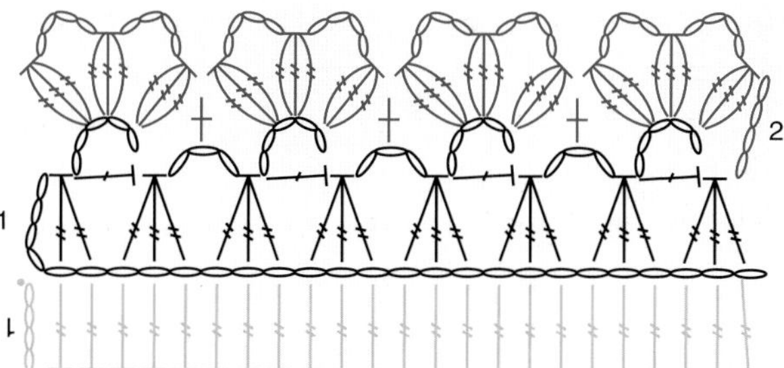

glory

▼ **2TC (2-Tr Cluster)** (Yo twice, insert hook into designated st, yo and draw up a lp, [yo and draw through 2 lps on hook] twice) twice, yo and draw through all 3 lps on hook.

3TC (3-Tr Cluster) (Yo twice, insert hook into designated st, yo and draw up a lp, [yo and draw through 2 lps on hook] twice) 3 times, yo and draw through all 4 lps on hook.

Flowers

Make a ch to desired length in a multiple of 6 sts + 5.

Row 1 (WS) 2TC in 5th ch from hook, *skip 5 ch, 2TC in next ch, ch 4, sl st in same ch, ch 4, 2 TC in same ch; rep from *, end last rep 3TC in last ch. Turn.

Row 2 Ch 4, 2TC in same st, [ch 4, 1 sc in 4th ch from hook] 4 times, 3TC in same st, *skip next 2 ch-4 sps, 3TC in next 2TC, [ch 4, 1 sc in 4th ch from hook] 4 times, 3TC in same st; rep from * to end.

Fasten off.

Heading

With RS facing, working along foundation ch, attach B to right-hand edge.

Row 1 Ch 2 (counts as 1 hdc), 1 hdc in next ch and in each ch to end. Turn.

Row 2 Ch 2, 1 hdc in next hdc and in each hdc to end.

Fasten off.

glory

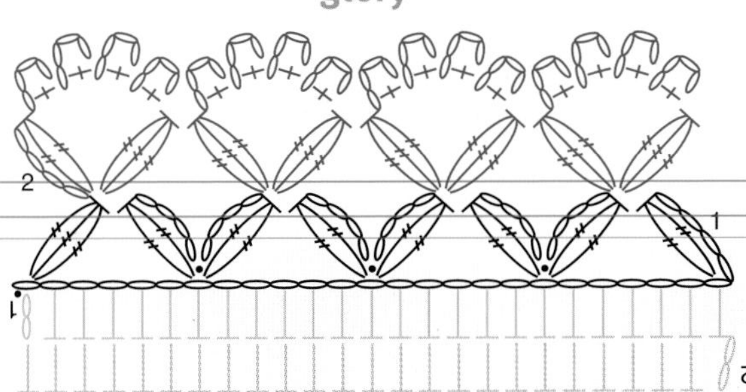

lucky leaves

▸ **First chain**

First leaf

Rnd 1 With A, ch 9, 1 sc in 2nd ch from hook, 1 dc in next 3 ch, 1 sc in next 2 ch, sl st in next ch, 3 sl st in last ch (working around to other side of foundation ch), 1 sl st in next ch, 1 sc in next 2 ch, 1 dc in next 3 ch, 1 sc in next ch. Do not fasten off.

Second leaf

Ch 1, sl st in 2nd ch of foundation ch of previous leaf.

Rep rnd 1 of first leaf.

Make leaves to desired length following instructions for second leaf.

Second chain

With B, work same as first chain.

Tack the 2 chains together where leaves meet.

Heading

With RS facing, attach A to right-hand edge in first dc of leaf.

Row 1 Ch 4 (counts as 1 tr), 1 tr in the next 2 dc, *ch 5, 1 tr in next 3 dc of next leaf; rep from * to end. Turn.

Row 2 Ch 3, 1 dc in next 2 tr, *1 dc in next 5 ch, 1 dc in next 3 tr; rep from * to end.

Fasten off.

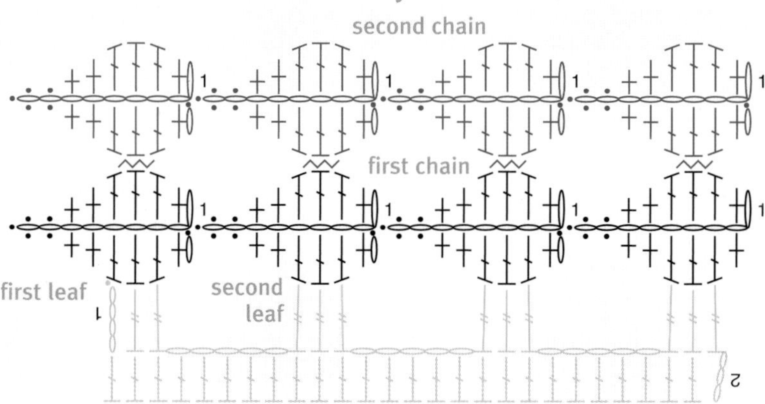

double layer petal edge

▼ **Colors** A, B and C

(multiple of 8 sts + 5)

Edging

With A, make a ch to desired length in a multiple of 8 sts + 6.

Rnd 1 1 Sc in 2nd ch from hook, *ch 5, skip 3 ch, 1 sc in next ch; rep from *, end 2 sc in last ch (working around to other side of foundation ch), **ch 5, skip 3 ch, 1 sc in next ch; rep from ** to end.]. Turn.

Row 2 Ch 5, 1 sc in first ch-5 lp, *8 dc in next ch-5 lp, 1 sc in next ch-5 lp; rep from *, end ch 5, sl st in last sc. Turn.

Rnd 3 Ch 3, *3 dc in first ch-5 lp*, ch 1, 1 sc in next sc, *[ch 1, 1 dc] in next 8 dc, ch 1, 1 sc in next sc; rep from *, ch 1, 4 dc in last ch-5 sp, ch 1 (working around to other side of edging), *8 dc in next ch-5 lp, 1 sc in next ch-5 lp; rep from *, end *8 dc in last ch-5 lp, ch 1.* Join with sl st in top of beg ch-3. Turn.

Row 4 Ch 5, skip next dc, 1 dc in next dc, *ch 5, skip 4 dc, 1 dc in next dc, ch 5, skip next [dc, sc, dc], 1 dc in next dc; rep from *, end ch 5, skip last dc, sl st in ch-1 sp. Turn.

Row 5 Ch 5, *1 sc in next ch-5 lp, 8 dc in next ch-5 lp; rep from *, end 1 sc in last ch-5 lp, ch 5, sl st in ch-1 sp. Turn.

Row 6 Ch 3, 3 dc in first ch-5 lp, 1 sc in next sc, *[1 dc, ch 4, 1 sc in 4th ch from hook] in next 8 dc, 1 sc in next sc; rep from *, end 4 dc in last ch-5 lp.

Fasten off.

Heading

Fold edging along foundation ch, with smaller ruffle over picot ruffle. Attach B to first ch-3 sp of foundation ch at right-hand edge.

Row 1 Ch 1, *5 sc in ch-3 sp; rep from * to end. Turn.

Rows 2 and 3 Ch 2 (counts as 1 hdc), 1 hdc in next st and in each st to end. Turn.

Fasten off.

Flower

With C, ch 4. Join with sl st in first ch to form a ring.

Rnd 1 *Ch 8, 1 sc in ring; rep from * 4 times more—5 petals.

Rnd 2 Ch 1, *8 sc in next ch-8 lp, 1 sc in next sc; rep from * around.

Join with sl st to first sc.

Fasten off.

Make desired number of flowers with A and B.

With A, sew flower to heading and make a french knot (see page 195) at center of flower.

double layer petal edge

edging

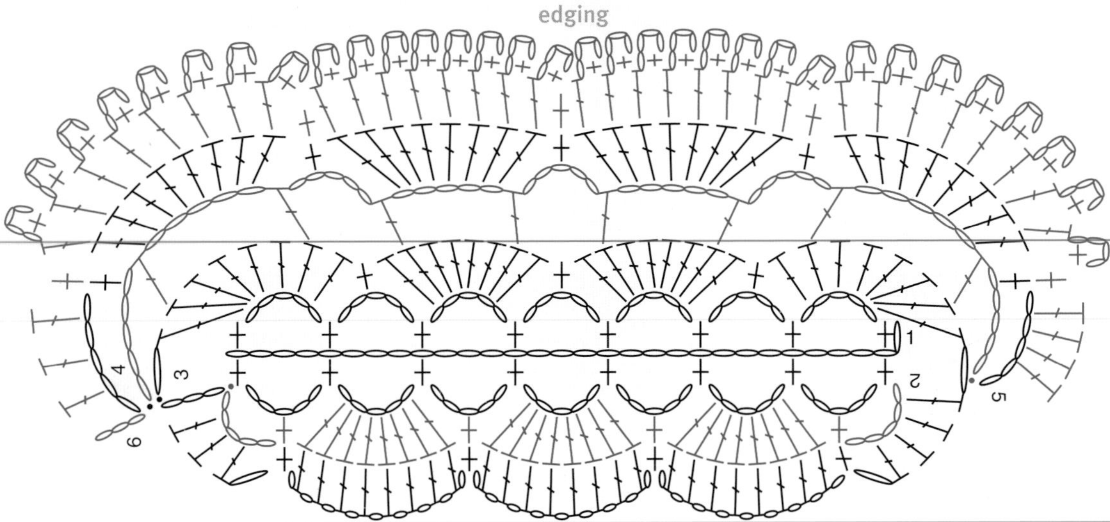

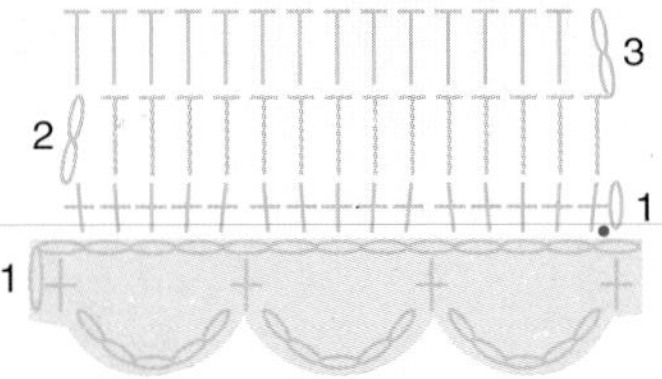

heading

flower power

▶ **Colors** A and B

Flower

With A, ch 7. Join with sl st in first ch to form a ring.

Row 1 Ch 3, 2 dc in ring, *ch 7, 3 dc in ring; rep from * 3 times more, ch 7. Join with sl st in top of beg ch-3–*5 petals*.

Fasten off A. Attach B in center dc of any 3-dc group.

Row 2 Ch 1, 1 sc in same sp, [8 dc in next ch-7 lp, ch 3, sl st in dc just made, 8 dc in same lp, 1 sc in center dc of next 3-dc group] twice, *16 dc in next ch-7 lp, 1 sc in center dc of next 3-dc group next loop; rep from * twice more.

Join with sl st in first sc.

Fasten off.

Make desired number of flowers.

Joining band

With RS facing, attach B to right-hand picot of any flower.

Row 1 Ch 1, 1 sc in same picot, *ch 8, 1 sc in picot of next petal, ch 8, 1 sc in first picot of next flower; rep from * until all flowers have been joined, end ch 8, 1 sc in picot of last picot. Turn.

Row 2 Ch 3, (counts as 1 dc), *1 dc in next 8 ch, 1 dc in next sc; rep from * to end. Turn.

Row 3 Ch 5, skip 2 dc, 1 dc in next dc, *ch 2, skip 2 dc, 1 dc in next dc; rep from * to end.

Fasten off.

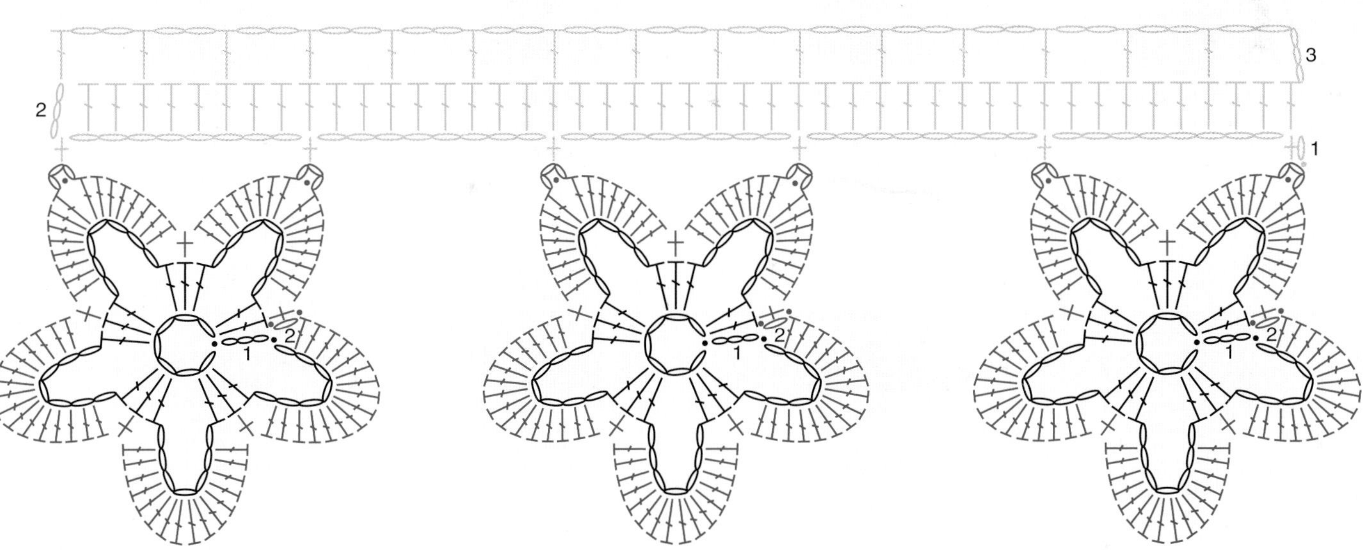

cosmos

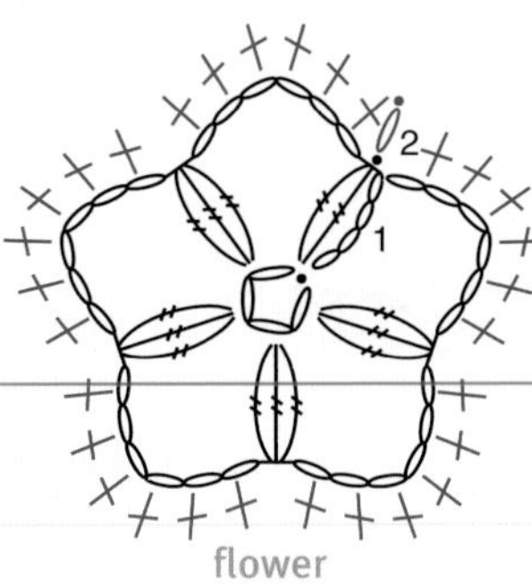

flower

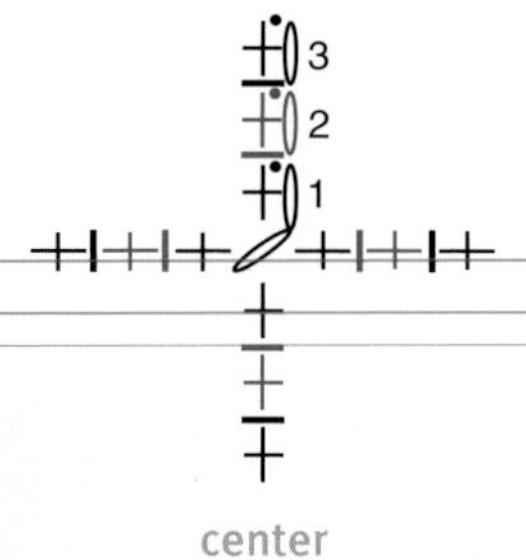

center

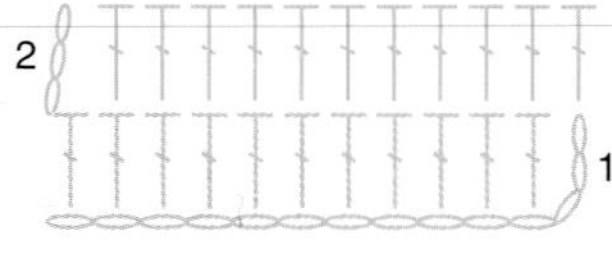

base

cosmos

E Colors A, B and C

Note *Size of flower is determined by size of hook and yarn used.*

2TC (2-Tr Cluster) (Yo twice, insert hook into designated st, yo and draw up a lp, [yo and draw through 2 lps on hook] twice) twice, yo and draw through all 3 lps on hook.

3TC (3-Tr Cluster) (Yo twice, insert hook into designated st, yo and draw up a lp, [yo and draw through 2 lps on hook] twice) 3 times, yo and draw through all 4 lps on hook.

Base

With A, make a ch to desired length.

Row 1 1 dc in 4th ch from hook and in each ch to end. Turn.

Rows 2–6 Ch 3 (counts as 1 dc), 1 dc in next dc and in each dc to end. Turn. Fasten off.

Flower

With B, ch 4. Join with sl st in first ch to form a ring.

Row 1 Ch 4, 2TC in ring, ch 6, [3TC, ch 6] 4 times in ring. Join with sl st in top of first TRC—*5 petals.*

Row 2 Ch 1, *6 sc in next ch-6 sp; rep from * around. Join with sl st in first sc. Fasten off.

Make desired number of flowers.

Center

With C, ch 2.

Rnd 1 4 sc in 2nd ch from hook. Join with sl st in first sc.

Rnd 2 Ch 1, 1 sc in front lp of first sc and in each sc around. Join with sl st in first sc.

Rep rnd 2 to desired size.

Fasten off, leaving a long tail.

Finishing

Slip tails from center through center of flower and through base or project. Tie on WS to secure.

happy garden

E **Note** *Size of flower is determined by size of hook and yarn used.*

Base

Make a ch to desired length.

Row 1 1 hdc in 3rd ch from hook and in each ch to end. Turn.

Rows 2–10 Ch 2 (counts as 1 hdc), 1 hdc in next hdc and in each hdc to end. Turn.

Fasten off.

Flower

Ch 5.

Row 1 Sl st in first ch, *ch 8, sl st in same ch; rep from * 4 times more—*5 petals.*

Row 2 *8 sc in next ch-8 lp; rep from * around. Join with sl st in first sc.

Fasten off.

Finishing

Use french knots (see page 195) to make centers for flowers while sewing to base or project.

happy garden

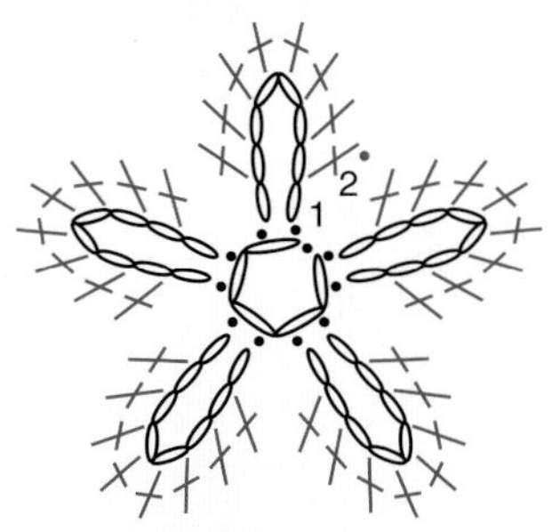

flower

sunflower

E **Colors** A, B, C and D

Note *Size of flower is determined by size of hook and yarn used.*

Base

With A, make a ch to desired length.

Row 1 1 hdc in 3rd ch from hook and in each ch to end. Turn.

Rows 2–5 Ch 2 (counts as 1 hdc), 1 hdc in next hdc and in each hdc to end. Turn.

Fasten off.

Flower

With B, ch 4. Join with sl st in first ch to form a ring.

Rnd 1 Ch 1, 7 sc in ring. Join with sl st in first sc.

Rnd 2 Ch 1, 2 sc in each sc around—14 sc. Join with sl st in first sc.

Rnd 3 *Ch 6, 1 sc in second ch from hook, 1 hdc in next ch, 1 dc in next ch, 1 tr in next 2 ch, skip next sc of rnd 2, sl st in next sc; rep from * around, ending last rep with sl st in base of beg ch-6—*7 petals.*

Fasten off.

Make desired number of flowers.

Leaf

With C, ch 8.

Rnd 1 1 sc in 2nd ch from hook, 1 hdc in next ch, 1 dc in next ch, 1 tr in next ch, 1 dc in next ch, 1 hdc in next ch, 3 sc in next ch (working around to other side of foundation ch), 1 hdc in next ch, 1 dc in next ch, 1 tr in next ch, 1 dc in next ch, 1 hdc in next ch, 1 sc in last ch. Join with sl st in first sc.

Fasten off.

Finishing

With D, attach sunflowers to base or project with french knots (see page 195) scattered over center of flower. Tack leaves to heading or project along center vein.

sunflower

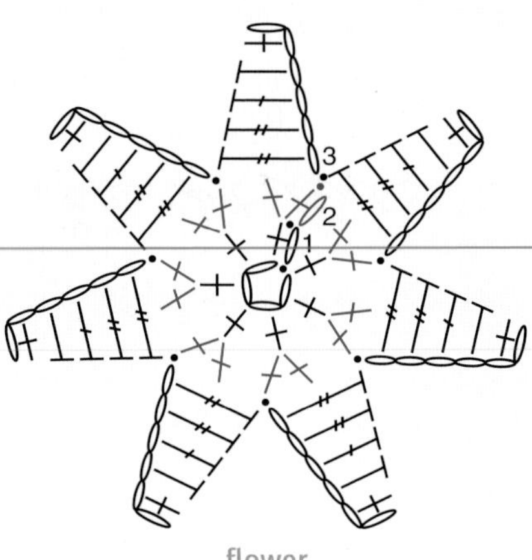

flower

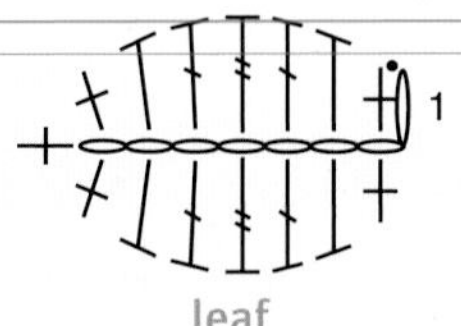

leaf

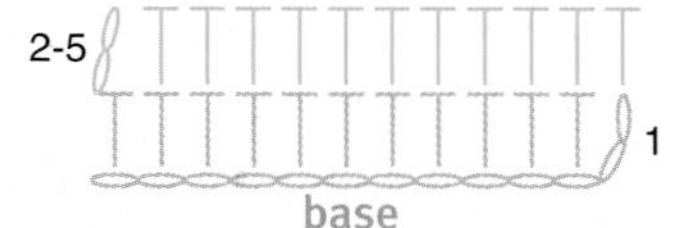

base

english garden

E **Colors** A, B and C

Note *Size of flower is determined by size of hook and yarn used.*

Base

With A, make a ch to desired length.

Row 1 1 hdc in 3rd ch from hook and in each ch to end. Turn.

Rows 2–8 Ch 2 (counts as 1 hdc), 1 hdc in next hdc and in each hdc to end. Turn.

Fasten off.

Flower

Beg DCL (Beg Dc Cluster) [Yo, insert hook into designated st, yo and draw up a lp, yo and draw through 2 lps on hook] twice, yo and draw through all 3 lps on hook.

DCL (Dc Cluster) [Yo, insert hook into designated st, yo and draw up a lp, yo and draw through 2 lps on hook] 3 times, yo and draw through all 4 lps on hook.

With B, ch 8. Join with sl st in first ch to form a ring.

Rnd 1 Ch 1, 10 sc in ring. Join with sl st to first sc.

Rnd 2 Ch 3, beg DCL in same sp, *ch 5, skip next sc, **DCL in next sc; rep from * around, ending last rep at **—*5 petals.* Join with sl st in first DCL.

Rnd 3 Ch 1, *[1 sc, ch 3] 3 times in next ch-5 lp, 1 sc in same lp; rep from * around. Join with sl st in first sc.

Fasten off.

Make desired number of flowers.

Leaf

With C, ch 9.

Row 1 1 sc in 2nd ch from hook, 1 dc in next 3 ch, 1 sc in next 2 ch, sl st in next ch, 3 sl st in last ch (working around to other side of foundation ch), sl st in ch, 1 sc in next 2 ch, 1 dc in next 3 ch, 1 sc in next ch.

Fasten off.

Make desired number of leaves.

Finishing

Position flowers and leaves as desired on base or project and sew in place.

english garden

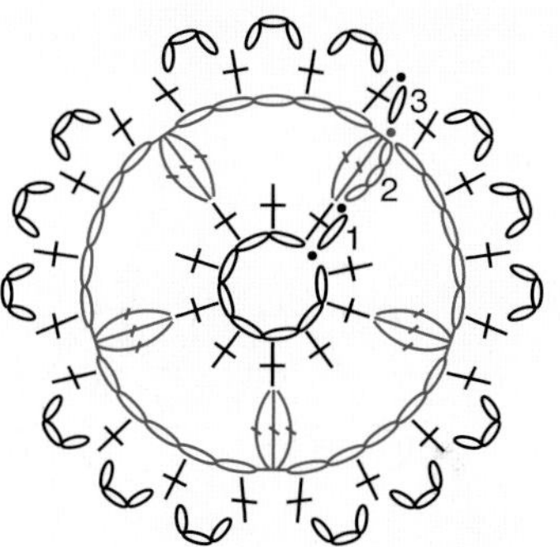

flower

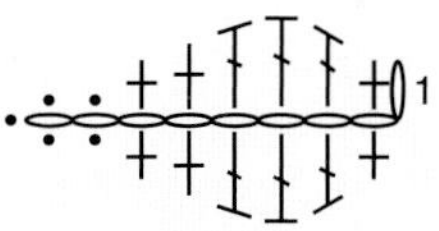

leaf

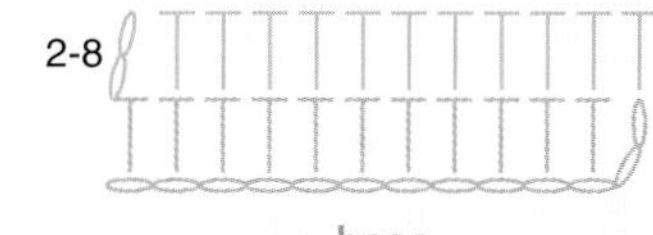

base

fringes

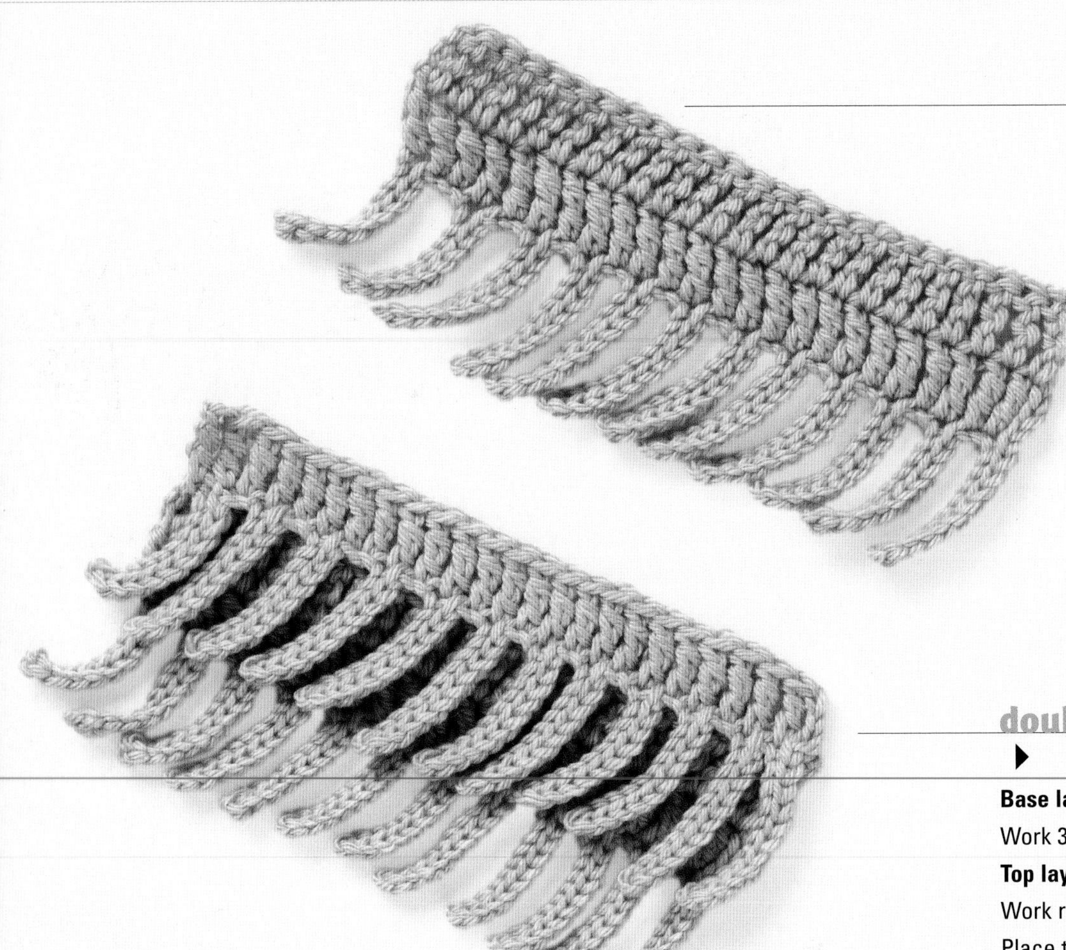

eyelash fringe

Fringe

Ch 11.

Row 1 Sl st in 2nd ch from hook and in each ch to end, *ch 12, sl st in 2nd ch from hook and in next 9 ch; rep from * for desired length.

Cont to row 2 of heading, working along straight length of fringe.

Heading

Row 2 Ch 4, 1 tr in next st and in each st to end. Turn.

Row 3 Rep row 2.

Fasten off.

eyelash fringe

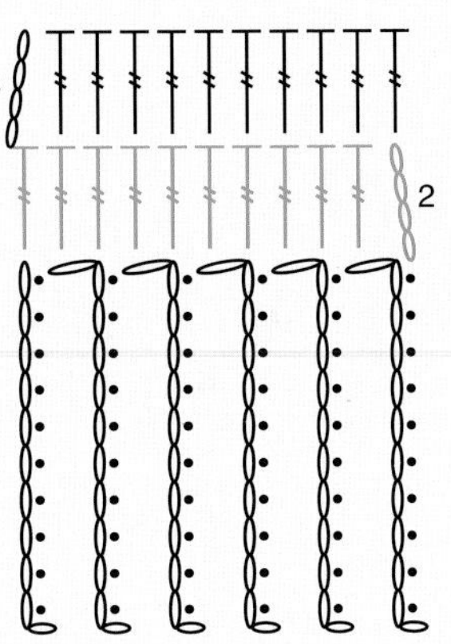

double layered eyelash fringe

Base layer

Work 3 rows of Eyelash Fringe (see above).

Top layer

Work row 1 of Eyelash Fringe.

Place top layer over base layer and work row 2 through both layers to join.

Fasten off.

double layered eyelash fringe

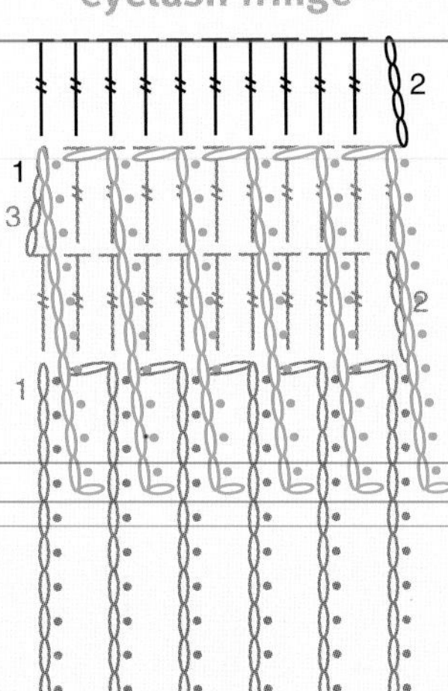

looped fringe with filet band

looped fringe with filet band

▼ (multiple of 4)

Fringe

Make a ch to desired length.

Row 1 1 sc in 2nd ch from hook and in each ch to end. Turn.

Row 2 Ch 1, wrap yarn over left index finger, twice clockwise, insert hook in first sc, *draw up both strands of lps on finger to 1"/2.5cm, remove finger with lp in back, yo and through all 3 lps on hook—(*loop st made*); rep from * to end. Turn.

Row 3 Ch 1, 1 sc in each st to end. Turn.

Filet band

Row 4 Ch 4, 1 tr in next sc, *ch 3, skip 3 sc, 1 tr in next sc; rep from *, end 1 tr in last st. Turn.

Rows 5 and 6 Ch 4, *1 tr in next tr, ch 3, skip ch-3 sp; rep from *, end 1 tr in last 2 tr. Turn.

Row 7 Ch 1, 1 sc in same tr, *1 sc in next tr, 3 sc in next ch-3 sp; rep from *, end 1 sc in last 2 tr. Fasten off.

layered looped fringe

▼ Make a ch to desired length in a multiple of 4 sts.

Row 1 1 sc in 2nd ch from hook and in each ch to end. Turn.

Row 2 Ch 1, wrap yarn over left index finger twice clockwise, insert hook in first sc, *draw up both strands of lp on finger to 1"/2.5cm, remove finger, with lps in back, yo and through all 3 lps on hook—(*loop st made*); rep from * to end. Turn.

Row 3 Ch 1, 1 sc in each st to end. Turn.

Rep rows 2 and 3 for as many layers as desired.

layered looped fringe

double fringe

▼ **Colors** A and B

(multiple of 3 sts + 2)

Note This edging can be worked directly onto a project or into a chain and attached.

Base

With A, make a ch to desired length in a multiple of 3 sts.

Row 1 1 sc in 2nd ch from hook and in each ch to end. Turn.

Cont to row 2 of fringe.

Fringe

With WS facing, attach yarn to right-hand edge of project or heading.

Row 1 Ch 1, 1 sc in next st and in each st across. Turn.

Row 2 Ch 14, 1 sc in next sc, *skip next sc, 1 sc in next sc, ch 14, 1 sc in next sc; rep from * to end.

Fasten off A. With RS facing, attach B to right-hand edge (row 2 loops will be pointing up).

Row 3 *Ch 10, 1 sc in next skipped sc of row 1; rep from *, end ch 10, 1 sc into last sc of row 1.

For heading, continue below.

Fasten off.

Heading

Rotate piece to work along foundation ch.

Row 1 Ch 1, 1 sc in first ch and in each ch to end. Turn.

Row 2 Ch 2, 1 hdc in next sc and in each sc to end.

Fasten off.

double fringe

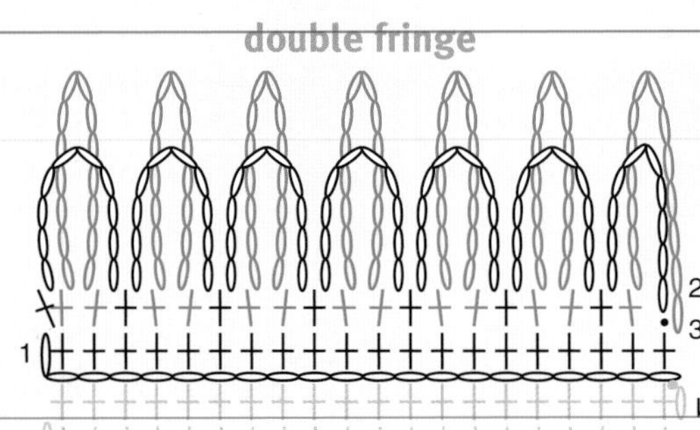

dangling hearts

E Colors A and B

Joining strip

With A, ch 5.

Row 1 1 hdc in 3rd ch from hook and in each ch to end. Turn.

Row 2 Ch 2, 1 hdc in next hdc and in each hdc to end. Turn.

Rep row 2 to desired length.

Heart

With B, ch 2.

Rnd 1 6 sc in 2nd ch from hook—6 sc. Join with sl st in first sc.

Rnd 2 Ch 1, 2 sc in next 3 sc, 3 sc in next sc, 2 sc in next 2 sc, 1 dc in center space. Do not join, cont work in rows. Turn.

Row 3 1 sc in next 2 sc, sl st in next 3 sc, 3 sc in next sc, sl st in next 3 sc, 1 sc in next 2 sc, skip next sc, 1 dc in last sc. Turn.

Rnd 4 Ch 1, 1 sc in dc, 1 sc in next 2 sc, 1 sc in next 3 sl st, 1 sc in next sc, 3 sc in next sc, 1 sc in next sc, 1 sc in next 3 sl st, 1 sc in next 2 sc, 1 sc in dc, 2 sc down side of same dc, sc3tog over inner curve of heart, 2 sc up side of next dc. Join with sl st in next st.

Fasten off.

Make desired number of hearts.

Join hearts

With B, insert hook into center of heart, pull up a lp and ch 5. Fasten off. Using tails, sew to joining strip or directly onto project.

dangling hearts

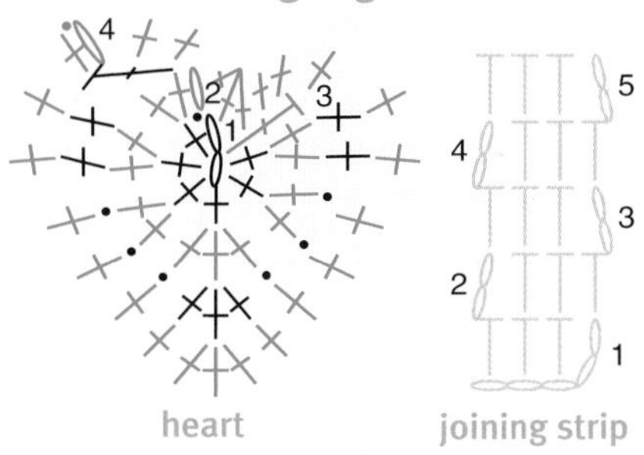

bobble fringe

▼ Colors A and B

(multiple of 2 sts + 1)

6TC (6-Tr Cluster) (Yo twice, insert hook in designated st and draw up a lp, [yo and draw lp through 2 lps on hook] twice) 6 times, yo and draw lp through all 7 lps on hook.

Note This edging can be worked directly onto a project or onto the heading as shown and attached.

Heading

Make a ch to desired length in a multiple of 3 + 4.

Row 1 1 hdc in 3rd ch from hook and in each ch to end. Turn.

Row 2 Ch 2, 1 hdc in next hdc and in each hdc to end. Turn.

Rep row 2 to desired length.

Cont to row 1 of fringe.

Fringe

With RS facing, attach B to right-hand edge of heading or project.

Row 1 (RS) Ch 4, skip next st, 6TC in next st, *ch 3, skip 2 sts, 6TC in next st; rep from *, end skip next st, 1 tr in last st.

Fasten off B. With RS facing, attach A to top of ch-4 at right-hand edge.

Row 2 Ch 20, 1 sc in top of first cluster*, [ch 20, 1 sc in ch-3sp] twice, ch 20, 1 sc in top of next cluster; rep from *, end ch 20, 1 sc in last tr.

Fasten off.

bobble fringe

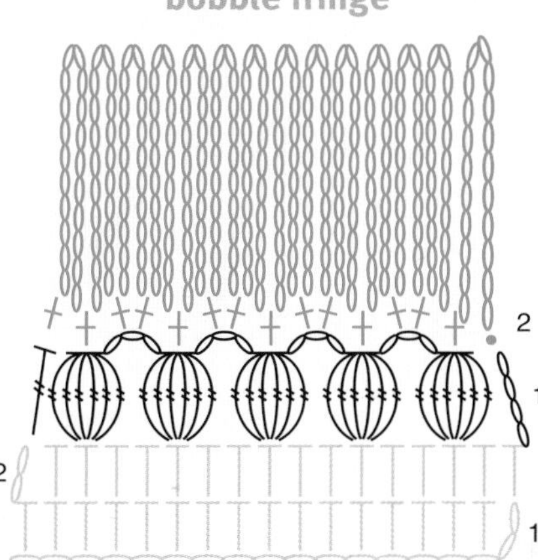

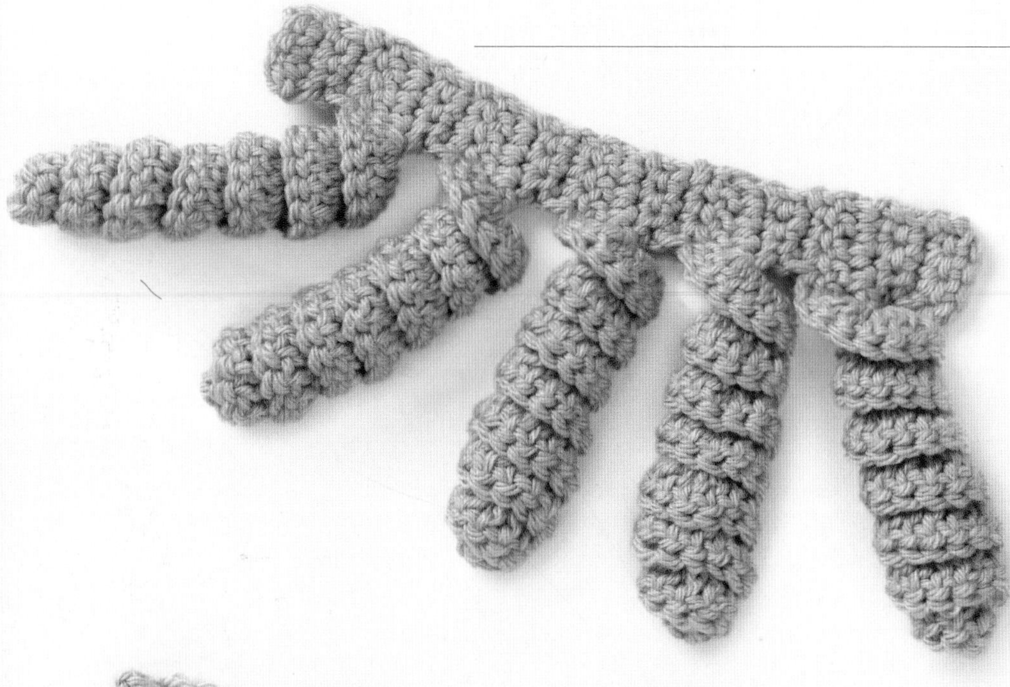

basic corkscrew

▶ Ch 5.

Heading

Row 1 1 sc in 2nd ch from hook, 1 sc in each ch to end—4 sc. Turn.

Rows 2, 3 and 4 Ch 1, 1 sc in each sc to end—4 sc. Turn.

Corkscrew

Row 5 Ch 24, 3 dc in 4th ch from hook, 4 dc in next 20 ch. Turn.

Rep rows 2–5 to length desired.

Fasten off.

basic corkscrew

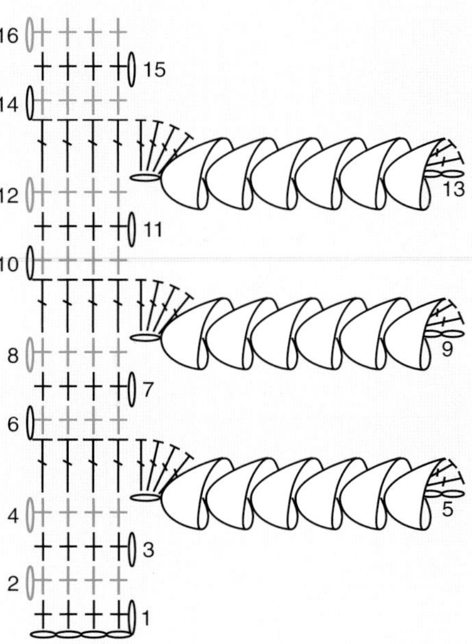

keyhole corkscrew

E Ch 12.

Row 1 5 dc in 4th ch from hook, *4 dc in next ch; rep from * to last ch, sc in last ch. Do not fasten off.

Keyhole

Ch 4. Join with sl st to first ch to form a ring.

Rnd 1 Ch 1, 8 sc in ring. Join with sl st in first sc. Fasten off.

keyhole corkscrew

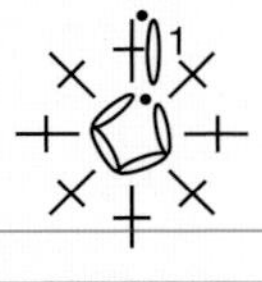

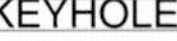

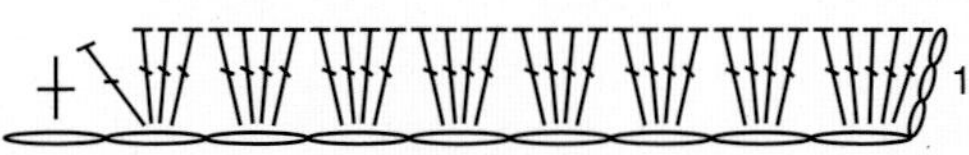

CORKSCREW

edged corkscrew

▶ **Colors** A and B

(Sample made with ch 60 for corkscrew and ch 26 for heading)

Corkscrew

With A, make a ch to desired length and follow instructions for **Basic Corkscrew** (see page 116). Count the curls to determine length of chain for heading.

Band

With B, ch 6 for each multiple of 5 curls plus 4 more.

Row 1 1 tr in 5th ch from hook and in each ch to end. Turn.

Row 2 Ch 1, 1 sc in first tr and in each tr to end. Turn.

Row 3 Ch 1, 1 sc in first sc, ch 5, sl st in top of first st of Corkscrew, 1 sc in each ch of ch-5, *sc in next 6 sc of heading, ch 5, skip 4 curls, sl st in top st of next curl, 1 sc in each ch of ch-5; rep from *, ending last rep with sl st in top of last st of Corkscrew, 1 sc in each ch of ch-5, sl st into sides of rows 1 and 2 to foundation ch.

Fasten off.

edged corkscrew

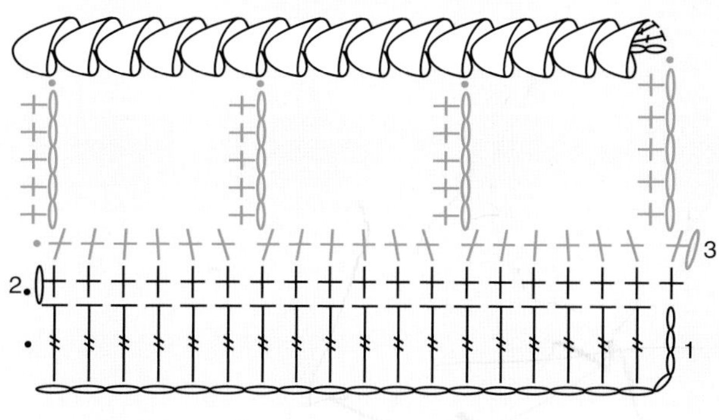

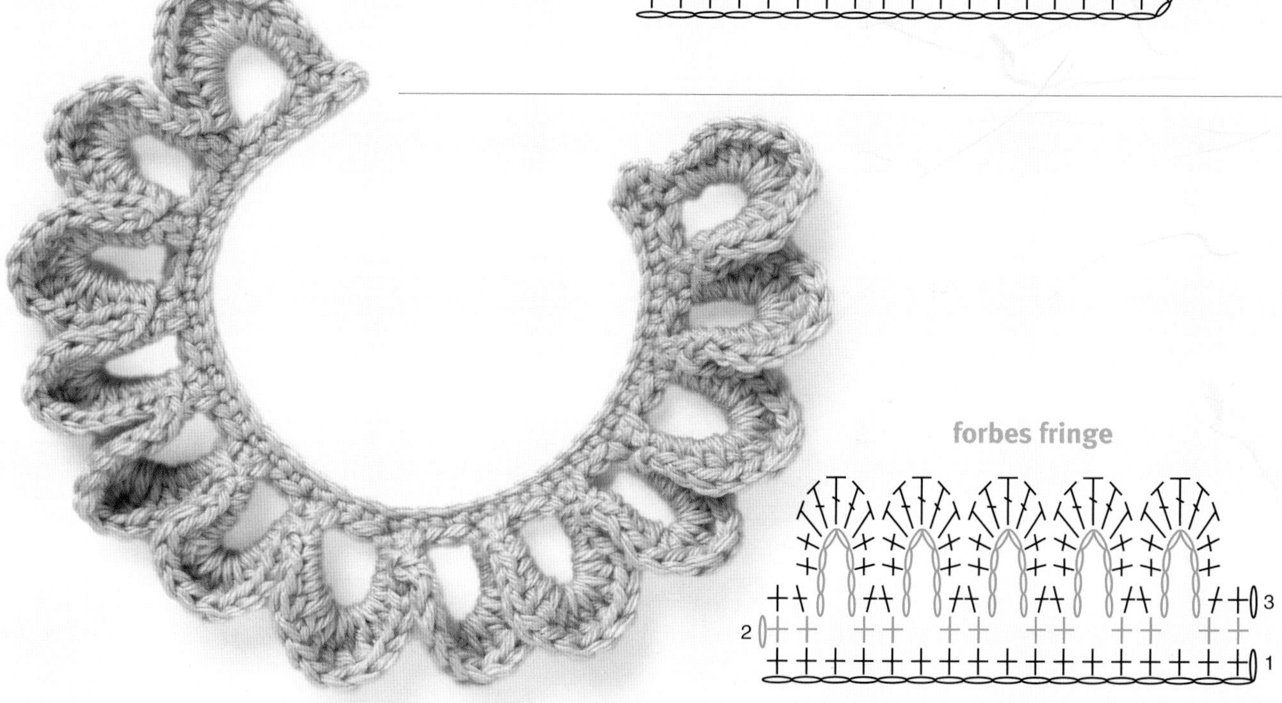

forbes fringe

▼ (multiple of 3 sts + 2)

Note This edging can be worked directly onto a project or into a chain and attached.

For chain

Make a ch to desired length in a multiple of 3 sts.

Row 1 1 sc in 2nd ch from hook and in each ch to end. Turn. Cont to row 2 of fringe.

Fringe

With RS facing, attach yarn to right-hand edge of project.

Row 1 Ch 1, 1 sc in each st to end. Turn.

Row 2 Ch 1, 1 sc in first 2 sc, *ch 8, skip 1 sc, 1 sc in next 2 sc; rep from * to end. Turn.

Row 3 Ch 1, 1 sc in first 2 sc, *[2 sc, 1 hdc, 3 dc, 1 hdc, 2 sc] in ch-8 lp, 1 sc in next 2 sc; rep from * to end.

Fasten off.

forbes fringe

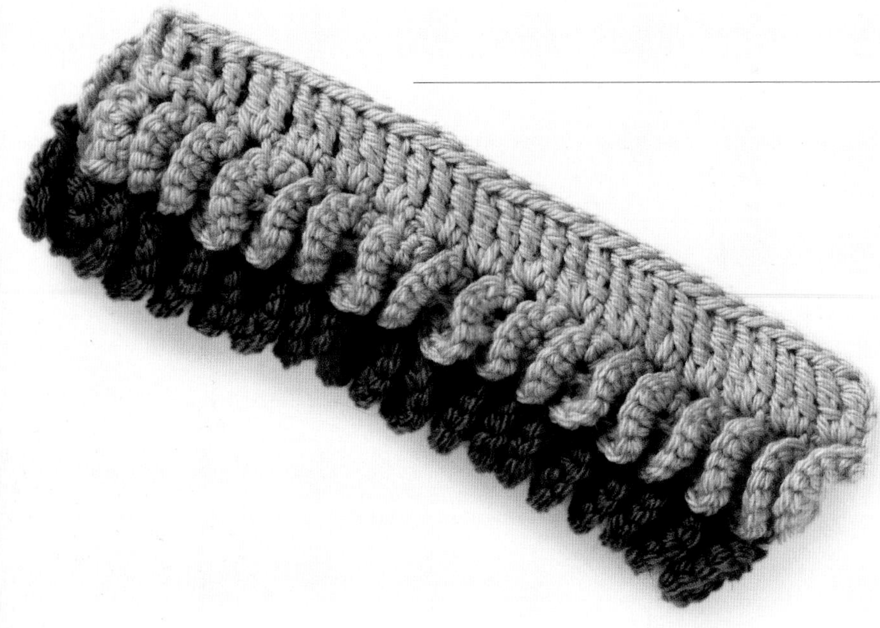

layered edged corkscrew

▶ **Colors** A and B

(Sample made with ch 24 for corkscrew)

Base layer

Corkscrew

With B, make a ch to desired length and follow instructions for Basic Corkscrew (see page 116).

Heading

Join A in top of one st on first curl.

Row 1 *Ch 3, sl st in top of one st on next curl; rep from * to end. Turn.

Row 2 Ch 4 (counts as tr), 1 tr in first ch-3 sp, *2 tr in next ch-3 sp; rep from * to end. Turn.

Row 3 Ch 4, 1 tr in each tr to end.

Fasten off.

Top layer

Corkscrew

With A, make a corkscrew same as base layer.

Base

With A, work same as base layer heading through row 2.

Row 3 Holding both pieces together, sl st in each st to end working through both layers to join.

Fasten off.

layered edged corkscrew

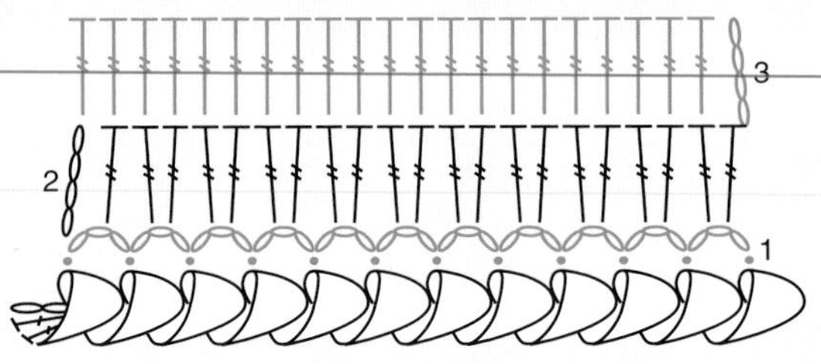

base layer

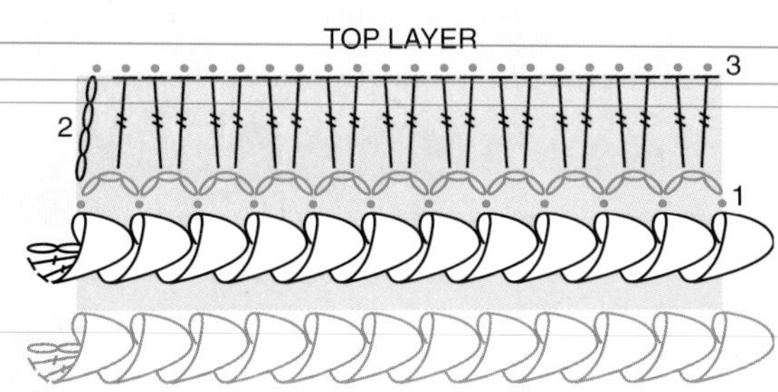

corkscrew scallops

▲ **Colors** A and B

Corkscrews

With A and B, make desired number of Basic Corkscrews (see page 116).

Join corkscrews

Row 1 Join A with sl st to beg of first corkscrew, ch 5, sl st to end of first corkscrew, *ch 3, sl st to beg of next corkscrew, ch 5, sl st to end of next corkscrew; rep from * until all corkscrews are joined. Turn.

Row 2 Ch 1, *5 sc in ch-5 sp, 3 sc over ch-3 sp; rep from *, end last rep 5 sc in ch-5 sp. Turn. Fasten off.

Band

Row 3 Join B with sl st to end of row 2, ch 4, 3 tr in same sc, *ch 4, 4 tr in 2nd sc of 3-sc group; rep from *, end last rep ch 4, 4 tr in last sc. Turn.

Row 4 Ch 4, 1 tr in next tr, 1 tr in each tr and ch to end. Fasten off.

corkscrew scallops

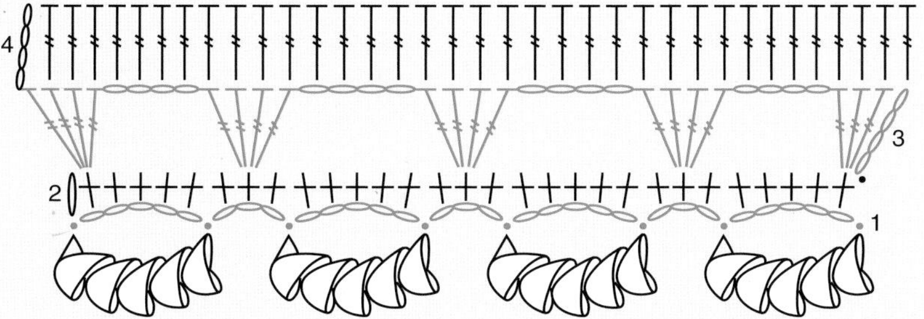

bow ties

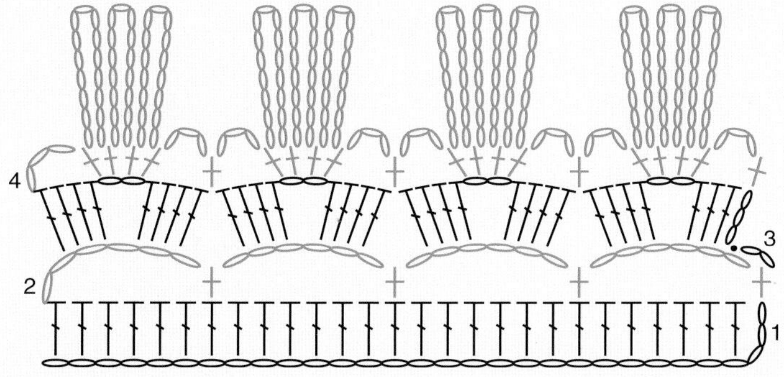

bow ties

▼ (multiple of 7 sts + 1)

Make a ch to desired length in a multiple of 7 sts + 2.

Row 1 1 dc in 4th ch from hook and in each ch to end. Turn.

Row 2 *Ch 6, skip 6 dc, 1 sc in next dc; rep from * to end. Turn.

Row 3 Ch 2, sl st in first lp, ch 3, [3 dc, ch 2, 4 dc] in same lp, *[4 dc, ch 2, 4 dc] in next lp; rep from * to end. Turn.

Row 4 *Ch 3, 1 sc into ch-2 sp, [(ch 15, 1 sc) in same sp] 3 times, ch 3, 1 sc in sp between next two 4-dc groups; rep from *, end last rep 1 sc in top of beg ch-3. Fasten off.

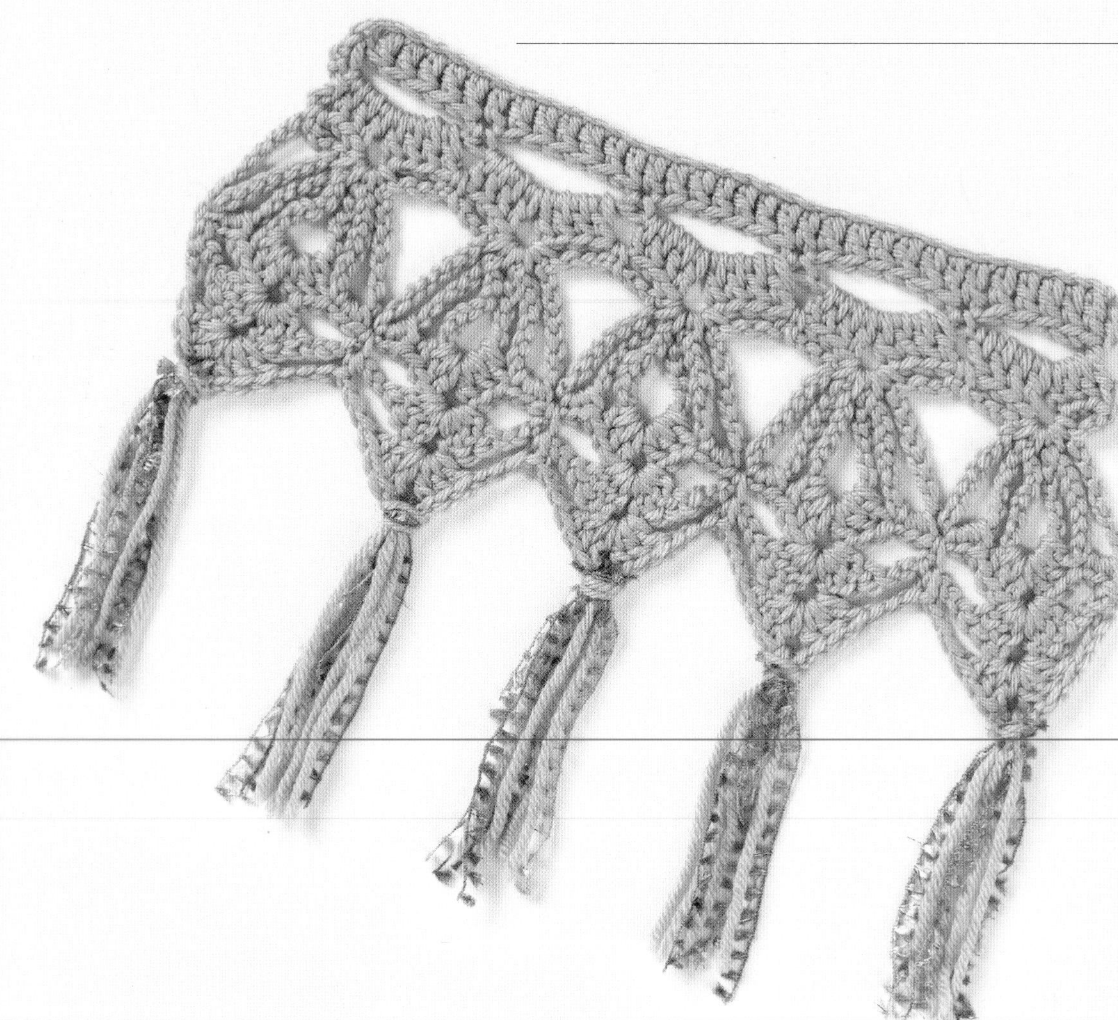

fancy lanterns

▼ **Colors** A and B

(multiple of 7 sts + 1)

With A, make a ch to desired length in a multiple of 7 sts + 2.

Row 1 1 dc in 4th ch from hook and in each ch to end. Turn.

Row 2 *Ch 6, skip next 6 dc, 1 sc in next dc; rep from * to end. Turn.

Row 3 Ch 2, sl st in first lp, ch 3, [3 dc, ch 2, 4 dc] in same lp, *[4 dc, ch 2, 4 dc] in next lp; rep from * to end. Turn.

Row 4 *Ch 3, 1 sc in ch-2 sp, [(ch 15, 1 sc) in same sp] 3 times, ch 3, 1 sc in sp between next two 4-dc groups; rep from *, end last rep sc in top of beg ch-3.

Row 5 Ch 8, *3 sc in first lp, [3 dc, ch 2, 3 dc] in next lp, 3 sc in next lp; rep from * to end. Turn.

Row 6 *Ch 3, [3 dc, ch 2, 3 dc] in next ch-2 sp, ch 3, 1 sc in sp between next two 3-sc groups; rep from *, end last rep 1 sc in top of beg ch-8. Turn.

Row 7 *Ch 3, [3 dc, ch 2, 3 dc] in ch-2 sp, ch 3, 1 sc in next sc; rep from *, end last rep sl st in top of beg ch-3.

Fasten off.

Fringe

Using A and B, cut 7"/18cm lengths of yarn, two in each color for each point. Fold the 4 strands in half and insert lps through ch-2 sp of last row, then insert ends through lps, pull through and tighten. Trim if needed.

fancy lanterns

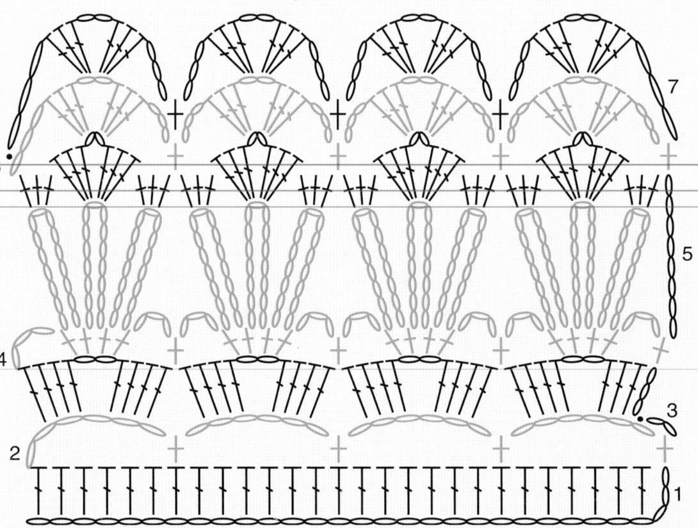

giggy fringe

▶ Ch 11.

Row 1 1 sc in 8th ch from hook, ch 4, skip 2 ch, 1 sc in last ch. Turn.

Row 2 Ch 13, 1 sc in ch-4 sp, ch 4, 1 sc in ch-7 sp. Turn.

Row 3 Ch 13, 1 sc in ch-4 sp, ch 4, 1 sc in ch-13 sp. Turn.

Row 4 Ch 6, 1 sc in ch-4 sp, ch 4, 1 sc in ch-13 sp. Turn.

Row 5 Ch 6, 1 sc in ch-4 sp, ch 4, 1 sc in ch-6 sp. Turn.

Row 6 Ch 13, 1 sc in ch-4 sp, ch 4, 1 sc in ch-6 sp. Turn.

Rep rows 3–6 for desired length, ending with row 5.

Border rnd Ch 1, 3 sc in ch-4 sp, 3 sc in ch-6 sp. Rotate to work along length of piece, *ch 6, 2 sc in ch-13 lp; rep from * to end. Rotate to work to end beginning edge, ch 6, 3 sc in ch-7 sp, 3 sc in ch-2 sp. Rotate to work to end opposite length, *ch 6, 2 sc in ch-13 lp; rep from * to end, ch 6, sl st in first sc of border row. Fasten off or continue as desired.

Band

With RS facing, join yarn in first ch-6 loop on left-hand side of Border Rnd.

Row 1 Ch 2, 1 hdc in same st, 1 hdc in each ch and sc, end 1 sc in first 2 ch ch-6 corner sp. Turn.

Row 2 Ch 2, 1 hdc in next hdc and in each hdc to end. Turn.

Row 3 Ch 1, 1 sc in each hdc to end.

Fasten off.

Fringe

Cut three 6"/15 cm lengths of yarn for each 2 sc on bottom edge of border rnd. Fold strands in half and insert lps at each 2 sc, then insert ends through lps, pull through and tighten. Trim if needed.

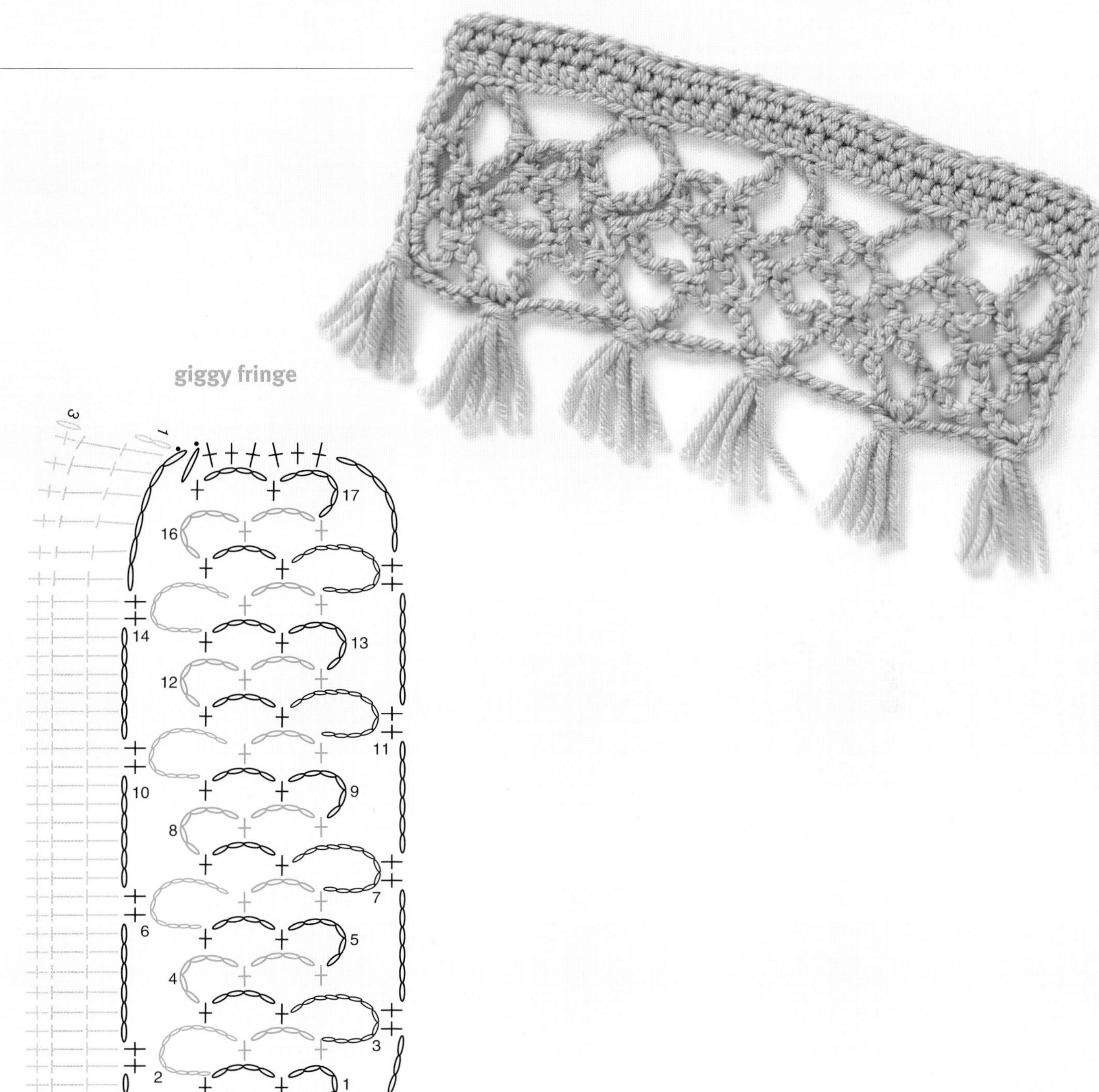

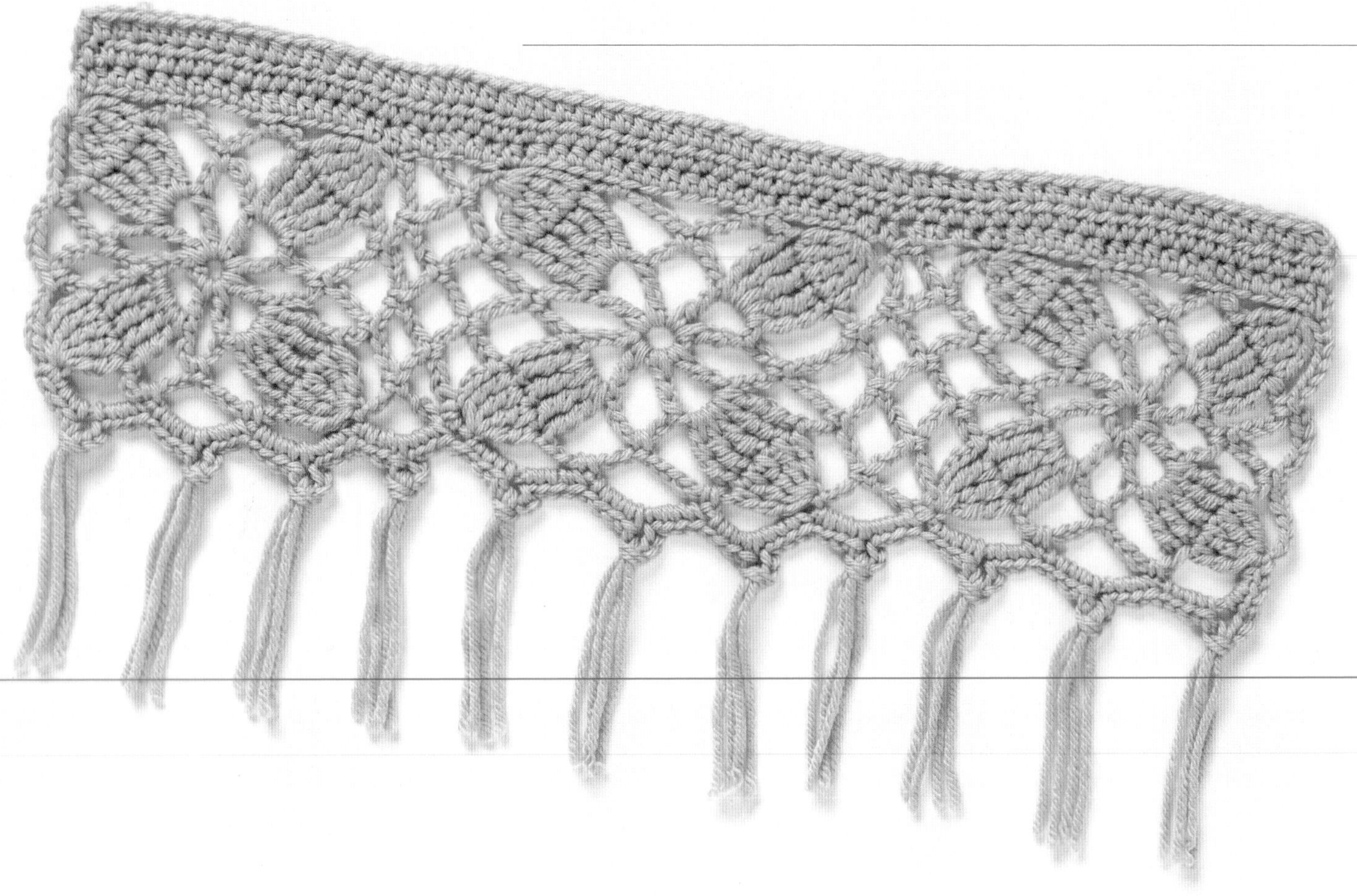

long french fringe

Beg Tr Cluster Ch 4, (yo twice, insert hook in next tr and draw up a lp, [yo, draw through 2 lps] twice) 4 times, yo, draw lp through all 5 lps on hook.

Tr Cluster (Yo twice, insert hook in next tr and draw up a lp, [yo, draw through 2 lps] twice) 5 times, yo, draw lp through all 6 lps on hook.

First motif

Ch 6. Join with sl st to form a ring.

Rnd 1 Ch 7 (counts as 1 tr, ch 3), [1 tr, ch 6, 1 tr, ch 3] 3 times in ring, 1 tr in ring, ch 6. Join with sl st in 4th ch of beg ch-7.

Rnd 2 Ch 5, 4 dtr in next ch-3 sp, *ch 6, 1 sc in next ch-6 sp, ch 6, 5 dtr in next ch-3 sp; rep from * twice more, ch 6, 1 sc in next ch-6 sp, ch 6. Join with sl st in top of beg ch-5.

Rnd 3 Beg tr cluster over first 5 dtr, *[ch 6, 1 sc in next ch-6 sp] twice, ch 6, tr cluster over next 5 dtr; rep from * twice more, [ch 6, 1 sc in next ch-6 sp] twice, ch 6. Join with sl st in top of beg tr cluster. Fasten off.

Second and all following motifs

Work same as first motif through row 3.

Do not fasten off.

With RS facing, place previous motif below current one and work from right to left.

Joining row Ch 6, sl st in corresponding tr cluster of previous motif, sl st to center of next ch-6 sp, *ch 3, 1 sc in next corresponding ch-6 sp of current motif, ch 3, 1 sc in next ch-6 sp of previous motif; rep from * once more, ch 3, 1 sc in next corresponding ch-6 sp of current motif, sl st to next tr cluster, ch 6, sl st in top of corresponding tr cluster of previous motif. Fasten off.

Lower edge

With RS facing, join yarn in top of first tr cluster at right-hand side.

Row 1 Ch 1, [4 sc, ch 3, 4 sc] in each ch-6 sp to end. Fasten off.

Band

With RS facing, working along opposite edge, join yarn in top of first tr cluster at right-hand side.

Row 1 Ch 2, 1 hdc in each ch, sc and tr cluster to end. Turn.

Rows 2 and 3 Ch 2, 1 hdc in next hdc and each hdc to end. Turn

Fasten off.

Fringe

Follow instructions for fringe on page 121, using two strands of yarn inserted into each ch-3 sp. Trim to desired length.

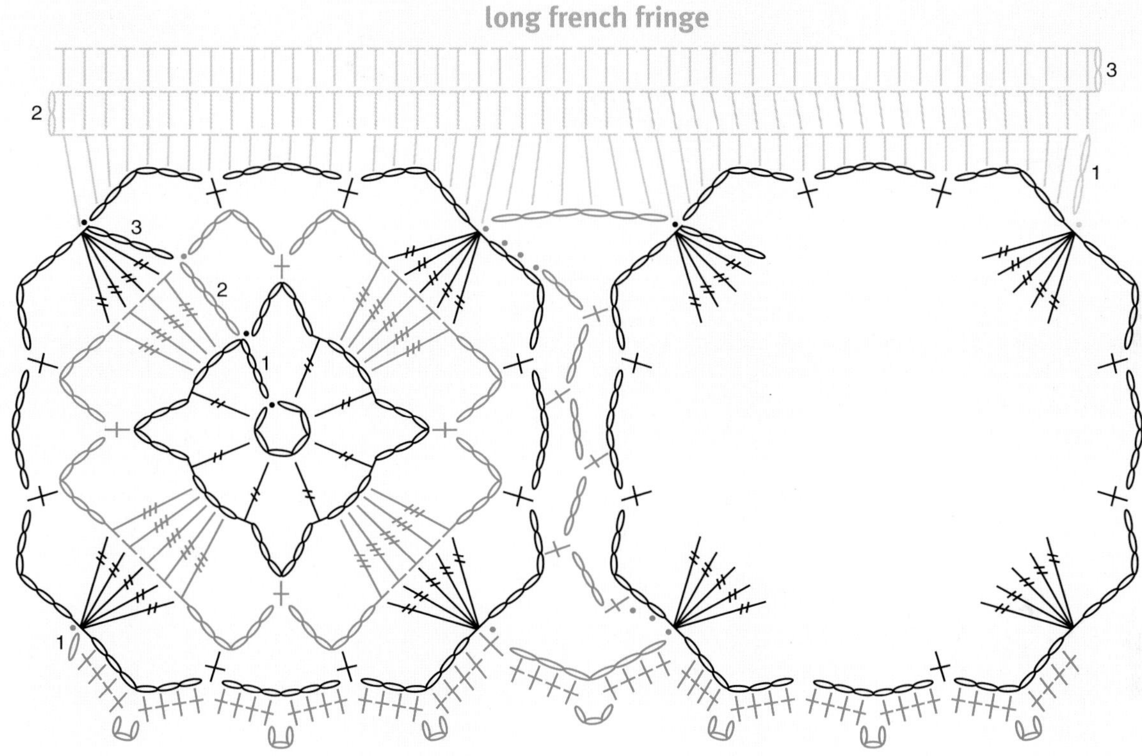

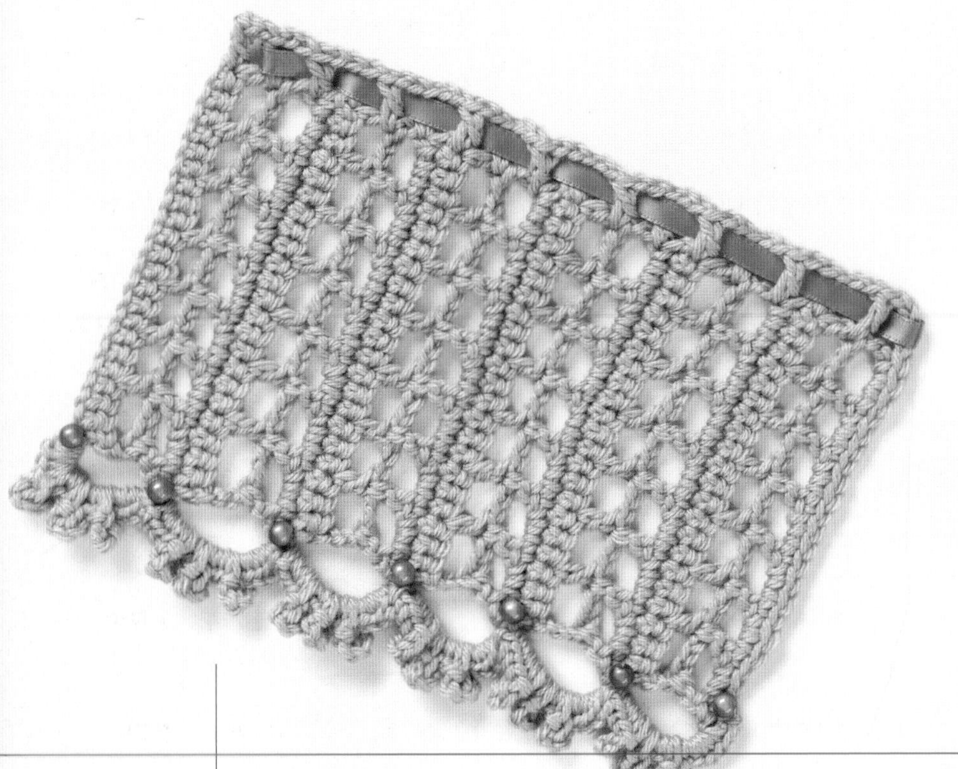

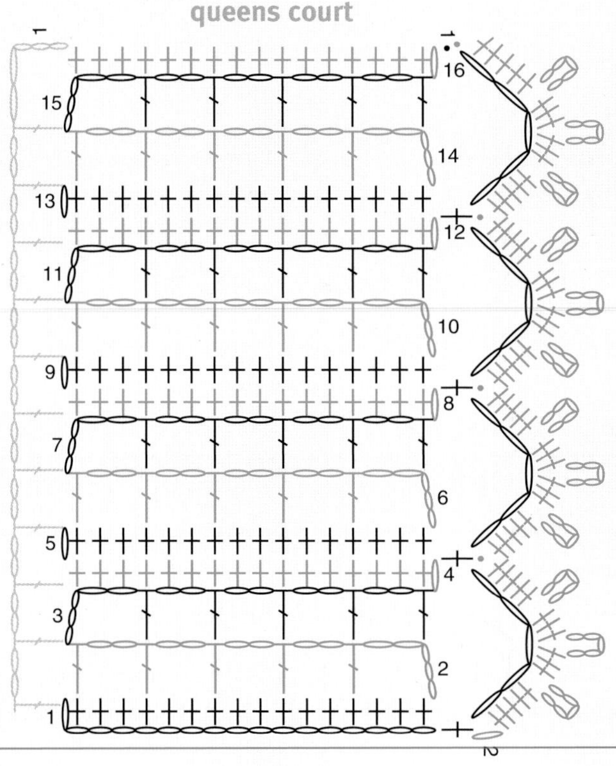

queens court

▶ (multiple of 3 sts + 1)

Make a chain to desired depth in a multiple of 3 sts + 2.

Row 1 1 sc in 2nd ch from hook and in each ch to end. Turn.

Row 2 Ch 5 (counts as 1 dc, ch 2), skip next 2 sc, 1 dc in next sc, *ch 2, skip next 2 sc, 1 dc in next sc; rep from * to end. Turn.

Row 3 Ch 5 (counts as 1 dc, ch 2), *1 dc in next dc, ch 2; rep from *, end 1 dc in 3rd ch of beg ch-5. Turn.

Row 4 Ch 1, 1 sc in first dc, *2 sc in next ch-2 sp, 1 sc in next dc; rep from *, end last rep 1 sc in 3rd ch of beg ch-5. Turn.

Row 5 Ch 1, 1 sc in each sc to end. Turn.

Rep rows 2–5 for length desired, ending with row 4. *Do not fasten off.*

Top Edge

Rotate to work along side length of piece.

Row 1 Ch 5, skip next row-end dc, *1 dc in top of next dc, ch 2, 1 dc in top of next sc, ch 2, 1 dc in base of next sc; rep from *, end last rep 1 dc in top of last sc.

Fasten off.

Scalloped edge

With WS facing, attach yarn to first st at right-hand side.

Row 1 *Ch 5, 1 sc between ends of next 2 sc rows; rep from *, end 1 sc in end of last sc row. Turn.

Row 2 Ch 1, *(5 sc, ch 5, [3 sc, ch 5] twice, 5 sc) in ch-5 lp, sl st in next sc; rep from * to end.

Fasten off.

Optional Thread satin ribbon in and out of spaces in top edge. Sew beads to top of each scallop in edging, if desired.

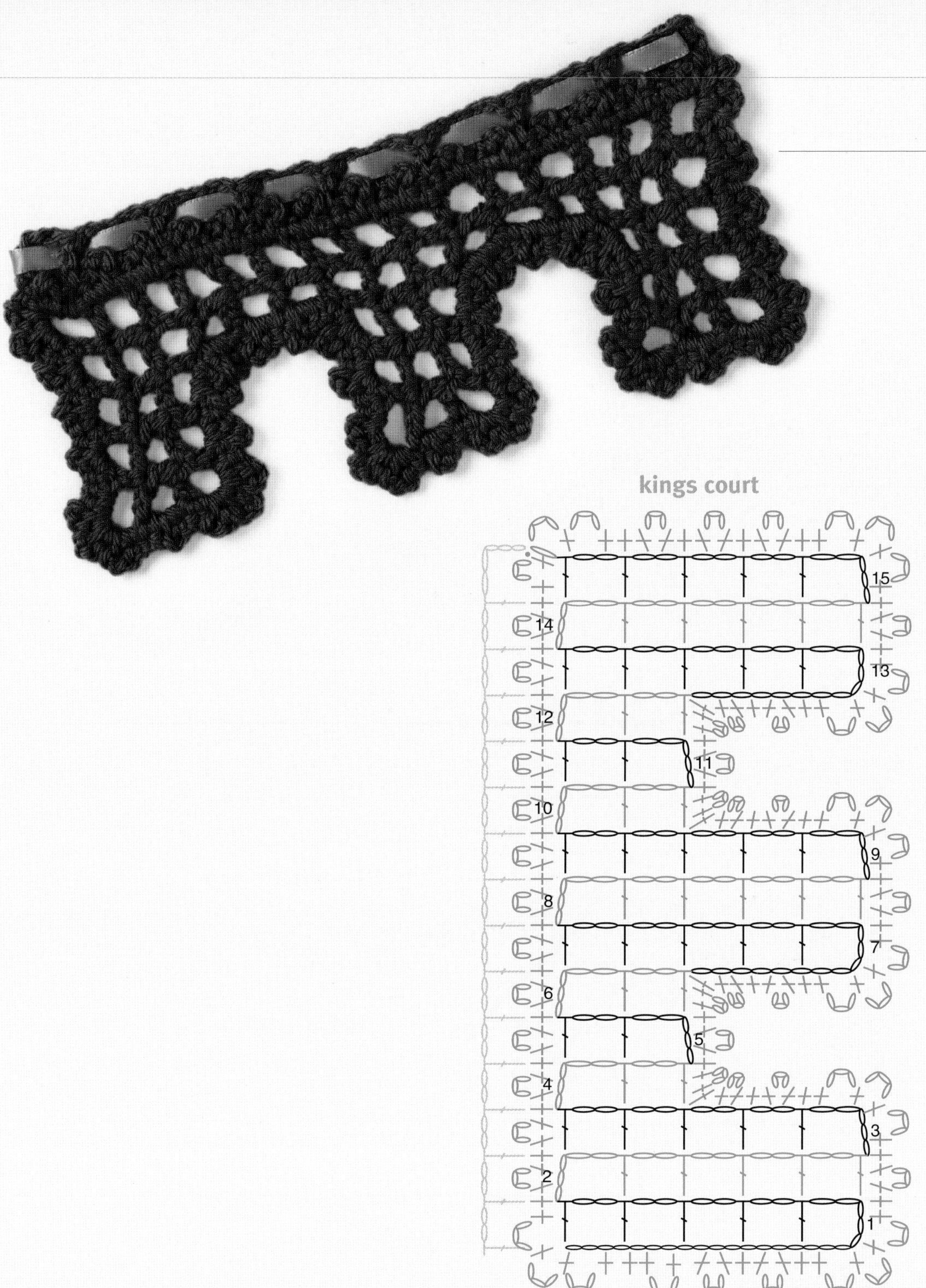

kings court

▶ Ch 20.

Row 1 1 dc in 8th ch from hook, *ch 2, skip 2 ch, 1 dc in next ch; rep from * to end. Turn.

Row 2 Ch 5 (counts as 1 dc, ch 2), [1 dc in next dc, ch 2] 4 times, 1 dc in 5th ch of beg ch-7. Turn.

Row 3 Ch 5 (counts as 1 dc, ch 2), [1 dc in next dc, ch 2] 4 times, 1 dc in 3rd ch of beg ch-5. Turn.

Row 4 Ch 5 (counts as 1 dc, ch 2), 1 dc in next dc, ch 2, 1 dc in next dc. Turn.

Row 5 Ch 5 (counts as 1 dc, ch 2), 1 dc in next dc, ch 2, 1 dc in 3rd ch of beg ch-5. Turn.

Row 6 Ch 5 (counts as 1 dc, ch 2), 1 dc in next dc, ch 2, 1 dc in 3rd ch of beg ch-5. Turn.

Row 7 Ch 13, 1 dc in 8th ch from hook, ch 2, skip 2 ch, 1 dc in next ch, [ch 2, 1 dc in next dc] 3 times, end last rep 1 dc in 3rd ch of beg ch-5. Turn.

Rep rows 2–7 to desired length, ending with row 3. Do not turn, do not fasten off.

Border row

Rotate to work across **top edge**. Ch 1, *[1 sc, ch 3, 1 sc] in next space, 1 sc at base of dc row; rep from * to corner sp.

Rotate to work **corner and side edge** [1 sc, ch 3] 3 times in corner sp, 1 sc in same sp, *1 sc in next dc, [1 sc, ch 3, 1 sc] in next sp; rep from * to next corner sp.

Rotate to work **corner and lower edge** *[1 sc, ch 3] 3 times in corner sp, 1 sc in same sp, 1 sc in top of dc row, [1 sc, ch 3, 1 sc] in next sp, 1 sc in top of dc row, [1 sc, ch 3] 3 times in corner sp, 1 sc in same sp, 1 sc in next dc, ([1 sc, ch 3, 1 sc] in next sp, 1 sc in next dc) 7 times; rep from *, end last rep work between ( ) 4 times, ch 3. Join with sl st to first sc.

Do not fasten off.

Eyelet Row

Working across top edge only, ch 5, *skip [1 sc, ch 3, 1 sc], 1 dc in next sc, ch 2; rep from * to end.

Fasten off.

Optional Thread satin ribbon in and out of spaces in eyelet row.

heartfelt fringe

▼ (multiple of 4 sts + 3)

Note This edging can be worked directly onto a project or into a chain and attached.

Band

Make a ch to desired length in a multiple of 4 sts.

Row 1 1 hdc in 3rd ch from hook and in each ch to end. Turn.

Row 2 Ch 2, 1 hdc in next hdc and in each hdc to end. Turn.

Row 3 Rep row 2.

Cont to row 1 of fringe.

Fringe

With WS facing, attach yarn to right-hand edge of band or project.

Row 1 *Ch 6, skip next st or ch, 1 sc in next st or ch; rep from * to end. Turn.

Row 2 Ch 1, sl st in first ch-6 lp, ch 3, 6 dc in same lp, *1 dc in next ch-6 loop, ch 10, [3 dc, ch 3] twice, sl st in 4th ch from hook, ch 7, 1 dc in same space, 7 dc in next ch-6 lp; rep from * to end.

Fasten off.

heartfelt fringe

clever clover fringe

▲ **Colors** A and B

(multiple of 6 sts + 4)

With A, make a ch to desired length in a multiple of 6 sts + 7.

Row 1 1 tr in 5th ch from hook and in each ch to end. Turn.

Row 2 Ch 3, 1 dc in next 4 tr, *ch 10, sl st in 6th ch from hook to form a ring, 1 sc, [1 dc, 2 tr, 1 dc, 1 sc] 3 times in ring, sl st in last 3 ch of ch-10, 1 dc in next 6 tr; rep from *, end last rep 1 dc in last 5 tr.

Row 3 Ch 4, 1 tr in each dc to end.

Fasten off.

Optional For additional layer, attach B and rep rows 2–3, alternating positions of clovers.

clever clover fringe

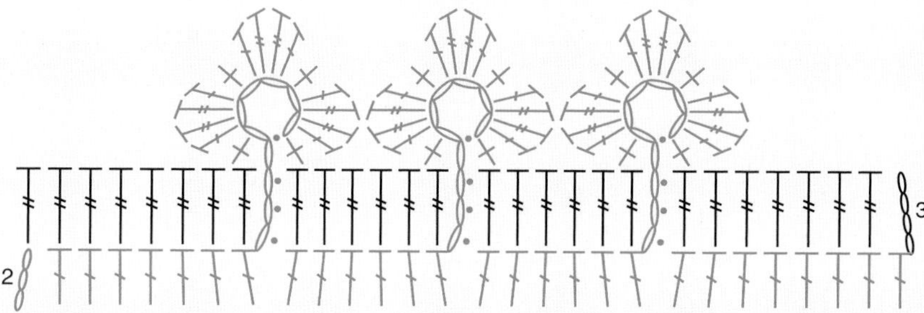

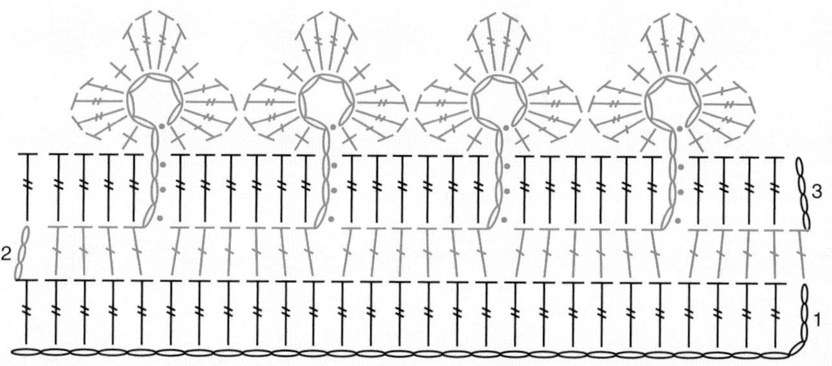

spotted piggy tails

▲

Base (optional)

Make a ch to desired length.

Row 1 1 sc in 2nd ch from hook and in each ch to end. Turn.

Row 2 Ch 1, 1 sc in each sc to end. Turn.

Rep row 2 for desired length.

Tails

Winding st [Yo, bring hook under last 3 ch and draw up a lp] 9 times, yo and draw through all 19 lps on hook. Ch 13.

Row 1 Work winding st around last 3 ch, sl st in 4th ch from hook, ch 3, *work winding st around last 3 ch, sl st in sp between winding sts; rep from * twice more, end last rep sl st in same ch as first winding st, ch 10.

Make piggy tails in quantity and colors as desired.

Using tails, attach piggy tails as desired, alternating colors and positions.

spotted piggy tails

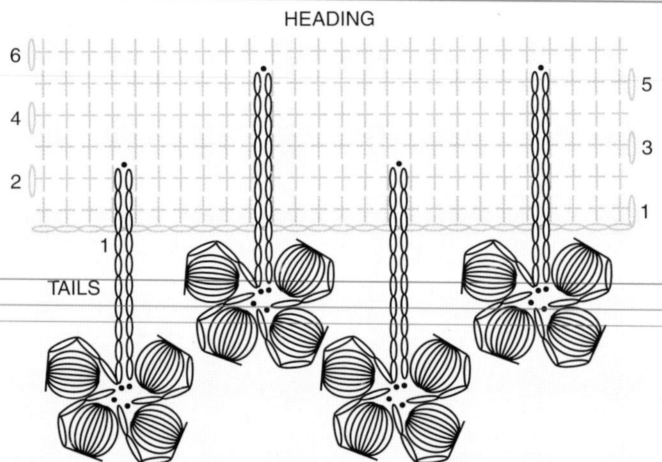

piggy tails

E Heading

Make a ch to desired length.

Row 1 1 hdc in 3rd ch from hook and in each ch to end. Turn.

Row 2 Ch 2, 1 hdc in next hdc and in each hdc to end. Turn.

Rep row 2 for desired length.

Tails

Winding st [Yo, bring hook under last 3 ch and draw up a lp] 9 times, yo and draw through all 19 lps on hook. Ch 13.

Row 1 Work winding st around last 3 ch, sl st in 4th ch from hook, ch 3, *work winding st around last 3 ch, sl st in sp between winding st; rep from * once more, ending sl st in same ch as first winding st, ch 10. Fasten off.

Using tails, attach piggy tails evenly across edge of heading.

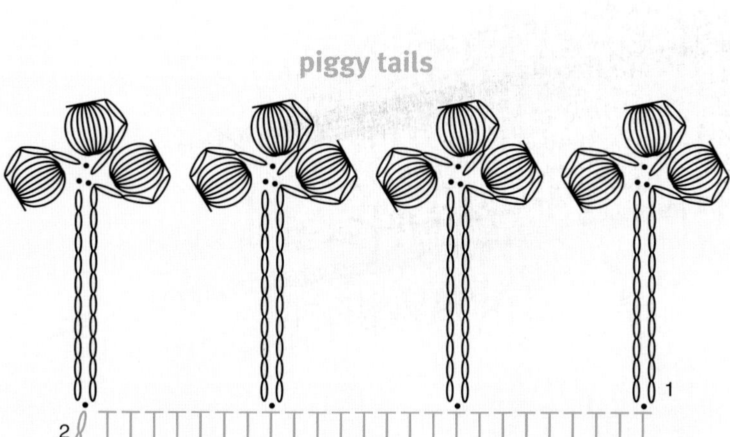

reina I

▼ **Colors** A and B

Materials Polyfill

Note This edging can be worked directly onto a project or onto a band as shown and attached.

Band

With A, make a ch to desired length.

Row 1 1 dc in 4th ch from hook and in each ch to end. Turn.

Row 2 Ch 3, 1 dc in front lp of next dc and in each dc to end. Turn.

Row 3 Ch 3, 1 dc in back lp of next dc and in each dc to end. Turn.

Rep rows 2 and 3 to desired length.

Balls

With A or B, make the slip knot so the tail end can tighten the loop. Ch 2.

Rnd 1 8 sc in 2nd ch from hook. Join with sl st to first sc.

Rnd 2 Ch 1, 2 sc in each sc around—16 sc. Join with sl st to first sc.

Rnds 3 and 4 Ch 1, 1 sc in each sc around. Join with sl st to first sc. Place Polyfill into ball.

Rnd 5 Ch 1, sc2tog around—8 sc. Join with sl st to first sc.

Rnd 6 Ch 1, 1 sc in each sc around. Join with sl st to first sc.

Fasten off, leaving a 12"/30.5cm tail. Thread tail through each st, pulling taut to close opening and secure.

Attach balls

Using tail, ch 8, sl st in project or band where desired, sl st in each ch back to ball. Fasten off.

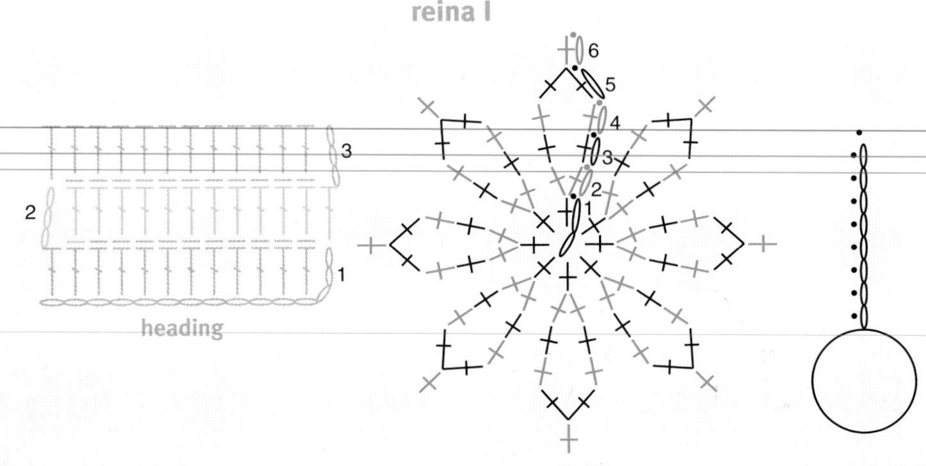

reina II

▼ (multiple of 8 sts + 1)

Materials Polyfill

9-dc cluster Yo, insert hook into next st and draw up a lp, yo and draw through 2 lps on hook, [yo, insert hook into same st and draw up a lp, yo and draw through 2 lps on hook] 8 times, yo and draw through all 10 lps on hook.

Cluster strip

Make a ch to desired length in a multiple of 8 sts + 2.

Row 1 1 sc in 2nd ch from hook and in each ch to end. Turn.

Row 2 Ch 1, 1 sc in next sc and in each sc to end. Turn.

Row 3 Ch 5, *skip next sc, 9-dc cluster in next sc, ch 2, skip next sc, 1 dc in next sc, ch 2; rep from *, end last rep ch 2, skip next sc, 1 dc in last st. Turn.

Row 4 Ch 1, 1 sc in first dc, *1 sc in next ch sp, 1 sc in top of next cluster, 1 sc in next ch sp, 1 sc in next dc; rep from * end 1 sc in 3rd ch of beg ch-5. Turn.

Row 5 Rep row 2.

Fasten off.

Balls

Work same as Reina I (see page 130).

Fasten off, leaving a 40"/101.5cm tail. Thread tail through each st, pulling taut to close opening and secure.

Attach balls

First ball Using tail, ch 9, sl st in 3rd sc in cluster strip above first cluster, sl st in each ch back to ball, ch 9, skip next cluster, sl st in sc in cluster strip above next cluster, sl st in each ch back to ball. Fasten off.

Second and subsequent balls Using tail, ch 9, sl st in sc in cluster strip above skipped cluster, sl st in each ch back to ball, ch 9, skip next 2 clusters, sl st in sc in cluster strip above next cluster, sl st in each ch back to ball. Fasten off.

Last ball Using tail, ch 9, sl st in sc in cluster strip above skipped cluster, sl st in each ch back to ball, ch 9, skip next cluster, sl st in sc in heading above last cluster, sl st in each ch back to ball. Fasten off.

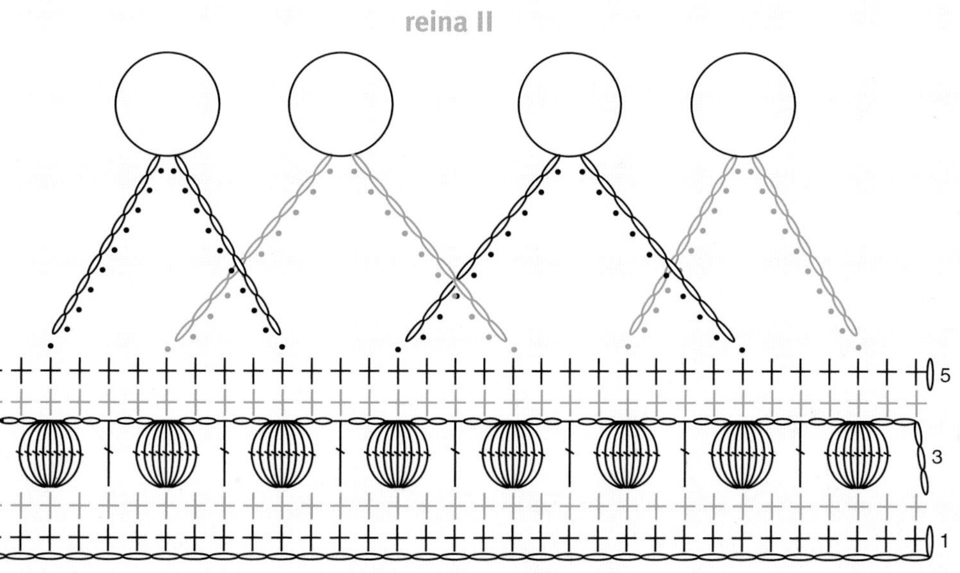

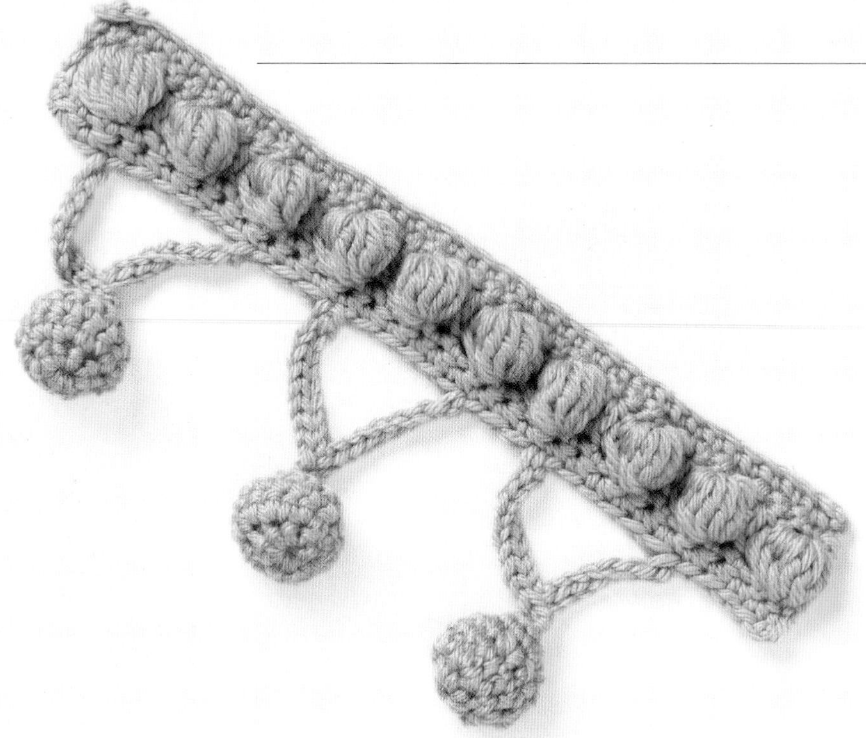

reina III

E (multiple of 12 sts + 1)

Materials Polyfill

Cluster Strip

Make a ch to desired length in a multiple of 12 sts + 2.

Work same as Reina II (see page 131).

Balls

Work same as Reina I (see page 130).

Attach balls

Using tail, ch 13, sl st in 3rd sc in cluster strip above first cluster, sl st in each ch back to ball, ch 13, skip next cluster, sl st in sc in cluster strip above next cluster, sl st in each ch back to ball. Fasten off.

Rep above to attach balls to heading, skipping 3 sc between attachments.

reina 3

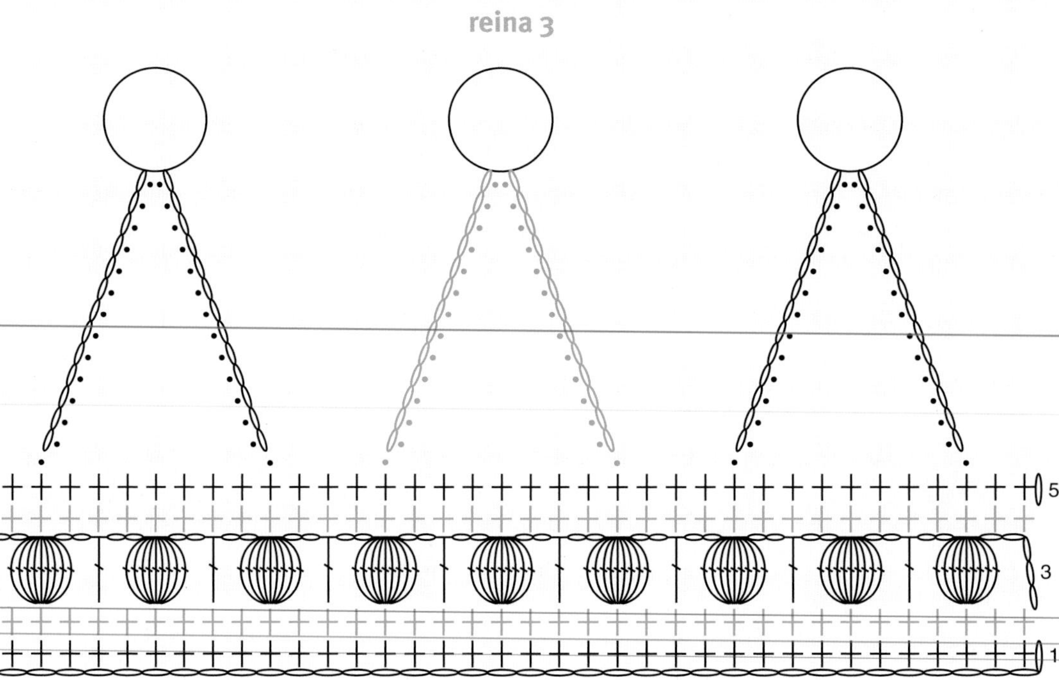

raindrops

▼ **Colors** A and B

(multiple of 8 sts + 1)

Fringe

With A, make a ch to length desired in a multiple of 8 sts + 7.

Row 1 1 sc in 4th ch from hook—(*picot made*), ch 8, 1 sc in 4th ch from hook—(*picot made*), ch 2, skip 10 ch of foundation ch, 1 sc in next ch from first picot—(*picot lp made*), *ch 6, picot, ch 8, picot, ch 2, skip 7 ch of foundation ch, 1 sc in next ch—(*picot lp made*); rep from * to end. Turn.

Row 2 Ch 8, picot, ch 8, picot, ch 2, *1 sc between picots of next picot lp, ch 6, picot, ch 8, picot, ch 2; rep from *, end 1 sc between picots of last picot lp. Turn.

Row 3 Rep row 2.

Fasten off A.

Squares

Row 1 With B, ch 6, 1 sc between picots of first picot lp on left side. Turn.

Row 2 Ch 1, 1 sc in first sc, working in chain-bar, 1 sc in each ch to end—7 sc. Turn.

Rows 3, 4, 5 and 6 Ch 1, 1 sc in each sc to end. Turn.

Row 7 Ch 1, 1 sc in each sc to end. Do not turn.

Rep rows 1–7 until all picot lps of fringe have been worked.

Fasten off.

Top row

Attach B to right-hand edge of fringe at opposite side of foundation ch.

Row 1 Ch 2, 1 hdc in next ch in in each ch across.

Fasten off.

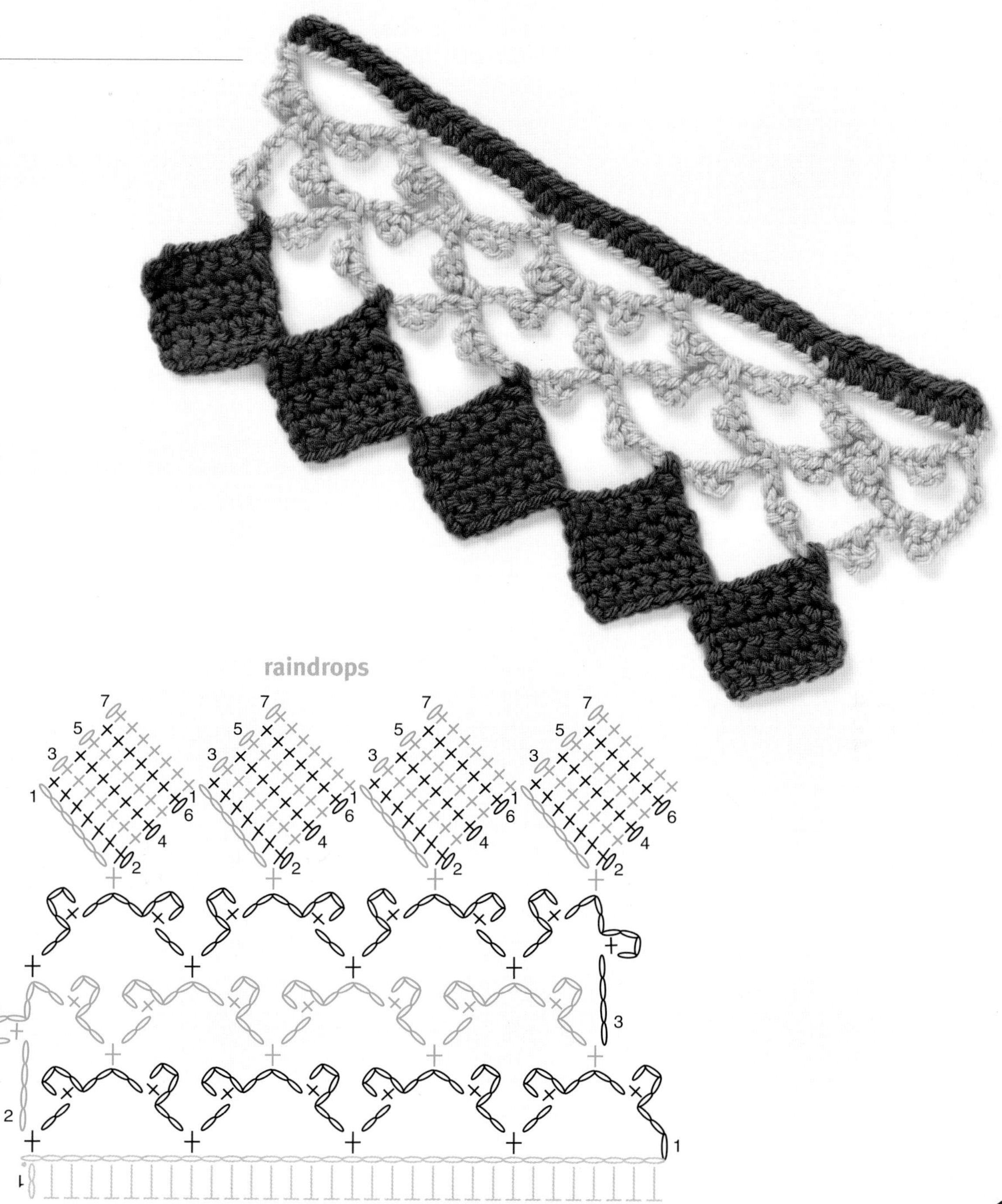

fuzzy tails bunny fringe

▲ **Colors** A and B

Materials Beads for eyes

Body and head

With A, ch 4. Join with sl st in first ch to form a ring.

Rnd 1 Ch 3 (counts as 1 dc), 11 dc in ring. Join with sl st in top of beg ch-3—12 dc. Turn.

Rnd 2 Ch 3, 3 dc in next dc, *ch 5, sl st in 2nd ch from hook, 1 sc in next 2 ch, sl st to base of ch-5; rep from * for second ear.

Fasten off.

Tail

With B, ch 3. Join with sl st in first ch to form a ring.

Rnd 1 Working in spiral rnds, ch1, 1 sc in each st around. Rep rnd 1 until tail is desired size. Join with sl st to first sc.

Fasten off, leaving a 4"/10cm tail.

Joining Strip

Join A to tip of first ear of first bunny.

Row 1 Ch 1, 1 sc in same st, ch 3, 1 sc in tip of second ear, *ch 4, 1 sc in tip of first ear of next bunny, ch 3, 1 sc in tip of second ear; rep from * until all bunnies have been joined. Turn.

Row 2 Ch 3, 1 dc in each ch and sc to end. Turn.

Row 3 Ch 3, 1 dc in each dc to end.

Fasten off.

Sew on beads. Using tails, sew tail to body of bunny.

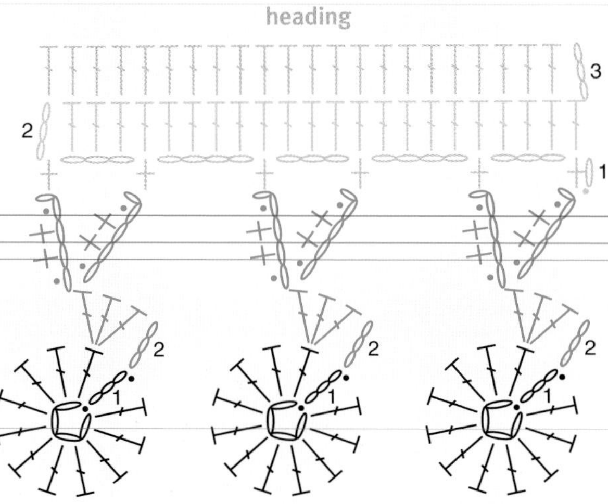

donut fringe

▲ **Donut** (make number desired)

Ch 8. Join with a sl st in first ch to form a ring.

Row 1 Ch 3, 19 dc in ring. Join with sl st in top of beg ch-3.

Fasten off.

Joining donuts

Attach yarn to any st of first donut.

Joining row Ch 1, 1 sc in same st, 1 sc in next 2 sts, *ch 3, 1 sc in 3 sts of next donut; rep from * until all donuts are joined. Turn.

Heading

Row 1 Ch 4, 1 tr in next sc, 1 tr in each sc and ch to end.

Fasten off.

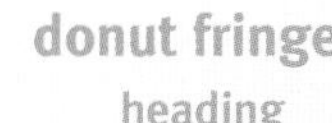

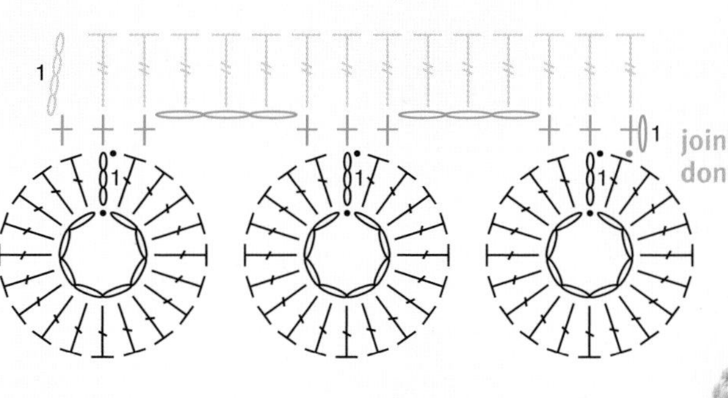

floral donut fringe

▲ **Colors** A and B

Large floral donut

With A, ch 8. Join with a sl st in first ch to form a ring.

Row 1 Ch 3, 19 dc in ring. Join with sl st in top of beg ch-3.

Fasten off A. Attach B in same sp.

Row 2 Ch 1, 1 sc in same sp, *ch 3, 1 sc in next st; rep from * around, ch 8, sl st in each ch back to donut. Join with sl st in base of ch-8.

Fasten off.

Make desired number of donuts.

Small donut

With A, ch 8. Join with a sl st in first ch to form ring.

Row 1 Ch 3, 19 dc in ring. Join with sl st in top of beg ch-3.

Fasten off A. Attach B in same sp.

Row 2 Sl st in back lps only of each dc around, ch 8, sl st in each ch back to donut. Join with sl st in base of ch-8.

Fasten off.

Make desired number of donuts.

Heading

Make a ch to desired length.

Row 1 1 tr in 5th ch from hook and in each ch to end.

Fasten off.

Attach ends of ch-8 tails of donuts to heading as desired.

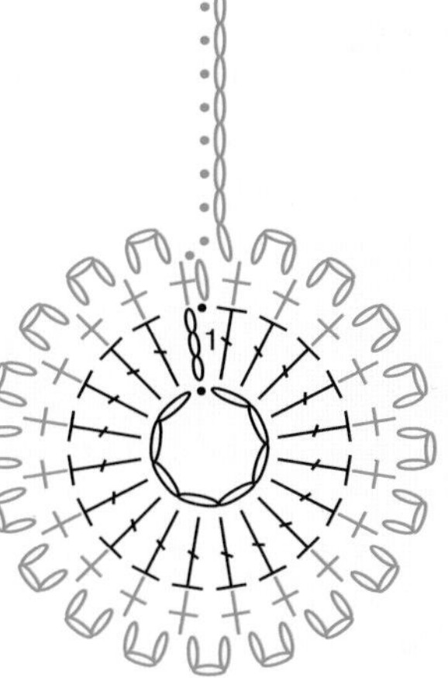

large floral donut

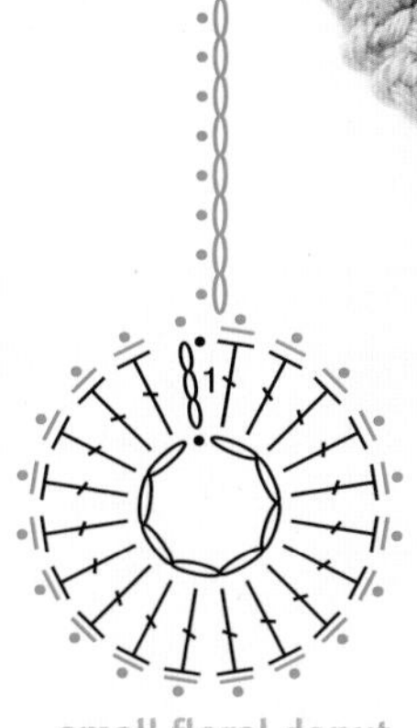

small floral donut

finger lace fringe

Panel

Ch 16.

Row 1 1 dc in 7th ch from hook, *ch 2, skip 2 ch, 1 dc in next ch; rep from * to end—4 ch sps. Turn.

Row 2 Ch 1, [1 sc in dc, 2 sc in first ch-2 sp] 3 times, 1 sc in dc, 10 sc in last sp (working around to other side of foundation ch), [1 sc in dc, 2 sc in next ch-2 sp] 3 times, 1 sc in last dc—30 sc. Turn.

Row 3 Ch 1, 1 sc in each sc to end. Turn.

Row 4 Ch 1, 1 sc in first 4 sc, [ch 3, sl st in 3rd ch from hook, 1 sc in next 4 sc] twice, [ch 3, sl st in 3rd ch from hook, 1 sc in next 3 sc] twice, [ch 3, sl st in 3rd ch from hook, 1 sc in next 4 sc] 3 times.

Fasten off.

Make desired number of panels.

Joining strip

With RS facing, and working along straight edge of panel, attach yarn to right-hand edge.

Row 1 Ch 1, *1 sc into side of first 2 sc rows, skip next row-end sc, 2 sc into side of dc, skip next row-end sc, 1 sc into side of last 2 sc rows, ch 2; rep from * until all panels are joined, omitting ch 2 after last panel. Turn.

Row 2 Ch 5 (counts as 1 dc, ch 2), skip next sc, 1 dc in next sc, ch 2, skip next sc, 1 dc in next sc, *ch 2, skip next sc, 1 dc in first ch, [ch 2, skip next ch, 1 dc in next sc] 3 times; rep from *, end ch 2, 1 dc in last sc. Turn.

Row 3 Ch 1, 3 sc in first ch-2 sp and in each ch-2 sp to end.

Fasten off.

falling leaves

Leaf

Ch 26.

Rnd 1 1 sc in 2nd ch from hook, *ch 4, skip 3 ch, 1 dc in next ch, ch 4, skip 3 ch, 1 tr in next ch, ch 4, skip 3 ch, 1 dtr in next ch, ch 4, skip 3 ch, 1 tr in next ch, ch 4, skip 3 ch, 1 dc in next ch, ch 4, skip 3 ch, 1 sc in next ch, rotate to cont along opposite side of foundation chain, ch 4, 1 sc in same ch, ch 4, skip 3 ch, 1 dc in next ch, ch 4, skip 3 ch, 1 tr in next ch, ch 4, skip 3 ch, 1 dtr in next ch, ch 4, skip 3 ch, 1 tr in next ch, ch 4, skip 3 ch, 1 dc in next ch, ch 4, skip 3 ch, 1 sc in last ch. Join with sl st in first sc.

Fasten off.

Make desired number of leaves.

Joining leaves

With RS facing, attach yarn to joining sl st.

Row 1 Ch 1, * ([3 sc, ch 3, 3 sc] in next ch-4 space) 6 times**, [3 sc, ch 4, sl st in 4th ch from hook, 3 sc] in next ch-4 sp; rep from * to **. Join with sl st in first sc, ch 24, sl st in joining sl st of next leaf, ch 1; rep from * until all leaves are joined, ending with sl st in last sc. Turn.

Row 2 *([3 sc, ch 4, sl st in 4th ch from hook] 8 times, 3 sc) around ch-24; rep from * until each ch-24 has been covered, end sl st to first sc of first leaf.

finger lace fringe

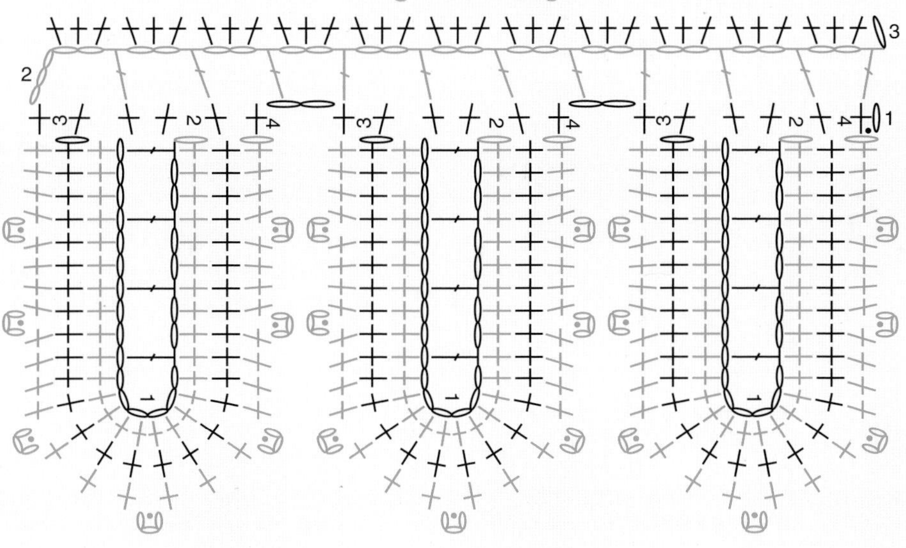

falling leaves

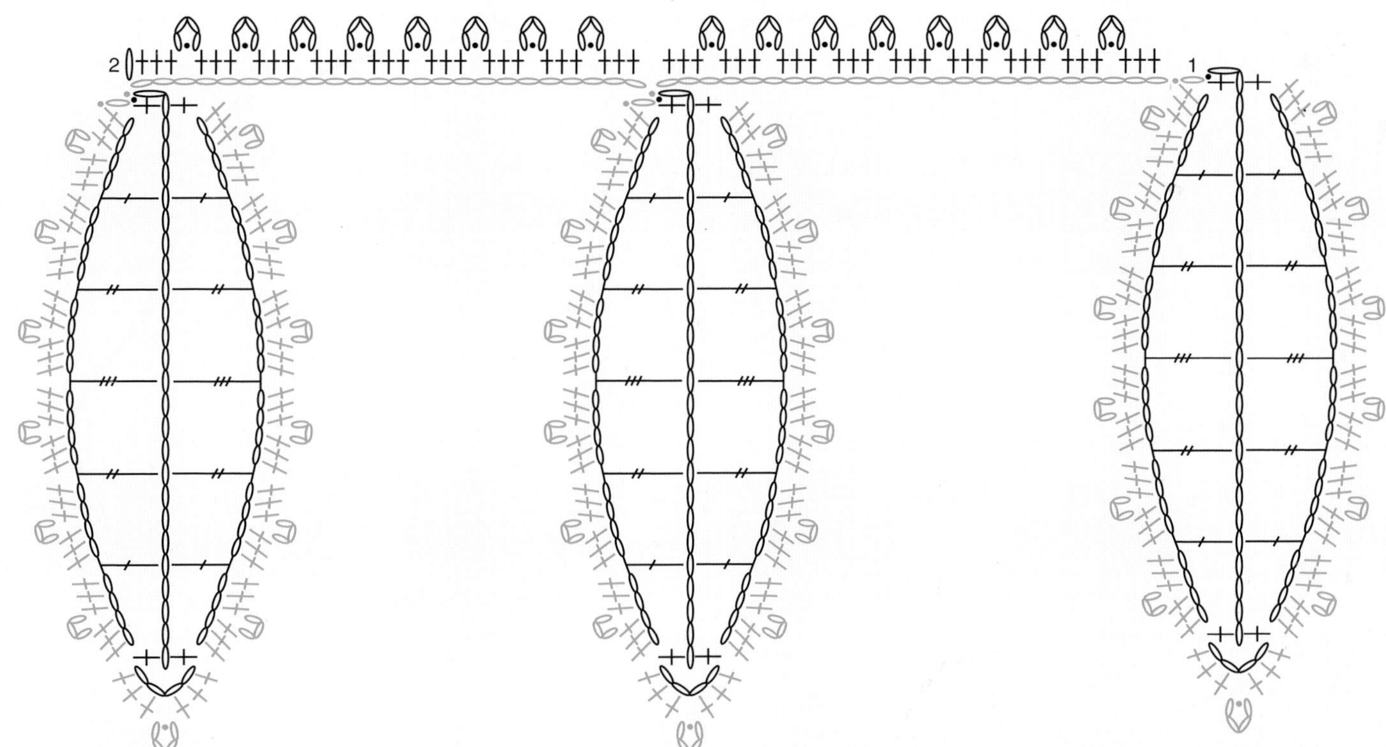

pickle fringe

▲ **Colors** A and B

Pickle

With A, ch 19.

Row 1 1 sc in 2nd ch from hook and in each ch to last ch, 3 sc in last ch (working around to other side of foundation ch), 1 sc in each ch to end—37 sc. Turn.

Row 2 Ch 1, 1 sc in back lp of each sc to 3-sc group, 2 sc in back lp of next 3 sc, 1 sc in back lp of each sc to end—40 sc. Turn.

Fasten off A. Attach B.

Row 3 Ch 1, 1 sc in first sc, [ch 4, skip next 3 sc, 1 sc in next sc] 5 times, ch 4, skip next 2 sc, 1 sc in next sc, [ch 4, skip next 3 sc, 1 sc in next sc] 4 times.

Fasten off.

Make desired number of pickles.

Joining strip

With RS facing, and working along straight edge of pickle, attach A to right-hand edge.

Row 1 Ch 1, 1 sc in first row-end sc, *1 sc into side of next 4 sc rows, ch 4, skip first row-end sc of next pickle; rep from * until all pickles are joined, omitting ch 4 after last pickle, 1 sc in last row-end sc. Turn.

Row 2 Ch 4, 1 tr in next 4 sc, *ch 4, skip next ch-4 lp, 1 tr in next 4 sc; rep from *, end ch 4, sl st in last sc. Turn.

Row 3 Ch 1, 4 sc in ch-4 sp, ch 2, *1 hdc in next 4 tr, 1 sc in next 4 ch; rep from *, end 1 hdc in next 4 tr, ch 2, 4 sc in ch-4 sp.

Fasten off.

pickle fringe

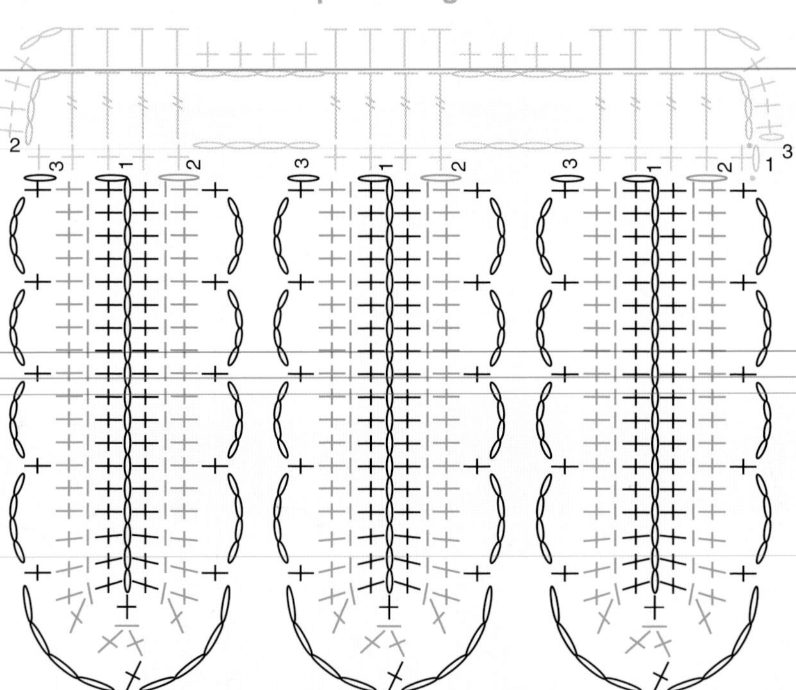

layered cactus flaps

Large flaps

Ch 12.

Row 1 1 sc in 2nd ch from hook and in each ch to last ch, 3 sc in last ch (working around to other side of foundation ch), 1 sc into each ch to end—23 sc. Turn.

Row 2 Ch 1, 1 sc in back lp of each sc to 3-sc group, 2 sc in next 3 sc, 1 sc in back lp of each st to end—26 sc. Turn.

Row 3 Ch 1, 1 sc in first sc, *ch 4, skip 2 sc, 1 sc in next st] 4 times, ch 4, 1 sc in next sc, [ch 4, skip 2 sc, 1 sc in next sc] 4 times.

Fasten off.

Work desired number of flaps.

Small flaps

Ch 8.

Row 1 1 sc in 2nd ch from hook and in each ch to last ch, 3 sc in last ch (working around to other side of foundation ch), 1 sc into each ch to end—15 sc. Turn.

Row 2 Ch 1, 1 sc in back lp of each sc to 3-sc group, 2 sc in next 3 sc, 1 sc in back lp of each st to end—18 sc. Turn.

Row 3 Ch 1, 1 sc in first sc, [ch 4, skip 2 sc, 1 sc in next st] twice, ch 4, skip 1 sc, 1 sc in next sc, [ch 4, skip 2 sc, 1 sc in next sc] 3 times.

Fasten off.

Work same number as large flaps less one.

Joining strip

With RS facing, and working along straight edge of large flap, attach yarn to right-hand edge.

Row 1 Ch 1, 1 sc into side of first 5 sc rows, *place small flap over last sc row and working through both layers, 1 sc into side of next sc row, 1 sc into side of next 4 sc rows, place large flap under last sc row and working through both layers, 1 sc into side of next sc row, 1 sc into side of next 4 sc rows; rep from * until all flaps are joined, ending 1 sc into side of last sc row of last large flap.

Row 2 Ch 4 (counts as 1 tr), 1 tr in next 4 sc, *ch 2, skip next sc, 1 tr in next 4 sc; rep from *, end last rep 1 tr in last 5 sc. Turn.

Row 3 Ch 1, 1 sc in first 5 tr, *1 sc in next ch-2 sp, 1 sc in next 4 tr; rep from *, end last rep 1 sc in last 5 tr.

Fasten off.

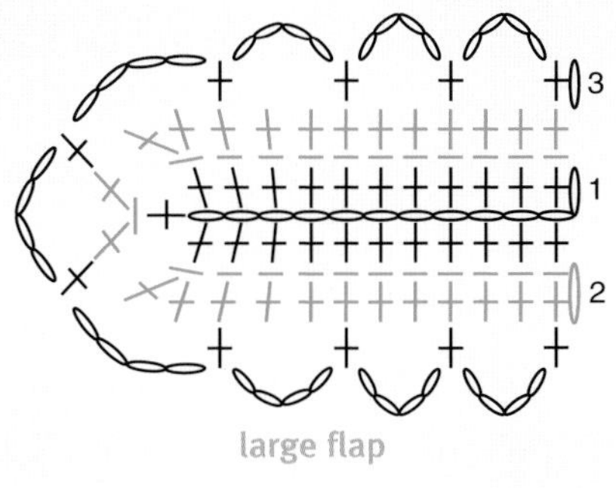

large flap

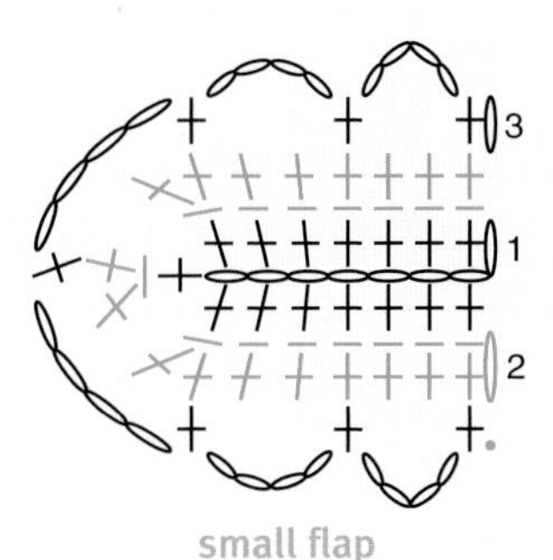

small flap

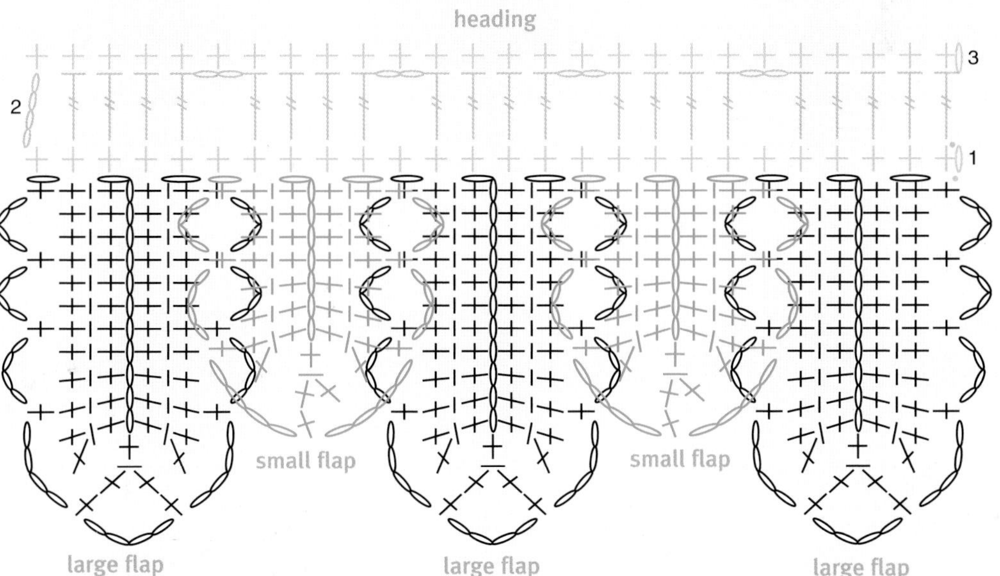

bobble flap fringe

▲ **Colors** A, B, C and D

Popcorn 5 dc in same st, remove hook from lp and insert in top of first dc of 5-dc group, replace lp on hook, yo and draw through both lp and st.

Flap

Ch 10.

Row 1 1 sc in 2nd ch from hook and in each ch to end—9 sc. Turn.

Row 2 Ch 1, 1 sc in each st to end. Turn.

Row 3 Ch 1, 1 sc in first 4 sts, popcorn in next st, 1 sc in last 4 sts. Turn.

Row 4 Ch 1, 1 sc in first 3 sts, popcorn in next st, 1 sc in next st, popcorn in next st, 1 sc in last 3 sts. Turn.

Row 5 Rep row 3.

Rows 6 and 7 Rep row 2.

Fasten off.

Joining strip

With WS facing and working along side edge of flap, attach yarn to right-hand edge.

Row 1 Ch 1, *7 sl st into side of sc rows evenly across, ch 2; rep from * until all flaps have been joined, omitting ch 2 after last flap. Turn.

Row 2 Ch 4, 1 tr in next sl st, 1 tr in each sl st and ch to end.

Fasten off.

Push popcorns to RS of panels.

bobble flap fringe

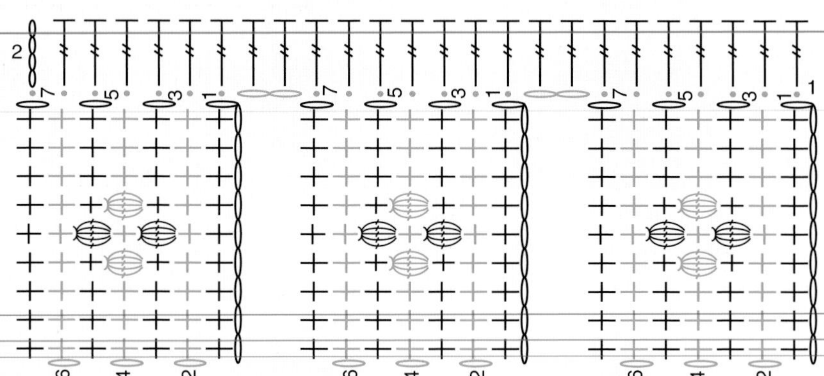

kaleidoscope fringe

▲ **Colors** A, B, C and D

Circles

With first color, ch 2.

Rnd 1 7 sc in 2nd ch from hook—7 sc. Join with sl st to first sc.

Fasten off first color and attach 2nd color.

Rnd 2 Ch 3, 1 dc in same st, 2 dc in each sc around—14 dc. Join with sl st in top of beg ch-3

Fasten off 2nd color and attach 3rd color.

Rnd 3 Ch 3, 1 dc in same st, 2 dc in each dc around—28 dc. Join with sl st in top of beg ch-3.

Fasten off.

Work desired number of circles.

Joining strip

With RS facing, attach yarn in any dc of first circle.

Row 1 Ch 1, 1 sc in same dc, 1 sc in next 3 dc, *ch 4, 1 sc in next 4 dc of next circle; rep from * until all circles have been joined. Turn.

Row 2 Ch 1, 1 sc in each sc and ch to end. Turn.

Row 3 Ch 4, 1 tr in next sc, ch 2, skip next 2 sc, *1 tr in next 4 sc, ch 4, skip 4 sc; rep from *, end last rep ch 2, skip 2 sc, 1 tr in last 2 sc.

Fasten off.

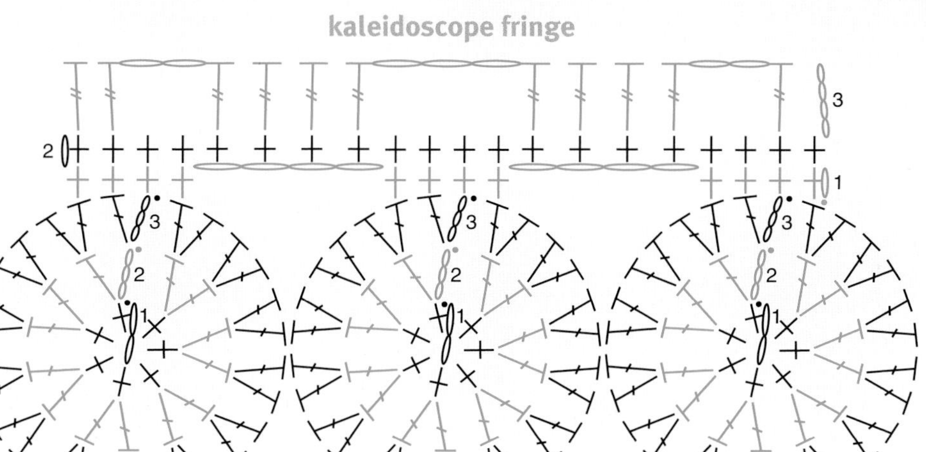

beary face

E **Colors** A, B and C

Materials Embroidery needle and black floss

Face

Ch 2.

Row 1 6 sc in 2nd ch from hook. Join with sl st in first sc.

Row 2 Ch 1, 1 sc in first sc, 2 sc in next 2 sc, 1 sc in next sc, 2 sc in next 2 sc—10 sc. Join with sl st to first sc.

Rows 3 and 5 Ch 1, 1 sc in each sc around. Join with sl st to first sc.

Row 4 Ch 1, 1 sc in first sc, *2 sc in next sc, 1 sc in next sc; rep from *, end 2 sc in last sc—15 sc. Join with sl st to first sc.

Row 6 Ch 1, 1 sc in first 2 sc, *2 sc in next sc, 1 sc in next 2 sc; rep from *, end 2 sc in last sc—20 sc. Join with sl st to first sc.

Row 7 Ch 1, 1 sc in next 3 sc (first ear), ch 1, sl st in same st, sl st in next 4 sc, ch 1, 1 sc in next 3 sc (2nd ear). Turn.

Row 8 Ch 1, 1 sc in first 3 sc, ch 1, sl st in next 5 sl st, ch 1, 1 sc in next 3 sc, ch 1, sl st in base of ear.

Fasten off.

Embroider eyes, nose and mouth.

Make desired number of faces.

Base

Make a ch to desired length.

Row 1 1 dc in 4th ch from hook and in each ch to end. Turn.

Row 2 Ch 3, 1 dc in next dc and in each dc to end. Turn.

Rep row 2 for desired length.

Fasten off.

With matching yarn, sew faces to heading or project as desired.

beary face

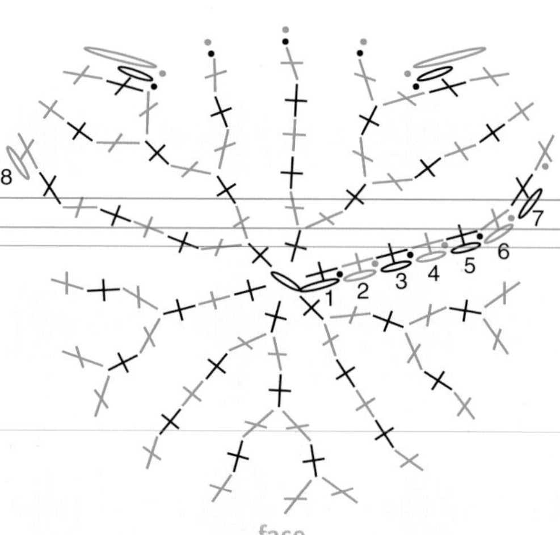

face

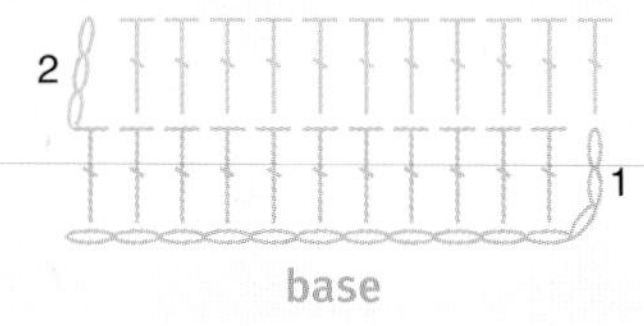

base

serendipity fringe

▶ **Note** Flowers and balls are worked separately and then attached between leaves. Leaves are worked connected to fringe band.

Flower

Ch 4. Join with sl st in first ch to form a ring.

Rnd 1 Ch 6 (counts as 1 dc, ch 3), *[1 dc, ch 3] 5 times in ring. Join with sl st to 3rd ch of beg ch-6.

Rnd 2 Ch 1, [1 sc, 1 dc, 3 tr, 1 dc, 1 sc] in each ch-3 sp. Join with sl st to first sc.

Fasten off

Ball

Ch 4.

Rnd 1 5 dc in 3rd ch from hook—6 dc.

Rnd 2 Working in a spiral, 2 sc in each sc around—12 sc.

Rnd 3 1 sc in each sc around.

Rnd 4 Sc2tog around—6 sc.

Rnd 5 Sc2tog around—3 sc.

Ch 5, fasten off.

Band with leaf

*Ch 24.

Row 1 1 sc in 2nd ch from hook, 1 hdc in next 3 ch, 1 dc in next 5 ch, 1 hdc in next 3 ch, 1 sc in next ch. Turn, leaving rem 10 ch unworked.

Row 2 Ch 3, [skip next st, 1 dc in next st, ch 3] 5 times, sl st in last st—6 ch-3 sps. Turn.

Row 3 Sl st in ch-3 sp, 3 sc in same sp, [1 sc in next dc, 3 sc in next ch-3 sp] 5 times.

Rep from * for desired number of leaves. On last leaf ch 11 and turn.

Next row 1 sc in 2nd ch from hook and in next 9 ch, *1 sc in side of each sc at end of leaf, 1 sc in next 10 ch; rep from * to end. Turn.

Next row Ch 2, 1 hdc in next sc and in each sc to end.

Fasten off.

Finishing

Using tails, attach flowers and balls along sc edge of heading between leaves.

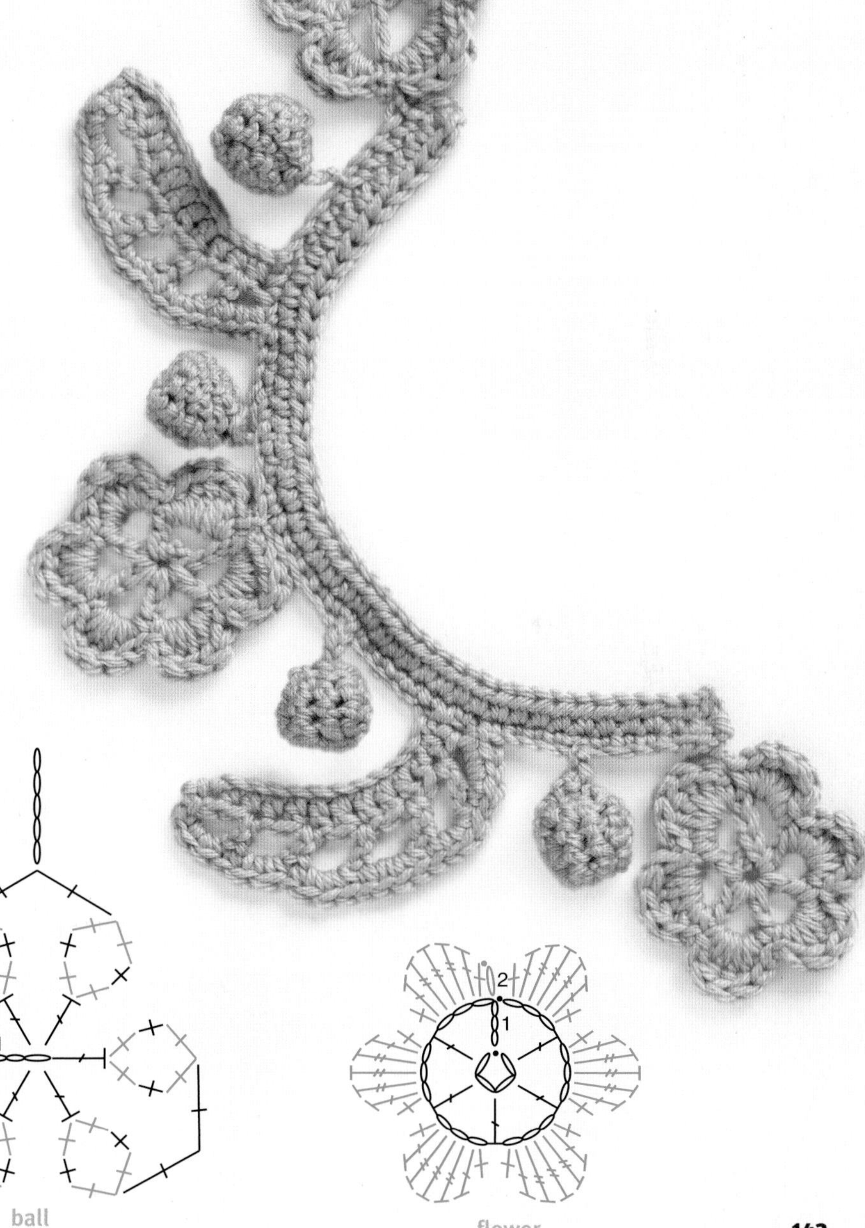

serendipity fringe

band with leaf

ball

flower

goodness grapes

Materials

1⅓ oz/10g ball each (approx 49yd/45m) of DMC #5 Perle Cotton in #3608 pink, #8837 purple, #924 dk green and #3348 lt green

Six ½"/1.25cm plastic rings for each grape bunch

C/2 (2.75mm) crochet hook

Sewing needle and matching thread

Grape (make 6 grapes for each cluster)

Attach yarn to ring.

Row 1 Ch 1, 15 sc in ring to cover. Join with sl st in first sc.

Fasten off.

Matching rings and sewing thread, sew 6 rings together to form each grape cluster.

Vines (make 1 for each bunch)

Follow instructions in Basic Corkscrew (see page 116), beginning with ch 12.

Leaf chain

Follow instructions in Cherry Jam (see page 145) for leaf chain, beginning with a ch in a multiple of 14 for each grape cluster + 2 in dk green. Work row 1 with dk green and row 2 with lt green, attaching vines after first then every other leaf as pictured.

Sew a grape cluster behind each vine.

goodness grapes
leaf chain

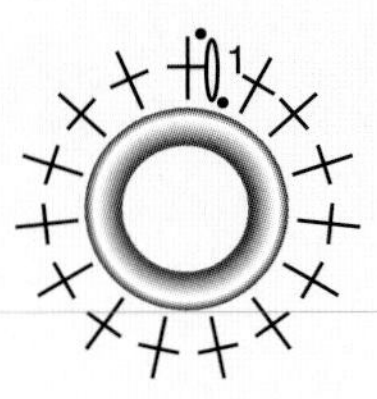

grape

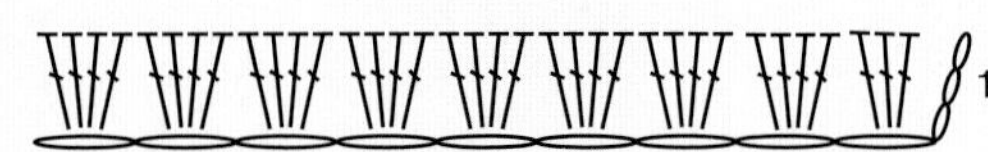

vines

cherry jam

▶ **Colors** A and B

Cherry

With A, ch 3. Join with sl st in first ch to form a ring.

Row 1 Ch 3, 10 dc in ring. Join with sl st in top of beg ch-3. Fasten off.

Make desired number of cherries in a multiple of 2.

Stem

Attach B to any st on cherry. Ch 10, sl st in 2nd ch from hook and in each ch back to cherry. Fasten off.

Leaf chain

With B, make a ch in a multiple of 7 for each pair of cherries + 9.

Row 1 Sl st in 2nd ch from hook, *1 sc in next ch, 1 hdc in next ch, 2 dc in next 2 ch, 1 hdc in next ch, 1 sc in next ch, sl st in next ch; rep from * to end.

Row 2 Ch 1 (working around to other side of foundation ch), *1 sc in next ch, 1 hdc in next ch, 2 dc in next 2 ch, 1 hdc in next ch, 1 sc in next ch, remove lp from hook and insert hook into ends of 2 cherry stems, replace lp onto hook, sl st in next ch drawing lp through all lps on hook; rep from * to end, omitting cherries in last sl st. Fasten off.

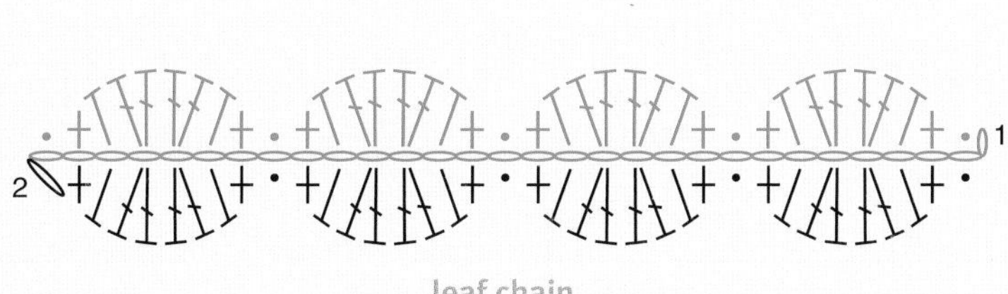

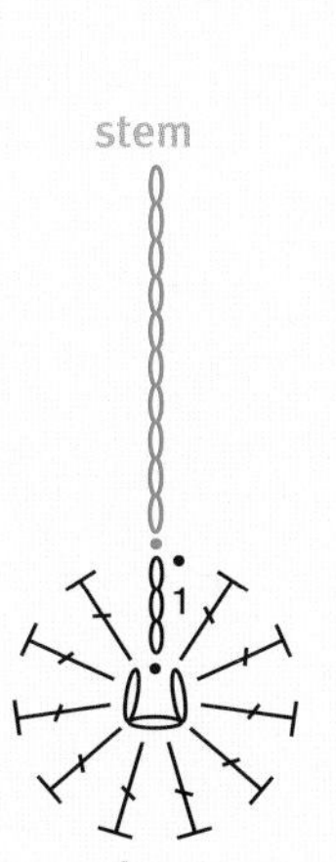

interlocked circles

▶ **Colors** A and B

First circle

Ch 26. Join with sl st in first ch to form a ring.

Row 1 Ch 3, *1 dc in next 4 ch, 2 dc in next ch; rep from * around—31 sc. Join with sl st in top of beg ch-3.

Fasten off.

Second circle

Ch 26. Insert end of ch through previous circle. Join with sl st in first ch to form a ring.

Work same as first circle.

Rep second circle instructions for desired number of circles.

Band

Attach yarn in any dc of first circle.

Row 1 Ch 1, 1 sc in same dc, 1 sc in next 4 dc, *1 sc in next 5 dc across top of next circle; rep from * until all circles have been worked. Turn.

Row 2 Ch 3 (counts as 1 dc), 1 dc in next sc and in each sc to end. Turn.

Row 3 Ch 3, 1 dc in next dc and in each dc to end.

Fasten off.

interlocked circles

heading

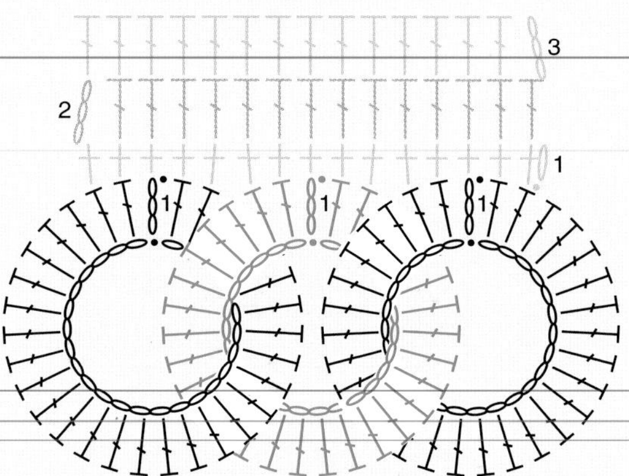

circles

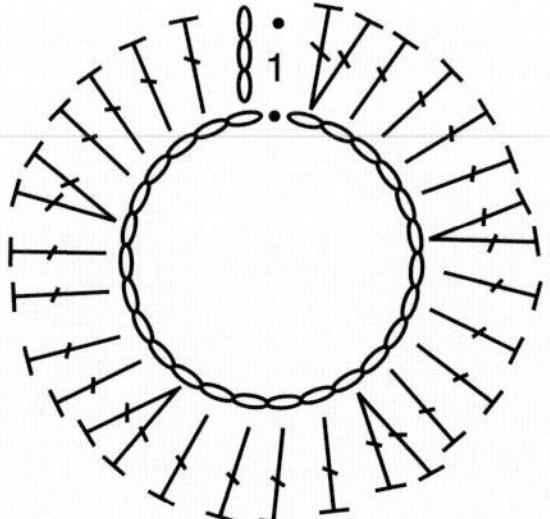

first circle

looped fringe circles

First circle

Ch 26. Join with sl st in first ch to make a ring.

Loop Ch 4, 1 dc in 2nd ch from hook, ch 1, 1 dc in next ch, sl st in next ch, sl st in first ch of ring.

Row 1 Ch 3, *1 dc in next 2 ch, 2 dc in next ch, 1 dc in next 2 ch; rep from * to end—31 dc. Join with sl st in top of beg ch-3.

Fasten off.

Second circle

Ch 26. Insert end of ch through previous circle. Join with sl st in first ch to form a ring.

Work same as first circle.

Rep second circle instructions for desired number of circles.

Fringe

Cut nine 7"/18cm lengths of yarn for each loop made. Fold in half and insert yarn lps from front to back into loop on circle, slip ends through lps and tighten. Rep for each circle. Trim ends if necessary.

looped fringe circles

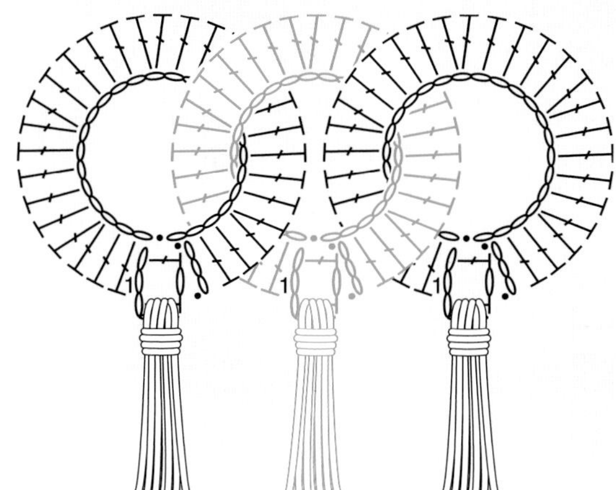

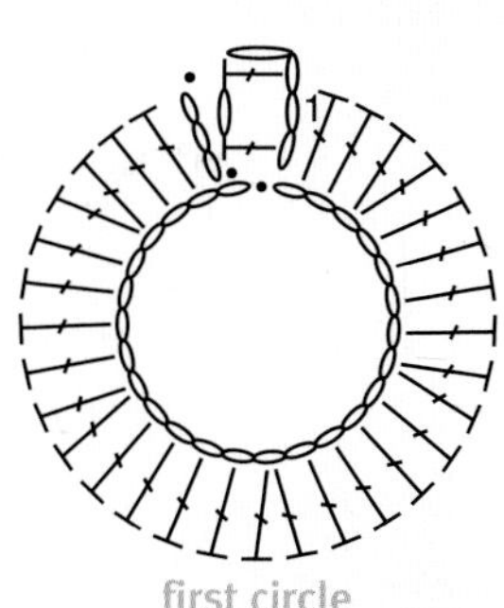

first circle

dangling leaves fringe

▲

Large leaf

Ch 14.

Row 1 Sl st in 2nd ch from hook, 1 sc in next 3 ch, 1 hdc in next 2 ch, 1 dc in next 3 ch, 2 hdc in next 2 ch, 1 sc in next ch, 3 sc in last ch (working around to other side of foundation ch), 1 sc in next ch, 1 hdc in next 2 ch, 1 dc in next 3 ch, 1 hdc in next 2 ch, 1 sc in next 3 ch, sl st in last ch. Fasten off.

Center ridge Working along foundation ch on RS of leaf, sl st in each ch to end, ch 6 for stem. Fasten off.

Small leaf

Ch 8.

Row 1 Sl st in 2nd ch from hook, 1 sc in next ch, 1 hdc in next ch, 1 dc in next ch, 1 hdc in next ch, 1 sc in next ch, 3 sc in last ch (working around to other side of foundation ch), 1 sc in next ch, 1 hdc in next ch, 1 dc in next ch, 1 hdc in next ch, 1 sc in next ch, sl st in last ch. Fasten off.

Center ridge Working along foundation ch on RS of leaf, sl st in each ch to end, Ch 6 for stem. Fasten off.

Band

Ch 4.

Row 1 Ch 4, *sl st in end of large leaf stem, ch 4, sl st in end of small stem, ch 4; rep from * until all leaves have been joined. Turn.

Row 2 Ch 5, 1 hdc in 3rd ch from hook, 1 hdc in each ch and sl st to end. Turn.

Row 3 Ch 2, 1 hdc in next hdc and in each hdc to end. Fasten off.

dangling leaves fringe

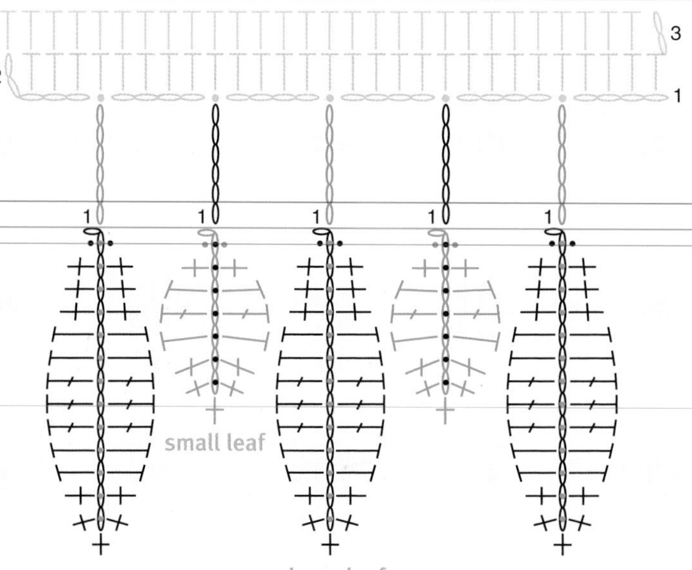

classic cotton rings

Materials

1⅓ oz/10g ball each (approx 49yd/45m) of DMC #5 Perle Cotton in #924 dk green and #3348 lt green

1⅛"/28mm plastic rings

Size C/2 (2.75mm) crochet hook

Sewing needle and matching thread

First row of rings

With A, attach thread to first ring.

Row 1 Ch 1, *15 sc in ring to cover half of ring; rep from * into half the desired number of rings.

Fasten off A and attach B to last ring.

Rep row 1 in reverse order back to first ring.

Fasten off.

Second row of rings

Work same as first row.

With sewing needle and thread, attach second row of rings to first row. Sew directly onto project or work attached band.

Band

Counting from right to left, attach A to 6th B sc of first ring.

Row 1 Ch 1, 1 sc in same sc, 1 sc in next 4 sc, *ch 4, skip next 5 sc of next ring, 1 sc in next 5 sc; rep from * in each ring to end. Turn.

Row 2 Ch 3 (counts as 1 dc), 1 dc in next sc and in each sc and ch to end. Turn.

Row 3 Ch 3 (counts as 1 dc), 1 dc in next dc and in each dc to end. Turn.

Rep row 3 to desired length.

Fasten off.

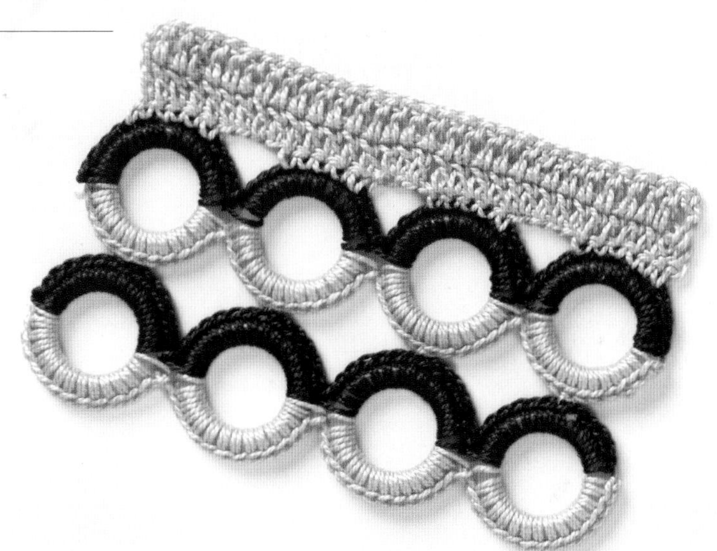

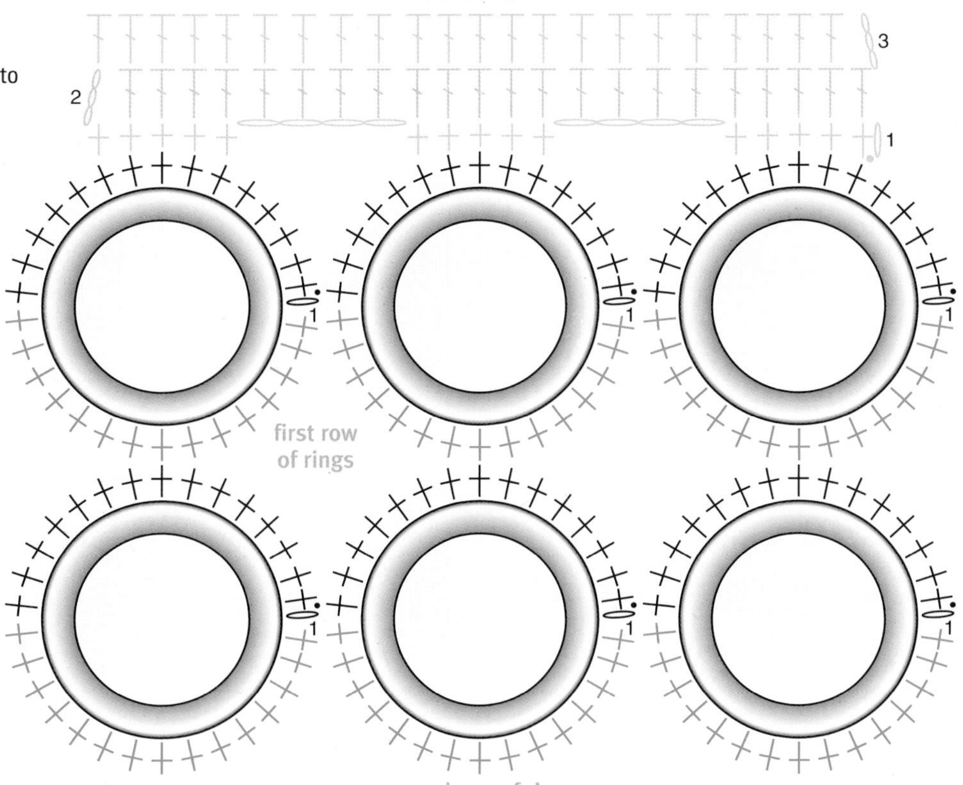

multicolor rings

E **Colors** your choice

Materials

½"/1.25cm and 1⅛"/28mm plastic rings or size desired

Sewing needle and matching thread

Small (large) ring

Attach yarn to ring.

Row 1 Ch 1, 15 (19) sc in ring. Join with sl st to first sc.

Fasten off.

Make desired number of rings in your choice of colors.

Place rings in random order and sew together.

Heading (Optional)

Make a ch to desired length.

Row 1 1 dc in 4th ch from hook and in each ch to end. Turn.

Row 2 Ch 3, 1 dc in next dc and in each dc to end. Turn.

Fasten off.

Sew rings to project.

multicolor rings

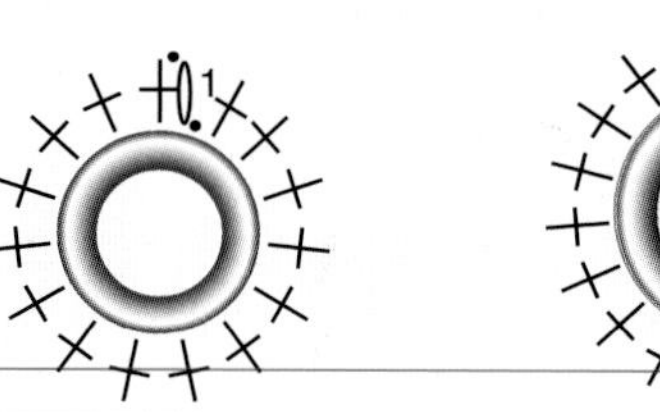

small ring

large ring

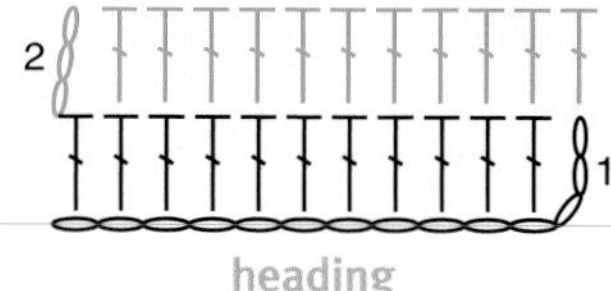

heading

points &

scallops

classic scallop

Colors A and B

(multiple of 6 sts + 1)

Edging

With A, make a foundation ch to desired length in a multiple of 6 sts + 2.

Row 1 Sl st in 2nd ch from hook, *skip 2 ch, 5 dc in next ch, skip 2 ch, sl st in next ch; rep from * to end. Fasten off.

Heading

With RS facing, attach B to right-hand edge of foundation ch.

Row 1 Ch 4, 1 tr in next ch and in each ch to end. Fasten off.

classic scallop

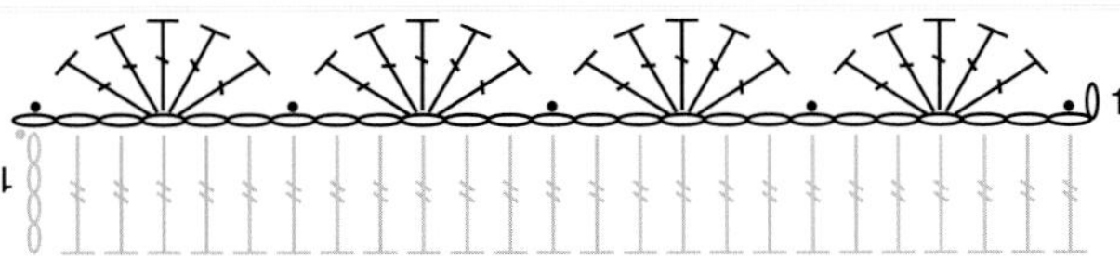

layered scallop I

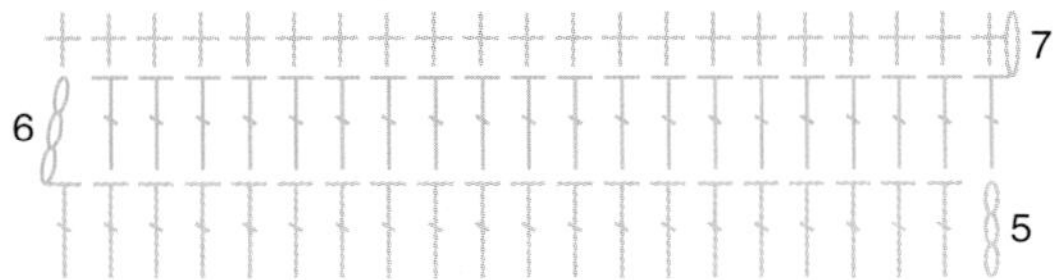

continued base

second row of scallops

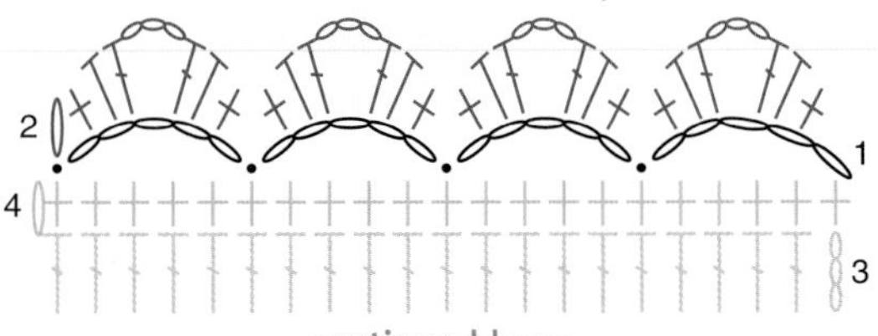

continued base

first row of scallops

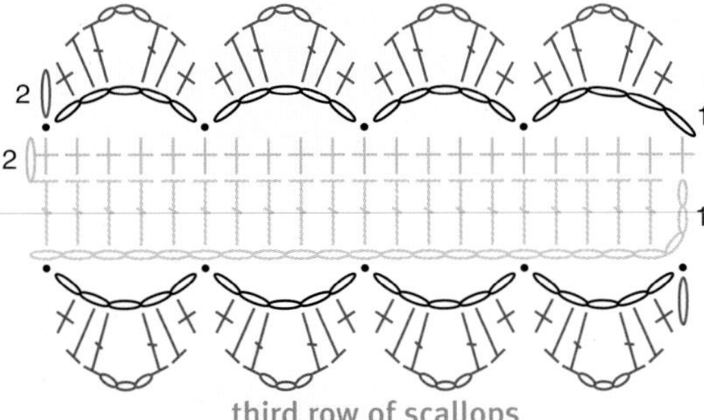

third row of scallops

layered scallop I

(multiple of 5 sts + 1)

Note This edging can be worked directly onto a project or onto the stitch pattern as shown and attached.

Base

Make a ch to desired length in a multiple of 5 sts + 3.

Row 1 1 dc in 4th ch from hook and in each ch to end. Turn.

Row 2 Ch 1, 1 sc in first dc and in each dc to end. Turn.

Cont to row 1 of edging.

First row of scallops

Row 1 *Ch 5, skip next 4 sts, sl st in next st; rep from * to end. Turn.

Row 2 Ch 1, *[1 sc, 1 hdc, 1 dc, ch 3, 1 dc, 1 hdc, 1 sc] in next ch-5 sp; rep from * to end. Turn.

Continued base

Row 3 Ch 3, 1 dc in next sc of row 2 and in each sc to end. Turn.

Row 4 Ch 1, 1 sc in first dc and in each dc to end. Turn.

2nd row of scallops

Work same as first row of scallops.

Continued base

Rows 5 and 6 Rep row 3 of cont'd heading.

Row 7 Rep row 4 of cont'd heading

Fasten off.

3rd row of scallops

With WS facing, attach yarn to right-hand edge of foundation ch. Work same as first row of scallops, end sl st to base of beg ch-5. Fasten off.

layered scallop II

▼ (multiple of 5 sts + 1)

Colors A and B

Base

With A, make a ch to desired length in a multiple of 5 sts + 3.

Row 1 1 dc in 4th ch from hook and in each ch to end. Turn.

Row 2 Ch 1, 1 sc in first dc and in each dc to end. Turn.

Cont to row 1 of edging.

First row of scallops

Drop A and pick up B.

Row 1 *Ch 5, skip next 4 sts, sl st in next st; rep from * to end. Turn.

Row 2 Ch 1, *[1 sc, 1 hdc, 1 dc, ch 3, 1 dc, 1 hdc, 1 sc] in next ch-5 sp; rep from * to end. Turn.

Continued base

Drop B and pick up A.

Row 3 Ch 3, 1 dc in next sc of row 2 and in each sc to end. Turn.

Row 4 Ch 1, 1 sc in first dc and in each dc to end. Turn.

2nd row of scallops

With A, work same as first row of scallops.

Continued base

Drop A and pick up B.

Rows 5 and 6 Rep row 3 of cont'd heading.

Row 7 Rep row 4 of cont'd heading

Fasten off.

3rd row of scallops

With WS facing, attach A to right-hand edge of foundation ch. Work same as first row of scallops, end sl st to base of beg ch-5. Fasten off. Fold over base.

layered scallop II

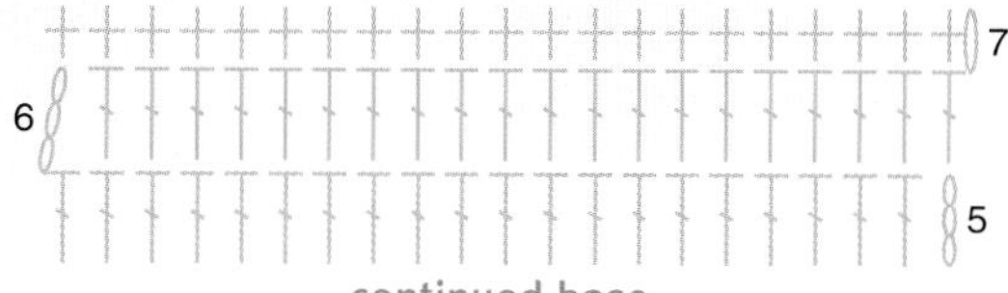

continued base

second row of scallops

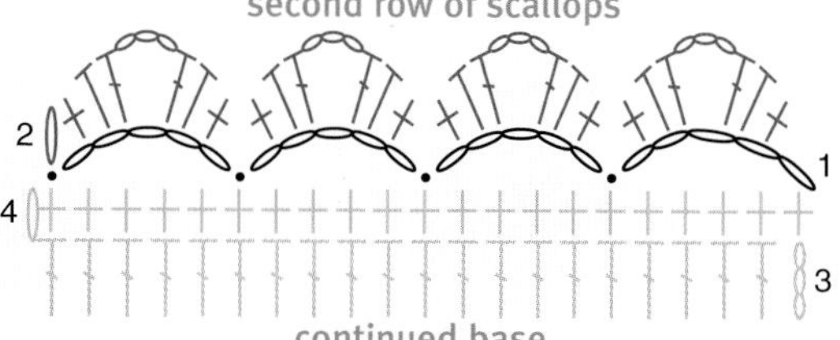

continued base

first row of scallops

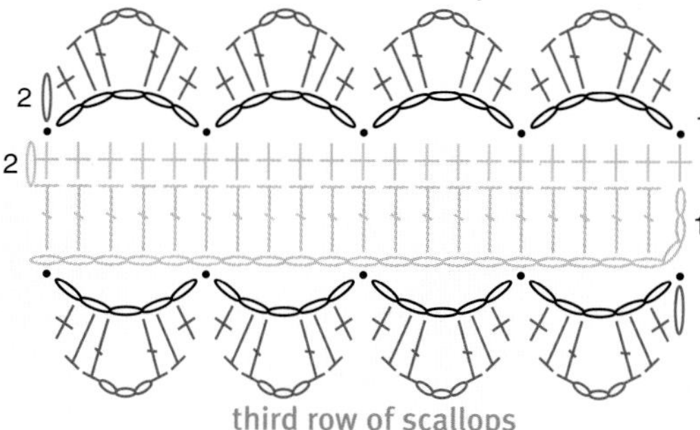

third row of scallops

nugget scallop

▼ (multiple of 8 sts + 1)

TCL (Tr Cluster) (Yo twice, insert hook in designated st and draw up a lp, [yo and draw through 2 lps on hook] twice) 3 times, yo and draw through all 4 lps on hook.

DTCL (Double Tr Cluster) *(Yo twice, insert hook in designated st and draw up a lp, [yo and draw through 2 lps on hook] twice) 3 times; rep from * in next designated st, yo and draw through all 7 lps on hook.

Make a ch to desired length in a multiple of 8 sts + 3.

Row 1 1 dc in 4th ch from hook and in each ch to end. Turn.

Row 2 Ch 5 (counts as 1 dc, ch 2), skip next 2 dc, *1 dc in next 3 dc, ch 2, skip 2 dc, 1 dc in next dc, ch 2, skip 2 dc; rep from *, end last rep 1 dc in dc. Turn.

Row 3 Ch 4, TCL in next ch-2 sp, ch 9, *DTCL over next 2 ch-2 sp, ch 9; rep from *, end [TCL, 1 tr] in last ch-2 sp. Turn.

Row 4 Ch 1, sl st in top of first TCL, *[1 sc, 1 hdc, 7 dc, 1 hdc, 1 sc] in ch-9 lp; rep from *, end sl st in top of last TCL.

Fasten off.

Optional Add beads where scallops and clusters join.

nugget scallop

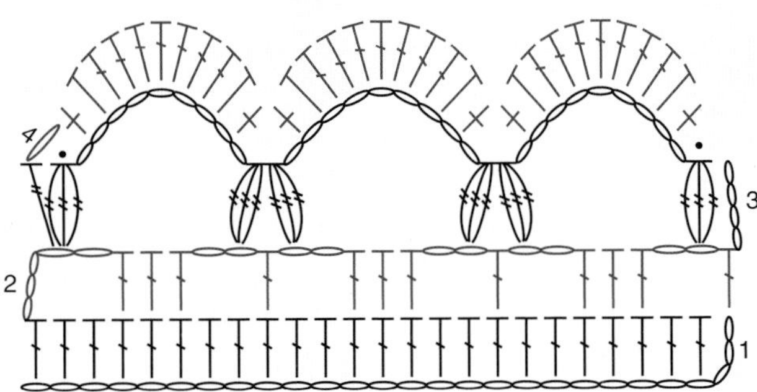

russian scallop

▲ (multiple of 6 sts + 1)

Make a ch to desired length in a multiple of 6 sts + 5.

Row 1 1 tr in 7th ch from hook, *ch 1, skip 1 ch, 1 tr in next ch; rep from * to end. Turn.

Row 2 Ch 3 (counts as 1 dc), skip first ch-1 sp, *[4 tr, ch 2, 4 tr] in next tr, skip next ch-1 sp, 1 dc in next tr, skip next ch-1 sp; rep from *, end last rep 1 dc in 5th ch of beg ch-6. Turn.

Row 3 Ch 1, 1 sc in same st, *ch 7, 1 sc in ch-2 sp; rep from *, end ch 7, 1 sc in top of beg ch-3. Turn.

Row 4 Ch 1, 1 sc in first sc, *[1 dc, 7 tr, 1 dc] in next ch-7 lp, 1 sc in next sc; rep from * to end.

Fasten off.

Optional Weave ribbon through top rows.

russian scallop

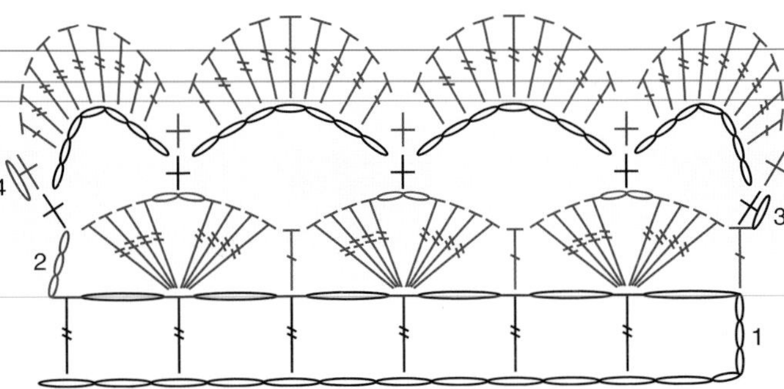

bodice scallop

▼ **Colors** A and B

(multiple of 9 sts + 1)

Heading

With A, make a ch to desired length in a multiple of 9 sts + 2.

Row 1 1 hdc in 3rd ch from hook and in each ch to end. Turn.

Row 2 Ch 2, 1 hdc in front lp of next hdc and in front lp of each hdc to end. Turn.

Row 3 Ch 2, 1 hdc in back lp of next hdc and in back lp of each hdc to end. Turn.

Cont to row 1 of edging.

Scallop

Row 1 (WS) With B, ch 2, 1 hdc in next hdc and in each hdc to end. Turn.

Fasten off B and attach A.

Row 2 With A, ch 1, 1 sc in first hdc and in each hdc to end. Turn.

Row 3 With A, ch 1, 1 sc in first sc, *ch 8, skip next 8 sc, 1 sc in next sc; rep from * to end. Turn.

Row 4 With A, ch 1, 1 sc in first sc, *[1 sc, 2 hdc, 3 dc, 3 tr, 3 dc, 2 hdc, 1 sc] in next ch-8 lp, 1 sc in next sc; rep from * to end. Fasten off A. With RS facing, join B at right-hand edge of edging.

Row 5 With B, ch 1, sc2tog, *1 sc in next 5 sts, [sl st, ch 4, sl st] in next 3 tr, 1 sc in next 5 sts, sc3tog; rep from *, end last rep sc2tog.

Fasten off.

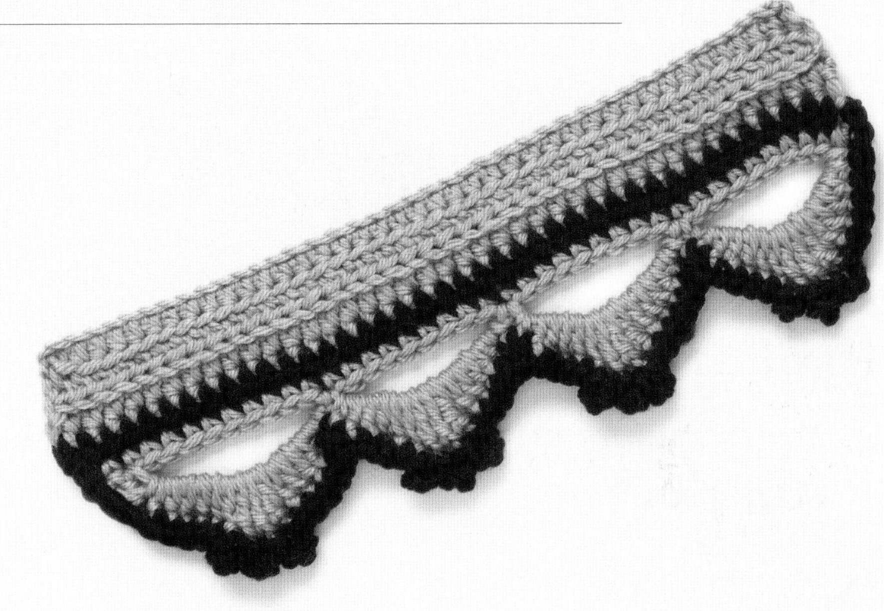

bodice scallop

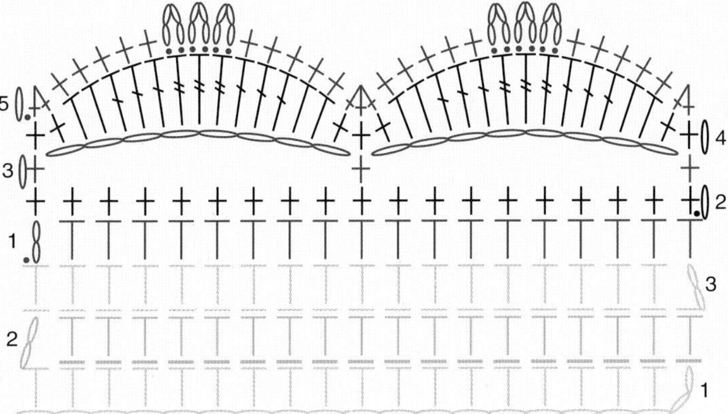

bold scallop

Colors A, B and C
(multiple of 10 sts + 1)

Scallop

With A, make a ch to desired length in a multiple of 10 sts + 2.

Row 1 (RS) With A, 1 sc in 2nd ch from hook, *skip next 4 ch, 12 tr in next ch, skip next 4 ch, 1 sc in next ch; rep from * to end. Turn.

Fasten off A. Attach B in top of first tr.

Row 2 With B, ch 3, 2 dc in same tr, 2 dc in next 11 tr, *sl st in next sc, 2 dc in next 12 tr; rep from * to end.

Fasten off.

Heading

With RS facing and working along foundation ch, attach C in top of first dc at right-hand edge of row 2.

Row 1 Ch 2 (counts as 1 hdc), 1 hdc into side of dc, 1 hdc into side of sc, 1 hdc in each ch to end, 1 hdc into side of sc, 2 hdc into side of dc. Turn.

Rows 2 and 3 Ch 2 (counts as 1 hdc), 1 hdc in next hdc and in each hdc to end. Turn.

Fasten off.

bold scallop

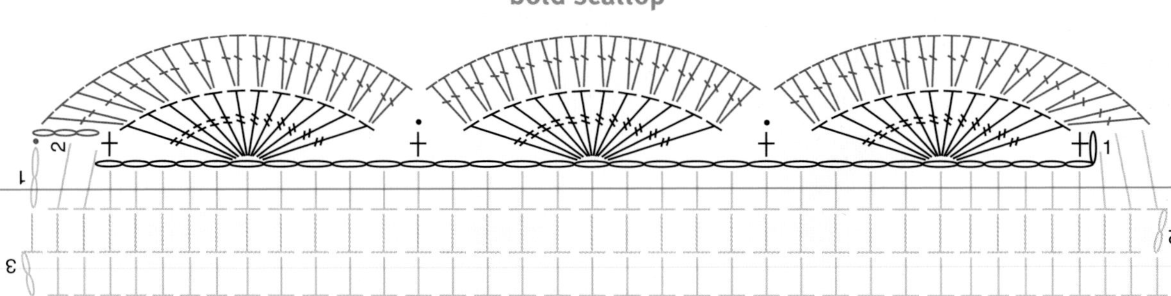

topsy turvy

Make a ch to desired length in a multiple of 2 sts.

Row 1 1 Sc in 2nd ch from hook and in each ch to end. Turn.

Row 2 *Ch 5, skip next sc, sl st in next sc; rep from * to end. Turn.

Row 3 Ch 1, *1 sc in next ch-5 sp, [ch 3, 1 sc] 5 times in same sp; rep from * to end.

Fasten off.

topsy turvy

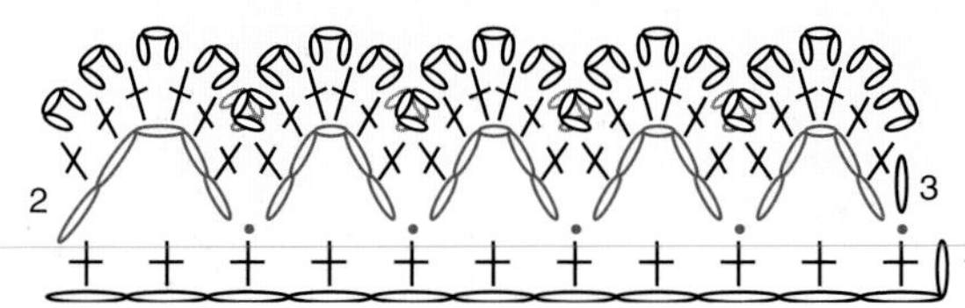

cameo scallop

Scallop

Ch 16.

Row 1 1 Tr in 12th ch from hook. Turn.

Row 2 Ch 4, 24 tr in ring, skip next 3 ch of beg ch-16, sl st in last ch. Turn.

Row 3 *Ch 4, skip next tr, 1 sc in next tr; rep from * to end, leaving beg ch-4 unworked—12 lps.

Row 4 Ch 20, 1 tr in 12th ch from hook. Turn.

Row 5 Ch 4, 24 tr in ring, skip 3 ch of beg ch-20, sl st in next ch.

Row 6 Join to previous scallop by ch 2, sl st in last ch-4 lp of previous scallop, ch 2, skip next tr of current scallop, 1 sc in next tr, *ch 4, skip next tr, 1 sc in next tr; rep from * to end, leaving beg ch-4 unworked—12 lps including joining lp.

Rep rows 4–6 for length desired. Turn and cont to row 1 of heading, working along top edges of scallops.

Band

Row 1 Ch 6, *[1 tr, ch 5, 1 tr] in side of tr in ring, ch 3, [1 tr, ch 5, 1 tr] in ch-4 sp between scallops, ch 3; rep from *, end last rep 1 tr in last ch-4 lp of last scallop. Turn.

Row 2 Ch 1, *1 sc in next tr, ch 3, skip next ch-3 sp, 1 sc in next tr, ch 5, skip next ch-5 lp; rep from *, end last rep ch 3, skip next ch-3 sp, 1 sc in 3rd ch of beg ch-6. Turn.

Row 3 Ch 2 (counts as 1 hdc), 2 hdc in first ch-3 sp, *5 hdc in next ch-5 sp, 3 hdc in next ch-3 sp; rep from * to end. Turn.

Rows 4 and 5 Ch 2 (counts as 1 hdc), 1 hdc in next hdc and in each hdc to end. Turn.

Fasten off.

Optional If desired, run a strand of beads through stitches between rows 2 and 3 of band.

cameo scallop

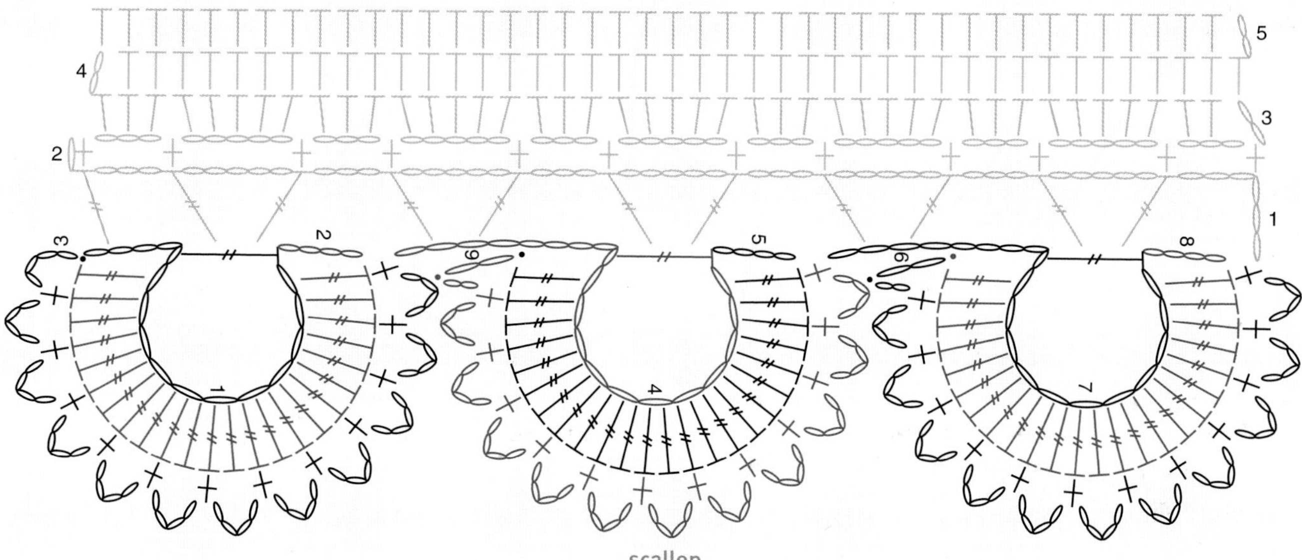

scallop

eileen's edge

14mm pearl beads

Make a ch to desired length in a multiple of 11 sts + 2.

Row 1 1 sc in 2nd ch from hook and in next 5 ch, *ch 5, 1 sc in next 11 ch; rep from *, end last rep ch 5, 1 sc in last 6 ch. Turn.

Row 2 Ch 1, 1 sc in first 3 sc, *ch 3, 9 tr in next ch-5 lp, ch 3, skip 3 sc, 1 sc in next 5 sc; rep from *, end last rep 1 sc in last 3 sc. Turn.

Row 3 *Ch 5, skip next tr, 1 tr in next tr [ch 1, 1 tr in next tr] 7 times, ch 5, skip 2 sc, 1 sc in next sc; rep from * to end. Turn.

Row 4 Ch 1, *5 sc in ch-5 lp, [1 sc in next ch-1 sp, ch 3] 6 times, 1 sc in next ch-1 sp, [5 sc in next ch-5 lp]; rep from * to end.

Fasten off.

Heading

With RS facing, attach yarn to right-hand edge of scallop.

Row 1 Ch 4, 1 tr in next foundation ch and in each ch to end.

Fasten off.

Optional If desired, sew a bead over each ch-5 lp of row 1 of scallop.

eileen's edge

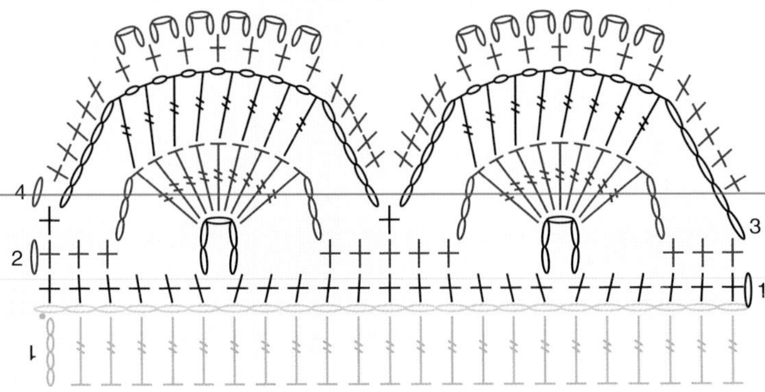

lila

Colors A and B

Scallop

TCL (Tr Cluster) (Yo twice, insert hook in designated st and draw up a lp, [yo and draw through 2 lps on hook] twice) 3 times, yo and draw through all 4 lps on hook.

With A, ch 11.

Row 1 TCL in 11th ch from hook. Turn.

Row 2 Ch 5, 1 dc in TCL. Turn.

Row 3 Ch 10, TCL in dc. Turn.

Rep rows 2 and 3 to length desired, ending with row 3. Do not turn.

Finishing row Working along straight edge of scallop, ch 5, *[TCL, ch 3, TCL] in next ch-5 lp, ch 3; rep from *, end last rep ch 5, sl st in base of first TCL.

Fasten off A and attach B.

Picot row Working around to opposite side, **([3 sc, ch 3] 3 times in next ch-10 lp, 3 sc in same lp, 1 sc in dc sp of row 2; rep from **, ending last rep 3 sc in same lp.

Cont to row 1 of heading.

Top row

Row 1 With B, ch 7 (working around to straight edge of scallop), *3 dc in next ch-5 lp, 1 dc in next TCL; rep from *, end 3 dc in last ch-5 lp, ch 7, sl st in first sc of picot row.

Fasten off.

If desired, sew a bead at the center of each flower.

lace shell

Scallop

Ch 11.

Row 1 3 dc in 11th ch from hook. Turn.

Rows 2, 3 and 4 Ch 5, 3 dc in first dc. Turn.

Row 5 Ch 10, 3 dc in first dc. Turn.

Rep rows 2–5 for length desired with an uneven number of ch-10 loops.

Finishing rnd Work across edge opposite to ch-10 lps as foll: *Ch 5, [1 dc, ch 2, 1 dc] in next ch-5 lp; rep from *, end ch 5, sl st in base of first 3-dc group. Cont around to opposite edge, sl st in next ch-10 lp, ch 4 (counts as 1 dc, ch 1), [1 dc in same lp, ch 1] 5 times, 1 dc in same lp,*ch 3, 1 sc in next ch-5 lp, ch 3, 1 dc in next ch-10 lp, [ch 1, 1 dc in same lp] 6 times; rep from * to end. Turn.

Picot row Ch 1, *1 sc in next ch-1 sp, [ch 3, 1 sc in next ch-1 sp] 5 times, [3 sc in next ch-ch-3 sp] twice; rep from *, end 1 sc in next ch-1 sp, [ch 3, 1 sc in next ch-1 sp] 5 times. Fasten off.

Band

With RS facing, attach yarn to right-hand edge of straight edge.

Row 1 Ch 3, 2 dc in first sp, *2 dc in next ch-2 sp, 5 dc in next ch-5 sp; rep from *, end last rep 3 dc in last sp. Fasten off.

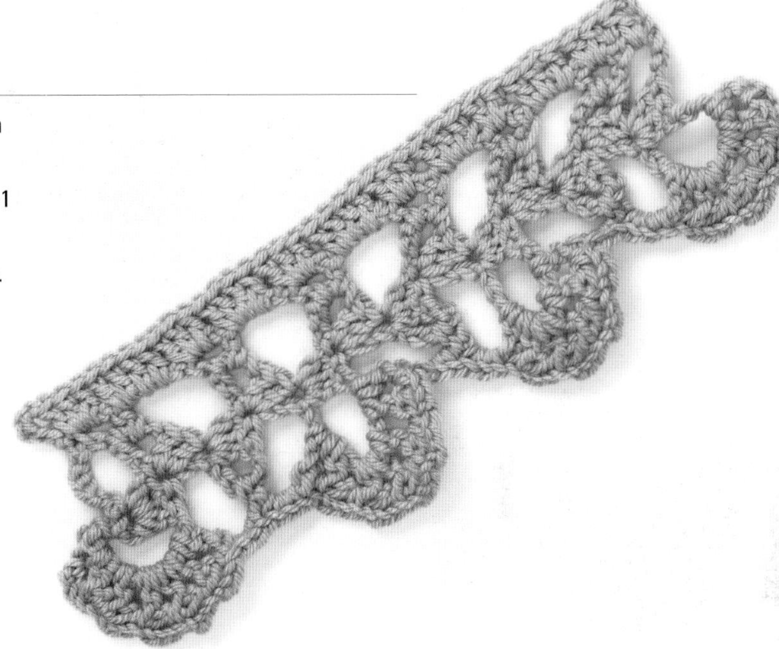

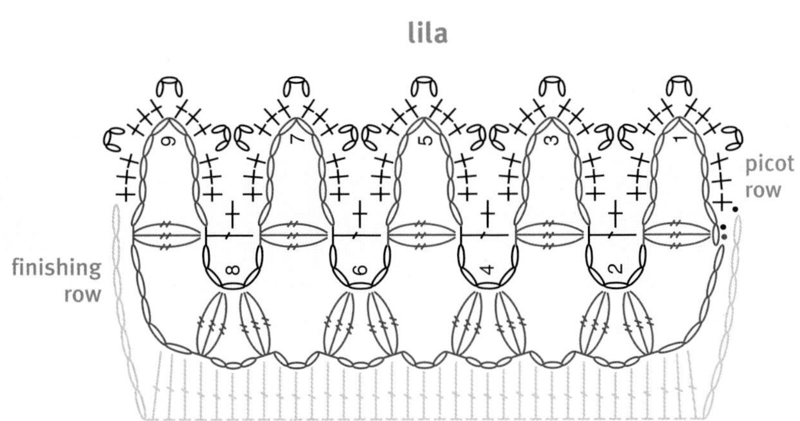

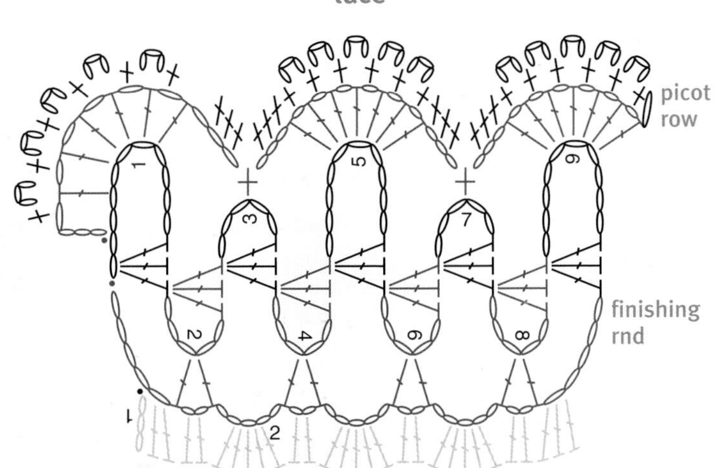

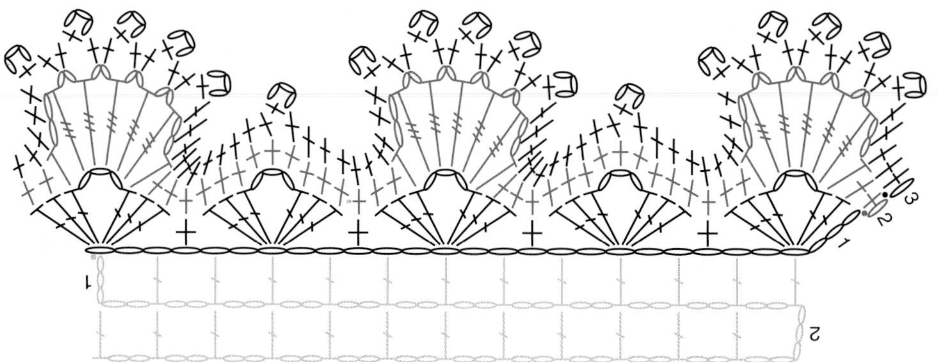

princess anne

▼ (multiple of 12 sts + 2)

Colors A and B

Scallop

With A, make a ch to desired length in a multiple of 12 sts + 4).

Row 1 [2 dc, ch 3, 3 dc] in 4th ch from hook, *skip 2 ch, 1 sc in next ch, skip 2 ch, [3 dc, ch 3, 3 dc] in next ch; rep from * to end. Fasten off A. With RS facing, attach B to top of beg ch-3 of row 1.

Row 2 Ch 1, 1 sc in same st, 1 sc in next dc, *1 hdc in next dc, ch 2, [1 dtr, ch 2] 4 times in next ch-3 sp, 1 dtr in same sp, ch 2, 1 hdc in next dc**, 1 sc in next 6 sts, 3 sc in next ch-3 sp, 1 sc in next 6 sts; rep from *, end last rep at **, 1 sc in last 2 sts. Fasten off B. With RS facing, attach A to first sc of row 2.

Row 3 Ch 1, 1 sc in same st, 1 sc in next 2 sts, *2 sc in next ch-2 sp, [ch 3, 1 sc in last sc made, 2 sc in next ch-2 sp] 4 times, ch 3, 1 sc in last sc made, 2 sc in next ch 2 sp, **1 sc in next 8 sts, ch 3, 1 sc in last sc made, 1 sc in next 8 sts; rep from *, end last rep at **, 1 sc in last 3 sts.

Fasten off,

Heading

With A and RS facing, working along foundation ch, attach yarn to right-hand edge.

Row 1 Ch 5 (counts as 1 dc, ch 2), *skip 1 ch, 1 dc in next ch, ch 2; rep from *, end 1 dc in last ch. Turn.

Row 2 Ch 5, *1 dc in next dc, ch 2; rep from *, end 1 dc in 3rd ch of beg ch-5. Fasten off.

Sew beads as desired.

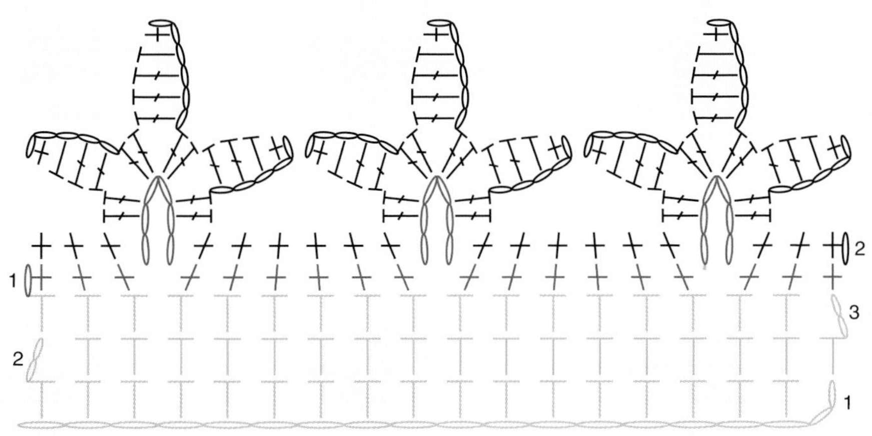

twinkle

▼ **Colors** A and B

(multiple of 6 sts)

Note This edging can be worked directly onto a project or into a chain and attached.

Band

With A, make a ch in a multiple of 6 sts + 1.

Row 1 1 hdc in 3rd ch from hook and in each ch to end. Turn.

Rows 2 and 3 Ch 2 (counts as 1 hdc), 1 hdc in next hdc and in each hdc to end. Turn.

Fasten off.

Scallop

With WS facing, attach B to right-hand edge of project or chain a multiple of 6 sts.

Row 1 Ch 1, 1 sc in first 3 sts or ch, *ch 6, 1 sc in next 6 sts or ch; rep from *, end ch 6, 1 sc in last 3 sts or ch. Turn.

Row 2 Ch 1, 1 sc in first 3 sc, *2 dc in next ch-6 lp, ch 5, 1 sc in 2nd ch from hook, 1 hdc in next ch, 1 dc in next 2 ch, 2 dc in same lp (first point made), ch 6, 1 sc in 2nd ch from hook, 1 hdc in next ch, 1 dc in next 3 ch, 2 dc in same lp (2nd point made), ch 5, 1 sc in 2nd ch from hook, 1 hdc in next ch, 1 dc in next 2 ch, 2 dc in same lp (3rd point made), 1 sc in next 6 sc; rep from *, end last rep 1 sc in last 3 sc.

Fasten off.

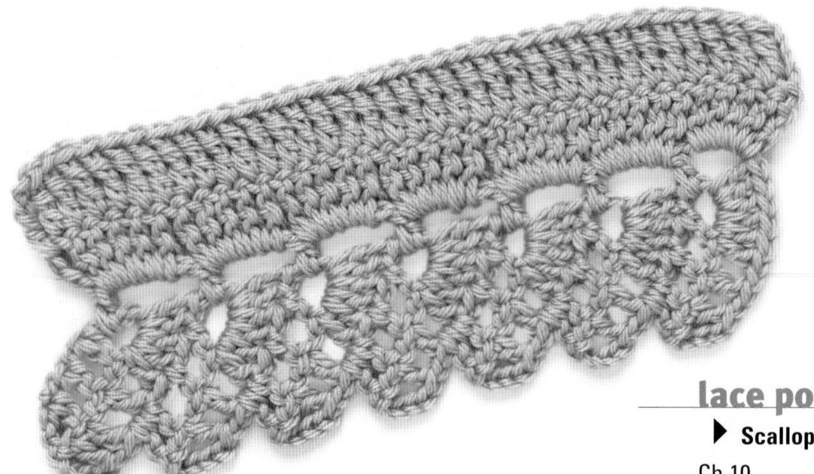

lace points

Scallop

Ch 10.

Row 1 1 dc in 6th ch from hook, ch 1, skip 1 ch, 1 dc in next ch, ch 1, skip 1 ch, [1 dc, ch 1, 1 dc] in last ch. Turn.

Row 2 Ch 4, [1 dc in next dc, ch 1] twice, 1 dc in next dc, 5 dc in ch-6 sp. Turn.

Row 3 Ch 5, 1 dc in next dc, [ch 1, skip 1 dc, 1 dc in next dc] twice, ch 1, 1 dc in ch-1 sp. Turn.

Rep rows 2 and 3 to desired length ending with row 2.

Do not turn.

Cont to row 1 of heading.

Band

Row 1 Working along straight edge of scallop, ch 7 (counts as 1 dc, ch 4), 1 dc in first ch-5 sp, *ch 4, 1 dc in next ch-5 sp; rep from * to end. Turn.

Row 2 Ch 4 (counts as 1 tr), 4 tr in first ch-4 sp, *5 tr in next ch-4 sp; rep from * to end. Turn.

Row 3 Ch 4, 1 tr in next tr and in each tr to end.

Fasten off.

lace points

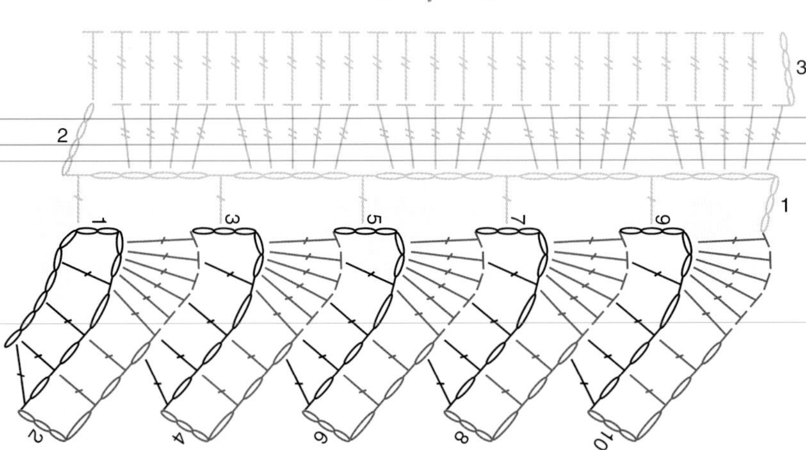

shade

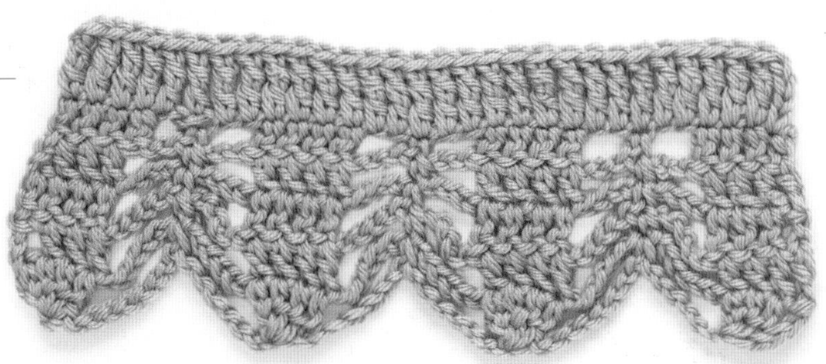

▼ (multiple of 9 sts + 4)

Beg DCL (Beg Dc Cluster) [Yo, insert hook in designated st and draw up a loop, yo and draw through 2 lps on hook] 3 times, yo and draw through all 4 lps on hook.

DCL (Dc Cluster) [Yo, insert hook in designated st and draw up a loop, yo and draw through 2 lps on hook] 4 times, yo and draw through all 5 lps on hook.

Scallop

Make a ch to desired length in a multiple of 9 sts + 6.

Row 1 1 Dc in 4th ch from hook, 1 dc in next 2 ch, *ch 3, skip 2 ch, 1 sc in next ch, ch 3, skip 2 ch, 1 dc in next 4 ch; rep from * to end. Turn.

Row 2 Ch 3, 1 dc in next 3 dc, *ch 4, 1 sc in next sc, ch 4, 1 dc in next 4 dc; rep from * to end. Turn.

Row 3 Ch 3, 1 dc in next 3 dc, *ch 5, 1 sc in next sc, ch 5, 1 dc in next 4 dc; rep from * to end. Turn.

Row 4 Ch 3, 1 dc in next 3 dc, *ch 6, 1 sc in next sc, ch 6, 1 dc in next 4 dc; rep from * to end. Turn.

Row 5 Ch 3, Beg DCL over next 3 dc, *ch 7, 1 sc in next sc, ch 7, DCL over next 4 dc; rep from * to end.

Fasten off.

Heading

Working across foundation ch, attach yarn to right-hand edge.

Row 1 Ch 4, 1 tr in next ch and in each ch to end.

Fasten off.

shade

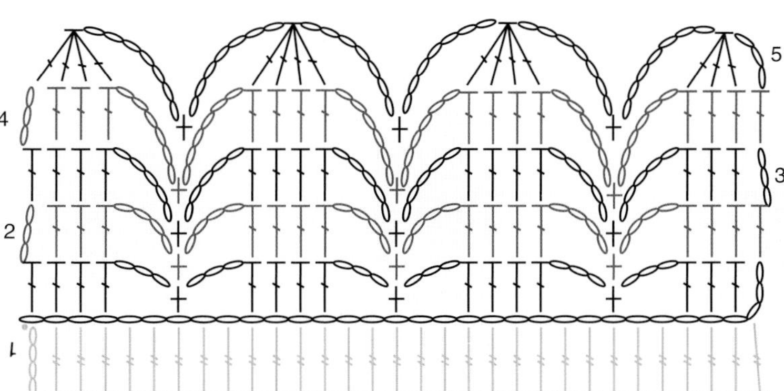

pomegranate

▼ (multiple of 10 sts + 2)

TCL (Tr Cluster) (Yo twice, insert hook in designated st and draw up a lp, [yo and draw through 2 lps on hook] twice) 7 times, yo and draw through all 8 lps on hook.

Scallop

Make a ch to desired length in a multiple of 10 sts + 3.

Row 1 1 Sc in 2nd ch from hook, *ch 5, 1 sc in next 5 ch; rep from *, end last rep ch 5, 1 sc in last ch. Turn.

Row 2 Ch 1, sl st in first sc, sl st in first 2 ch of ch-5 lp, ch 1, 2 sc in same lp,*ch 3, 7 tr in next ch-5 lp, ch 3, 3 sc in next ch-5 lp; rep from *, end last rep 2 sc in last ch-5 lp. Turn.

Row 3 Ch 1, 1 sc in first sc, *ch 7, TCL over next 7 tr, ch 7, skip next sc, 1 sc in next sc; rep from *, end last rep 1 sc in last sc. Turn.

Row 4 Ch 1, *7 sc in next ch-7 lp, [ch 7, 1 sc in 7th ch from hook] 3 times, 7 sc in next ch-7 lp; rep from * to end.

Fasten off.

Heading

Working across foundation ch of scallop, attach yarn to first ch.

Row 1 Ch 4, 1 tr in next ch and in each ch to end. Fasten off.

pomegranate

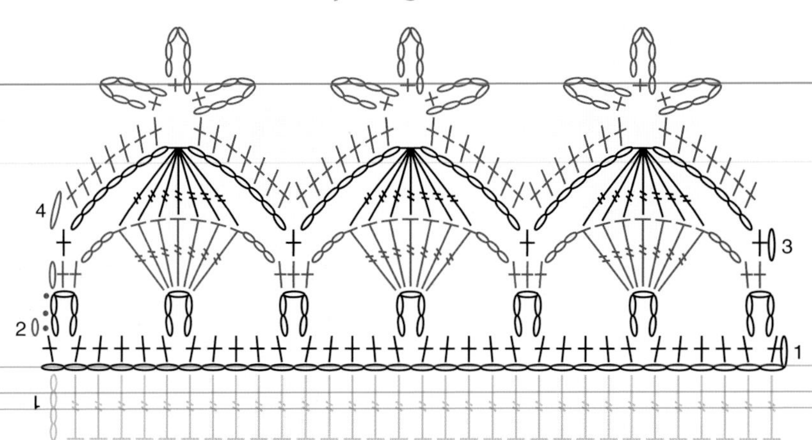

pleasure

▲ **TCL (Tr Cluster)** (Yo twice, insert hook in designated st and draw up a lp, [yo and draw through 2 lps on hook] twice) 3 times, yo and draw through all 4 lps on hook.

Scallop

Ch 11.

Row 1 TCL in 11th ch from hook. Turn.

Row 2 Ch 5, TCL in TCL. Turn.

Row 3 Ch 10, TCL in TCL. Turn.

Rep rows 2 and 3 to length desired.

Finishing row Working along edge of scallop, ch 3*, [7 dc, ch 5, 7 dc] in next ch-10 lp; rep from *, end 1 dc in base of first TCL. Turn.

Next row Ch 7, *[1 dc, ch 2, 1 sc in just made dc] 4 times in ch-5 lp, 1 dc in same lp**, ch 2 [1 dc, ch 3, 1 dc, ch 2] in space between next two 7-tr groups; rep from *, end last rep at **, ch 7, sl st in top of beg ch-3. Fasten off.

Top rows

Attach yarn to first ch-3 lp on straight edge of scallop.

Row 1 Working along straight edge of scallop, ch 3, 2 dc in same sp, *ch 6, 3 dc in next ch-5 sp; rep from *, end last rep ch 6, 3 dc into side of last dc of finishing row. Turn.

Row 2 Ch 3 (counts as 1 dc), 1 dc in next 2 dc, *ch 6, 1 dc in next 3 dc; rep from * to end. Turn.

Row 3 Ch 2 (counts as 1 hdc), 1 hdc in next 2 dc, *6 hdc in next ch-6 sp, 1 hdc in next 3 dc; rep from * to end. Turn.

Rows 4 and 5 Ch 2 (counts as 1 hdc), 1 hdc in next hdc and in each hdc to end. Turn.

Fasten off.

Optional If desired, add dangling beads in-between scallops.

pleasure

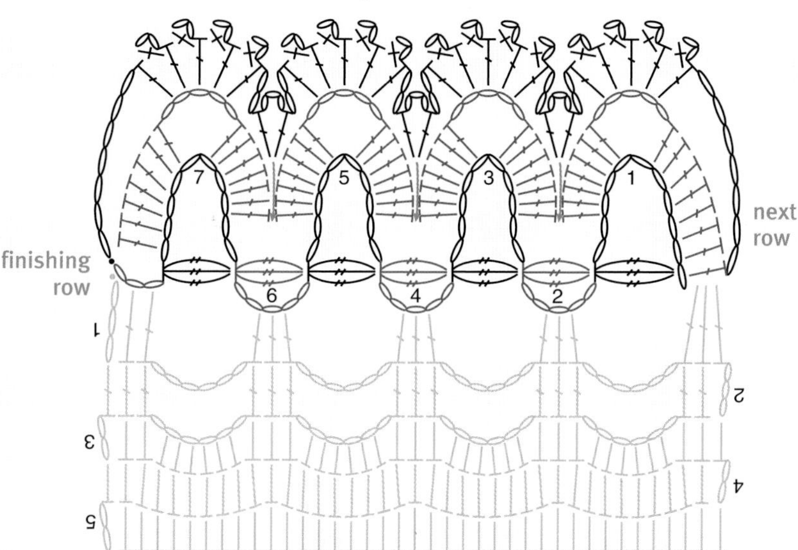

crown points

▶ **Colors** A and B

Edging

Triangle

Note Each triangle is made separately.

Ch 2.

Row 1 1 sc in 2nd ch from hook. Turn.

Row 2 Ch 1, 2 sc in sc. Turn.

Rows 3 through 9 Ch 1, 2 sc in first sc, 1 sc in each sc to end. Turn.

Do not turn after row 9—9 sc.

Rotate to work along sloping sides of triangle.

Finishing row Ch 1, 1 sc into edge of next 8 rows, 6 dc in tip of triangle, drop lp and insert hook in top of first dc, pick up dropped lp, yo and draw through both lps on hook, 1 sc into edge of next 8 rows. Join with sl st in first sc of row 9.

Fasten off.

Make desired number of triangles.

Joining row

Attach B to right-hand top edge of first triangle.

Row 1 (join triangles) Ch 3, 1 dc in next sc and in each sc to end; rep from * for each triangle. Turn.

Row 2 Ch 3, 1 dc in next dc and in each dc to end. Fasten off.

crown points

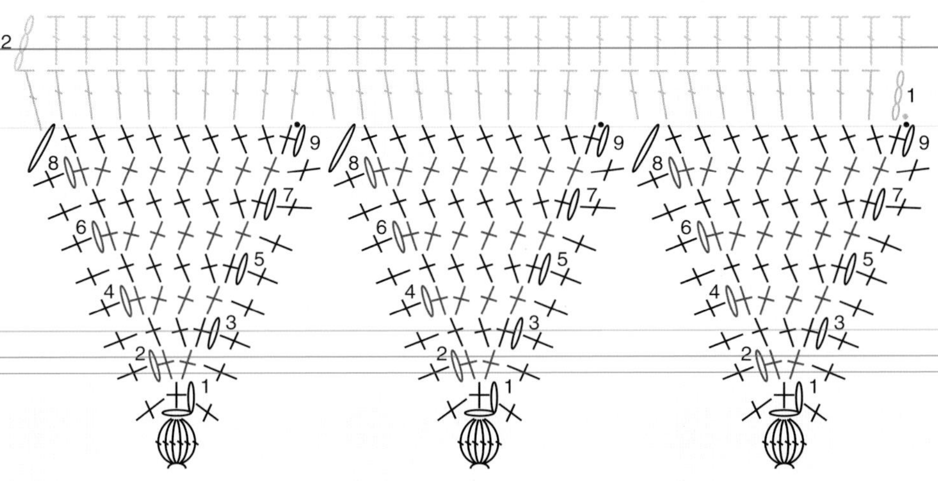

jester points

▶ **Colors** A, B, C and D

Edging

Triangle

Note Each triangle is made separately in color desired.

Ch 2.

Row 1 1 sc in 2nd ch from hook. Turn.

Row 2 Ch 1, 2 sc in sc. Turn.

Rows 3, 4, 5, 6 and 7 Ch 1, 2 sc in first sc, 1 sc in each sc to end. Turn.

Do not turn after row 7—7 sc.

Rotate to work along sloping sides of triangle.

Finishing row Ch 1, 1 sc into edge of next 6 rows, 3 sc in tip of triangle, 1 sc into edge of next 6 rows. Join with sl st in first sc of row 7.

Fasten off.

Make desired number of triangles.

Band

Attach yarn to right-hand top edge of first triangle.

Row 1 (join triangles) Ch 1, *1 sc in first sc and in each sc to end; rep from * for each triangle. Turn.

Row 2 Ch 3, 1 dc in next sc and in each sc to end. Fasten off.

jester points

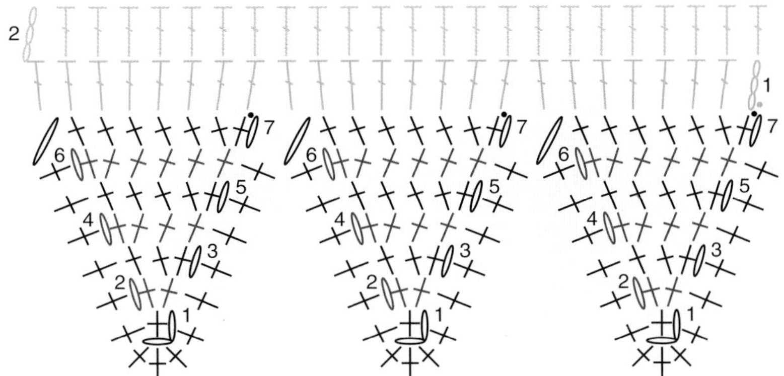

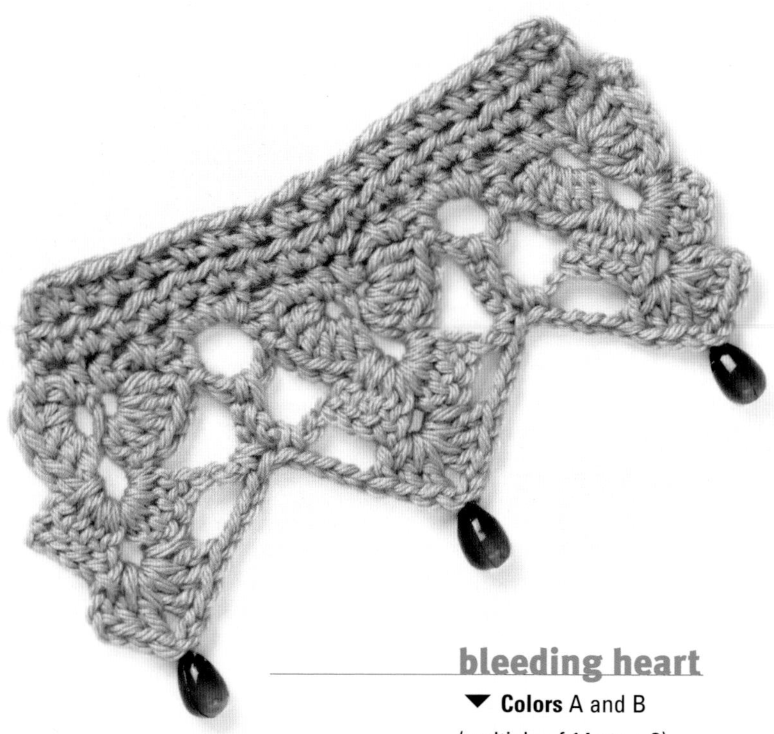

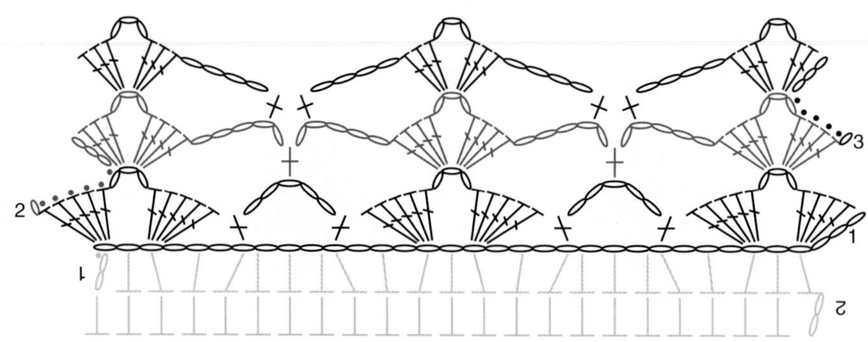

bleeding heart

▼ **Colors** A and B

(multiple of 14 sts + 3)

Edging

With A, make a ch in a multiple of 14 sts + 6.

Row 1 4 dc in 4th ch from hook, *ch 3, skip 1 ch, 5 dc in next ch, skip 3 ch, 1 sc in next ch, ch 5, skip 3 ch, 1 sc in next ch, skip 3 ch, 5 dc in next ch; rep from *, end ch 3, skip 1 ch, 5 dc in last ch. Turn.

Row 2 Ch 1, sl st in first 5 dc, sl st in ch-3 sp, ch 3, 3 dc in same sp, ch 3, 4 dc in same place, *ch 5, 1 sc in ch-5 loop, ch 5, [4 dc, ch 3, 4 dc] in next ch-3 sp; rep from * to end. Turn.

Row 3 Ch 1, sl st in first 4 dc, sl st in ch-3 sp, ch 3, 2 dc in same sp, ch 3, 3 dc in same sp, *ch 4, 1 sc in next 2 ch-5 sp, ch 4, [3 dc, ch 3, 3 dc] in next ch-3 sp; rep from * to end. Fasten off.

Top rows

Working across foundation ch, attach B to right-hand edge in space made by last dc of row 1.

Row 1 Ch 2 (counts as 1 hdc), *1 hdc in next 2 ch of foundation ch, 1 hdc in next ch-3 sp, 1 hdc in next ch at base of sc, 3 hdc in next ch-3 sp, 1 hdc in next ch at base of sc, 1 hdc in ch-3 sp, 1 hdc in next ch; rep from *, end 1 hdc in last 2 ch of foundation ch. Turn.

Rows 2 and 3 Ch 2 (counts as 1 hdc), 1 hdc in next hdc and in each hdc to end. Turn.

Fasten off.

Optional If desired, add a dangling bead at each point.

window box

▼ (multiple of 5 sts + 2)

CL (Cluster) [Yo, insert hook in st and draw up a lp, yo and draw through 2 lps on hook] twice, yo and draw through all 3 lps on hook.

Scallop

Make a ch to desired length in a multiple of 5 sts + 3.

Row 1 1 sc in 2nd ch from hook, 1 sc in next ch, *ch 3, skip 3 ch, 1 sc in next 2 ch; rep from * to end. Turn.

Row 2 Ch 1, 1 sc in first 2 sts, *ch 3, skip next ch-3 sp, 1 sc in next 2 sts; rep from * to end. Turn.

Row 3 Ch 3, 1 dc in next st, *ch 3, skip next ch-3 sp, 1 dc in next 2 sts; rep from * to end. Turn.

Rows 4–7 Rep rows 2 and 3.

Row 8 Rep row 2.

Row 9 Ch 3, 1 dc in next sc, *ch 6, CL over next 2 sc; rep from * to end. Turn.

Fasten off A. Attach B to right-hand edge.

Row 10 Ch 1, 1 sc in first CL, 2 sc in next ch-6 lp, *[ch 3, 1 sc] 5 times in same lp, 2 sc in same lp, ** 2 sc in next ch-6 lp; rep from *, end last rep at **, 1 sc in top of beg ch-3.

Fasten off.

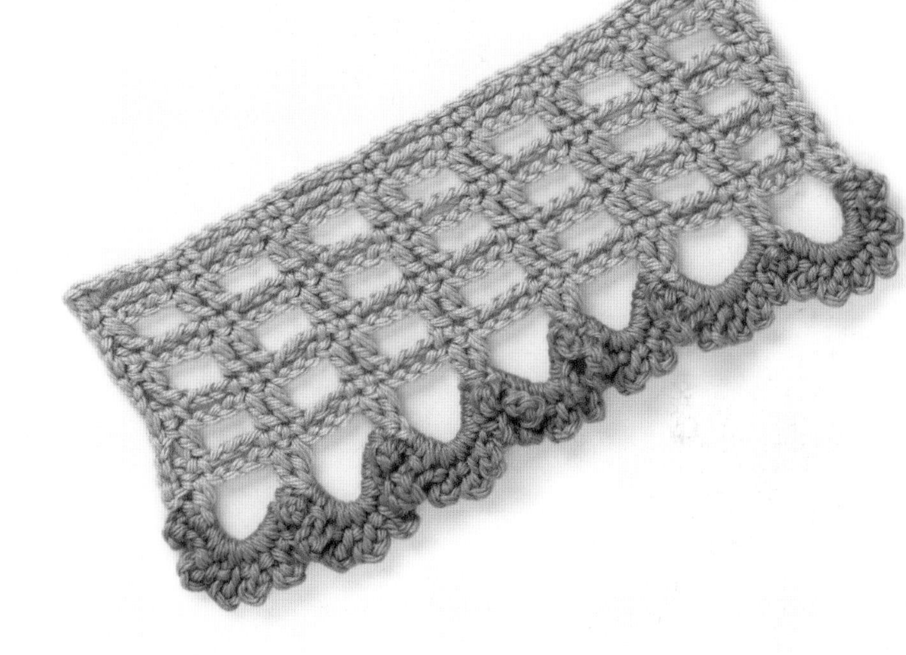

window box

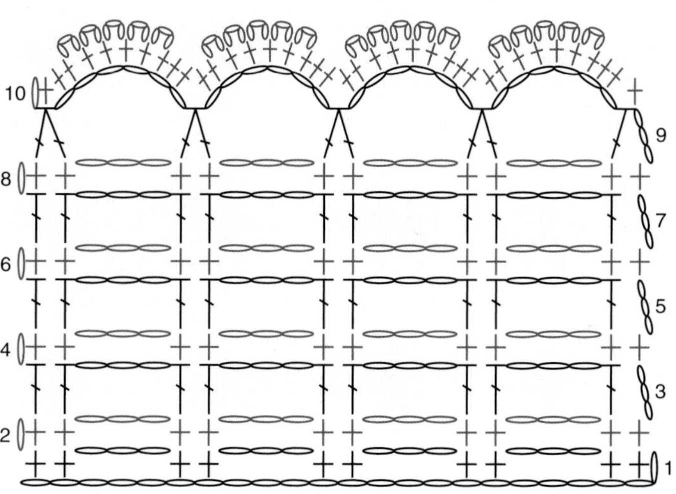

fanny may

▼ (multiple of 13 sts)

Scallop

Make a ch to desired length in a multiple of 13 sts.

Row 1 1 dc in 4th ch from hook and in next 3 ch, 3 dc in next ch, 1 dc in next 5 ch, *skip 2 ch, 1 dc in next 5 ch, 3 dc in next ch, 1 dc in next 5 ch; rep from * to end. Turn.

Row 2 Ch 3, skip next dc, 1 dc in next 4 dc, 3 dc in next dc, 1 dc in next 5 dc, *skip 2 dc, 1 dc in next 5 dc, 3 dc in next dc, 1 dc in next 5 dc; rep from *, end last rep 1 dc in next 4 dc, skip 1 dc, 1 dc in top of beg ch-3. Turn.

Rep row 2 to desired length.

Row 5 (Picot row) Ch 3, skip next dc, 1 dc in next 4 dc, *[ch 5, 1 sc in dc just made, 1 dc in next dc] 6 times, skip 2 dc, [ch 5, 1 sc in dc just made, 1 dc in next dc] 5 times; rep from *, end [ch 5, 1 sc in dc just made, 1 dc in next dc] twice, 1 dc in next 3 dc, skip next dc, 1 dc in top of beg ch-3.

Fasten off.

fanny may

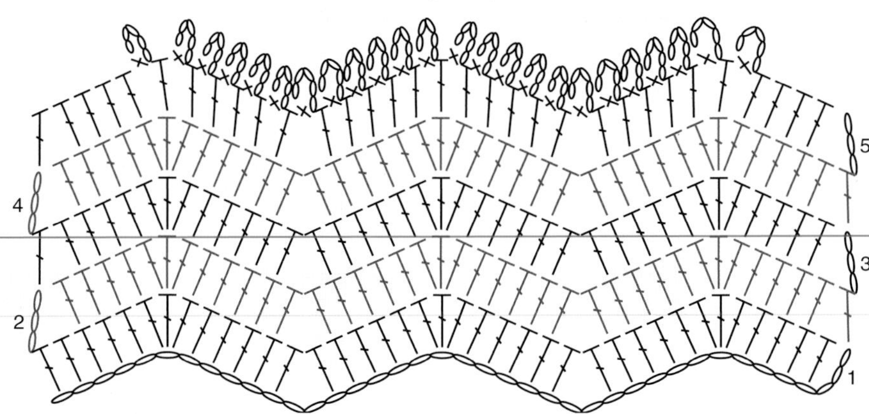

fanfare

▼ Scallop

Ch 11.

Row 1 *1 Dc in 5th ch from hook, ch 16; rep from * for desired length, end 1 dc in 5th ch from hook. Turn.

Row 2 Ch 9, *1 tr in next ch-4 lp, [ch 1, 1 tr] 6 times in same lp, ch 2, skip 5 ch, 1 sc in next ch, ch 2; rep from *, end 1 sc in last ch. Turn

Row 3 Ch 4, *[1 tr in next tr, ch 1] 3 times, [1 tr, ch 1] 3 times in next tr, [1 tr in next tr, ch 1] twice, 1 tr in next tr; rep from *, end 1 tr in 7th ch of beg ch-9. Turn.

Row 4 Ch 5 (counts as 1 tr, ch 1), skip next tr, *[1 tr in next tr, ch 1] 3 times, [1 tr, ch 1] 3 times in next tr, [1 tr in next tr, ch 1] twice, 1 tr in next tr, skip 2 tr; rep from *, end last rep skip 1 tr, 1 tr in top of beg ch-4. turn.

Row 5 Ch 1, 1 sc in first tr, [ch 3, 1 sc in next tr] 5 times, *ch 3, 1 sc in same tr, [ch 3, 1 sc in next tr] 3 times**, ch 3, 1 sc between next 2 tr, ch 3, skip next tr, 1 sc in next tr, [ch 3, 1 sc in next tr] 3 times; rep from *, end last rep at **, ch 3, 1 sc in next tr, ch 3, 1 sc in 4th ch of beg ch-6.

Fasten off.

Band

Working across foundation ch, attach yarn to right-hand edge.

Row 1 Ch 4, 1 tr in next ch and in each ch to end, working 2 tr into side of each dc.

Fasten off.

fanfare

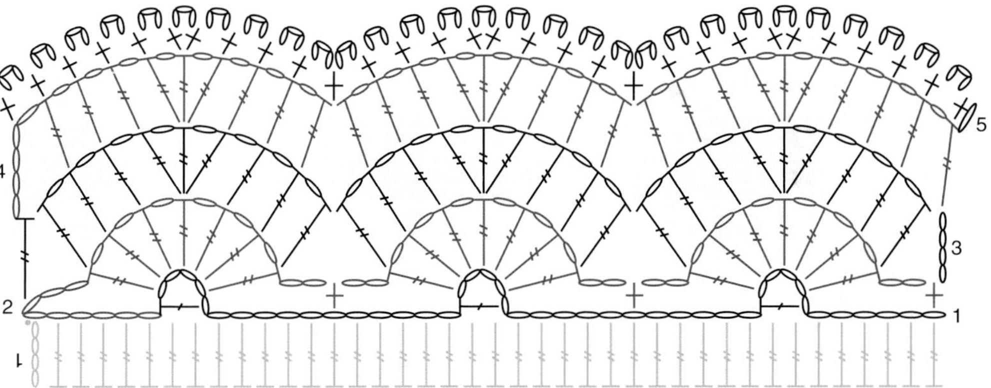

butterfly

▲ (multiple of 6 sts + 27)

Colors A and B

Butterfly

With A, ch 5.

Row 1 3 Dc in 3rd ch from hook, 1 sc in next ch, 3 dc in next ch. Ch 2 (working around to other side of foundation ch, sl st in ch with sc, *ch 7, 1 dc in 3rd ch from hook, 1 dc in next ch, 1 tr in next 2 ch, 1 dc in last ch, sl st in same ch with sc; rep from * once more, ch 5 for first antenna.

Fasten off. Re-attach yarn at base of first antenna and ch 5 for 2nd antenna. Fasten off.

Make desired number of butterflies.

Eyelet band

With B, ch 14.

Row 1 *Sl st in tip of left wing, ch 6; rep from * until all butterflies are attached, ch 14. Turn.

Row 2 1 hdc in 3rd ch from hook and in each ch to end. Turn.

Row 3 Ch 4, 1 tr in next 2 hdc, *ch 3, skip 3 hdc, 1 tr in next 3 hdc; rep from * to end.

Fasten off.

butterfly

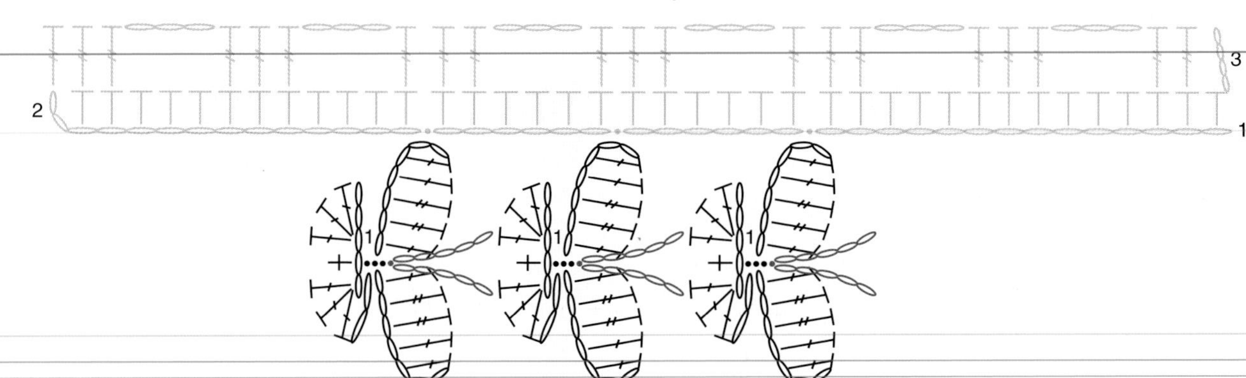

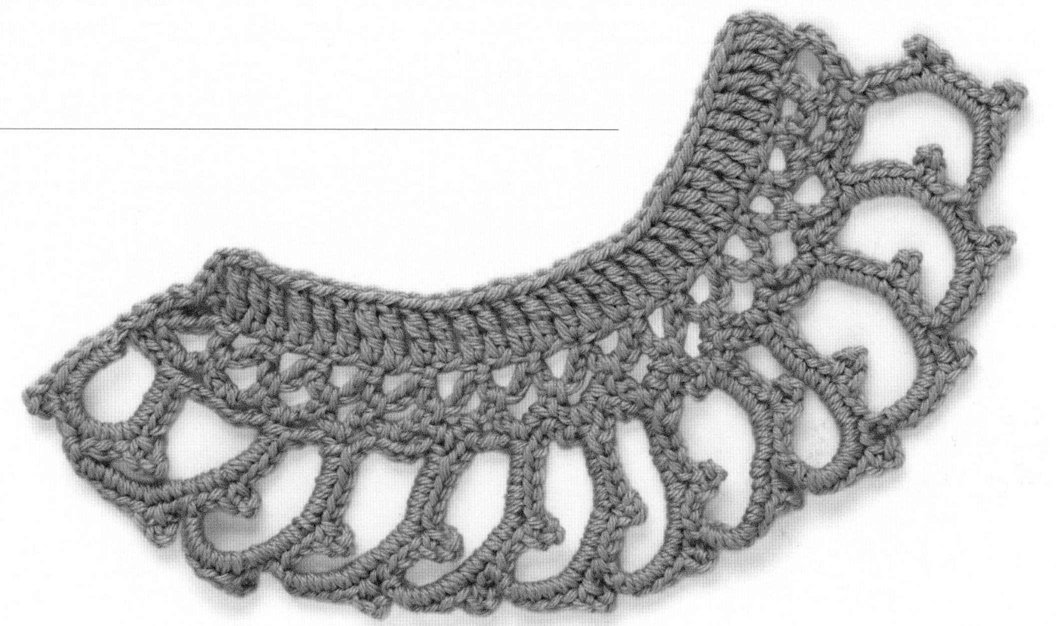

picot curve

▸ **Scallop**

Ch 5.

Row 1 1 Dc in 5th ch from hook, *ch 5, 1 dc in last dc made; rep from * to desired length,

ending with an even number of ch-5 lps.

Row 2 Ch 8, 1 sc in first ch-5 lp, *ch 5, 1 sc in next ch-5 lp; rep from * to end. Turn.

Row 3 Ch 6, 1 sc in first ch-5 lp, ch 12, sl st in base of beg ch-6, *5 sc in ch-12 lp, [ch 4, 1 sc in 4th ch from hook, 5 sc in same lp] twice, ch 2, 1 sc in same ch-5 lp**, ch 3, 1 sc in next ch-5 lp, ch 12, sl st in center sc between picots of previous chain; rep from *, ending last rep at **.

Fasten off.

Band

Working across dc edge of row 1, attach yarn to right-hand edge.

Row 1 Ch 4, 1 tr into side and base of each dc to end.

Fasten off.

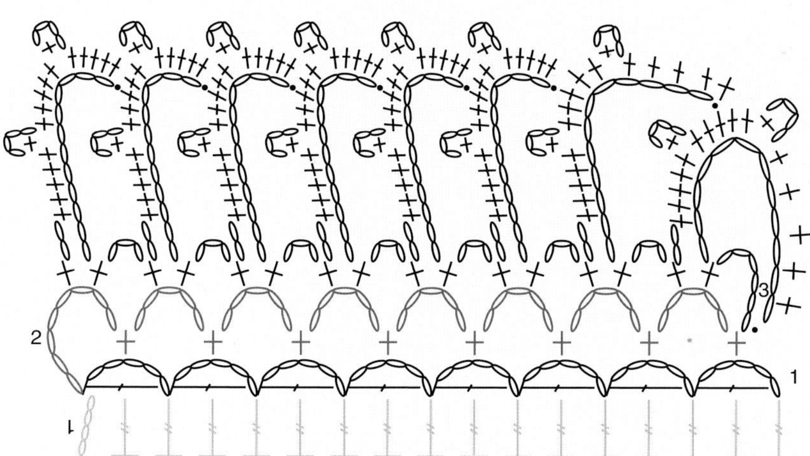

helmet

▶ **Colors** A and B

Points

With A, ch 11.

Row 1 1 Tr in 11th ch from hook. Turn.

Row 2 Ch 3, 5 dc in ring. Turn.

Row 3 Ch 11, 1 tr in 11th ch from hook. Turn.

Rep rows 2 and 3 to desired length, ending with row 2. Do not turn.

Finishing row Cont along length of points with loops, ch 3, [1 sc, ch 3, 3 dc, ch 5, 3 dc, ch 3, 1 sc] in same lp, *[1 sc, ch 3, 3 dc, ch 5, 3 dc, ch 3, 1 sc] in next lp; rep from *, end ch 3, 5 dc in same last lp. Do not turn.

Next row Cont along opposite length, *ch 3, 1 dc in base of next turning ch, ch 2, 1 dc in top of same turning ch; rep from * to end. Turn. Cont to row 1 of band.

Band

Row 1 With A, ch 1, 1 sc in first dc and in each ch and dc to end. Turn.

Fasten off A and attach B.

Row 2 With B, ch 4, 1 tr in next sc and in each sc to end.

Fasten off.

helmet

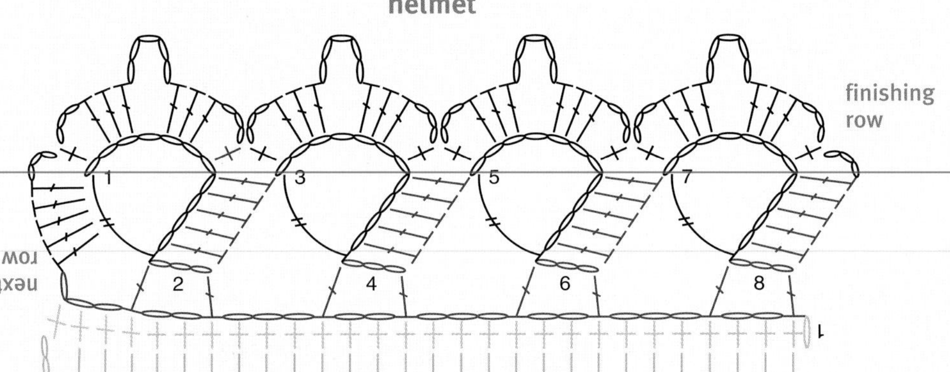

ripple looped points

▼ (multiple of 14 sts + 1)

Colors A and B

8mm round pearl beads

Ripple

With A, make a ch to desired length in a multiple of 14 sts + 2.

Row 1 With A, 2 sc in 2nd ch from hook, *1 sc in next 5 ch, skip 3 ch, 1 sc in next 5 ch, 3 sc in next ch; rep from *, end last rep 2 sc in last ch. Turn.

Row 2 Ch 1, 2 sc in first sc, *1 sc in next 5 sc, skip 2 sc, 1 sc in next 5 sc, 3 sc in next sc; rep from *, end last rep 2 sc in last sc. Turn.

Rep row 2, alternating 4 rows A with 4 rows B, to desired length.

Cont to row 1 of fringe.

Looped fringe

Row 1 [Ch 15, 1 sc in same sp] 3 times in first sc, *1 sc in next 5 sc, skip 2 sc, 1 sc in next 5 sc, [ch 15, 1 sc in same sp] 3 times in next sc; rep from * to end.

Fasten off.

Optional If desired, sew a bead to base of each fringe.

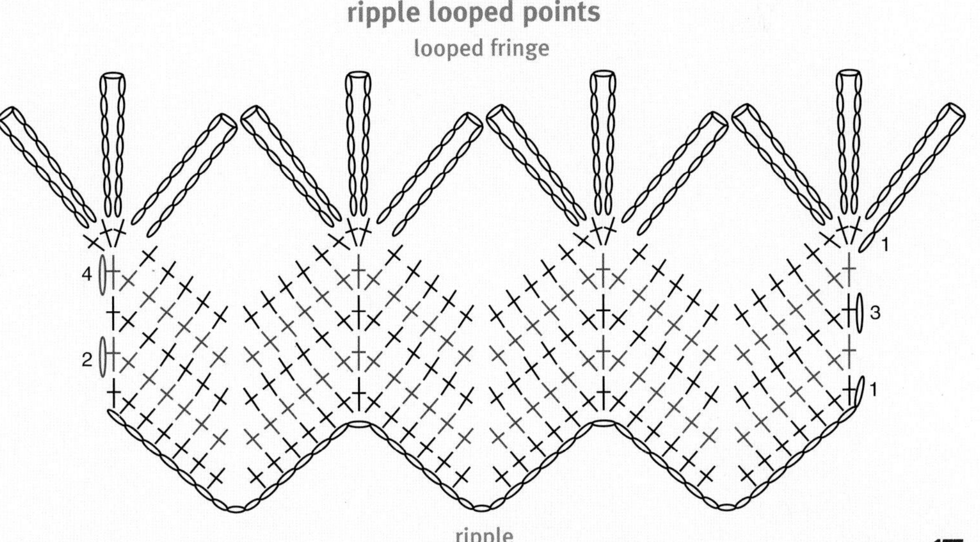

ripple bobble points

(multiple of 14 sts + 1)

Colors A, B and C

Ripple

Work same as Ripple Looped Points (see page 177), alternating 2 rows A, 2 rows B and 2 rows C. ending 1 row before desired finished length.

Bobble points

Row 1 Ch 1, 1 sc in first sc, *ch 3, [yo, bring hook under last ch-3 and draw up a lp] 9 times, yo and draw through all 19 lps on hook, sl st in same sc, 1 sc in next 5 sc, skip 2 sc, 1 sc in next 6 sc; rep from *, end, ch 3, [yo, bring hook under last ch-3 and draw up a lp] 9 times, yo and draw through all 19 lps on hook, sl st in same sc. Fasten off.

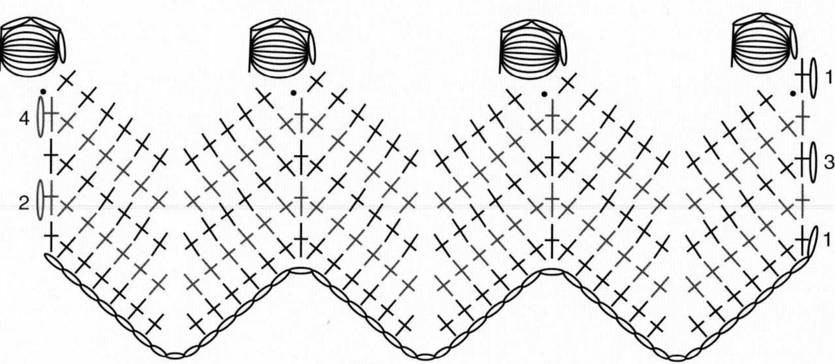

single points

Colors A and B

Top

With A, make a ch to desired length in a multiple of 5 sts + 2.

Row 1 1 Hdc in 3rd ch from hook and in each ch to end. Fasten off A. With RS facing, attach B to right-hand edge.

Row 2 Ch 1, 1 sc in same st and each st to end. Fasten off B. With RS facing, attach A to right-hand edge.

Row 3 Ch 2, 1 hdc in next st and each st to end. Fasten off. With RS facing, attach A to top of beg ch-2.

Points

Row 1 (RS) With A, ch 9, *1 sc in 2nd ch from hook, 1 hdc in next ch, 1 dc in next 2 ch, 1 tr in next 2 ch, 1 dtr in last ch *(point made)*, skip next 4 sts of heading, 1 sc in next st, ch 8; rep from *, end last rep omit ch 8.

Fasten off A. With RS facing, attach B to base of beg ch-9 of row 1.

Row 2 (RS) Ch 1, 1 sc in same st, *1 sc in next 7 foundation ch of point, 3 sc into ch-1 at tip, 1 sc in next 7 sts of point, 1 sc in next sc; rep from * to end.

Fasten off.

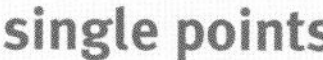

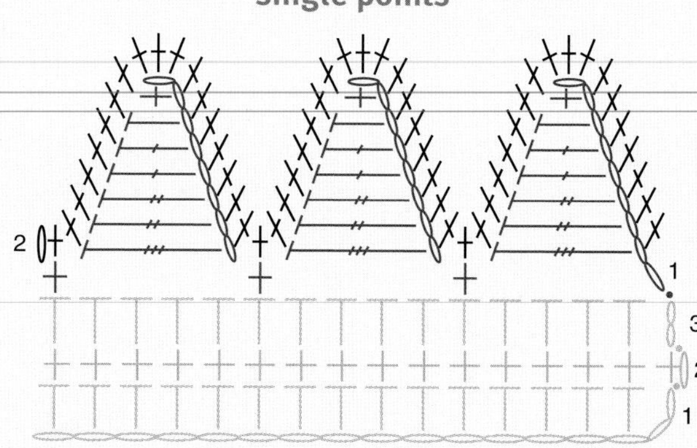

layered points

▶ **Colors** A and B

Backing

With A, make a ch to desired length in a multiple of 5 sts + 2.

Row 1 1 Hdc in 3rd ch from hook and in each ch to end. Turn.

Row 2 Ch 1, 1 sc in same st and each st to end. Turn.

Row 3 Ch 2, 1 hdc in next st and each st to end. Turn.

Rep rows 2 and 3 once more. Cont to points.

First row of points

Row 1 (RS) With A, ch 9, *1 sc in 2nd ch from hook, 1 hdc in next ch, 1 dc in next 2 ch, 1 tr in next 2 ch, 1 dtr in last ch *(point made)*, skip next 4 sts of backing, 1 sc in next st, ch 8; rep from *, end last rep omit ch 8. Fasten off A. With RS facing, attach B to base of beg ch-9 of row 1.

Row 2 (RS) Ch 1, 1 sc in same st, *1 sc in next 7 foundation ch of point, 3 sc into ch-1 at tip, 1 sc in next 7 sts of point, 1 sc in next sc; rep from * to end. Fasten off.

Second row of points

With WS facing, attach A to right-hand edge of foundation ch. Work same as rows 1 and 2 of points. Flip points over to RS.

Top band

With WS facing, attach A to right-hand edge of foundation ch.

Row 1 Ch 2, 1 hdc in next ch and in each ch to end. Turn.

Row 2 Ch 2, 1 hdc in next hdc and in each hdc to end.

Fasten off.

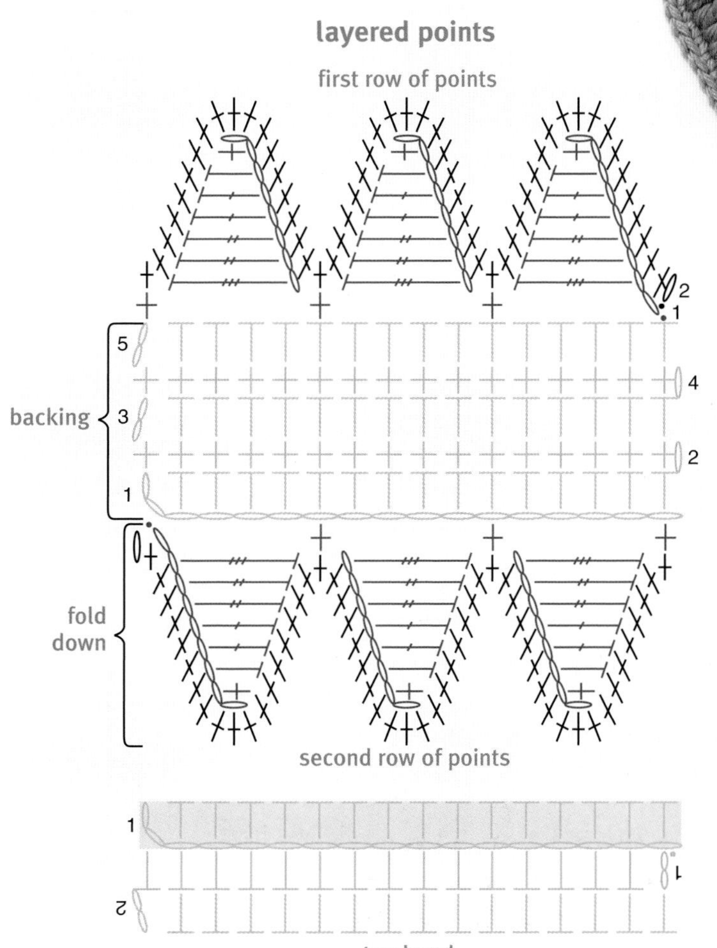

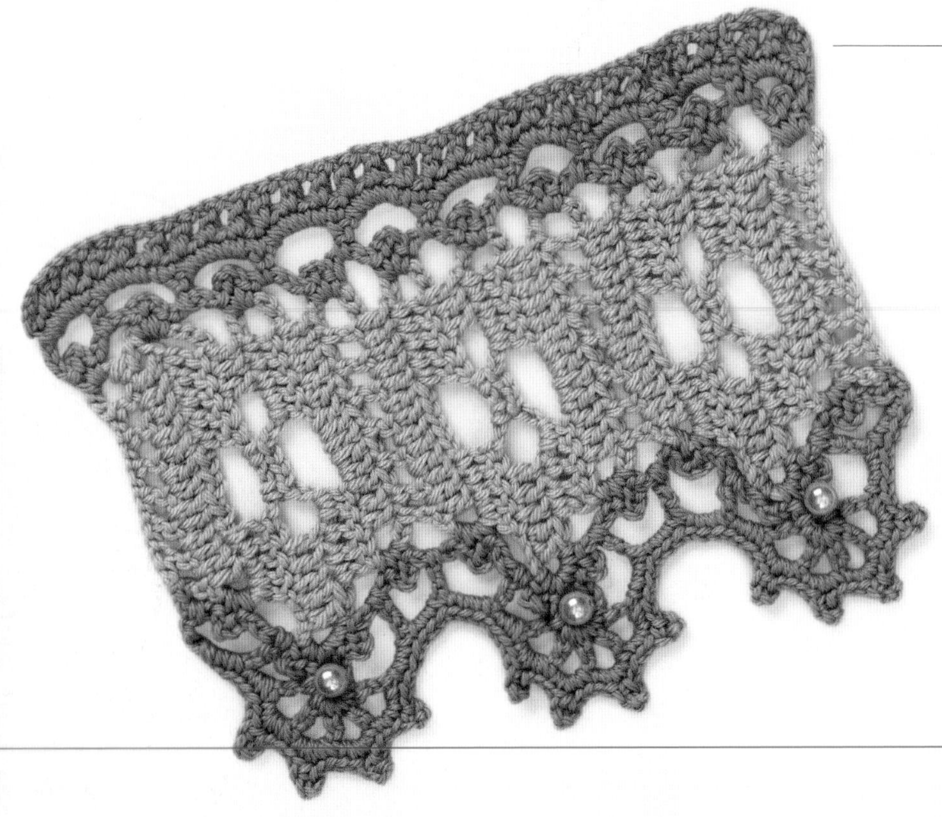

baroque point

▶ **Colors** A and B

Body

With A, ch 20.

Row 1 1 Dc in 8th ch from hook, [ch 1, skip next ch, 1 dc in next ch] 6 times. Turn.

Row 2 Ch 5, 1 dc in first dc, [1 dc in next ch-1 sp, 1 dc in next dc] 6 times. Turn.

Row 3 Ch 7, 1 dc in next 5 dc, ch 5, skip 5 dc, 1 dc in next 3 dc, 2 dc in ch-5 sp. Turn.

Row 4 Ch 7, 1 dc in 6th ch from hook, 1 dc in next ch, 1 dc in next 3 dc, ch 4, [1 sc, ch 3, 1 sc] in next ch-5 sp, ch 4, skip 2 dc, 1 dc in next 3 dc. Turn.

baroque point

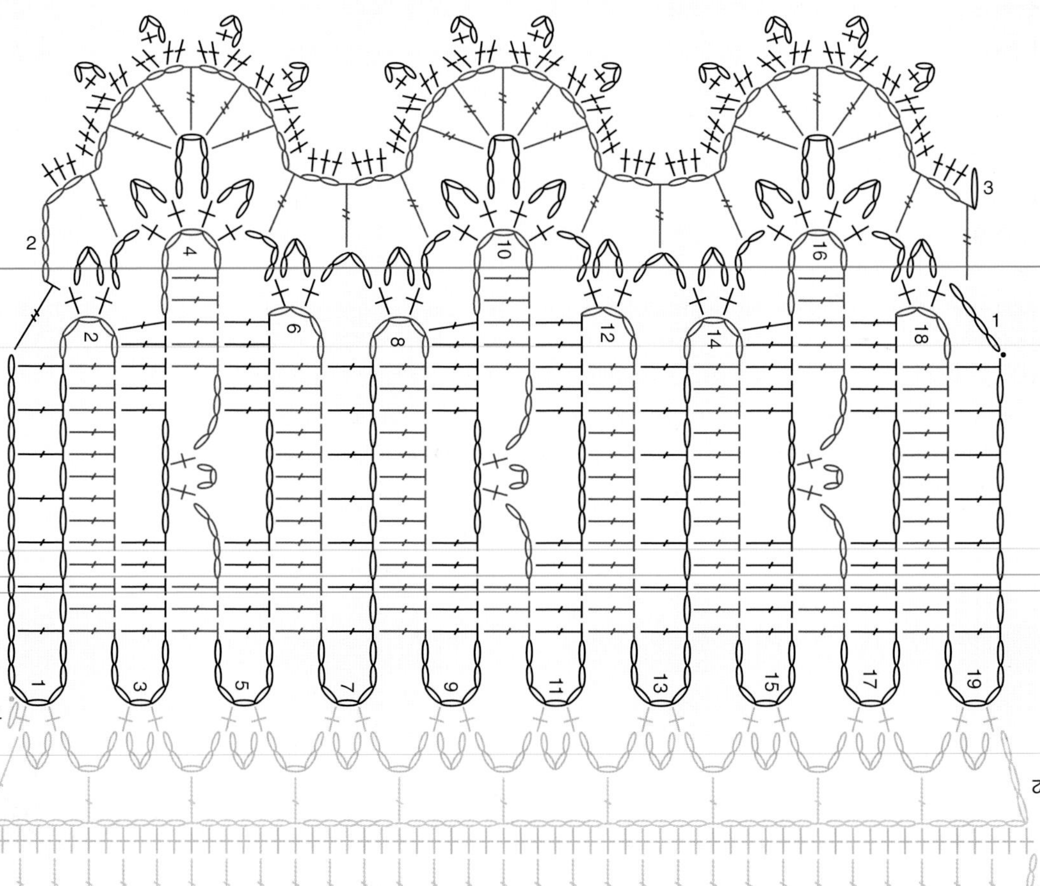

Row 5 Ch 7, 1 dc in next 3 dc, 2 dc in next ch-4 sp, ch 5, 2 dc in next ch-4 sp, 1 dc in next 3 dc. Turn.

Row 6 Ch 4, skip 2 dc, 1 dc in next 3 dc, 5 dc in ch-5 sp, 1 dc in next 5 dc. Turn.

Row 7 Ch 7, 1 dc in next dc, [ch 1, skip next dc, 1 dc in next dc] 6 times. Turn.

Rep rows 2–7 to desired length, ending with row 7.

Fasten off.

Heading

Working along length of body with ch-7 lps, attach B in first ch-7 lp.

Row 1 Ch 1, [1 sc, ch 4, 1 sc] in first lp, *ch 5, [1 sc, ch 4, 1 sc] in next lp; rep from * to end. Turn.

Row 2 Ch 8 (counts as 1 dc and ch 5), 1 dc in first ch-5 sp, *ch 5, 1 dc in next ch-5 sp; rep from *, end ch 4, 1 dc in last sc. Turn.

Row 3 Ch 1, 1 sc in first dc, *5 sc in next ch-5 sp; 1 sc in next dc; rep from * to end. Turn.

Row 4 Ch 4 (counts as 1 dc, ch 1), *skip next sc, 1 dc in next sc, ch 1; rep from *, end 1 dc in last sc.

Fasten off.

Edging

Working along opposite length of body, attach B to end of first row.

Row 1 Ch 4 (counts as 1 tr), *[1 sc, ch 4, 1 sc] in next turning ch sp, ch 4, [1 sc, ch 4, 1 sc, ch 7, 1 sc, ch 4, 1 sc] in next turning ch sp, ch 4, [1 sc, ch 4, 1 sc] in next turning ch sp, ch 4; rep from *, end last rep omit ch 4, 1 tr in end of foundation ch. Turn.

Row 2 Ch 6 (counts as 1 tr and ch 2), skip ch-4 lp, 1 tr in next ch-4 lp, *skip ch-4 lp (ch 2, 1 tr in next ch-4 in ch-7 lp] 5 times, [ch 2, skip ch-4 lp, 1 tr in next ch-4 lp] 3 times; rep from *, ending last rep with [ch 2, skip ch-4 lp, 1 tr in next ch-4 lp] twice. Turn.

Row 3 Ch 1, [3 sc in ch-2 sp] twice, *([2 sc, ch 3, 1 sc in 3rd ch from hook, 2 sc] in next ch-2 sp) 4 times, [3 sc in ch-2 sp] 4 times; rep from *, end last rep [3 sc in ch-2 sp] twice.

Fasten off.

Optional If desired, sew a pearl bead over each ch-7 sp of row 1 of edging.

patterns

STRIPED SWEATSHIRT JACKET

Sizes
S (M)

Finished bust: 31 (35)"/79 (89) cm
Finished length: 17 (18)"/43 (46) cm

Materials

- 2 7oz/200g balls (each approx 364yd/333m) of Naturally NZ/ Fibertrends *Alpine 10ply* (100% wool) each in #2012 gold (A) , #2001 olive (B), #2000 dk brown (C)
- 1 ball in #2013 white (D) (4)
- Size H/8 (5mm) crochet hook
- Stitch markers
- One 14 (16)" separating zipper in dk brown

Gauge
15.5 sts and 14.5 rows = 4"/10cm in sc

Body

Right half
With A, ch 101 (109).
Row 1 (RS) Sc in 2nd ch from hook and in each sc to end—100 (108) sc. Turn.
Row 2 Ch 1, 1 sc in each sc to end. Turn. Fasten off A.
Rep row 2 for pattern as foll: 1 more row A, 3 rows B, 3 rows C, 3 rows D, 3 rows C, 3 rows B, 10 (14) rows A—28 (32) rows total.
Fasten off.
Make left half same as right half.

Sleeve
With RS facing, working along last row of body, attach A to 30th (31st) st from right-hand side.
Row 1 Ch 1, 1 sc in same st and in next 41 (45) sc—42 (46) sc. Turn.
Row 2 Ch 1, 1 sc in each sc to end—42 (46) sc. Turn.
Rep row 2 for pattern as foll: 12 more rows A, 6 rows B, 6 rows C, 4 rows D, 6 rows C, 6 rows B, 2 rows A—44 rows.
With C, work 1 row reverse sc (see page TK).
Fasten off.
Rep for second half.

Hood
With A, ch 71.
Working in sc as for body, pattern 70 sc as foll: 2 rows A, 4 rows B, 3 rows C, 4 rows D, 3 rows C, 4 rows B, 4 rows A, 4 rows B, 4 rows C—32 rows.
Do not fasten off. Fold in half widthwise with RS together and sl st back seam closed.

Finishing
Align ch edge of right and left halves with RS together. Using A, sl st the center back seam from bottom edge for 43 (47) sts. Place markers at each front edge 18 (15) sts from center back neck.
Fold in half across sleeves and sl st side and sleeve seams, matching st colors with stripes.

Ribbing

Lower edge
With C, ch 9.
Row 1 Sc in 2nd ch from hook and in each ch to end—8 sc. Turn.
Row 2 Ch 1, 1 sc in back lp of each sc to end. Turn.
Rep row 2 for pattern as foll: 35 (42) more rows C, 4 rows B, 4 rows C, 2 rows D, 4 rows C, 4 rows B, 2 rows A, 4 rows B, 4 rows C, 2 rows D, 4 rows C, 4 rows B, 37 (44) rows C—112 (126) rows.
Fasten off.
Sew to lower edge of jacket, matching stripes at center back and st colors with stripes.

Cuffs (make 2)
With C, ch 7. Work same as lower edge ribbing with 6 sc for 32 (34) rows.
Sew ends together to form a ring. Matching seams, sew to sleeve openings, easing sleeve to fit.

Neck edging
With RS facing, attach C to lower right front corner.
Row 1 Ch 1, 1 sc in each sc around entire front opening, ending at lower left front corner. Do not turn. Do not fasten off.
Align center back seam of hood to center back seam of jacket and edges of hood to front markers. Sew to body, easing hood to fit.
Row 2 Ch 1, 1 reverse sc in each sc to end, including hood opening and ending at lower right front corner.
Fasten off.
Sew zipper into front opening. Make 2 Basic Corkscrews (see page TK), 1 each with A and B. Attach to zipper pull.

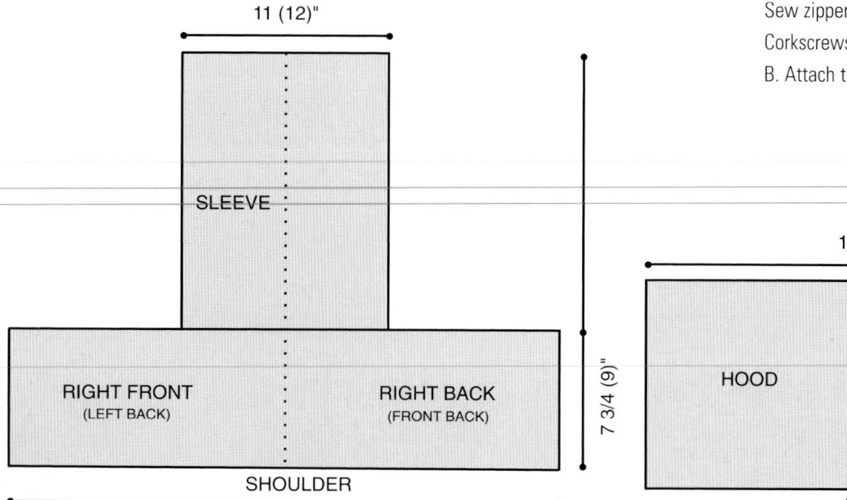

LITTLE RED JACKET

Sizes
S (M, L, 1X, 2X)

Finished Measurements
Bust 32 (36, 40, 44, 48)"
Length 17 (17.5, 18, 18.5, 19)"

Materials

- 5 (6, 7, 8, 9) 3.5oz/100g balls (each approx 215yds/198m) of Berroco, Inc.'s *Ultra Alpaca* (50% superfine alpaca/50% peruvian high-land wool) in #6234 cardinal (MC) (4)
- 1 ball in #6245 pitch black (CC)
- Size G/6 (4mm) crochet hook
- Three 1½"/38mm buttons
- Tapestry needle

Gauge
16 sts and 16 rows = 4"/10cm over Corded ridge st.

Stitch pattern

Corded Ridge St
Row 1 1 sc in 2nd ch from hook and in each ch to end. *Do not turn.*
Row 2 Ch 1, 1 reverse sc in next sc and in each sc to end. *Do not turn.*
Row 3 Ch 2, 1 hdc in *back lp* of next reverse sc and in back lp of each reverse sc to end. *Do not turn.*
Row 4 Working in sp between sts, ch 1, 1 reverse sc in next sp and in each sp to end,

1 reverse sc in top of beg ch-2.

Rep rows 3 and 4.

Left Side

Note Body is worked sideways in 2 pieces from side edge to center.

With MC, ch 100 (104, 108, 112, 116).

Rows 1–4 Work in pat st—99 (103, 107, 111, 115) sc.

Rows 5 through 22 (24, 28, 30, 32) Rep rows 3 and 4 of pat st.

Back

Next row Rep row 3 over first 48 (50, 52, 54, 56) sts.

Next row Rep row 4 over same 48 (50, 52, 54, 56) sts.

Rep last 2 rows 4 (5, 5, 6, 7) times more.

Fasten off.

Front

With RS facing, skip next 12 sts of row 22 (24, 28, 30, 32) and attach MC to next st.

Next row Ch 2, skip next st, 1 hdc in *back lp* next st and in each st to end—1 st decreased. *Do not turn.*

Next row Rep row 4.

Rep last 2 rows twice more.

Cont in pat over rem 36 (38, 40, 42, 44) sts for 4 (6, 6, 8, 10) rows more.

Fasten off.

Right Side

Work same as left side to back.

Front

Next row Ch 2, 1 hdc in *back lp* of first sc and in next 36 (38, 40, 42, 44) sc, skip next sc, 1 hdc in back lp of next sc—1 st decreased. *Do not turn.*

Next row Rep row 4.

Next row Ch 2, 1 hdc in *back lp* of first sc and in each sc to last 2 sc, skip next sc, 1 hdc in back lp of sc—1 st decreased. *Do not turn.*

Rep last 2 rows once more.

Cont in pat st over rem 36 (38, 40, 42, 44) sts for 5 (7, 7, 9, 11) rows more.

Fasten off.

Back

With RS facing, skip next 12 sts of row 22 (24, 28, 30, 32) and attach MC to next st.

Next row Rep row 3 over last 48 (50, 52, 54, 56) sts.

Next row Rep row 4 over same 48 (50, 52, 54, 56) sts.

Rep last 2 rows 4 (5, 5, 6, 7) times more.

Fasten off.

Sleeves

With RS facing and working along side edge of either side piece, skip first 15 sts and attach MC to next st.

Work rows 3 and 4 of pat st over center 69 (73, 77, 81, 85) sts for 7 (5, 3, 1, 1) rows. Cont in pat st, dec 1 st each side every row 3 until 41 (43, 43, 45, 45) sts rem, ending with row 3. Fasten off. Rep for other side piece.

Finishing

With RS together, sew sleeve, side and back seams using slip stitch.

Cuffs

With RS facing, attach CC to sleeve seam.

Rnd 1 Working in sp between sts, ch 1, 1 reverse sc in next sp and in each sp to end—41 (43, 43, 45, 45) sts. Join with sl st in first st.

Drop CC and attach MC.

Rnd 2 Ch 2, 1 hdc in *back lp* of next reverse sc and in *back lp* of each reverse sc to end. Join with sl st in top of beg ch-2.

Drop MC and pick up CC.

Rnds 3–6 Rep rnds 1 and 2.

Rnds 7 and 9 Rep rnd 1.

Rnds 8 and 10 Ch 2, 2 hdc in *back lp* of next reverse sc, 1 hdc in *back lp* of each reverse sc to end—43 (45, 45, 47, 47) sts after row 10. Join with sl st in top of beg ch-2.

Fasten off CC.

Rnds 11 and 13 With MC, rep rnd 1.

Rnds 12 and 14 Ch 3, 2 dc in *back lp* of next reverse sc, 1 dc in *back lp* of each reverse sc to end—45 (47, 47, 49, 49) sts after rnd 14. Join with sl st in top of beg ch-3.

Rnd 15 Rep row 1.

Do not fasten off. Cont to rnd 1 of ruffled edge.

Ruffled edge

For sizes M and L only, *skip 2 sts twice in rnd 1, then cont as written.*

Rnd 1 Ch 1, 1 sc in first reverse sc, *ch 3, skip next 3 sts, 1 sc in next st; rep from * to end. Join with sl st in first sc.

Rnd 2 Ch 1, 1 sc in first sc, *5 dc in next ch-3 sp, 1 sc in next sc; rep from *, end last rep omit 1 sc in next sc. Join with sl st in first sc.

Rnd 3 Ch 1, 1 sc in first sc, *ch 5, skip next 5 dc, 1 sc in next sc; rep from *, end last rep omit 1 sc in next sc. Join with sl st in first sc.

Rnd 4 Ch 1, 1 sc in first sc, *7 dc in next ch-5 sp, 1 sc in next sc; rep from *, end last rep omit 1 sc in next sc. Join with sl st in first sc. Fasten off MC and attach CC.

Rnd 5 With CC, ch 2, *1 hdc in next 3 dc, ch 3, skip next dc, 1 hdc in next 3 dc, sl st in next sc; rep from *, end last rep omit sl st in next sc. Join with sl st in base of beg ch-2. Fasten off.

Collar

With WS facing, attach MC to right-hand edge.

Row 1 Ch 1, work 78 (90, 90, 102, 114) sc evenly around neck opening. Turn.

Row 2 Ch 2, 1 hdc in *back lp* of next sc and in each sc to end. *Do not turn.*

Row 3 Working in sp between sts, ch 1, 1 reverse sc in next sp and in each sp to end. *Do not turn.*

Row 4 Ch 2, 1 hdc in *back lp* of next reverse sc and in *back lp* of each reverse sc to end. *Do not turn.*

Drop MC and attach CC.

Row 5 With CC, rep row 3.

Drop CC and pick up MC.

Row 6 With MC, rep row 4.

Drop MC and pick up CC

Rows 7, 8, 9 and 10 Rep rows 5 and 6.

Fasten off CC.

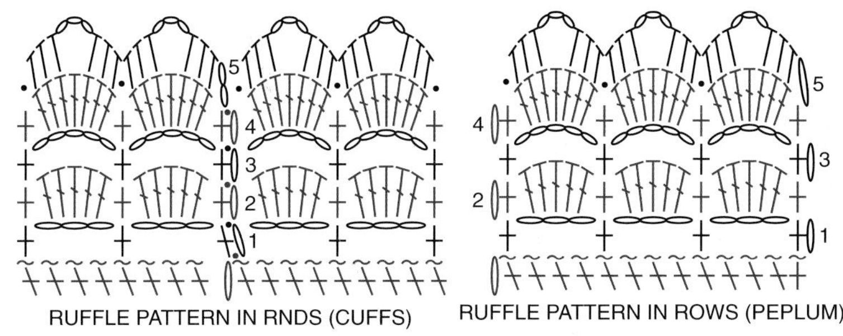

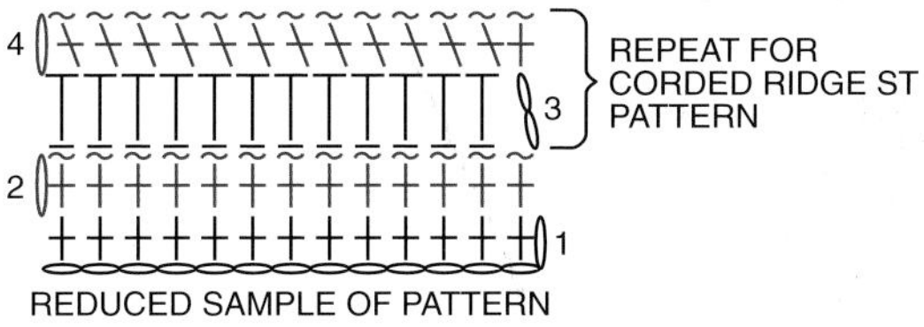

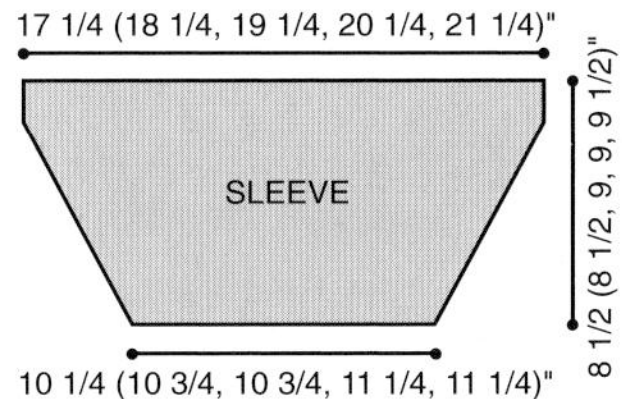

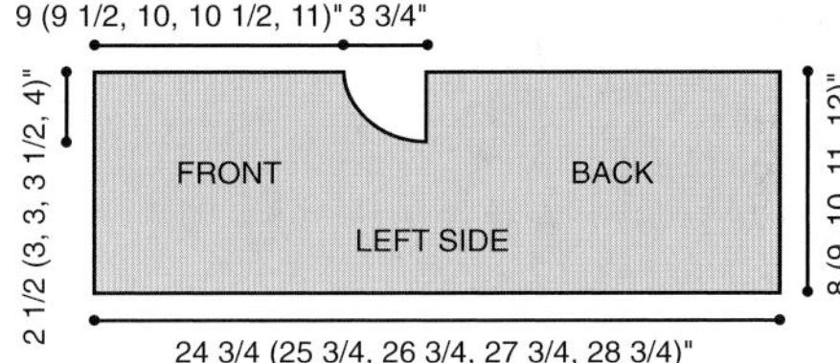

RUFFLE = 5" on Sleeve; 4 1/2" on Body.

Row 11 With MC, rep row 3.

Row 12 Ch 3, 1 dc in *back lp* of next reverse sc and in back lp of each reverse sc to end. Fasten off.

Peplum

With RS facing, attach MC to bottom of right front edge.

Row 1 Ch 1, work 117 (129, 145, 161, 173) reverse sc evenly across bottom edge. *Do not turn.*

Row 2 Ch 2, 1 hdc in *back lp* of next reverse sc and in *back lp* of each reverse sc to end. *Do not turn.*

Drop MC and attach CC.

Row 3 With CC, ch 1, working in sp between sts, 1 reverse sc in next sp and in each sp to end. *Do not turn.*

Drop CC and pick up MC.

Row 4 With MC, rep row 2.

Drop MC and pick up CC.

Rows 5, 6, 7 and 8 Rep rows 3 and 4.

Fasten off CC.

Row 9 With MC, rep row 3.

Row 10 Ch 3, 1 dc in *back lp* of next reverse sc and in *back lp* of each reverse sc to end.

Rows 11 and 12 Rep rows 9 and 10.

Row 13 Rep row 9.

Do not fasten off. Cont to row 1 of ruffled edge.

Ruffled edge

Row 1 Ch 1, 1 sc in first reverse sc, *ch 3, skip next 3 sts, 1 sc in next st; rep from * to end. Turn.

Row 2 Ch 1, 1 sc in first sc, *5 dc in next ch-3 sp, 1 sc in next sc; rep from * to end. Turn.

Row 3 Ch 1, 1 sc in first sc, *ch 5, skip next 5 dc, 1 sc in next sc; rep from * to end. Turn.

Row 4 Ch 1, 1 sc in first sc, *7 dc in next ch-5 sp, 1 sc in next sc; rep from * to end. Turn. Fasten off MC and attach CC.

Row 5 With CC, ch 1, *1 hdc in *back lp of* next 3 dc, ch 3, skip next dc, 1 hdc in *back lp* of next 3 dc, sl st in next sc; rep from * to end. Fasten off.

Button bands and edging

With WS facing, attach MC to right front at base of collar.

Row 1 Ch 10, skip 3 sts, [1 hdc in front lp of next 12 (13, 14, 15, 16) reverse sc, ch 10, skip 3 sts] twice, 1 hdc in front lp of last reverse sc. *Do not turn.*

Row 2 Ch 1, [10 reverse sc in ch-10 lp, 1 reverse sc in next 12 (13, 14, 15, 16) sp] twice, 10 reverse sc in ch-10 lp. Do not fasten off. Cont to work reverse sc evenly along edge of collar, in each sp across straight edge of collar, and evenly along opposite edge of collar. Sl st in first st of left front. Turn to work along left front edge with RS facing.

Row 1 Ch 2, 1 hdc in *back lp* of next reverse sc and in *back lp* of each reverse sc to top of ruffle. *Do not turn.*

Row 2 Ch 1, working in sp between sts, 1 reverse sc in next sp and in each sp to end. Fasten off.

Sew buttons to left front opposite button loops.

CASHMERE CAPELET

Size

Each panel measures approx 15"Wx26"L/38x66cm

Materials

- 6 1¾oz/50g skeins (each approx 125yds/114m) of Classic Elite Yarns *Lavish* (100% cashmere) in #10084 lavender (4)
- Size K/10.5 (6.5mm) crochet hook for capelet
- Size H/8 (5mm) crochet hook for flowers
- 2½ yd/2.25m purchased beaded fringe (optional)

Panel (make 2)

Ch 46.

Row 1 2 dc in 4th ch from hook, *ch 4, skip 5 ch, 5 dc in next ch; rep from *, end last rep 3 dc in last ch. Turn.

Row 2 Ch 3 (counts as 1 dc), skip first 3 dc, *[3 dc, ch 3, 3 dc] in next ch-4 sp, skip 5 dc; rep from *, end last rep skip 2 dc, 1 dc in top of beg ch-3. Turn.

Row 3 Ch 6 (counts as 1 dtr, ch 1), 5 dc in next ch-3 sp, *ch 4, 5 dc in next ch-3 sp; rep from *, end ch 1, 1 dtr in top of beg ch-3. Turn.

Row 4 Ch 5 (counts as 1 tr, ch 1), 3 dc in first ch-1 sp, *skip 5 dc, [3 dc, ch 3, 3 dc] in next ch-4 sp; rep from *, end skip 5 dc, 3 dc in last ch-1 sp, ch 1, 1 tr in 5th ch of beg ch-6. Turn.

Row 5 Ch 3 (counts as 1 dc), 2 dc in first ch-1 sp, *ch 4, 5 dc in next ch-3 sp; rep from *, end ch 4, 2 dc in last ch-1 sp, 1 dc in top of beg ch-3. Turn.

Rep rows 2–5 six times more.

Fasten off.

Sew panels together following diagram.

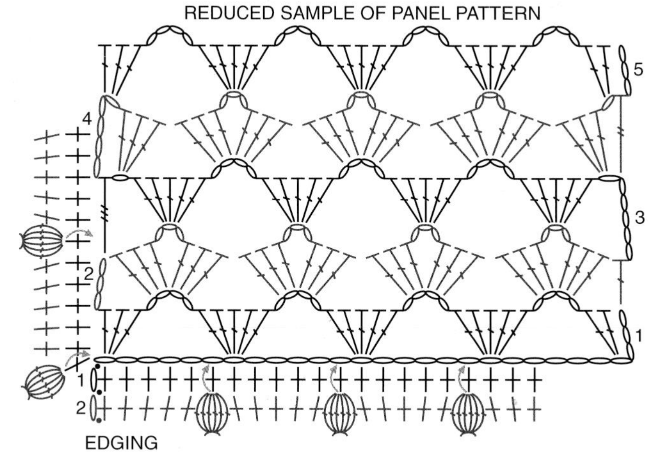

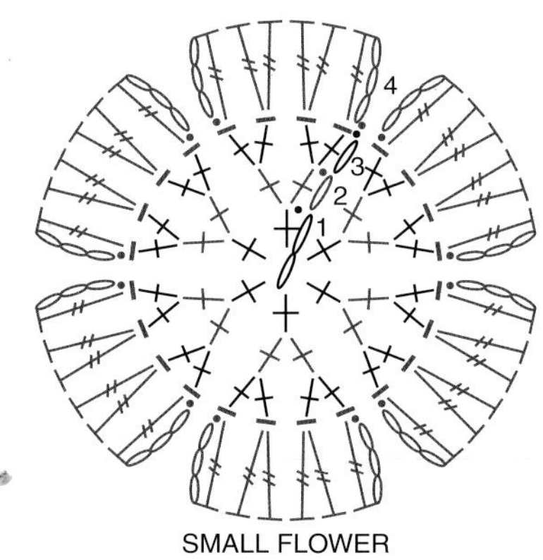

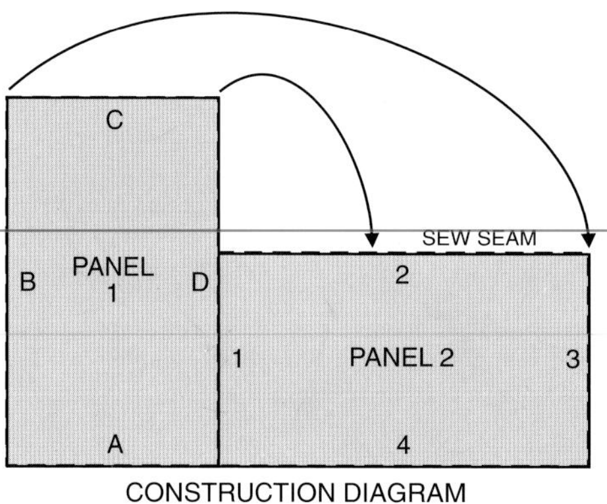

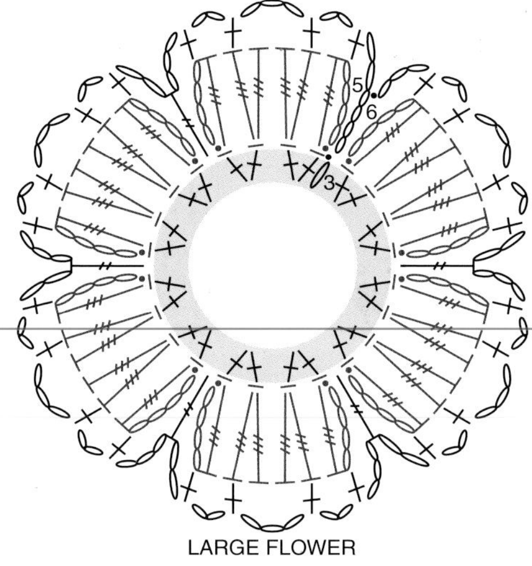

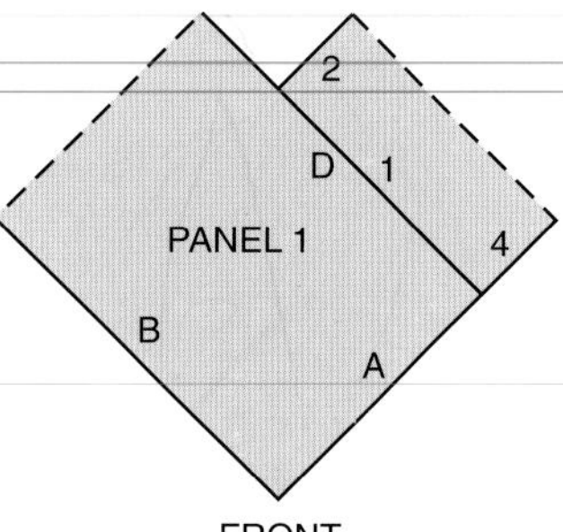

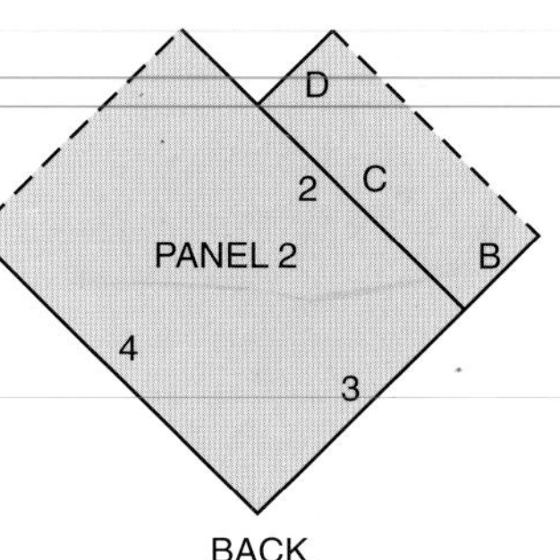

Edging

(multiple of 6 sts)

With RS facing, attach yarn to seam at neck edge.

Rnd 1 Ch 1, sc evenly around, working 3 sc at each outer corner, in a multiple of 6 sts. Join with sl st in first sc.

Rnd 2 Ch 1, *1 sc in next 5 sc, ch 1, 6 dc in next st 2 rows below, drop lp, insert hook in first dc of 6-dc group just made, draw dropped lp through st; rep from * around. Join with sl st in first sc.

Fasten off.

Rep edging around lower edge.

Small flower (make 5)

Ch 2.

Rnd 1 6 sc in 2nd ch from hook. Join with sl st to first sc.

Rnd 2 Ch 1, 2 sc in each sc around—12 sc. Join with sl st to first sc.

Rnd 3 Ch 1, 2 sc in each sc around—24 sc. Join with sl st to first sc.

Rnd 4 *Working in front lps only*, *[ch 3, 1 tr] in same sc, [2 tr in next sc] twice, 1 tr in next sc, ch 3, sl st in same sc, sl st in next sc; rep from * around—6 petals. Join with sl st in base of beg ch.

Fasten off.

Large flower (make 1)

Work rnds 1–4 of small flower.

Rnd 5 *Working in back lps only* of rnd 3, *[ch 4, 1 dtr] in same st, [2 dtr in next st] twice, 1 dtr in next st, ch 4, sl st in same st, sl st in next st; rep from * around—6 petals. Join with sl st in base of beg ch-4.

Rnd 6 Ch 6, *1 sc in top of ch-4 lp, ch 2, skip 1 dtr, 1 sc in next dtr, ch 3, skip 2 dtr, 1 sc in next dtr, ch 2, skip next dtr, 1 sc in top of ch-4, ch 3, 1 tr in sp at base of petal, ch 2; rep from * 5 times more, ending last rep 1 sc in top of ch-4, ch 3. Join with sl st in 4th ch of beg ch-6.

Fasten off.

Sew flowers along one side seam, with large flower at neck edge.

Optional Sew beaded fringe behind edging of entire lower edge.

MEDALLION MEDLEY

Size

Approx 64" x 40"/162.5 x 101.5cm

Materials

- 14 3½oz/100g skeins (each approx 170yd/156m) of Lion Brand *Vanna's Choice* (100% acrylic) in #99 linen (5)
- Size H/8 (5mm) crochet hook
- Size G/6 (4mm) crochet hook
- Polyfill
- Tapestry needle

Special stitches

Beg DC popcorn 5 dc in designated st, drop lp, insert hook into top of beg ch-3 and pick up dropped lp, drawing through dc.

DC Popcorn 6 dc in designated st, drop lp, insert hook into first dc of 6-dc group and pick up dropped lp, drawing through dc.

Beg DCL [Yo, insert hook in designated st and draw up a lp, yo and draw through 2 lps on hook] twice, yo and draw through all 3 lps.

DCL [Yo, insert hook in designated st and draw up a lp, yo and draw through 2 lps on hook] 3 times, yo and draw through all 4 lps.

Beg Tr popcorn 4 tr in designated st, drop lp, insert hook into top of beg ch-4 and pick up dropped lp, drawing through tr.

Tr popcorn 5 tr in designated st, drop lp, insert hook into first tr of 5-tr group and pick up dropped lp, drawing through tr.

Instructions

Make 36 medallions as follows:

Medallion 1

Large (make 2)

MEDALLION 1
LARGE

With larger hook, ch 5. Join with sl st in first ch to form a ring.

Rnd 1 Ch 1, 16 sc in ring. Join with sl st to first sc.

Rnd 2 Ch 5, skip next sc, *1 dc in next sc, ch 2, skip next sc; rep from * around. Join with sl st in 3rd ch of beg ch-5 - 8 dc and 8 ch-2 sps.

Rnd 3 Ch 3, 2 dc in same st, ch 2, *3 dc in next dc, ch 2; rep from * around. Join with sl st in top of beg ch-3.

Rnd 4 Ch 3, 1 dc in next dc, 2 dc in next dc, ch 2, *1 dc in next 2 dc, 2 dc in next dc, ch 2;

rep from * around. Join with sl st in top of beg ch-3.

Rnd 5 Ch 3, 1 dc in next 2 dc, 2 dc in next dc, ch 2, *1 dc in next 3 dc, 2 dc in next dc, ch 2; rep from * around. Join with sl st in top of beg ch-3.

Rnd 6 Ch 3, 1 dc in same st, 1 dc in next 3 dc, 2 dc in next dc, ch 2, *2 dc in next dc, 1 dc in next 3 dc, 2 dc in next dc, ch 2; rep from * around. Join with sl st in top of beg ch-3.

Rnd 7 Sl st in next dc, ch 3, 1 dc in next 4 dc, ch 2, 1 dc in next ch-2 sp, ch 2, skip next dc, *1 dc in next 5 dc, ch 2, 1 dc in next ch-2 sp, ch 2, skip next st; rep from * around. Join with sl st in top of beg ch-3—48 dc and 16 ch-2 sps.

Rnd 8 Sl st in next dc, ch 3, 1 dc in next 2 dc, ch 2, [1 dc in next ch-2 sp, ch 2] twice, skip next dc, *1 dc in next 3 dc, ch 2, [1 dc in next ch-2 sp, ch 2] twice, skip next dc; rep from * around. Join with sl st in top of beg ch-3—40 dc and 24 ch-2 sps.

Rnd 9 Ch 3, *skip next dc, 1 dc in next dc, ch 3, 1 dc in next ch-2 sp, [ch 2, 1 dc in ch-2 sp] twice, *ch 3, 1 dc in next dc; rep from *, end last rep omit 1 dc in next dc. Join with sl st in top of beg ch-3.

Rnd 10 Ch 3, 1 beg dc popcorn in sp between first 2 dc, *ch 3, 1 dc in next dc, [ch 2, 1 dc in next dc] twice, ch 3**, 1 dc popcorn in sp between next 2 dc; rep from *, end last rep at **. Join with sl st in top of beg ch-3.

Rnd 11 Ch 3, 1 dc in ch-1 behind first popcorn, [2 dc ch 2, 2 dc] in each dc and ch-1 behind each popcorn around, end with 2 dc in same sp as 1st dc, ch 2. Join with sl st in top of beg ch-3.

Small (make 3)

With smaller hook, work through rnd 8 of large medallion.

Rnd 9 Ch 3, 1 beg DCL over next 2 dc, *ch 3, 1 dc in next ch-2 sp, [ch 2, 1 dc in next ch-2 sp] twice, ch 3, 1 DCL over next 3 dc; rep from *, end [ch 2, 1 dc in next ch-2 sp] twice, ch 3. Join with sl st in top of beg ch-3.

Center ball (make 5)

With larger hook, ch 4. Join with sl st in first ch to form a ring.

Rnd 1 Ch 1, 2 sc in top lps only of each ch around.

Rnd 2 (inc) Working in a spiral,*1 sc in back lp of next sc, 2 sc in back lp of next sc; rep from * 3 times more—12 sc.

Rnds 3, 4 and 5 1 sc in back lp of each sc around.

Stuff with polyester filling.

Rnd 6 (dec) Working in back lps, *sc2tog; rep from * until 4 sts rem.

Fasten off, leaving a long tail for sewing. Sew 1 ball to center of each medallion.

Medallion 2 (make 3)

With larger hook, ch 9. Join with sl st in first ch to form a ring.

Rnd 1 Ch 1, 18 sc in ring. Join with sl st to first sc.

Rnd 2 Ch 3, 1 beg dc popcorn in same st, *ch 2, skip 1 sc, 1 dc popcorn in next sc; rep from * around, end ch 2, skip last sc. Join with sl st in top of beg ch-3—9 popcorns.

Rnd 3 Ch 5 (counts as 1 dc, ch 2), 1 dc in next ch-2 sp, *ch 2, 1 dc in next popcorn, ch 2, 1 dc in next ch-2 sp; rep from * around, end ch 2. Join with sl st in top of beg ch-3—18 dc and ch-2 sps.

Rnd 4 Ch 1, 1 sc in same st, 3 sc in first ch-2 sp, *1 sc in next dc, 3 sc in next ch-2 sp; rep from * around. Join with sl st in first sc—72 sc.

Rnd 5 Ch 1, 3 sc in back lp of same st, 1 sc in back lp of next 3 sc, *3 sc in back lp of next sc, 1 sc in back lp of next 3 sc; rep from * around. Join with sl st in first sc—18 points.

Rnd 6 Ch 1, 1 sc in first sc, *3 sc in next sc (center sc of 3-sc point), 1 sc in next 5 sc; rep from * around, end 1 sc in last 4 sc. Join with sl st in first sc.

Rnds 7–11 Ch 1, 1 sc in first sc, *1 sc in each sc to center of next 3-sc point), 3 sc in next sc; rep from *, end 1 sc in each sc to end. Join with sl st in first sc—15 sc between each 3-sc point. Place a marker in center sc on each side of motif.

Turn after rnd 11 and sl st in first 2 sc. You should be at the center point between 2 points.

Rnd 12 Ch 1, bring last point and next point tog with RS of medallion at inside of fold, working through both layers, 1 sc in back lp of next 5 sts, *ch 4, bring next point together with previous point, started in next marked

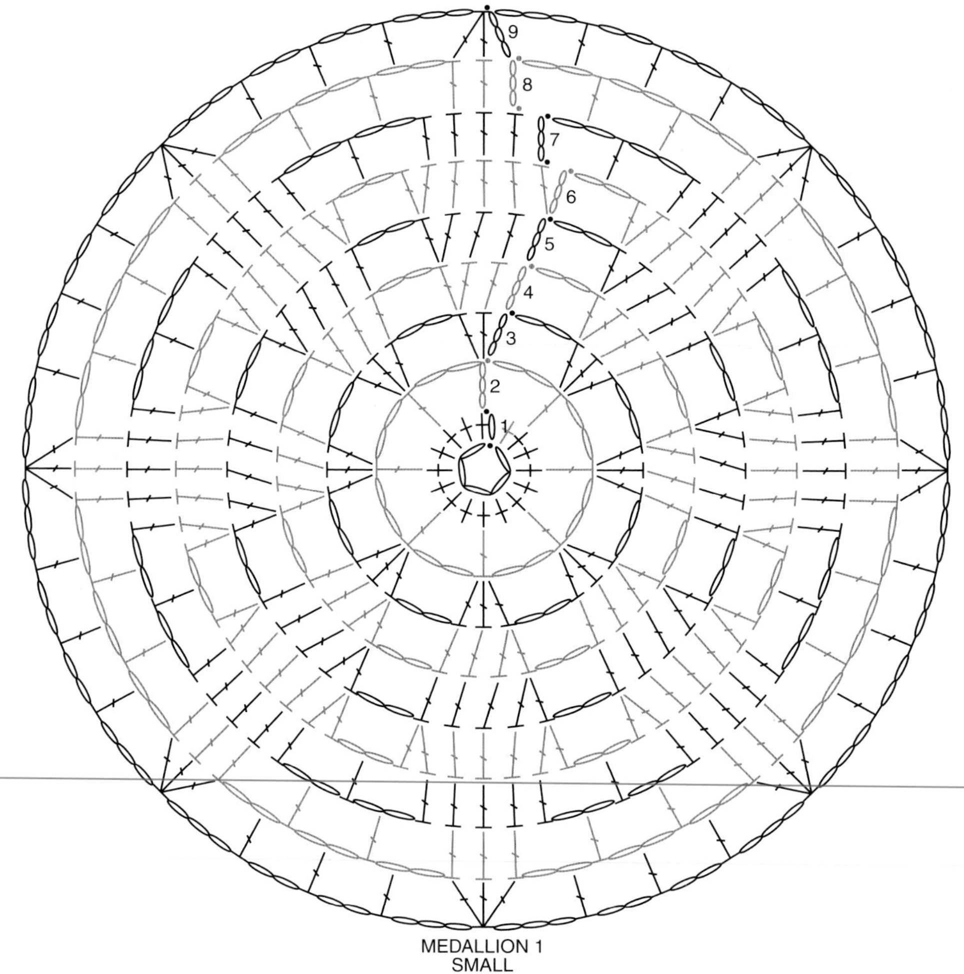

MEDALLION 1
SMALL

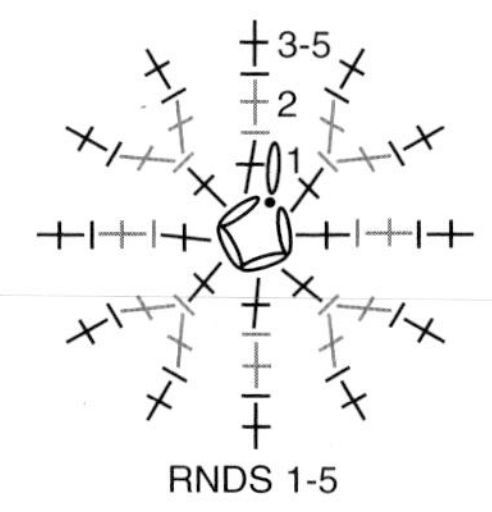

RNDS 1-5

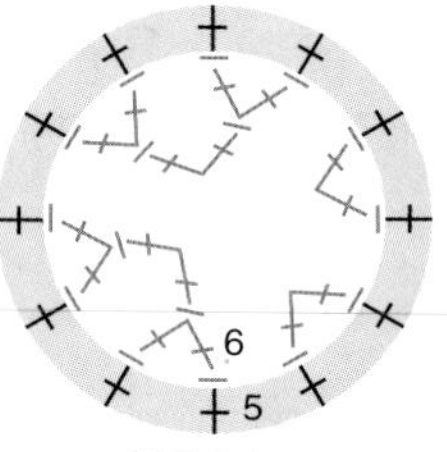

RNDS 6-7

MEDALLION 1
CENTER BALL

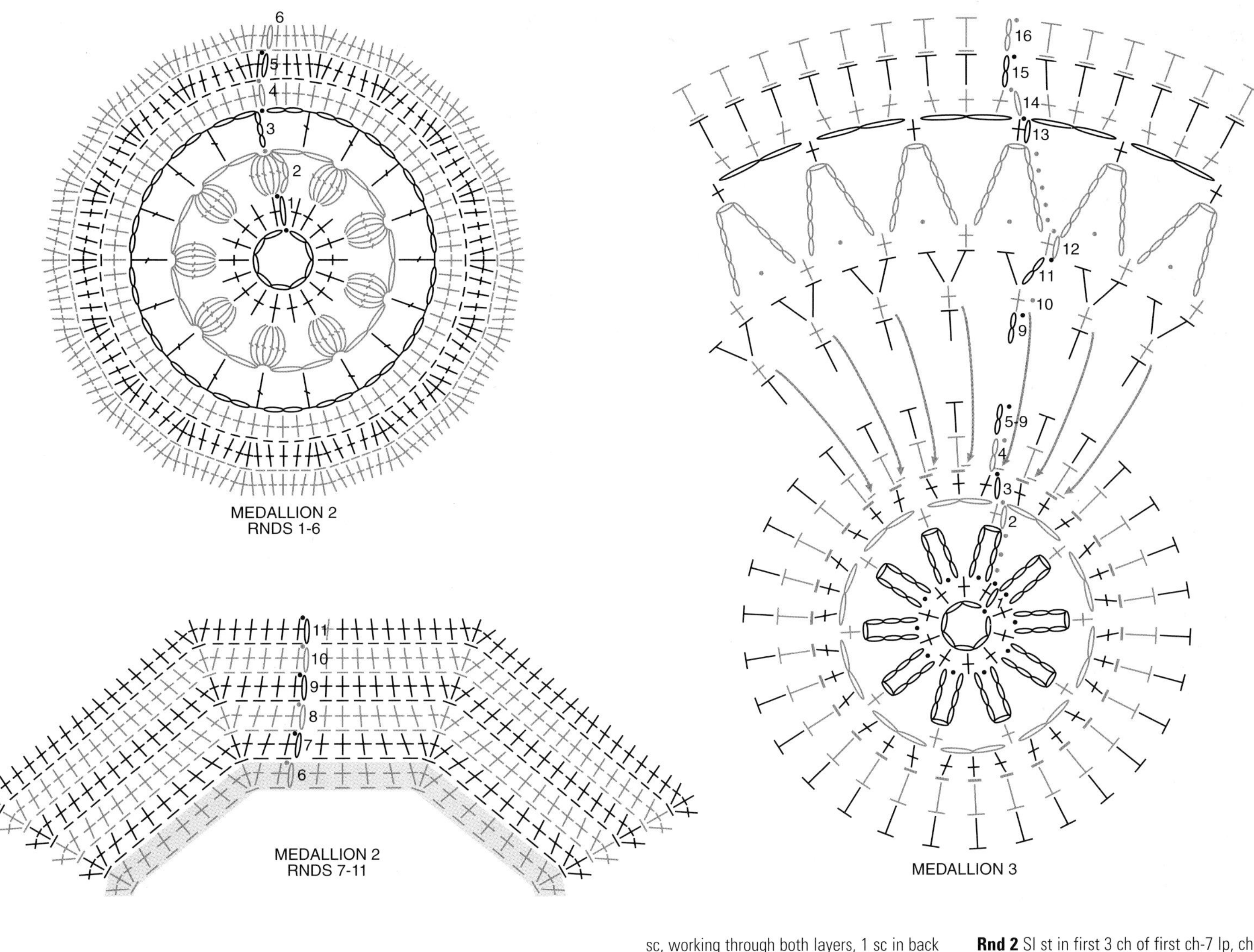

MEDALLION 2
RNDS 1-6

MEDALLION 2
RNDS 7-11

MEDALLION 3

MEDALLION 2
RND 12

sc, working through both layers, 1 sc in back lp of next 5 sc; rep from * until there are 18 folds, end ch 4. Join with sl st in first sc.
Fasten off.

Medallion 3 (make 4)

With larger hook, ch 7. Join with sl st in first ch to form a ring.

Rnd 1 Ch 1, *1 sc in ring, ch 7, sl st in sc just made; rep from * 9 times more—10 ch-7 lps. Join with sl st in first sc.

Rnd 2 Sl st in first 3 ch of first ch-7 lp, ch 1, 1 sc in same lp, *ch 2, 1 sc in next ch-7 lp; rep from * 8 times more, ch 2. Join with sl st in first sc.

Rnd 3 Ch 1, *3 sc in next ch-2 sp; rep from * around—30 sc. Join with sl st in first sc.

Rnd 4 Ch 2, 1 hdc in front lp of next sc and in front lp of each sc around. Join with sl st in top of beg ch-2.

Rnds 5–9 Ch 2, 1 hdc in each hdc around. Join with sl st in top of beg ch-2.

Rnd 10 Ch 1, bring rnd 9 together with rnd 3 with WS of medallion at inside of fold, working through sts of rnd 9 and corresponding unworked back lps of rnd 3, 1 sc in first st and in each st around. Join with sl st in first sc.

Rnd 11 Ch 2 (counts as 1 hdc), 1 hdc in first sc, 2 hdc in next sc and in each sc around—60 hdc. Join with sl st in top of beg ch-2.

Rnd 12 Ch 1, 1 sc in first hdc, *ch 11, sl st in sc just made, skip next hdc, 1 sc in next hdc; rep from * around—30 ch-11 lps. Join with sl st in first sc.

Rnd 13 Sl st in first 5 ch of first ch-11 lp, ch 1, 1 sc in same lp, *ch 2, 1 sc in next ch-11 lp; rep from * 28 times more, ch 2. Join with sl st in first sc.

Rnd 14 Ch 1, *3 sc in next ch-2 sp; rep from * around. Join with sl st to first sc.

Rnd 15 Ch 2, 1 hdc in next sc and in each sc around. Join with sl st in top of beg ch-2.

Rnd 16 Ch 2, 1 hdc in back lp of next hdc and in back lp of each hdc around. Join with sl st in top of beg ch-2.
Fasten off.

Medallion 4 (make 4)

With larger hook, ch 6. Join with sl st in first ch to form a ring.

Rnd 1 Ch 3 (counts as 1 dc), 19 dc in ring—20 dc. Join with sl st in top of beg ch-3.

Rnd 2 Ch 3 (counts as 1 dc), 1 dc in same st, 1 dc in back lp of next st, *2 dc in back lp of next st, 1 dc in back lp of next st; rep from * around—30 dc. Join with sl st in top of beg ch-3.

Rnd 3 Ch 1, 1 sc in same st, *ch 7, skip next dc, 1 sc in front lp of next dc; rep from *, end skip last dc. Join with sl st in first sc—15 ch-7 lps.

Rnd 4 Ch 3 (counts as 1 dc), 1 dc in same st, working in unworked back lps of rnd 2, *1 dc in next 3 sts, 2 dc in next st, ch 1, 2 dc in next st; rep from *, end 1 dc in next 3 sts, 2 dc in last st, ch 1—6 dc-groups. Join with sl st in top of beg ch-3.

MEDALLION 4
RNDS 4-10

MEDALLION 4
RNDS 1-3

Rnd 5 Working in back lps only, ch 3 (counts as 1 dc), 1 dc in same st, 1 dc in next 2 dc, 1 dc popcorn in next dc, 1 dc in next 2 dc, 2 dc in next dc, *ch 2, 2 dc in next dc, 1 dc in next 2 dc, 1 dc popcorn in next dc, 1 dc in next 2 dc, 2 dc in next dc; rep from *, end ch 2. Join with sl st in top of beg ch-3.

Rnd 6 Ch 3 (counts as 1 dc), 1 dc in same st, 1 dc in next 7 sts, 2 dc in next dc, ch 2, *2 dc in next dc, 1 dc in next 7 sts, 2 dc in next dc, ch 2; rep from * around—66 dc. Join with sl st in top of beg ch-3.

Rnd 7 Ch 3, 1 dc in same st, *1 dc in next 2 sts, 1 dc popcorn in next st, 1 dc in next 3 sts, 1 dc popcorn in next st, 1 dc in next 2 sts, 2 dc in next dc (last dc of group), ch 2, 2 dc in next dc (first dc of group); rep from *, end last rep ch 2. Join with sl st in top of beg ch-3.

Rnd 8 Ch 3, 1 dc in same st, 1 dc in next 11 sts, 2 dc in next dc (last dc of group), *ch 3, 2 dc in next dc (first dc of group), 1 dc in next 11 sts, 2 dc in next dc (last dc of group); rep from *, end ch 3. Join with sl st in top of beg ch-3.

Rnd 9 Ch 3, 1 dc in same st, *1 dc in next 2 dc, [1 dc popcorn in next dc, 1 dc in next 3 dc] twice, 1 dc popcorn in next dc, 1 dc in next 2 dc, 2 dc in next dc (last dc of group), ch 4, 2 dc in next dc (first dc of group); rep from *, end last rep ch 4. Join with sl st in top of beg ch-3.

Rnd 10 Ch 3, 1 dc in same st, *1 dc in next 15 sts, 2 dc in next st (last dc of group), ch 4, 2 dc in next dc (first dc of group); rep from *, end last rep ch 4. Join with sl st in top of beg ch-3.

Fasten off.

Medallion 5 (make 7)

With larger hook, ch 5. Join with sl st in first ch to form a ring.

Rnd 1 Ch 1, 16 sc in ring. Join with sl st to first sc.

Rnd 2 Ch 3 (counts as 1 dc), 1 beg dc popcorn in same st, *ch 2, skip next sc, 1 dc popcorn in next sc; rep from * around, end ch 2. Join with sl st in top of beg ch-3—8 popcorns.

Rnd 3 Ch 5 (counts as 1 dc, ch 2), *1 dc next ch-2 sp, ch 2**, 1 dc in top of next popcorn, ch 2; rep from * around, end last rep at **. Join with sl st in 3rd ch of beg ch-5.

Rnd 4 Ch 1, 1 sc in same st, *3 sc in next ch-2 sp, 1 sc in next dc; rep from * around, end 3 sc in last ch-2 sp. Join with sl st to first sc.

Rnd 5 Ch 3, 1 dc in back lp of next sc and in back lp of each sc around. Join with sl st in top of beg ch-3.

Fasten off.

Medallion 6 (make 3)

With larger hook, ch 7. Join with sl st in first ch to form 1 ring.

Rnd 1 Ch 1, *1 sc in ring, ch 7, sl st in sc just made; rep from * 9 times more. Join with sl st to first sc—10 lps.

Rnd 2 Ch 1, 1 sc in same st, ch 3, working behind lps of rnd 1, *1 sc in next sc between next two ch-7 lps, ch 3; rep from * 8 times more. Join with sl st to first sc.

Rnd 3 Ch 1, *3 sc in next ch-3 lp; rep from * 9 times more. Join with sl st to first sc.

Rnd 4 Ch 2, 1 hdc in next sc and in each sc around. Join with sl st in top of beg ch-2.

Rnd 5 Ch 2, 1 hdc in back lp of next hdc and in back lp of each hdc around. Join with sl st in top of beg ch-2.

Fasten off.

Medallion 7 (make 4)

With larger hook, ch 10. Join with sl st in first ch to form 1 ring.

Rnd 1 Ch 1, 20 sc in ring. Join with sl st to first sc.

Rnd 2 Ch 6 (counts as 1 tr, ch 2), *1 tr in next sc, ch 2; rep from * around. Join with sl st to first tr.

Rnd 3 Sl st in first ch-2 sp, ch 1, 2 sc in same sp and in each ch-2 sp around. Join with sl st to first sc—40 sc.

Rnd 4 Ch 5 (counts as 1 tr, ch 1), *1 tr in next sc, ch 1; rep from *around. Join with sl st in 4th ch of beg ch-5.

Rnd 5 Sl st in first ch-1 sp, ch 1, [1 sc, ch 9, 1

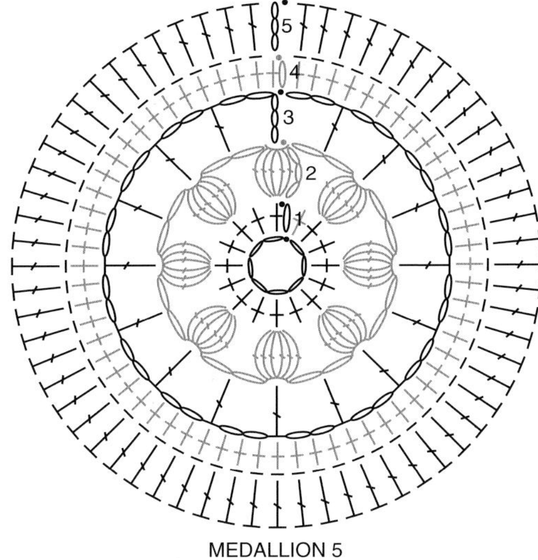

MEDALLION 5

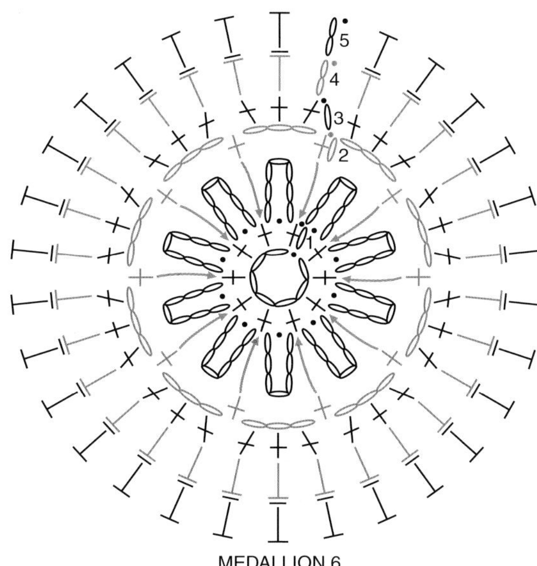

MEDALLION 6

MEDALLION 7

sc] in same ch-1 sp, ch 5, [1 sc, ch 5, 1 sc] in next ch-1 sp, *ch 5, skip next 2 ch-1 sps, [1 sc, ch 9, 1 sc] in next ch-1 sp, ch 5, [1 sc, ch 5, 1 sc] in next ch-1 sp; rep from * 8 times more, ch 5. Join with sl st to first sc.

Rnd 6 Sl st in first 4 ch of first ch-9 lp, ch 4, 1 beg tr popcorn in same lp, ch 5, skip next ch-5 lp, 1 sc in next ch-5 lp, *ch 5, 1 tr popcorn in next ch-9 lp, ch 5, skip next ch-5 lp, 1 sc in next ch-5 lp; rep from * 8 times more, ch 5. Join with sl st in top of beg ch-4.

Rnd 7 Ch 1, *5 sc in next ch-5 lp, 4 sc in next ch-5 lp; rep from * 9 times more. Join with sl st to first sc.

Rnd 8 Ch 1, 1 sc in back lp of first sc and in back lp of each sc around. Join with sl st to first sc.

Fasten off.

Medallion 8 (make 4)

With larger hook, ch 7. Join with sl st in first ch to form a ring.

Rnd 1 Ch 1, *1 sc in ring, ch 7, sl st in sc just made; rep from * 9 times more—10 lps. Join with sl st to first sc.

Rnd 2 Sl st in first 3 ch of first ch-7 lp, ch 1, [1 sc, ch 2] in same ch-7 lp and in each ch-7 lp around. Join with sl st in first sc.

Rnd 3 Ch 1, 3 sc in ch-2 sp and in each ch-2 sp around—30 sc. Join with sl st to first sc.

Rnd 4 Ch 2, 1 hdc in back lp of next sc and in back lp of each sc around. Join with sl st in top of beg ch-2.

Rnd 5 Ch 2, 1 hdc in next hdc and in each hdc around. Join with sl st in top of beg ch-2.

Rnd 6 Ch 1, 1 sc in first hdc and in each hdc around. Join with sl st to first sc.

Rnd 7 *Ch 12, sl st in next sc, sl st in back lp of same st; rep from * around, end ch 12, sl st in back lp of joining sl st—30 lps.

Rnd 8 Sl st in first 5 ch of first ch-12 lp, ch 1, 3 sc in same ch-12 lp, *3 sc in next ch-12 lp; rep from * around. Join with sl st to first sc—90 sc.

Rnd 9 Ch 2, 1 hdc in back lp of next sc and in back lp of each sc around. Join with sl st in top of beg ch-2.

Rnd 10 Ch 1, 1 sc in same st, 1 sc in back lp of next hdc and in back lps of each hdc around. Join with sl st to first sc.

Fasten off.

Ball fringe (make 10)

With larger hook, ch 4. Join with sl st in first ch to form a ring.

Rnd 1 Ch 1, 2 sc in top lps only of each ch around.

Rnd 2 (inc) Working in a spiral,*1 sc in back lp of next sc, 2 sc in back lp of next sc; rep from * 3 times more—12 sc.

Rnd 3 (inc) Cont in a spiral, *1 sc in back lp of next sc, 2 sc in back lp of next sc; rep from * 5 times more—18 sc.

Rnds 4–9 1 sc in back lp of each sc around. Stuff with polyester filling.

Rnd 10 (dec) Working in back lps, *sc2tog; rep from * until 3 sts rem.

Do not fasten off. Cont to rnd 1 of stem.

Stem

Rnd 1 Working in a spiral, 1 sc in back lp of each sc around.

Rep rnd 1 to desired length. Sl st in next sc.

Fasten off, leaving a long tail for sewing.

Pull stem taut.

Assembly

Using construction diagram as a guide, place medallions randomly over a rectangular area measuring approx 64" x 40"/162.5 x 101.5cm being sure that edges touch or overlap. Using tapestry needle and yarn, sew medallions in place. Sew 5 ball fringes to each narrow end of afghan, spacing evenly across.

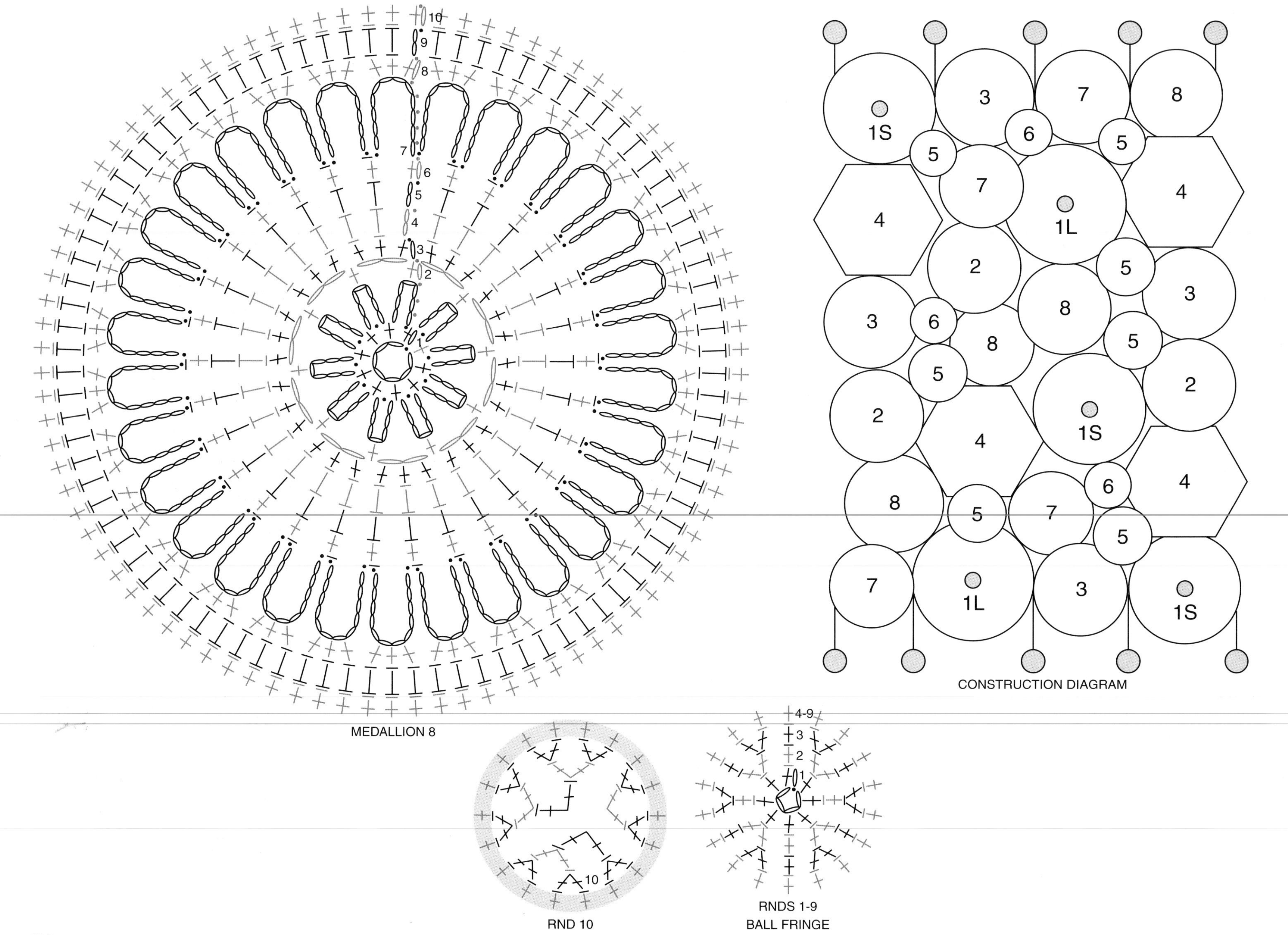

10
9
8
7
6
5
4
3
2
1
MEDALLION 8
1S
3
7
8
5
6
5
4
7
4
1L
2
5
3
3
6
8
8
5
5
2
2
4
1S
8
6
4
5
7
5
7
1L
3
1S
CONSTRUCTION DIAGRAM
10
RND 10
4-9
3
2
1
RNDS 1-9
BALL FRINGE

ECRU CRYSTAL SHOULDER CAPELET

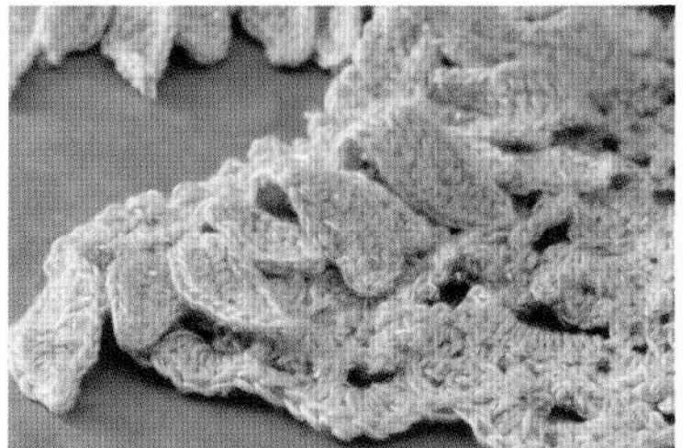

One size

- **Finished measurements** Approx 22"/56cm W at neck edge, 12"/30.5cm L

Materials

- 3 3½ oz/100g skeins (each approx 150yd/135m) of Tilli Tomas *Mariel's Crystals* (65% spun silk/35% swarovski crystals) in natural 4
- Size G/6 (4mm) crochet hook

Panel (make 2)

Ch 28.

Row 1 1 sc in 2nd ch from hook, [ch 5, skip next 3 ch, 1 sc in next ch] 6 times, ch 5, skip next ch, [1 sc, ch 5, 1 sc] in last ch (working around to other side of foundation ch), ch 5, skip next ch, 1 sc in next ch, [ch 5, skip next 3 ch, 1 sc in next ch] 6 times. Turn.

Row 2 Ch 1, 1 sc in first sc, ch 5, 1 sc in first ch-5 lp, [8 dc in next ch-5 lp, 1 sc in next ch-5 lp, ch 5, 1 sc in next ch-5 lp] twice, 9 dc in end ch-5 lp, [1 sc in next ch-5 lp, ch 5, 1 sc in next ch-5 lp, 8 dc in next ch-5 lp] twice, 1 sc in next ch 5 lp ch 2, 1 dc in last sc. Turn.

Row 3 Ch 8, [1 dc in next 8 dc, 1 sc in next ch-5-lp] twice, [1 dc, ch 1] in next 8 dc, 1 dc in next dc, [1 sc in next ch-5 lp, 1 dc in next 8 dc] twice, ch 4, 1 tr in last sc. Turn.

Row 4 Ch 1, 1 sc in tr, [ch 5, skip next 2 dc, 1 sc in next st] 6 times, ch 5, 1 sc in next dc, [ch 3, 1 sc in next dc] 3 times, ch 5, skip 1 dc, 1 sc in next dc, [ch 3, 1 sc in next dc] 3 times, ch 5, 1 sc in next sc, [ch 5, skip 2 dc, 1 sc in next st] 5 times, ch 2, 1 dc in 4th ch of beg ch-8. Turn.

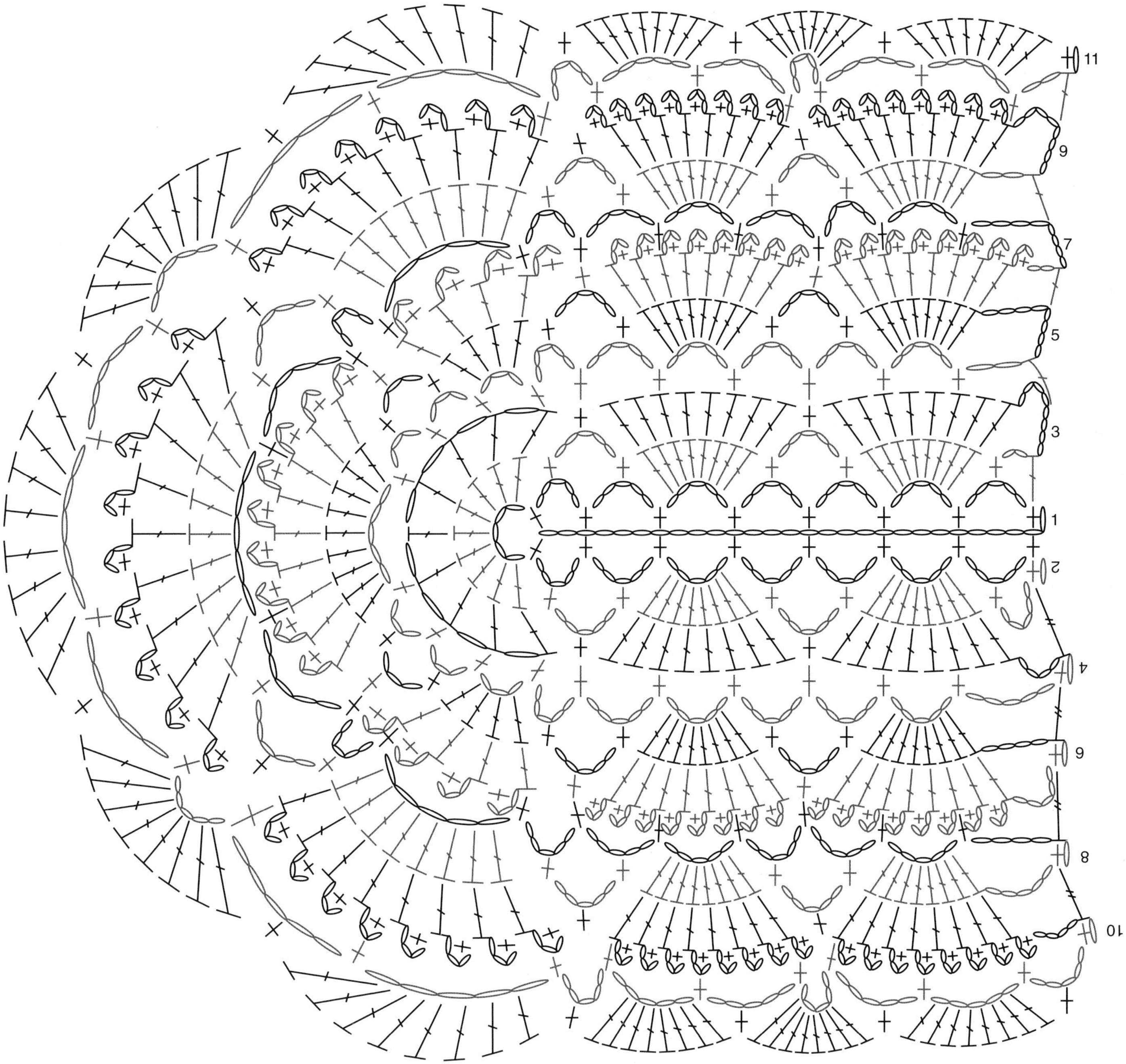

11 9 7 5 3 1 2 4 6 8 10

PANEL

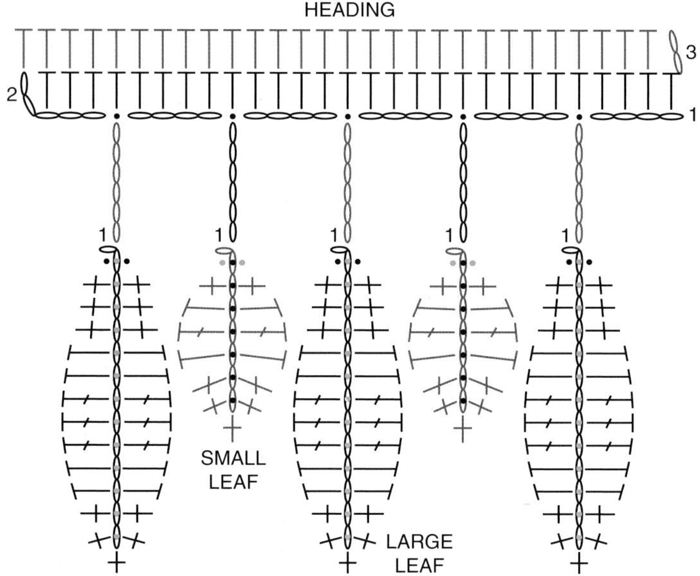

Row 5 Ch 8, [8 dc in next ch-5 lp, 1 sc in next ch-5 lp, ch 5, 1 sc in next ch-5 lp] twice, 4 dc in next ch-3 lp, 1 sc in next ch-3 lp, ch 3, 1 sc in next ch-3 lp, 9 dc in next ch-5 lp, 1 sc in next ch-3 lp, ch 3, 1 sc in next ch-3 lp, 4 dc in next ch-3 lp, [1 sc in next ch-5 lp, ch 5, 1 sc in next ch-5 lp, 8 dc in next ch-5 lp] twice, ch 4, 1 tr in last sc. Turn.

Row 6 Ch 1, 1 sc in tr, ch 5, ([1 dc in next dc, ch 3, 1 sc in 3rd ch from hook—(dc picot made)] 8 times, 1 sc in next ch-5 lp) twice, dc picot in next 4 dc, 1 sc in next ch-3 sp, dc picot in next 9 dc, 1 sc in next ch-3 sp, dc picot in next 4 dc, [1 sc in next ch-5 lp, dc picot in next 8 dc] twice, ch 2, 1 dc in 4th ch of beg ch-8. Turn.

Row 7 Ch 8, [skip 2 dc, 1 sc in next dc or sc, ch 5] 6 times, 1 sc in next dc, ch 5, skip 2 dc, 1 sc in next dc, ch 5, 1 sc in next sc, ch 5, skip 2 dc, 1 sc in next dc, ch 5, skip 3 dc, 1 sc in next dc, ch 5, skip 2 dc, 1 sc in next sc, ch 5, 1 sc in next dc, ch 5, skip 2 dc, 1 sc in next dc, ch 5, 1 sc in next sc, [ch 5, skip 2 dc, 1 sc in next dc or sc] 5 times, ch 4, 1 tr in last sc. Turn.

Row 8 Ch 1, 1 sc in tr, ch 5, [8 dc in next ch-5 lp, 1 sc in next ch-5 lp, ch 5, 1 sc in next ch-5 lp] 3 times, 9 dc in next ch-5 lp, [1 sc in next ch-5 lp, ch 5, 1 sc in next ch-5 lp, 8 dc in next ch-5 lp] 3 times, ch 2, 1 dc in 4th ch of beg ch-8. Turn.

Row 9 Ch 8, [dc picot in next 8 dc, 1 sc in next ch-5 lp] 3 times, dc picot in next 9 dc, [1 sc in next ch-5 lp, dc picot in next 8 dc] 3 times, ch 4, 1 tr in last sc. Turn.

Row 10 Ch 1, 1 sc in tr, [ch 5, 1 sc in next picot, ch 5, skip 3 picots, 1 sc in next picot, ch 5, skip 3 picots, 1 sc in next dc] 3 times, ch 5, 1 sc in next picot, [ch 5, skip 2 picots, 1 sc in next picot] twice, ch 5, skip next picot, 1 sc in next picot, [ch 5, 1 sc in next picot, ch 5, skip 3 picots, 1 sc in next picot, ch 5, skip 3 picots, 1 sc in next dc] 3 times, ch 2, 1 dc in 4th ch of beg ch-8. Turn.

Row 11 Ch 1, 1 sc in first dc, [8 dc in next ch-5 lp, 1 sc in next ch-5 lp] to end.

Fasten off.

Finishing

Place the 2 panels side by side with straight edges across the top. Using sl st, join for approx 1"/2.5cm from top edge.

Leaf edging

Attach yarn to right-hand edge.

Row 1 Ch 1, sc evenly across both pieces.

Fasten off.

Make dangling leaves fringe (see page 147) to match width of capelet.

Using sl st, attach fringe along sc row of edging.

BLACK AND SILVER SCARF

One size

Finished measurements

Approx 3¼"W x 48"L/8.5 x 122cm before edging

Materials

- 2 1¾oz/50g ball (each approx 170yd/155m) of Lang *Opal Lamé* (58% nylon/42% rayon) in #203 salt and pepper 
- Size F/5 (3.75mm) crochet hook
- 20 plastic rings (4 each ½"/12mm, ¾"/20mm, 1"/25mm, 1½"/38mm, 2"/50mm)
- Sewing needle and matching thread

Gauge

20 sts and 7 rows = 4"/10cm in pattern

Scarf

Ch 236.

Row 1 1 tr in 5th ch from hook and in next 3 ch, 3 tr in next ch, 1 tr in next 5 ch, *skip 2 ch, 1 tr in next 5 ch, 3 tr in next ch, 1 tr in next 5 ch; rep from * to end. Turn.

Row 2 Ch 4, skip next tr, 1 tr in next 4 tr, *3 tr in next tr, 1 tr in next 5 tr, skip 2 tr, 1 tr in next 5 tr; rep from *, end 3 tr in next tr, 1 tr in next 4 tr, skip next tr, 1 tr in top of beg ch-4. Turn.

Rep row 2 four times more.

Fasten off.

Edging

Attach yarn to ring.

Row 1 Ch 1, work enough sc in ring to cover completely. Join with sl st in first sc.

Fasten off.

Finishing

When all rings have been worked, divide in half and arrange in pattern as desired. Using sewing needle and thread, tack between rings to secure and attach to each end of scarf.

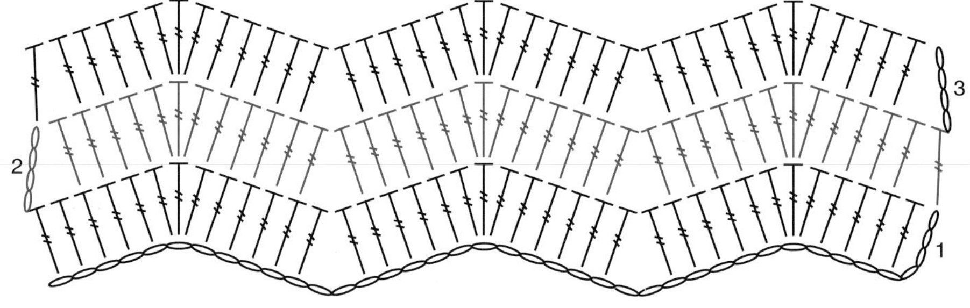

REDUCED SAMPLE OF SCARF PATTERN

RINGED HATBAND AND BRACELET

Finished measurements

- **Hatband** 25 Rings 17½"/44.5cm; Tie 25"/63.5cm after assembly
- **Bracelet** 5 Rings 5¼"/13.5cm; Tie 11"/28cm after assembly

Materials

- 1 skein (each approx 17yd/15m) of DMC *Pearl Cotton #3* (100% cotton) each in assorted colors
- Size C/2 (2.75mm) crochet hook
- 30 plastic rings 1⅛"/28mm

Note For more length, use more rings and longer ties.

Hatband

Ring

Attach yarn to ring.

Rnd 1 Ch 1, 30 sc in ring. Join with sl st to first sc.

Fasten off.

Make desired number of rings in assorted colors.

Tie

Ch 200.

Row 1 1 sc in 2nd ch from hook and in each ch to end.

Fasten off.

Bracelet

Ring

Work same as for hatband rings.

Tie

Ch 75.

Work same as for hatband tie.

Finishing

Assemble rings as desired. Following diagram, weave ties in and out of rings to interlock, leaving same length at either end for tying.

WEAVING TIE THROUGH RINGS

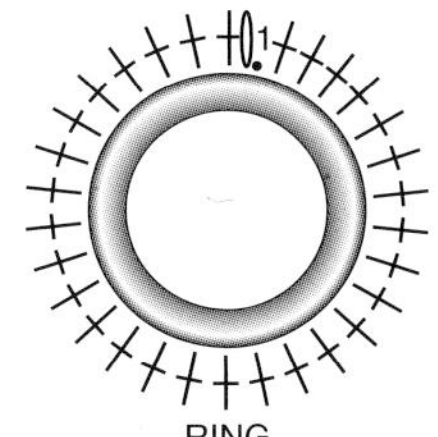

RING

PRINCESS ANNE VEST

One size

Bust measures 36"/91.5cm

Materials

- 9 1.75oz/50g balls (each approx 121 yd/109m) of GGH *Maxima* (100% wool) in #13 med teal (A)
- 1 ball in #9 lt teal (B)
- 2 balls in #14 dk teal (C)
- Size G/6 (4mm) crochet hook
- Size 4 (3.5mm) double-pointed needles
- Stitch markers

Gauge

16 sts and 10.5 rows = 4"(10cm) in pattern st

Body

With A, ch 202.

Row 1 (RS) Hdc in 3rd ch from hook and next 98 ch, 1 hdc in next ch and mark as center back, 1 hdc in each ch to end—201 sts. Turn.

Row 2 Ch 3 (counts as 1 dc), 1 dc in horizontal lp of next hdc and each hdc to center, [2 dc, ch 2, 2 dc] in next hdc (center back), 1 dc in horizontal lp of next hdc and each hdc to end. Turn.

Row 3 Ch 2 (counts as 1 hdc), 1 hdc in next dc and in each dc to center ch-2 sp, [2 hdc, ch 2, 2 hdc] in ch-2 sp, 1 hdc in next dc and in each dc to end. Turn.

Row 4 Ch 3 (counts as 1 dc), 1 dc in horizontal lp of next hdc and each hdc to center ch-2 sp, [2 dc, ch 2, 2 dc] in ch-2 sp, 1 dc in horizontal lp of next hdc and each hdc to end. Turn.

Rep rows 3 and 4 until there are 18 rows. Fasten off.

Back armhole shaping

With RS facing, working across last row of body, attach A to 40th st to right of center ch-2 sp.

Row 1 (RS) Ch 2, 1 hdc in next dc and in each dc to center ch-2 sp, [2 hdc, ch 2, 2 hdc] in ch-2 sp, 1 hdc in next 40 dc—84 hdc. Turn.

Row 2 Ch 3 (counts as 1 dc), skip next hdc, 1 dc in horizontal lp of next hdc and each hdc to center, [2 dc, ch 2, 2 dc] in next hdc (center back), 1 dc in horizontal lp of next hdc and each hdc to last 2 hdc, skip next hdc, 1 dc in last hdc. Turn.

Row 3 Ch 2 (counts as 1 hdc), 1 hdc in next dc and in each dc to center ch-2 sp, [2 hdc, ch 2, 2 hdc] in ch-2 sp, 1 hdc in next dc and in each dc to end. Turn.

Rep rows 2 and 3 twice more. Fasten off.

Side panels

Left front

With RS of body facing, Attach C to 16th st from right edge of row 18.

Row 1 Ch 4 (counts as 1 dc, ch 1), skip next st, 1 dc in next st, *ch 1, skip next st, 1 dc in next st; rep from * 9 times more—12 dc. Turn.

Row 2 Ch 2 (counts as 1 hdc), *1 hdc in ch-1 sp, 1 hdc in next dc; rep from * to end—23 hdc. Turn.

Row 3 Ch 3, 1 dc in horizontal loop of next hdc and in each hdc to end. Turn.

Row 4 Ch 2, 1 hdc in next dc and in each dc to end.

Fasten off.

Left back

With RS of body facing, attach C to right edge of last row of armhole shaping.

Work rows 1 through 4 of left front. Fasten off.

Right front

With RS of body facing, attach C to 38th st from left edge of row 18.

Work rows 1 through 4 of left front. Fasten off.

Right back

With RS of body facing, attach C to 23rd st from left edge of last row of armhole shaping. Work rows 1 through 4 of left front. Fasten off.

Right pocket

With A, ch 61.

Row 1 (RS) Hdc in 3rd ch from hook and in each ch to end—60 sts. Turn.

Row 2 Ch 3 (counts as 1 dc), 1 dc in horizontal lp of next hdc and each hdc to end. Turn.

Row 3 Ch 2 (counts as 1 hdc), skip next dc, 1 hdc in next dc and in each dc to end. Turn.

Row 4 Ch 3 (counts as 1 dc), 1 dc in horizontal lp of next hdc and each hdc to end. Turn.

Rep rows 3 and 4 until there are 18 rows—52 sts. Fasten off.

With RS facing, attach A to right-hand side of shaped edge. Ch 1, 1 hdc in side of each hdc row and 2 hdc in side of each dc row across. Fasten off.

Left pocket

With A, ch 61.

Row 1 (RS) Hdc in 3rd ch from hook and in each ch to end—60 sts. Turn.

Row 2 Ch 3 (counts as 1 dc), 1 dc in horizontal lp of next hdc and each hdc to end. Turn.

Row 3 Ch 2 (counts as 1 hdc), 1 hdc in next dc and in each dc to last 2 dc, skip next dc, 1 hdc in last dc. Turn.

Row 4 Ch 3 (counts as 1 dc), 1 dc in horizontal lp of next hdc and each hdc to end. Turn.

Rep rows 3 and 4 until there are 18 rows—52 sts. Fasten off.

With RS facing, attach A to right-hand side of shaped edge. Ch 1, 1 hdc in side of each hdc row and 2 hdc in side of each dc row across. Fasten off.

Hood

With A, ch 97.

Row 1 (RS) Hdc in 3rd ch from hook and in each ch to end—96 sts. Turn.

Row 2 Ch 3 (counts as 1 dc), 1 dc in horizontal lp of next hdc and each hdc to end. Turn.

Row 3 Ch 2 (counts as 1 hdc), 1 hdc in next dc and in each dc to end. Turn.

Rep rows 2 and 3 until there are 23 rows. Fasten off.

Finishing

Pockets

Align straight edge of WS right pocket with short edge of RS right front of body. Sew together matching rows. Fold up on RS so left edge meets and right edge overlaps seam. Tack in place.

Align straight edge of WS left pocket with short edge of RS left front of body. Sew together matching rows. Fold up on RS so right edge meets and left edge overlaps seam. Tack in place.

With RS facing, join A to base of right front pocket. Ch 1, 1 sc in each st across entire front edge, working through both layers of pockets at each end. Fasten off.

With RS facing, join A to base of left front pocket. Ch 1, 1 sc in each st of pocket, working through both layers. Fasten off.

With RS facing, join A to top edge of right front pocket. Ch 1, 1 sc in each st of pocket, working through both layers. Fasten off.

Sides

Join front and back side panels, matching sts.

Hood

Fold hood in half widthwise with RS together. Sew seam across last row. Place markers 7.5"/19cm from each side of center back neck of body. Match seam of hood to center back neck and sew hood in place between markers.

Edgings

Front edging

With RS facing, attach C to right front edge at top of pocket.

Row 1 Ch 1, 1 sc in each st across, working across right front edge, hood, and left front edge, ending at top of pocket. Turn.

Row 2 Ch 1, 1 sc in each st across, working across left front edge, hood, and right front edge, ending at top of pocket. Fasten off.

Armhole edging

With RS facing, attach A to side panel seam. Ch 2. Work 1 row hdc evenly around in a multiple of 12. Join with sl st to top of beg ch. Fasten off.

Attach B to same sp.

Row 1 Ch 3, [2 dc, ch 3, 3 dc] in same sp, *skip 2 sts, 1 sc in next st, sk 2 sts, [3 dc, ch 3, 3 dc] in next st; rep from *, end skip 2 sts, 1 sc in next st, skip 2 sts. Join with sl st in top of beg ch 3.

Fasten off B. With RS facing, attach C to same sp.

Row 2 Ch 1, 1 sc in same st, 1 sc in next dc, *1 hdc in next dc, ch 2, [1 dtr, ch 2] 4 times in next ch-3 sp, 1 dtr in same sp, ch 2, 1 hdc in next dc, 1 sc in next 5 sts, 3 sc in next ch-3 sp, 1 sc in next 5 sts; rep from *. Join with sl st to first sc.

Fasten off C. With RS facing, attach A to same sp.

Row 3 Ch 1, 1 sc in same st, 1 sc in next 2 sts, *2 sc in next ch-2 sp, [ch 3, 1 sc in last sc made, 2 sc in next ch-2 sp] 5 times, 1 sc in next 8 sts, ch 3, 1 sc in last sc made, 1 sc in next 8 sts; rep from *. Join with sl st to first sc. Fasten off.

Lower edging

Holding vest upside-down, beg at front edge of left pocket. With pocket opening facing down. Attach B to base of left-most hdc.

Row 1 Ch 3, [2 dc, ch 3, 3 dc] in same sp, *skip 1 st, 1 sc in next st, sk 1 st, [3 dc, ch 3, 3 dc] in next st; rep from * 5 times more across edge of pocket. Rotate to work across side and lower edges. [3 dc, ch 3, 3 dc] in side of hdc row of pocket, *skip 2 sts, 1 sc in next st, sk 2 sts, [3 dc, ch 3, 3 dc] in next st; rep from * 19 times more (skipping only 1 st if necessary so 3rd cluster rep will fall at center of side panel, 9th cluster rep at center back point, 15th cluster rep at center of side panel, and last cluster rep in side of hdc row of right pocket). Rotate to work across right pocket edge. [3 dc, ch 3, 3 dc] in base of right-most

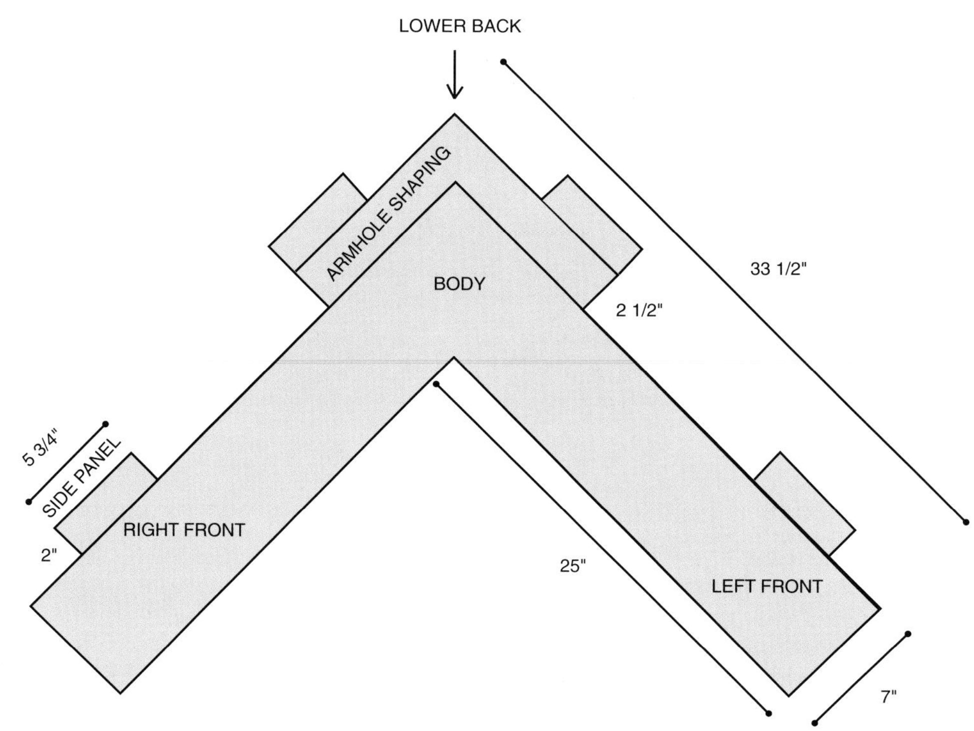

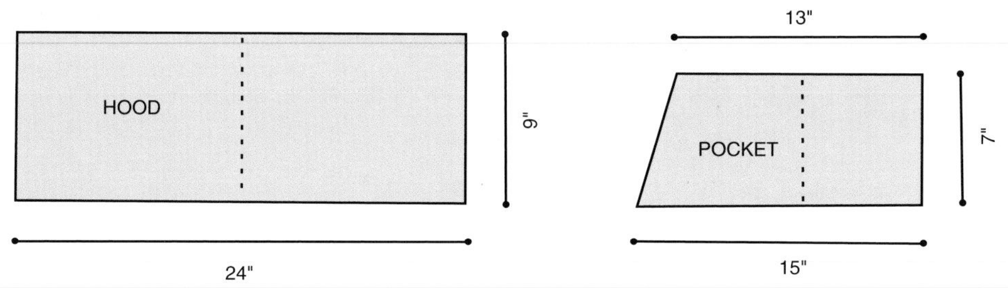

MANDARIN KNOT

hdc, *skip 1 st, 1 sc in next st, sk 1 st, [3 dc, ch 3, 3 dc] in next st; rep from * 5 times more across edge of pocket.

Fasten off B. With RS facing, attach C in top of beg ch of row 1.

Row 2 Ch 1, 1 sc in same st, 1 sc in next 2 sts, 3 sc in next ch-3 sp, *1 sc in next 5 sts, 1 hdc in next dc, ch 2, [1 dtr, ch 2] 4 times in next ch-3 sp, 1 dtr in same sp, ch 2, 1 hdc in next dc, 1 sc in next 5 sts, 3 sc in next ch-3 sp; rep from *, end 1 sc in last 3 sts.

Fasten off C. With RS facing, attach A in top of beg ch of row 2.

Row 3 Ch 1, 1 sc in same st, 1 sc in next 3 sts, ch 3, 1 sc in last sc made, *1 sc in next 7 sts, 2 sc in next ch-2 sp, [ch 3, 1 sc in last sc made, 2 sc in next ch-2 sp] 5 times, 1 sc in next 7 sts, ch 3, 1 sc in last sc made; rep from *, end 1 sc in last 4 sts.

Fasten off.

Using ends, tack down each side of edging.

Frog closure

Make 2 cords approximately 10"/25cm in length as follows:

With A, ch 2.

Row 1 3 sc in first ch.

Row 2 Working in a spiral, 1 sc in each sc around.

Rep row 2 to desired length.

Last row Sc3tog.

Fasten off.

Follow diagrams to form two sides of frog closure, one with a knot at the end and one with a loop at the end. Attach each side of frog closure to vest fronts.

T-SHIRT WITH CROCHETED EDGING

Finished measurements

Cuffs Approx 5½"/14cm D

Neck edging Approx 2"/5cm D

Materials

- 1 1¾ oz/50g ball (each approx 284yd/228m) of DMC *Cébélia* crochet cotton #10 (100% combed cotton) in #818 pale pink
- Size C/2 (2.75mm) crochet hook
- Purchased t-shirt
- Sewing needle and matching thread

Cuffs (make 2)

Make edging slightly longer than circumference of sleeve cuff following instructions for Baroque Point (see page 180).

Neck edging

Cross Tr (CT) [Yo] twice, insert hook in next st and draw up a lp, yo and draw through 2 lps, yo, skip next 2 sts, insert hook in next st and draw up a lp, [yo and draw through 2 lps] 4 times.

Make a ch slightly longer than circumference of neck opening in a multiple of 9 sts + 2.

Row 1 (WS) 1 sc in 2nd ch from hook and in each ch to end. Turn.

Row 2 Ch 4, skip next sc, *2 dc in next sc, CT, [ch 3, 1 sc in 3rd ch from hook—(*picot made*)] 3 times, 1 dc into centerjoint of CT just made, 2 dc in next sc, ch 3, skip next 3 sc; rep from *, end last rep with 1 dc into center joint of CT just made, 2 dc in next sc, ch 1, skip next sc, 1 dc in last sc. Turn.

Row 3 Ch 1, 1 sc in first dc, *ch 2, dtr in next picot, [ch 2, 1 dtr] 5 times in next picot, ch 2, 1 dtr in next picot, ch 2, 1 sc in next ch-3 sp; rep from *, end last rep 1 sc in 3rd ch of beg ch-4. Turn.

Row 4 Ch 1, [3 sc in next ch-2 sp] twice, *([2 sc, picot, 2 sc] in next ch-2 sp) 4 times, [3 sc in next ch-2 sp] 4 times; rep from *, end last rep [3 sc in next ch-2 sp] twice, sl st in top of last dc.

Fasten off.

Finishing

Optional If necessary, cut sleeves and hem to desired length minus depth measurement of cuffs before adding cuffs.

Baste straight edges of edgings and ease slightly to fit openings. With sewing needle and thread, sew in place. Sew side seams of edgings.

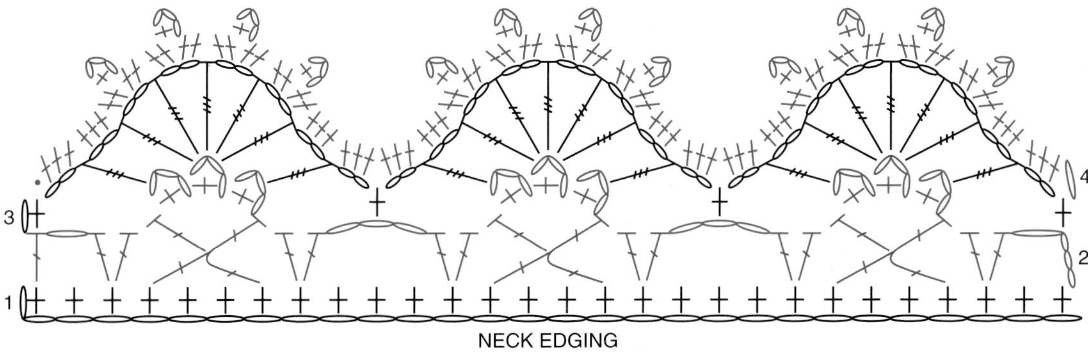

NECK EDGING

techniques

French Knot

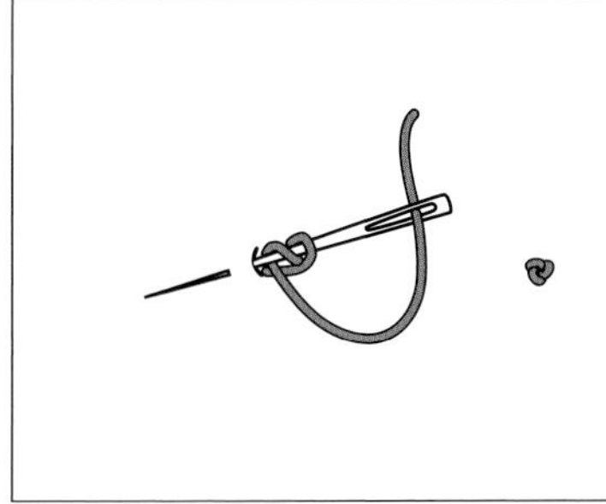

Lazy Daisy

resources

Lion Brand Yarn
34 West 15th Street
New York, NY 10011
www.lionbrand.com

Berroco, Inc.
14 Elmdale Road
P.O. Box 367
Uxbridge, MA 01569
www.berroco.com

Classic Elite Yarns
122 Western Avenue
Lowell, MA 01851
www.classiceliteyarns.com

Lang
distributed by Berroco, Inc.
www.langyarns.ch/en

DMC
77 South Hackensack Avenue
Bldg. 10F
South Kearny, NJ 07032
www.dmc.com

Tilli Tomas
72 Woodland Road
Boston, MA 02130
www.tillitomas.com

NICKY EPSTEIN'S

Crocheted Flowers

This eagerly awaited follow-up to the best-selling
Nicky Epstein's Knitted Flowers is inspiring crafters everywhere.
Nicky gives crocheters a collection of exquisite flowers to craft.
Crafters of all skill levels will use these designs to create
beautiful, fanciful flowers to wear and use to embellish their handicrafts.
A collection of innovative projects—including lanterns, a necklace,
a bag, gloves and a fabulous wedding dress—rounds out this beautiful book.
The best part? These flowers will last forever.

acknowledgments

Special thanks to my oldest friend—and now crochet consultant—Jo Brandon, whose tireless work and impressive crochet skills contributed immeasurably to this book.

Many thanks to:

- Rowan Yarns for their generosity, and to Lion Brand, Tilli Thomas, Lang, Berroco, DMC, Natural Wool, Muench, and Presencia
- Crocheters Maggie MacManus, Jackie Smyth and Nancy Henderson
- Photographer Jack Deutsch, whose skill and talent have made so many of my books look so beautiful
- The always-supportive staff at Sixth and Spring: Trisha Malcolm, Adina Klein, Carla Scott, Elaine Silverstein, Diane Lamphron, Erica Smith, and Sheena T. Paul
- Technical Editor Eve Ng, Illustrator Karen Manthey and Instructions checker Jeannie Chin
- And finally, thanks to my family and friends who keep the encouragement coming on a nonstop basis. You know who you are!

notes

notes